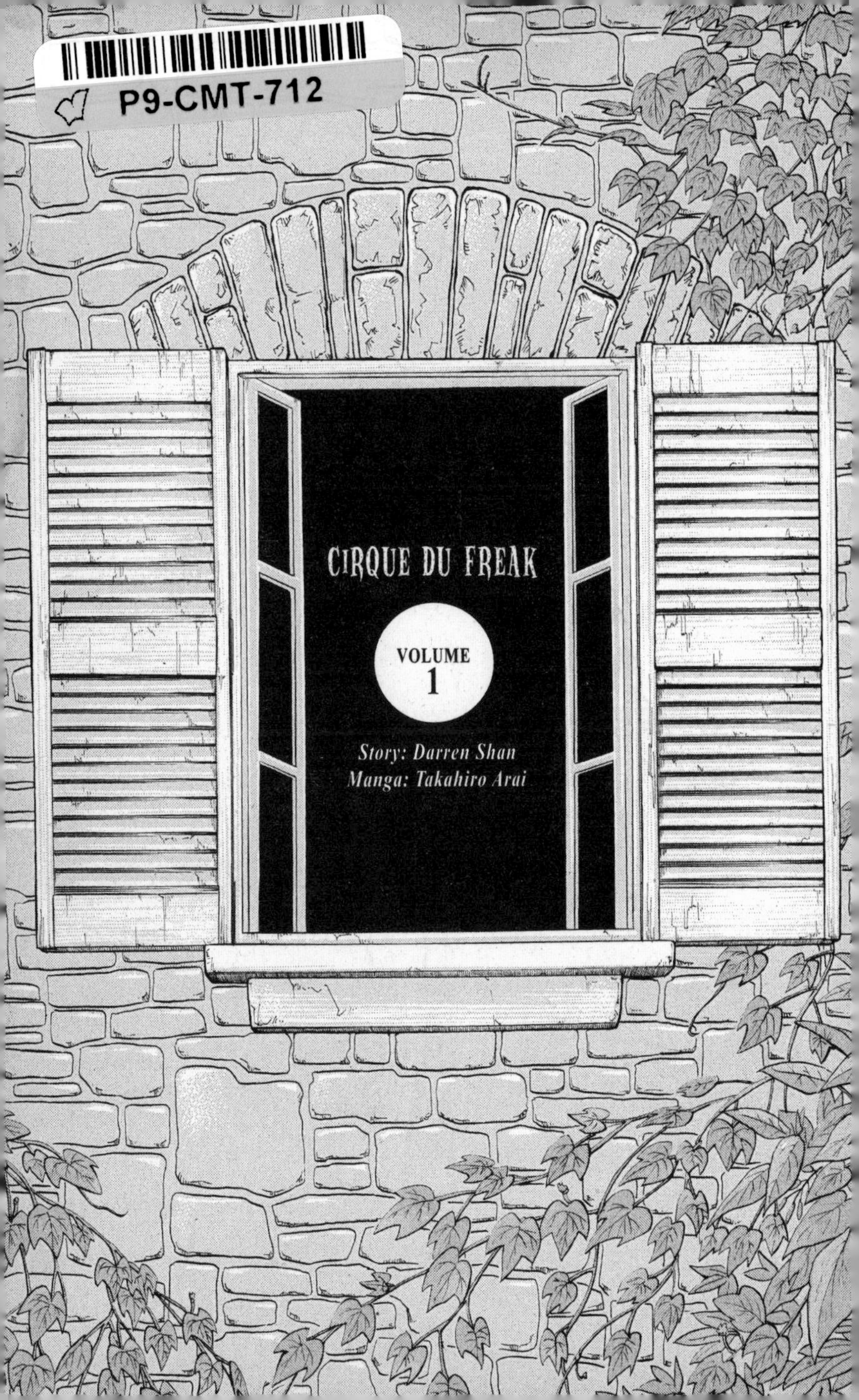
CIRQUE DU FREAK
VOLUME
1
Story: Darren Shan
Manga: Takahiro Arai

CIRQUE DU FREAK 1
CONTENTS

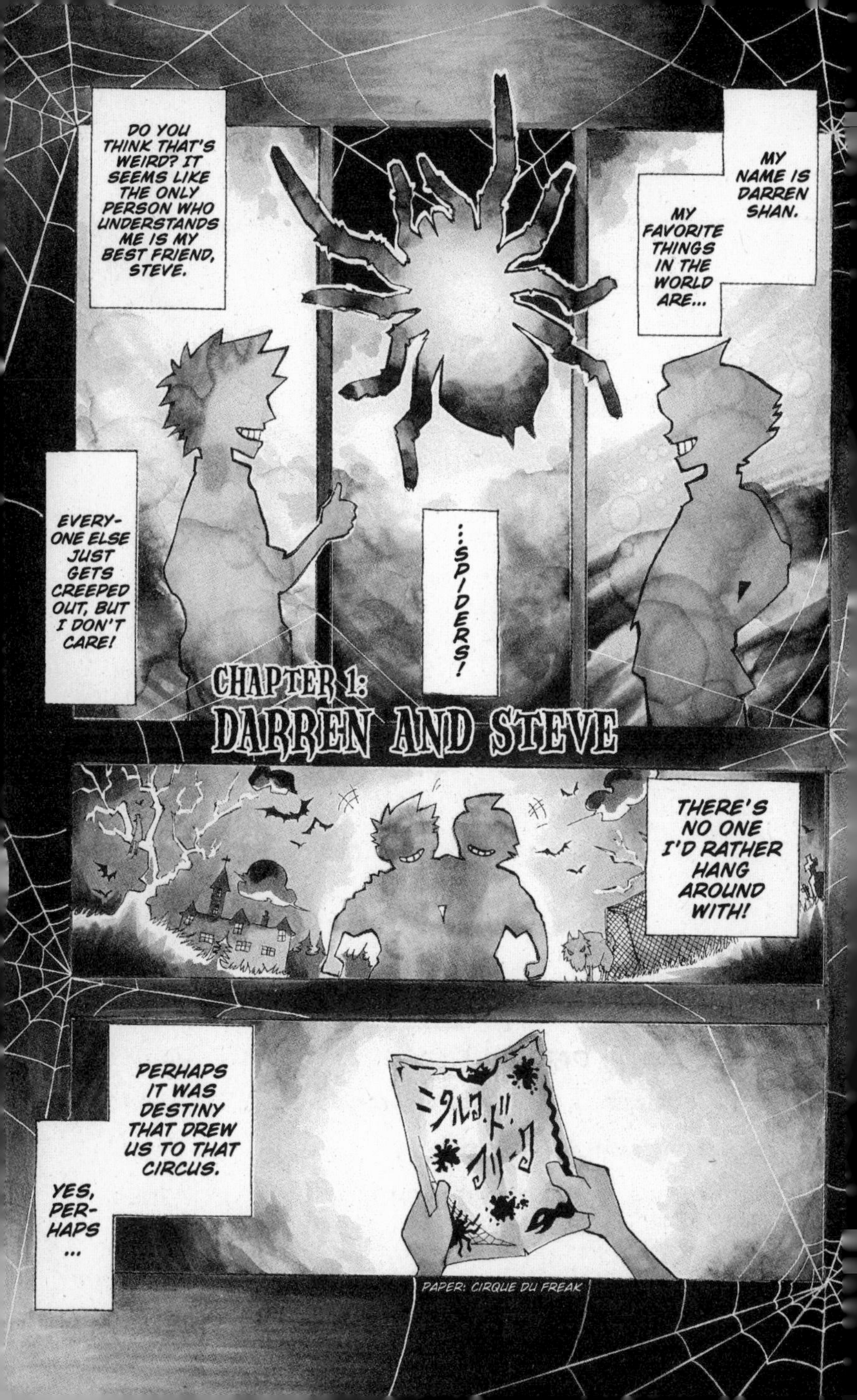
MY NAME IS DARREN SHAN.
MY FAVORITE THINGS IN THE WORLD ARE...
...SPIDERS!
DO YOU THINK THAT'S WEIRD? IT SEEMS LIKE THE ONLY PERSON WHO UNDERSTANDS ME IS MY BEST FRIEND, STEVE.
EVERY-ONE ELSE JUST GETS CREEPED OUT, BUT I DON'T CARE!
CHAPTER 1: DARREN AND STEVE
THERE'S NO ONE I'D RATHER HANG AROUND WITH!
PERHAPS IT WAS DESTINY THAT DREW US TO THAT CIRCUS.
YES, PER-HAPS ...
PAPER: CIRQUE DU FREAK

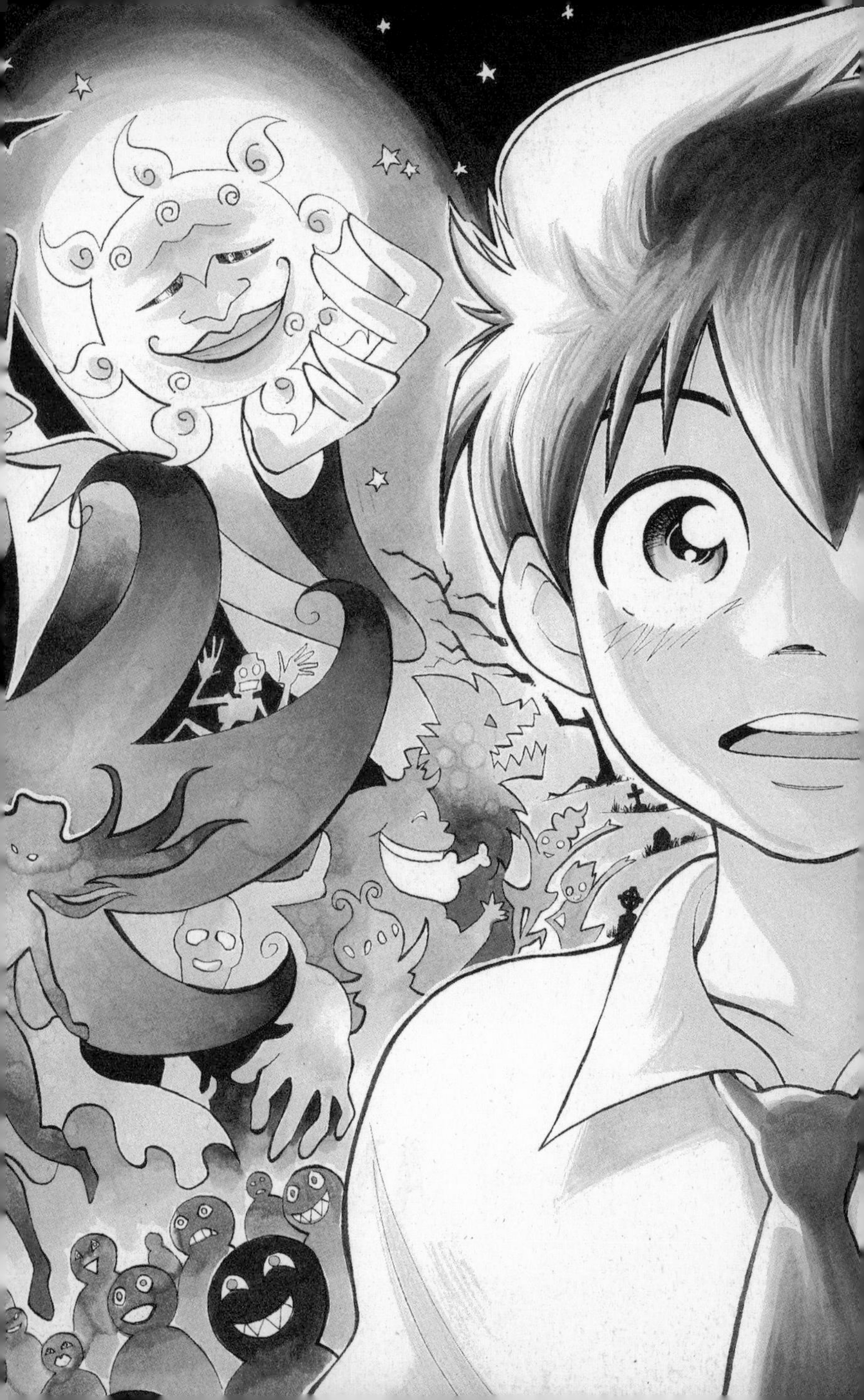

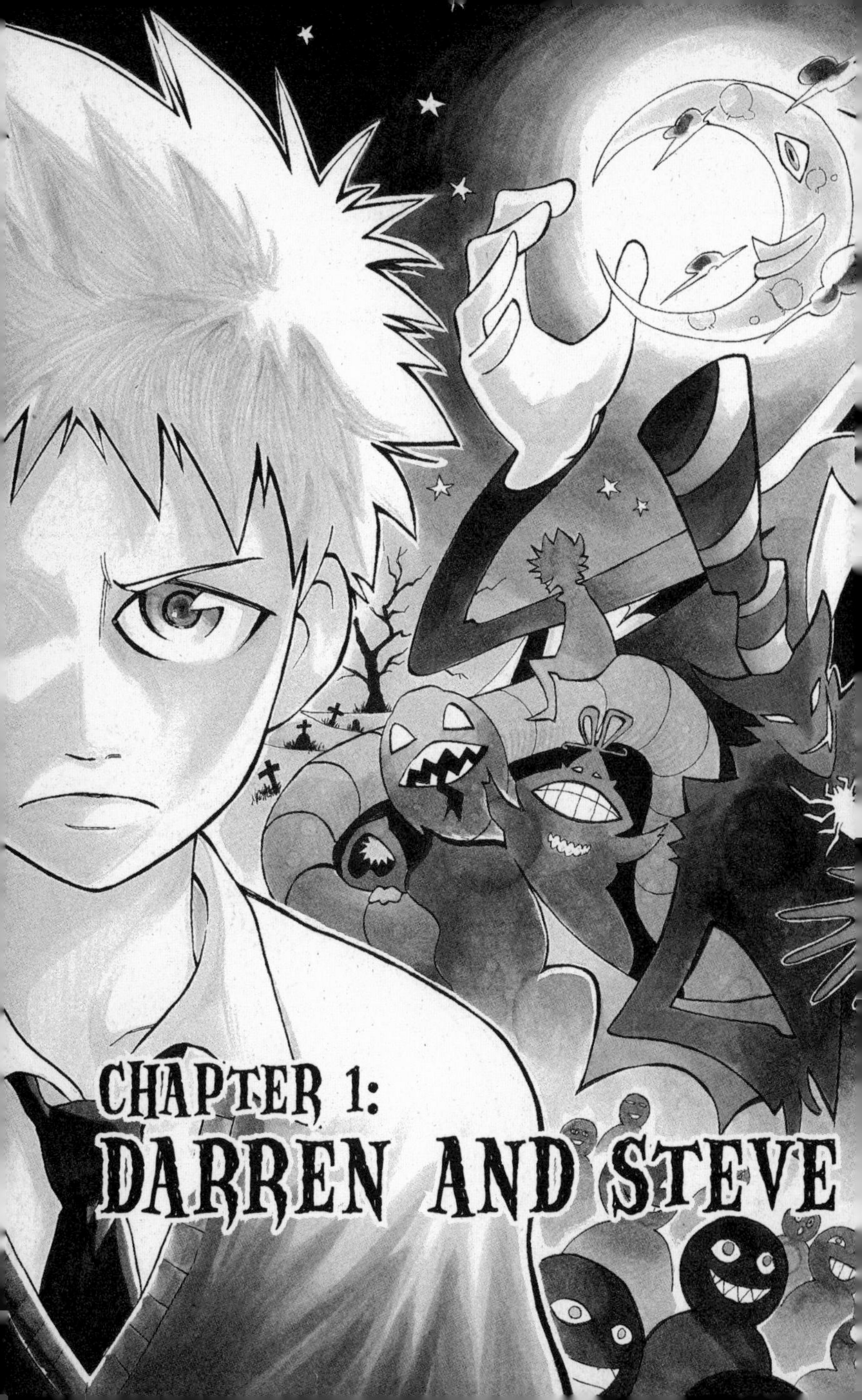
CHAPTER 1:
DARREN AND STEVE

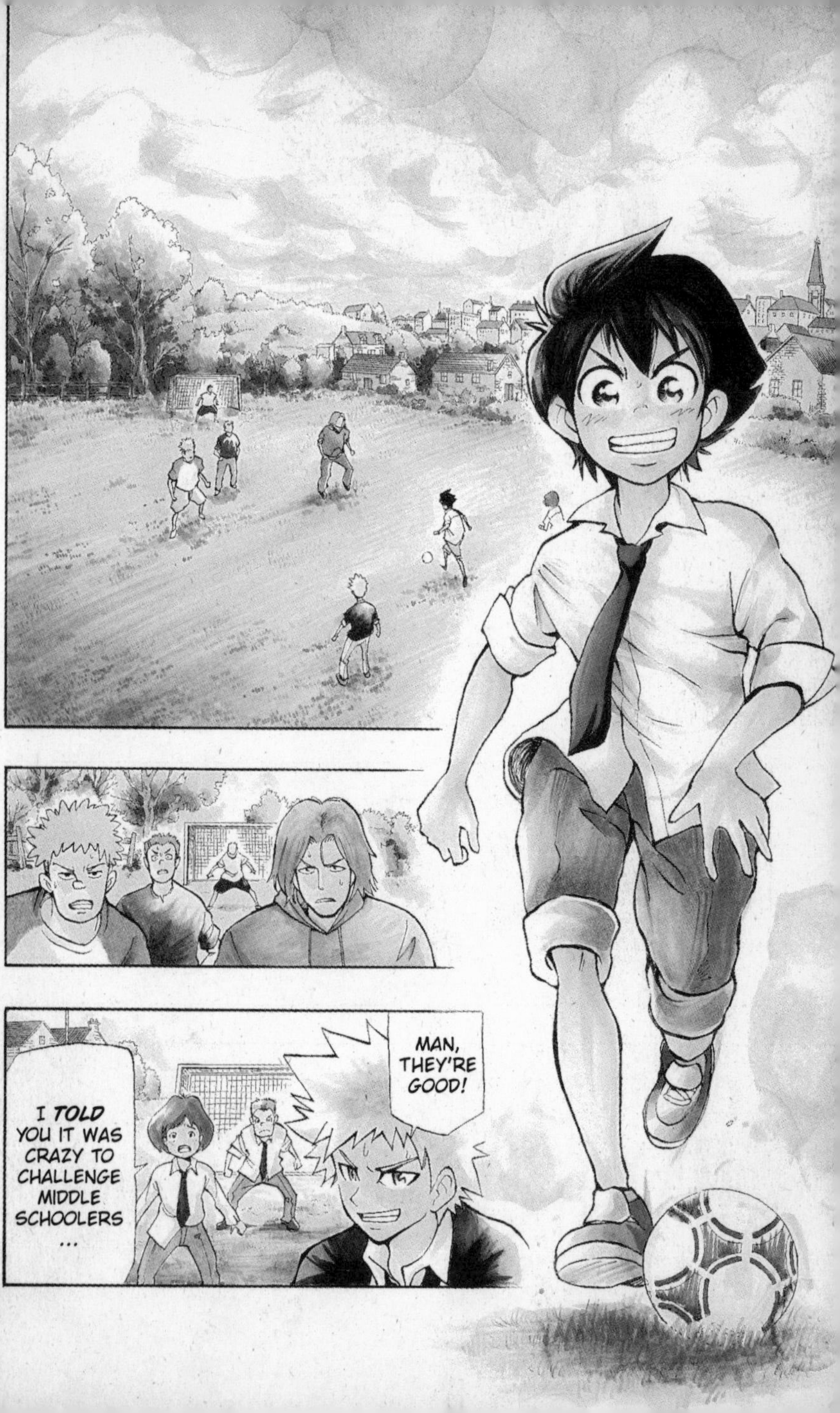
MAN, THEY'RE GOOD!
I *TOLD* YOU IT WAS CRAZY TO CHALLENGE MIDDLE SCHOOLERS ...

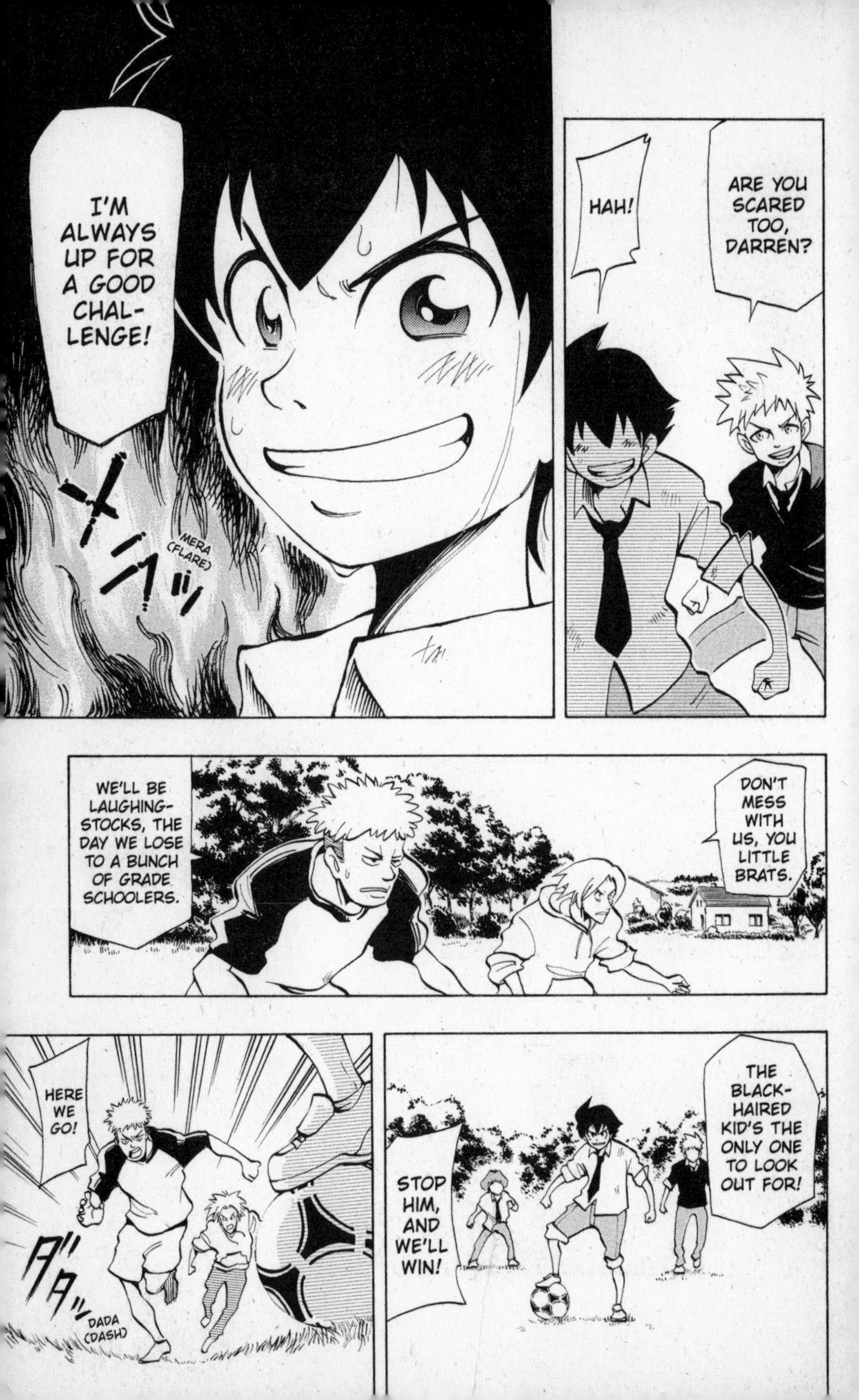
ARE YOU SCARED TOO, DARREN?
HAH!
I'M ALWAYS UP FOR A GOOD CHAL-LENGE!
MERA (FLARE)
DON'T MESS WITH US, YOU LITTLE BRATS.
WE'LL BE LAUGHING-STOCKS, THE DAY WE LOSE TO A BUNCH OF GRADE SCHOOLERS.
THE BLACK-HAIRED KID'S THE ONLY ONE TO LOOK OUT FOR!
STOP HIM, AND WE'LL WIN!
HERE WE GO!
DADA (DASH)

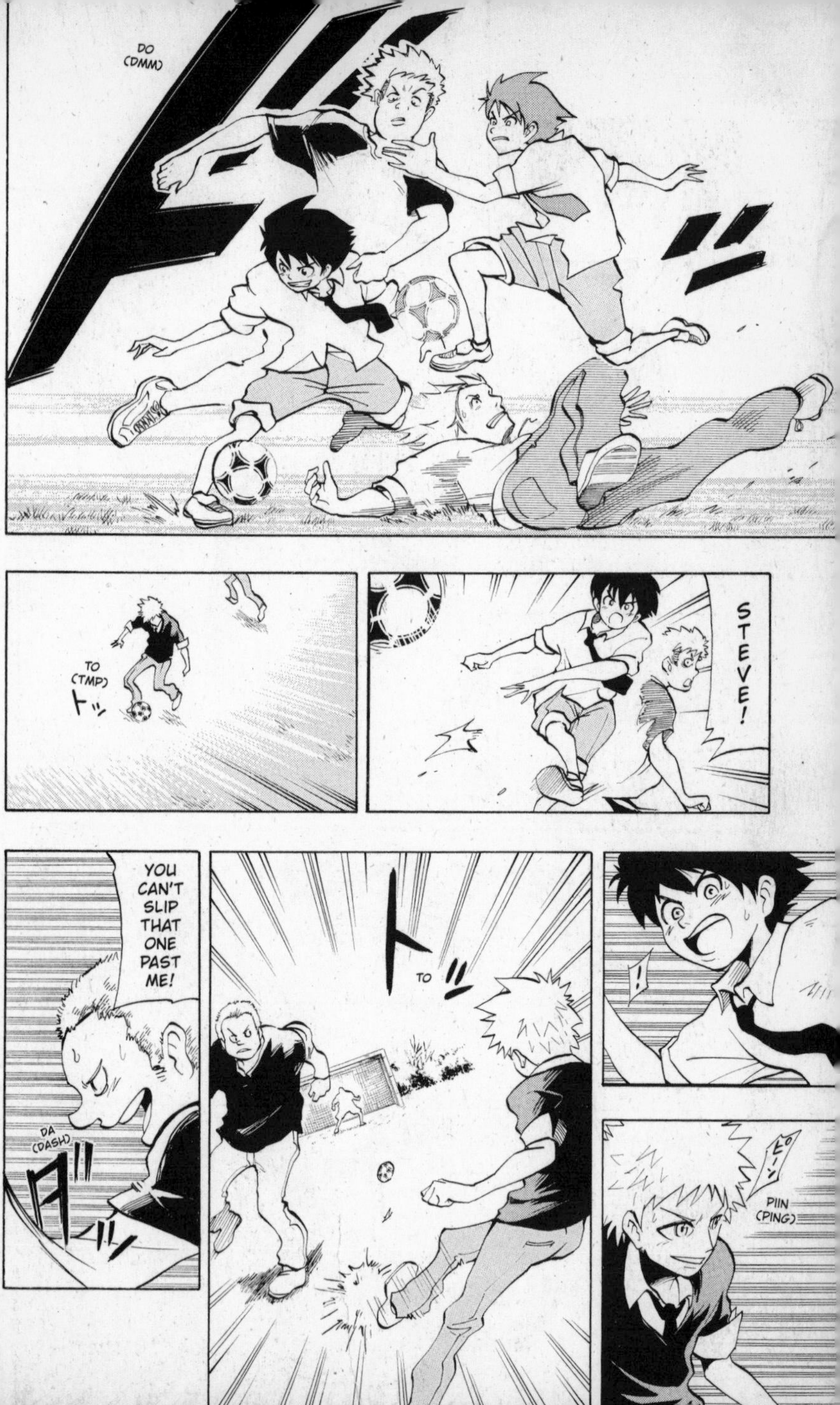
DO
(DMM)
STEVE!
TO
(TMP)
トッ
!
PIIN
(PING)
ピーン
TO
YOU CAN'T SLIP THAT ONE PAST ME!
DA
(DASH)

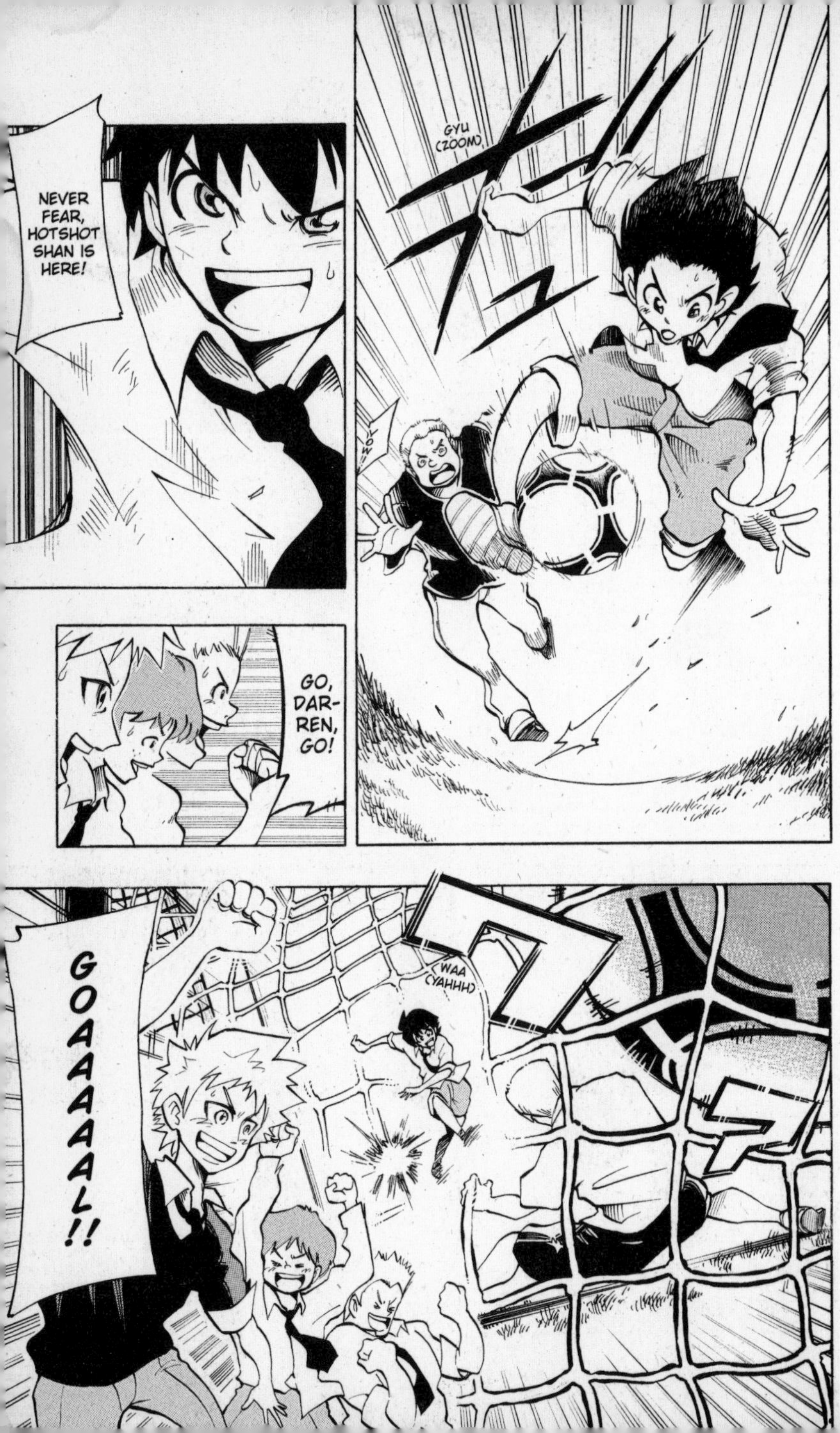
GYU (ZOOM)
YOW!!
NEVER FEAR, HOTSHOT SHAN IS HERE!
GO, DAR-REN, GO!
WAA (YAHHH)
GOAAAAAAL!!

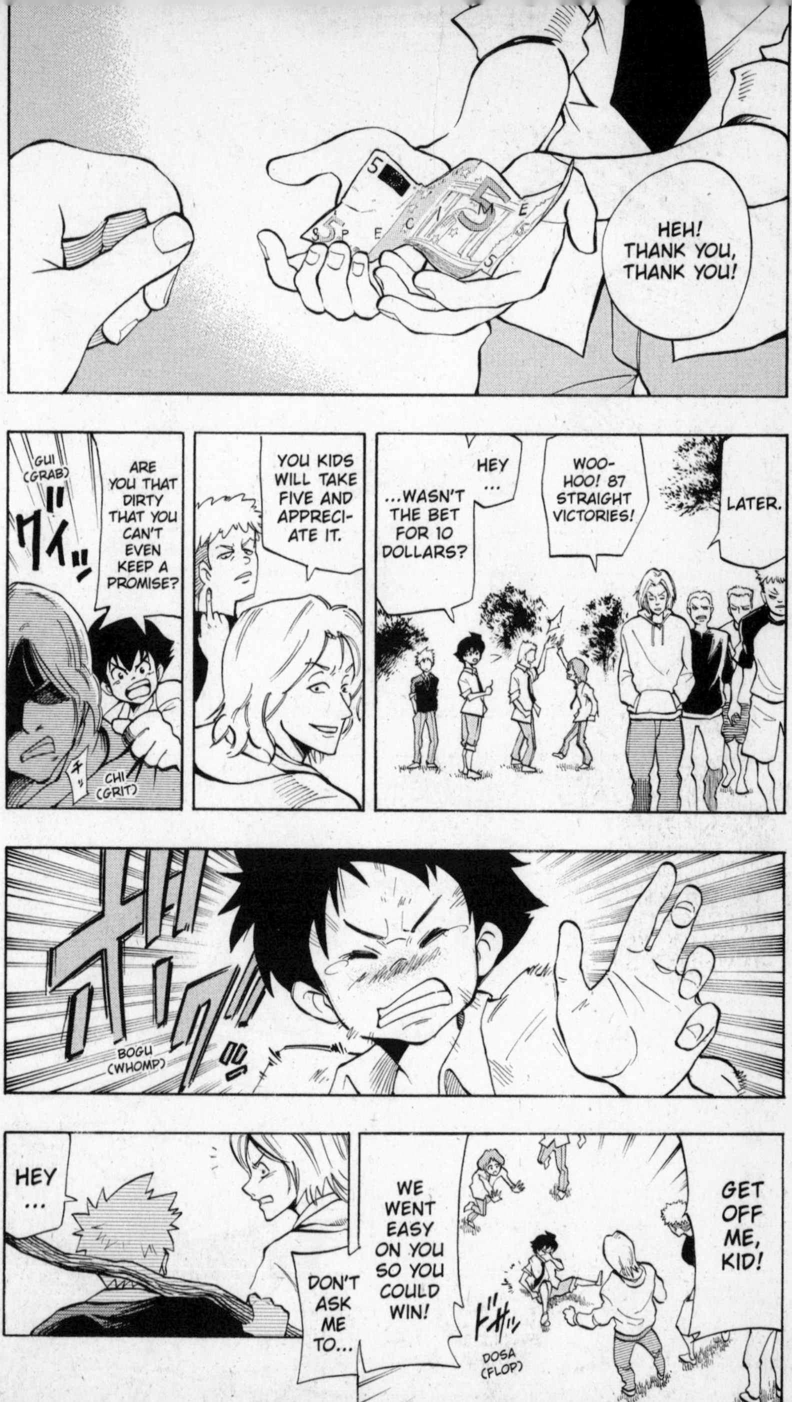
HEH! THANK YOU, THANK YOU!
LATER.
WOO-HOO! 87 STRAIGHT VICTORIES!
HEY ...
...WASN'T THE BET FOR 10 DOLLARS?
YOU KIDS WILL TAKE FIVE AND APPRECIATE IT.
ARE YOU THAT DIRTY THAT YOU CAN'T EVEN KEEP A PROMISE?
GUI (GRAB)
CHI (GRIT)
BOGU (WHOMP)
GET OFF ME, KID!
WE WENT EASY ON YOU SO YOU COULD WIN!
DOSA (FLOP)
DON'T ASK ME TO...
HEY ...

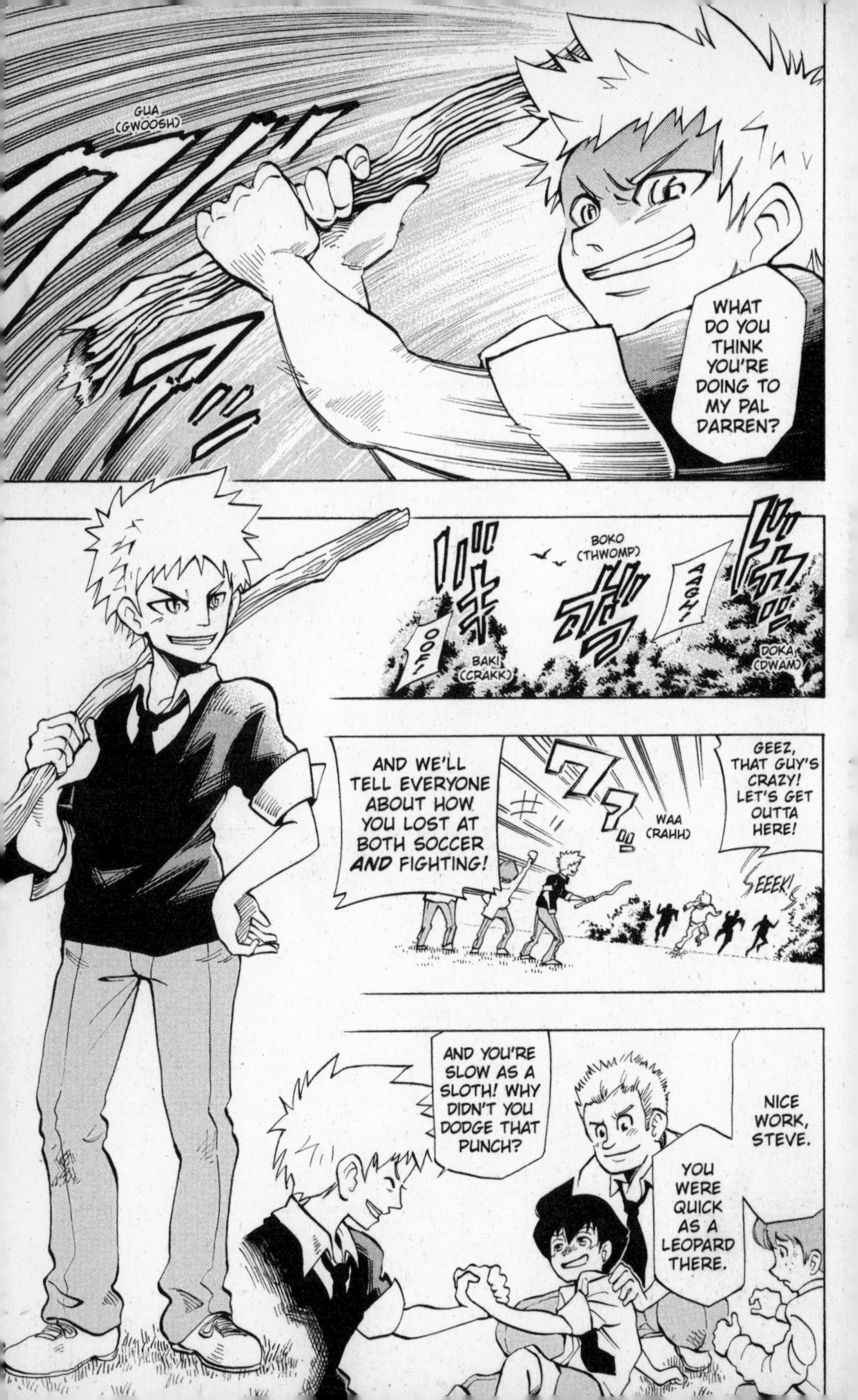
GUA (GWOOSH)
WHAT DO YOU THINK YOU'RE DOING TO MY PAL DARREN?
DOKA (DWAM)
AAGH!
BOKO (THWOMP)
BAKI (CRAKK)
OOF!
GEEZ, THAT GUY'S CRAZY! LET'S GET OUTTA HERE!
SEEEK!
WAA (RAHH)
AND WE'LL TELL EVERYONE ABOUT HOW YOU LOST AT BOTH SOCCER AND FIGHTING!
NICE WORK, STEVE.
YOU WERE QUICK AS A LEOPARD THERE.
AND YOU'RE SLOW AS A SLOTH! WHY DIDN'T YOU DODGE THAT PUNCH?

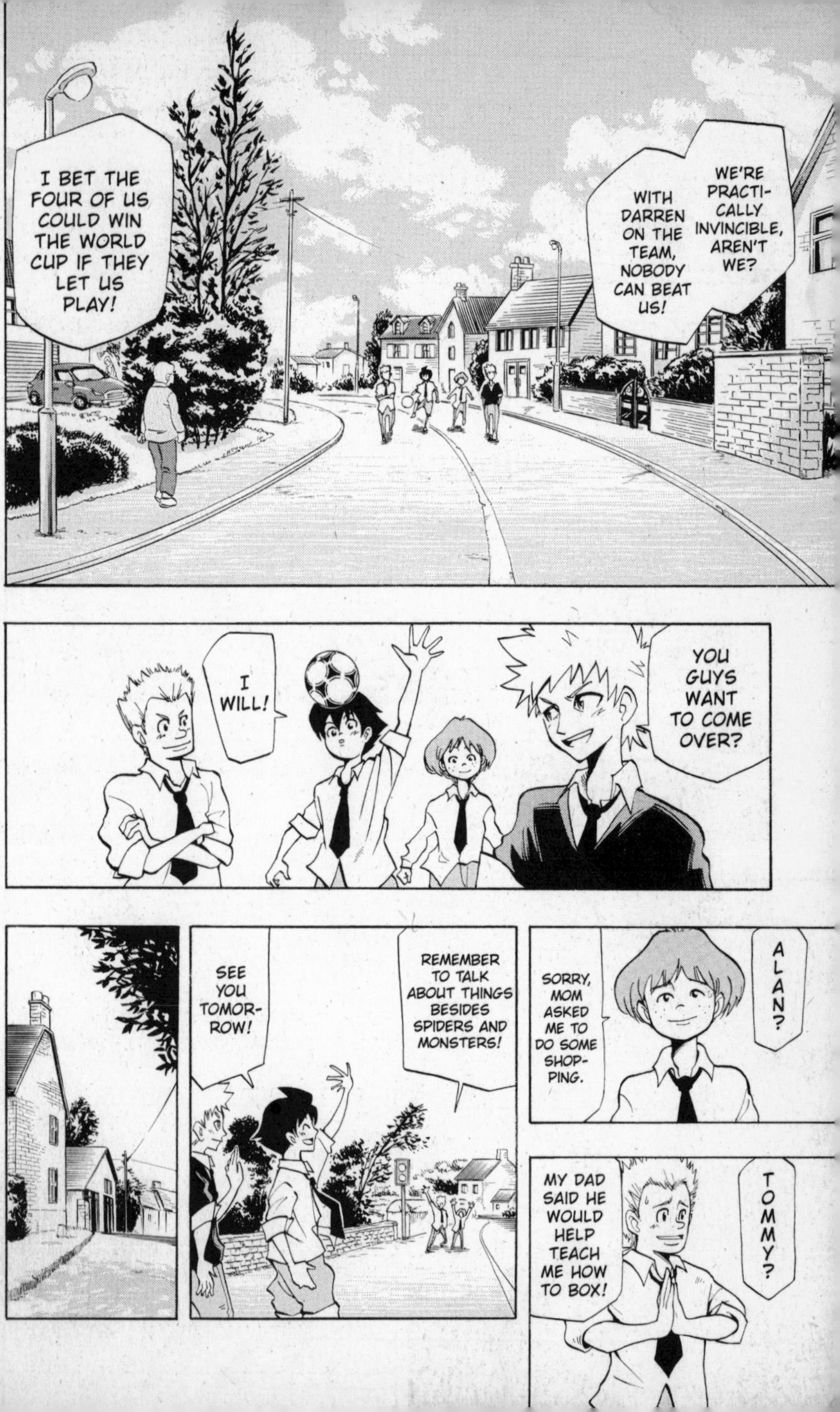
WE'RE PRACTI-CALLY INVINCIBLE, AREN'T WE?
WITH DARREN ON THE TEAM, NOBODY CAN BEAT US!
I BET THE FOUR OF US COULD WIN THE WORLD CUP IF THEY LET US PLAY!
YOU GUYS WANT TO COME OVER?
I WILL!
ALAN?
SORRY, MOM ASKED ME TO DO SOME SHOP-PING.
TOMMY?
MY DAD SAID HE WOULD HELP TEACH ME HOW TO BOX!
REMEMBER TO TALK ABOUT THINGS BESIDES SPIDERS AND MONSTERS!
SEE YOU TOMOR-ROW!

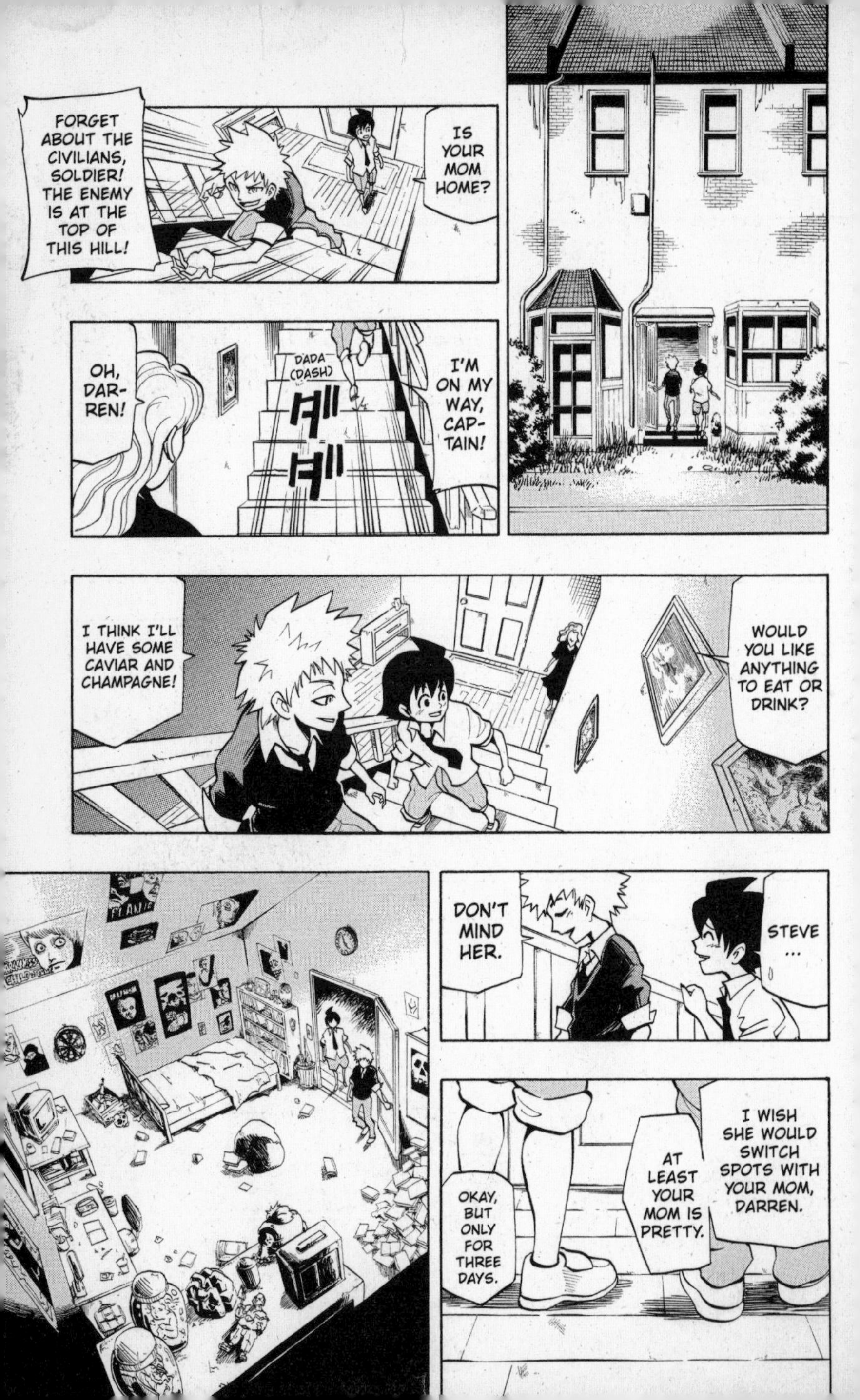
IS YOUR MOM HOME?
FORGET ABOUT THE CIVILIANS, SOLDIER! THE ENEMY IS AT THE TOP OF THIS HILL!
I'M ON MY WAY, CAPTAIN!
DADA (DASH)
OH, DAR-REN!
WOULD YOU LIKE ANYTHING TO EAT OR DRINK?
I THINK I'LL HAVE SOME CAVIAR AND CHAMPAGNE!
STEVE ...
DON'T MIND HER.
I WISH SHE WOULD SWITCH SPOTS WITH YOUR MOM, DARREN.
AT LEAST YOUR MOM IS PRETTY.
OKAY, BUT ONLY FOR THREE DAYS.

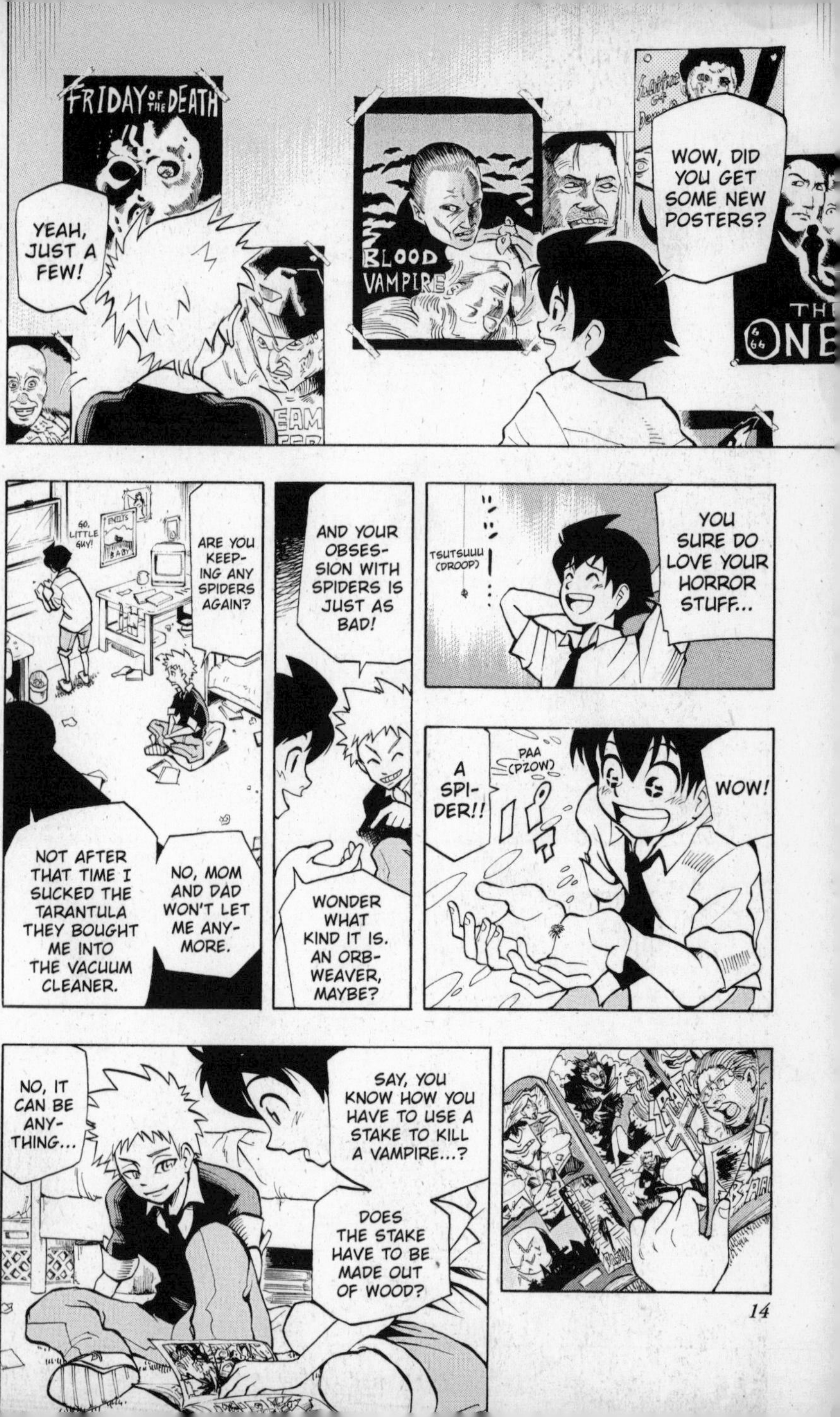
FRIDAY OF THE DEATH
BLOOD VAMPIRE
WOW, DID YOU GET SOME NEW POSTERS?
YEAH, JUST A FEW!
YOU SURE DO LOVE YOUR HORROR STUFF...
TSUTSUUU (DROOP)
WOW!
A SPI-DER!!
PAA (PZOW)
AND YOUR OBSES-SION WITH SPIDERS IS JUST AS BAD!
WONDER WHAT KIND IT IS. AN ORB-WEAVER, MAYBE?
ARE YOU KEEP-ING ANY SPIDERS AGAIN?
GO, LITTLE GUY!
NO, MOM AND DAD WON'T LET ME ANY-MORE.
NOT AFTER THAT TIME I SUCKED THE TARANTULA THEY BOUGHT ME INTO THE VACUUM CLEANER.
SAY, YOU KNOW HOW YOU HAVE TO USE A STAKE TO KILL A VAMPIRE...?
DOES THE STAKE HAVE TO BE MADE OUT OF WOOD?
NO, IT CAN BE ANY-THING...

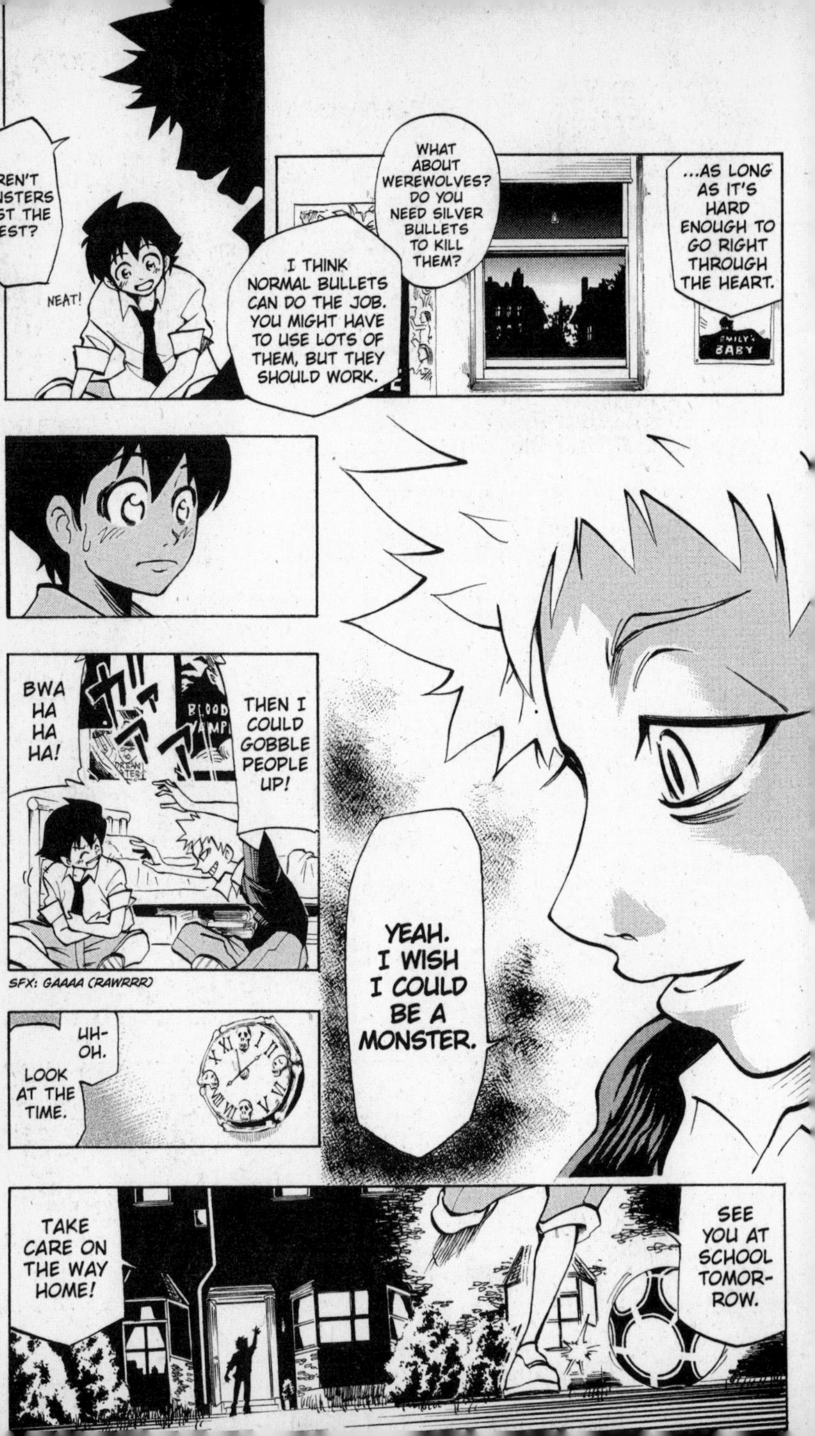
...AS LONG AS IT'S HARD ENOUGH TO GO RIGHT THROUGH THE HEART.
EMILY'S BABY
WHAT ABOUT WEREWOLVES? DO YOU NEED SILVER BULLETS TO KILL THEM?
I THINK NORMAL BULLETS CAN DO THE JOB. YOU MIGHT HAVE TO USE LOTS OF THEM, BUT THEY SHOULD WORK.
AREN'T MONSTERS JUST THE BEST?
NEAT!
YEAH. I WISH I COULD BE A MONSTER.
THEN I COULD GOBBLE PEOPLE UP!
BWA HA HA HA!
SFX: GAAAA (RAWRRR)
UH-OH.
LOOK AT THE TIME.
SEE YOU AT SCHOOL TOMOR-ROW.
TAKE CARE ON THE WAY HOME!

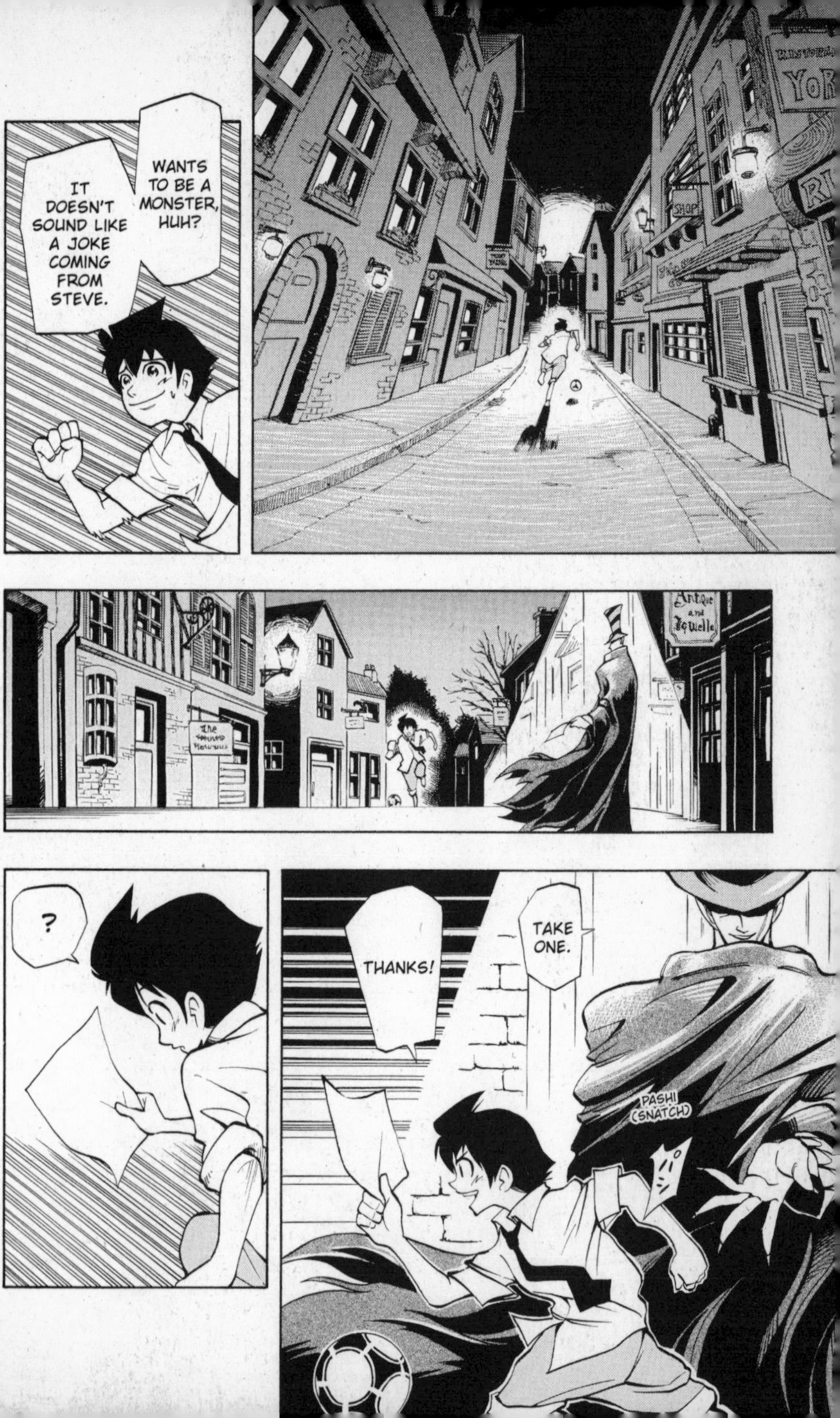
SHOP
WANTS TO BE A MONSTER, HUH?
IT DOESN'T SOUND LIKE A JOKE COMING FROM STEVE.
TAKE ONE.
THANKS!
PASHI (SNATCH)
!
?

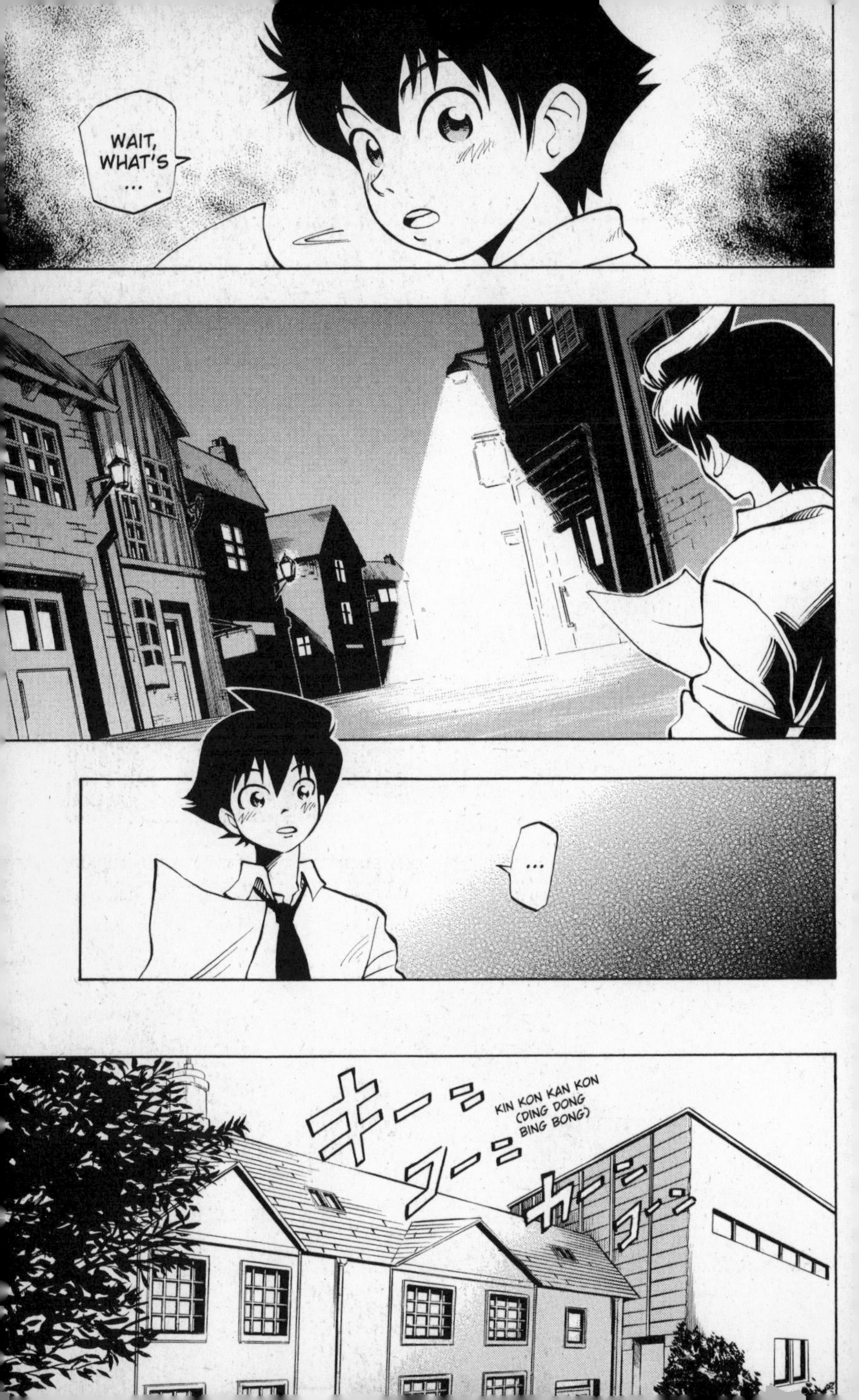
WAIT, WHAT'S ...
...
KIN KON KAN KON (DING DONG BING BONG)

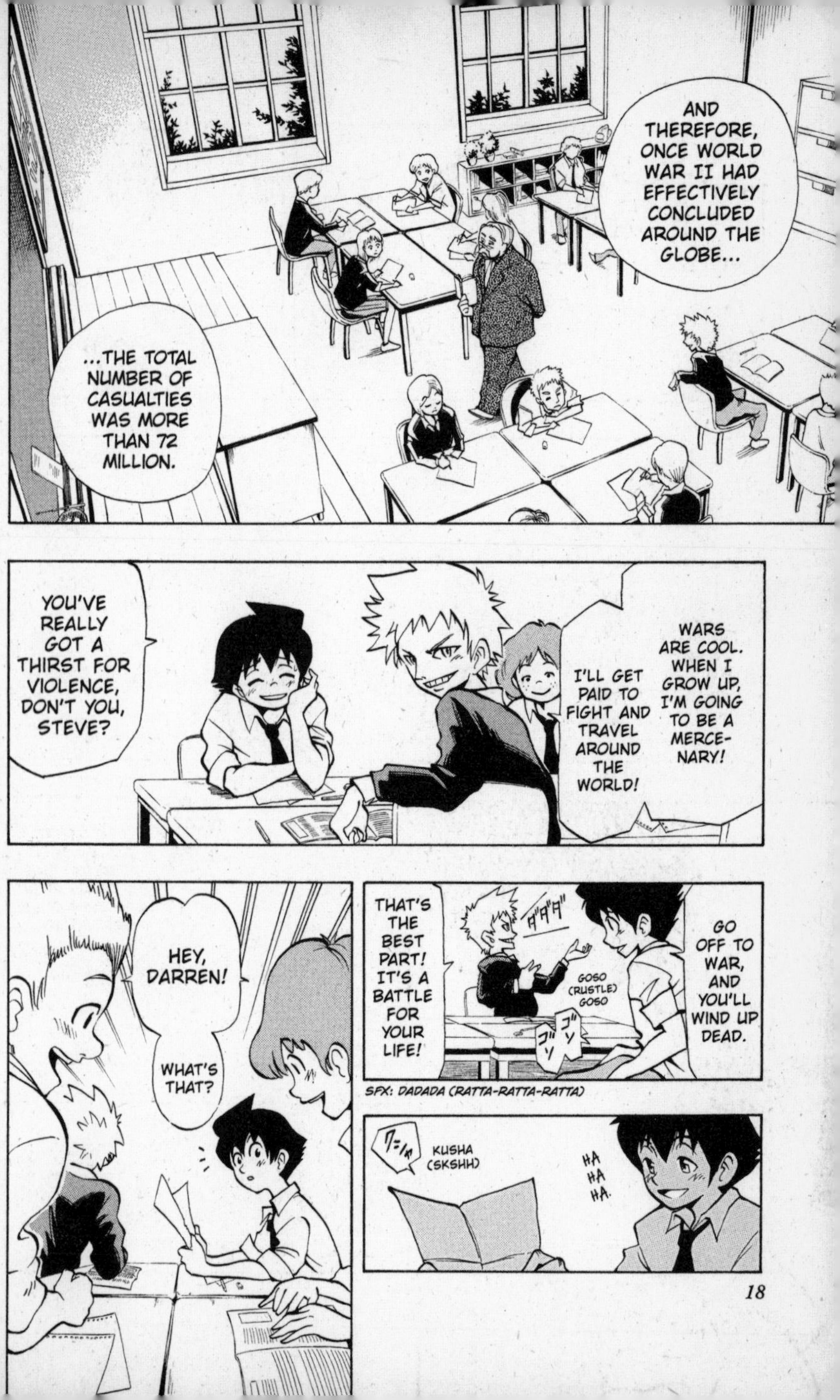
AND THEREFORE, ONCE WORLD WAR II HAD EFFECTIVELY CONCLUDED AROUND THE GLOBE...
...THE TOTAL NUMBER OF CASUALTIES WAS MORE THAN 72 MILLION.
WARS ARE COOL. WHEN I GROW UP, I'M GOING TO BE A MERCE-NARY!
I'LL GET PAID TO FIGHT AND TRAVEL AROUND THE WORLD!
YOU'VE REALLY GOT A THIRST FOR VIOLENCE, DON'T YOU, STEVE?
GO OFF TO WAR, AND YOU'LL WIND UP DEAD.
THAT'S THE BEST PART! IT'S A BATTLE FOR YOUR LIFE!
ダダダ
GOSO (RUSTLE) GOSO
ゴソ ゴソ
SFX: DADADA (RATTA-RATTA-RATTA)
HA HA HA.
クシャ
KUSHA (SKSHH)
HEY, DARREN!
WHAT'S THAT?

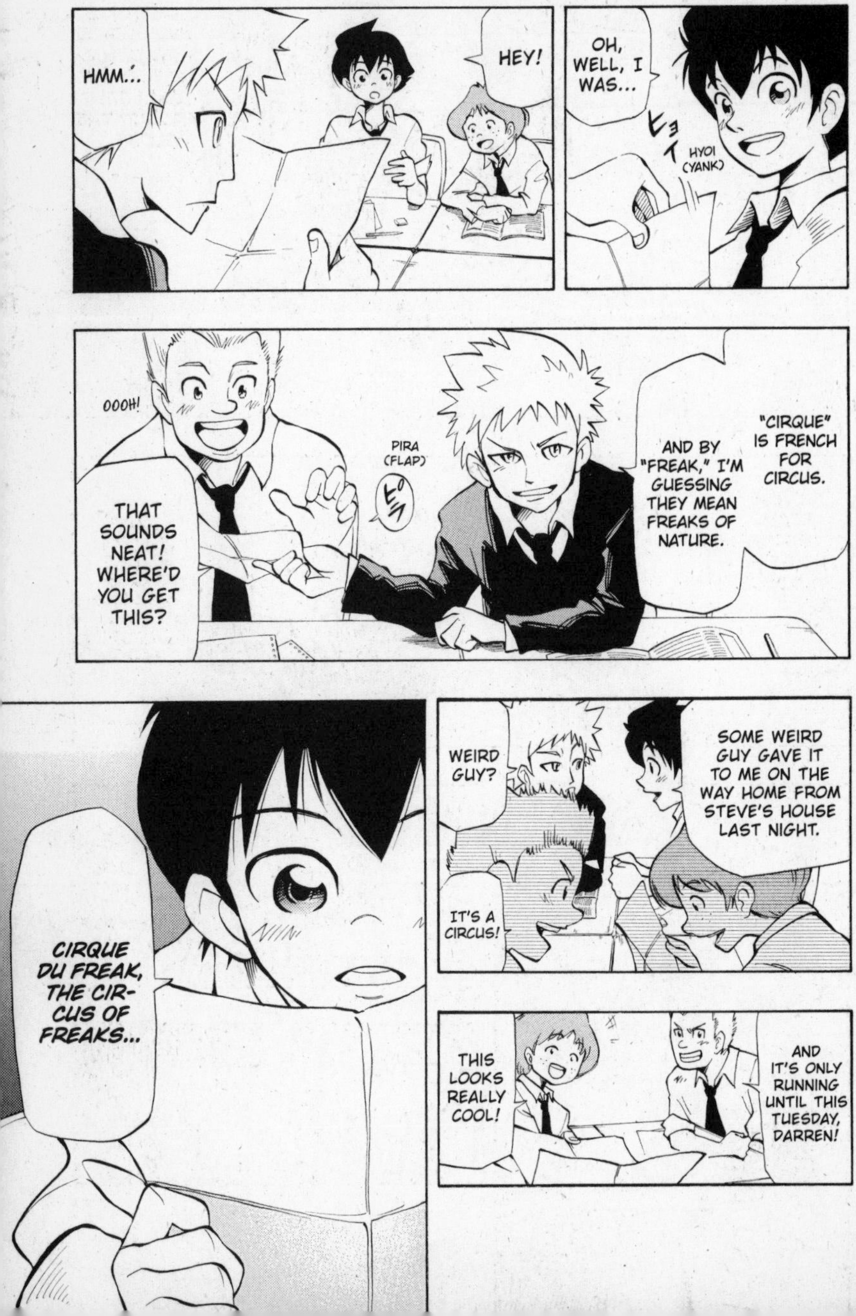
OH, WELL, I WAS...
ヒョイ
HYOI (YANK)
HEY!
HMM...
"CIRQUE" IS FRENCH FOR CIRCUS.
AND BY "FREAK," I'M GUESSING THEY MEAN FREAKS OF NATURE.
PIRA (FLAP)
ピラ
OOOH!
THAT SOUNDS NEAT! WHERE'D YOU GET THIS?
SOME WEIRD GUY GAVE IT TO ME ON THE WAY HOME FROM STEVE'S HOUSE LAST NIGHT.
WEIRD GUY?
IT'S A CIRCUS!
AND IT'S ONLY RUNNING UNTIL THIS TUESDAY, DARREN!
THIS LOOKS REALLY COOL!
CIRQUE DU FREAK, THE CIR-CUS OF FREAKS...

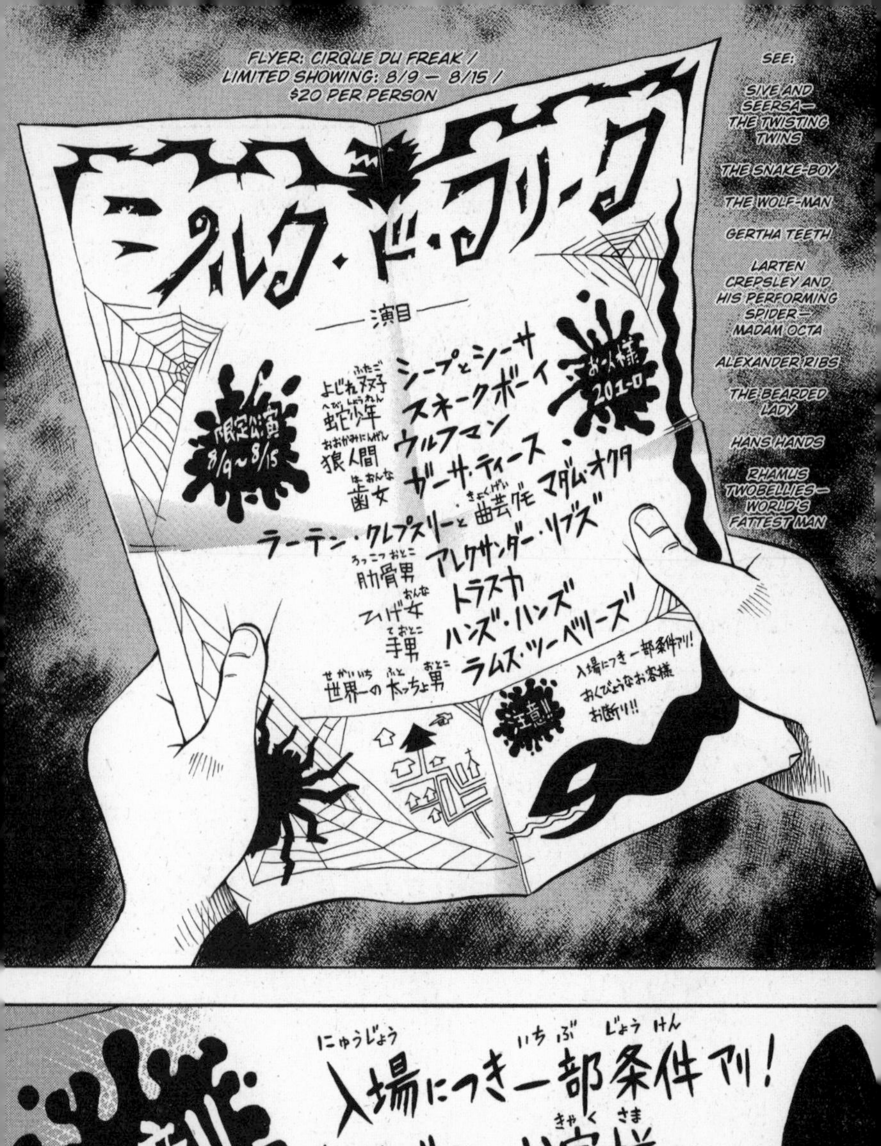
FLYER: CIRQUE DU FREAK / LIMITED SHOWING: 8/9 — 8/15 / $20 PER PERSON
SEE:
SIVE AND SEERSA—THE TWISTING TWINS
THE SNAKE-BOY
THE WOLF-MAN
GERTHA TEETH
LARTEN CREPSLEY AND HIS PERFORMING SPIDER—MADAM OCTA
ALEXANDER RIBS
THE BEARDED LADY
HANS HANDS
RHAMUS TWOBELLIES—WORLD'S FATTEST MAN
シルク・ド・フリーク
演目
限定公演 8/9~8/15
よじれ双子 シーブとシーサ
蛇少年 スネークボーイ
狼人間 ウルフマン
歯女 ガーサ・ティース
ラーテン・クレプスリーと曲芸グモ マダム・オクタ
肋骨男 アレクサンダー・リブズ
ヒゲ女 トラスカ
手男 ハンズ・ハンズ
世界一の太っちょ男 ラムス・ツーベリーズ
注意!!
入場につき一部条件アリ! おくびょうなお客様お断り!!
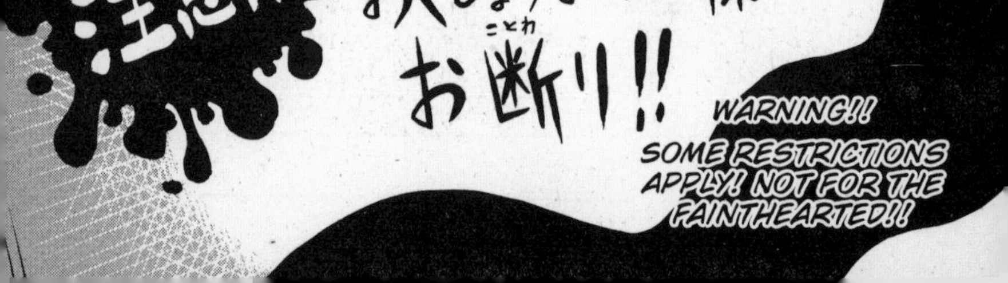
注意!!
入場につき一部条件アリ!
おくびょうなお客様
お断り!!
WARNING!! SOME RESTRICTIONS APPLY! NOT FOR THE FAINTHEARTED!!

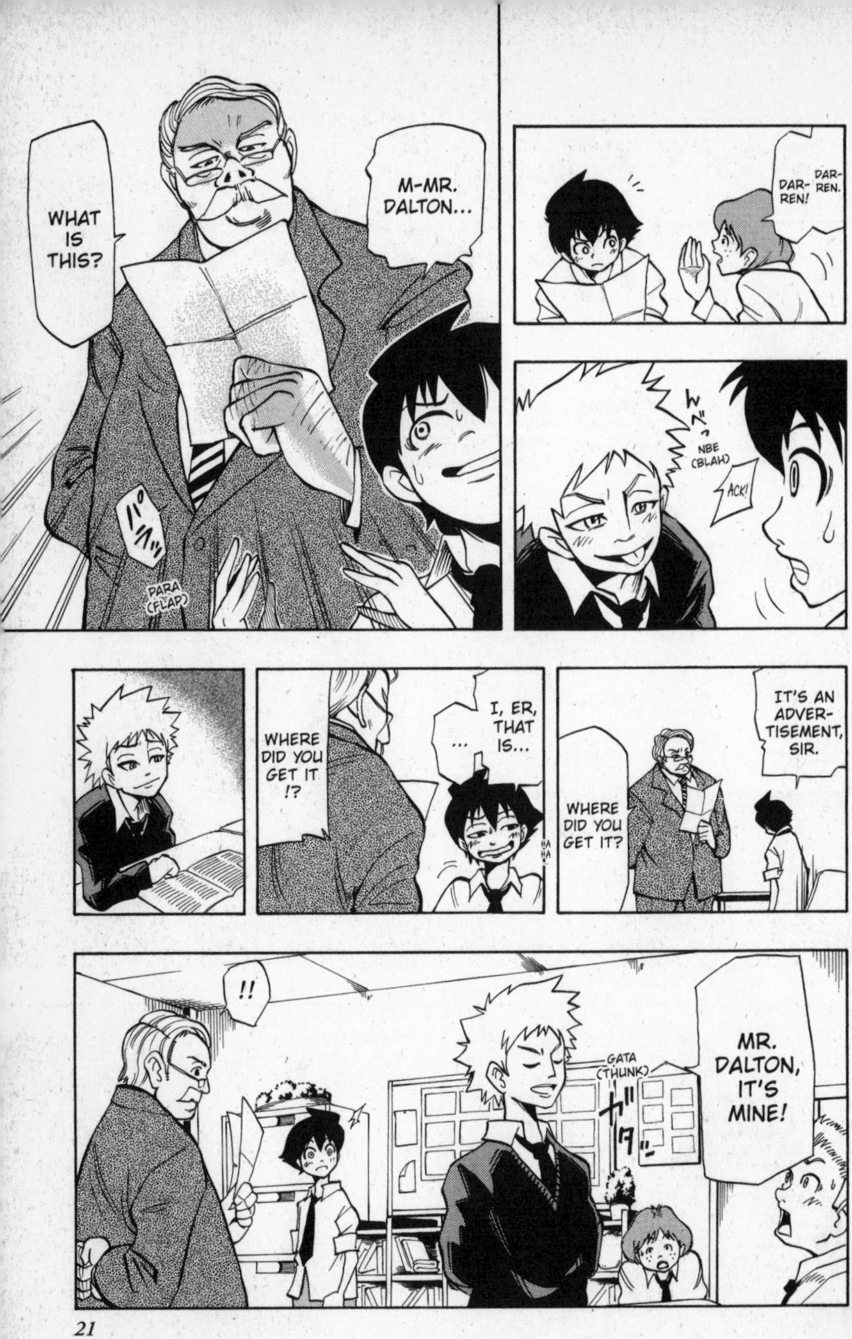
DAR-REN.
DAR-REN!
NBE (BLAH)
ACK!
M-MR. DALTON...
WHAT IS THIS?
PARA (FLAP)
IT'S AN ADVERTISEMENT, SIR.
WHERE DID YOU GET IT?
I, ER, THAT IS...
...
WHERE DID YOU GET IT !?
HAHAHA
MR. DALTON, IT'S MINE!
GATA (THUNK)
!!

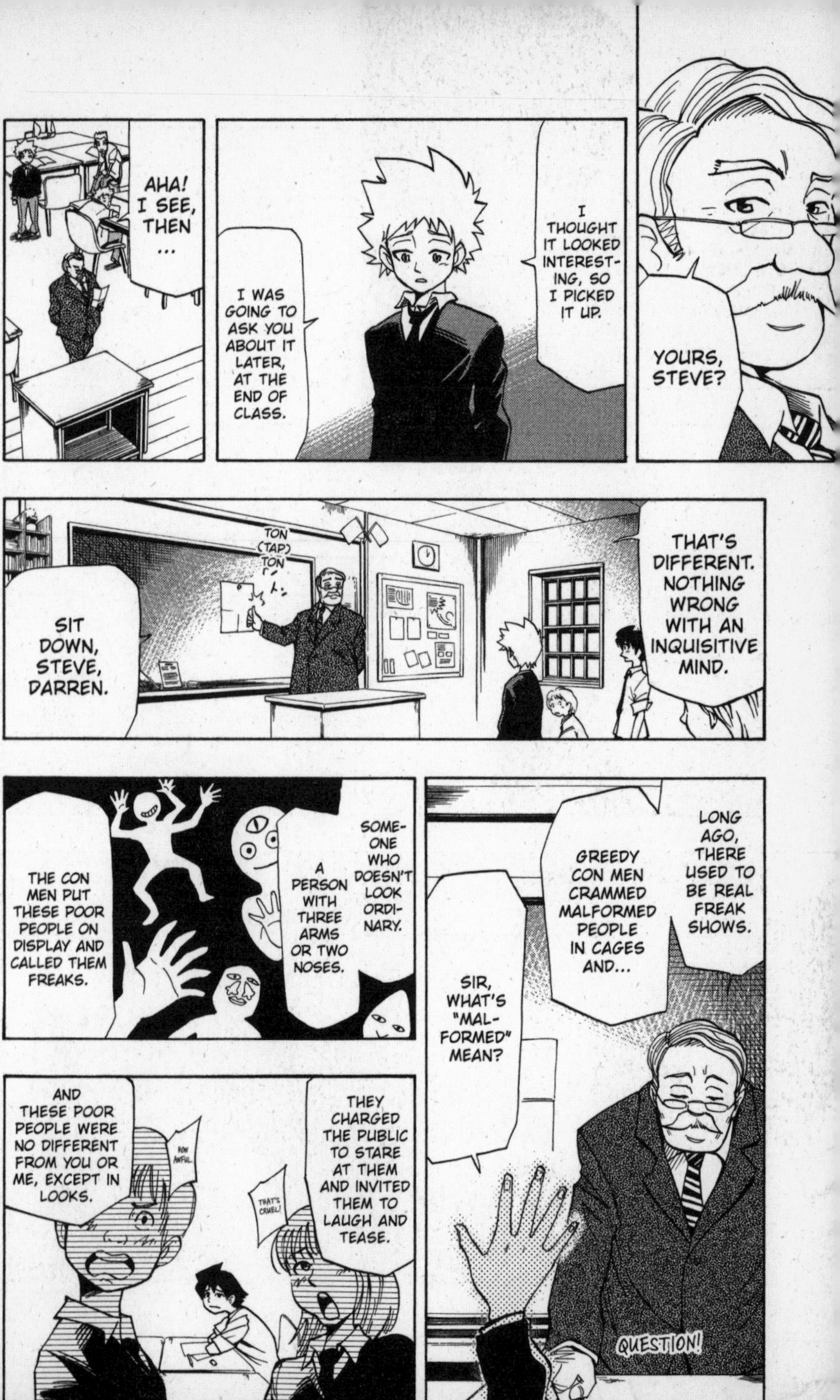
YOURS, STEVE?
I THOUGHT IT LOOKED INTERESTING, SO I PICKED IT UP.
I WAS GOING TO ASK YOU ABOUT IT LATER, AT THE END OF CLASS.
AHA! I SEE, THEN ...
THAT'S DIFFERENT. NOTHING WRONG WITH AN INQUISITIVE MIND.
TON (TAP) TON
SIT DOWN, STEVE, DARREN.
LONG AGO, THERE USED TO BE REAL FREAK SHOWS.
GREEDY CON MEN CRAMMED MALFORMED PEOPLE IN CAGES AND...
SIR, WHAT'S "MALFORMED" MEAN?
QUESTION!
SOMEONE WHO DOESN'T LOOK ORDINARY.
A PERSON WITH THREE ARMS OR TWO NOSES.
THE CON MEN PUT THESE POOR PEOPLE ON DISPLAY AND CALLED THEM FREAKS.
THEY CHARGED THE PUBLIC TO STARE AT THEM AND INVITED THEM TO LAUGH AND TEASE.
THAT'S CRUEL!
HOW AWFUL
AND THESE POOR PEOPLE WERE NO DIFFERENT FROM YOU OR ME, EXCEPT IN LOOKS.

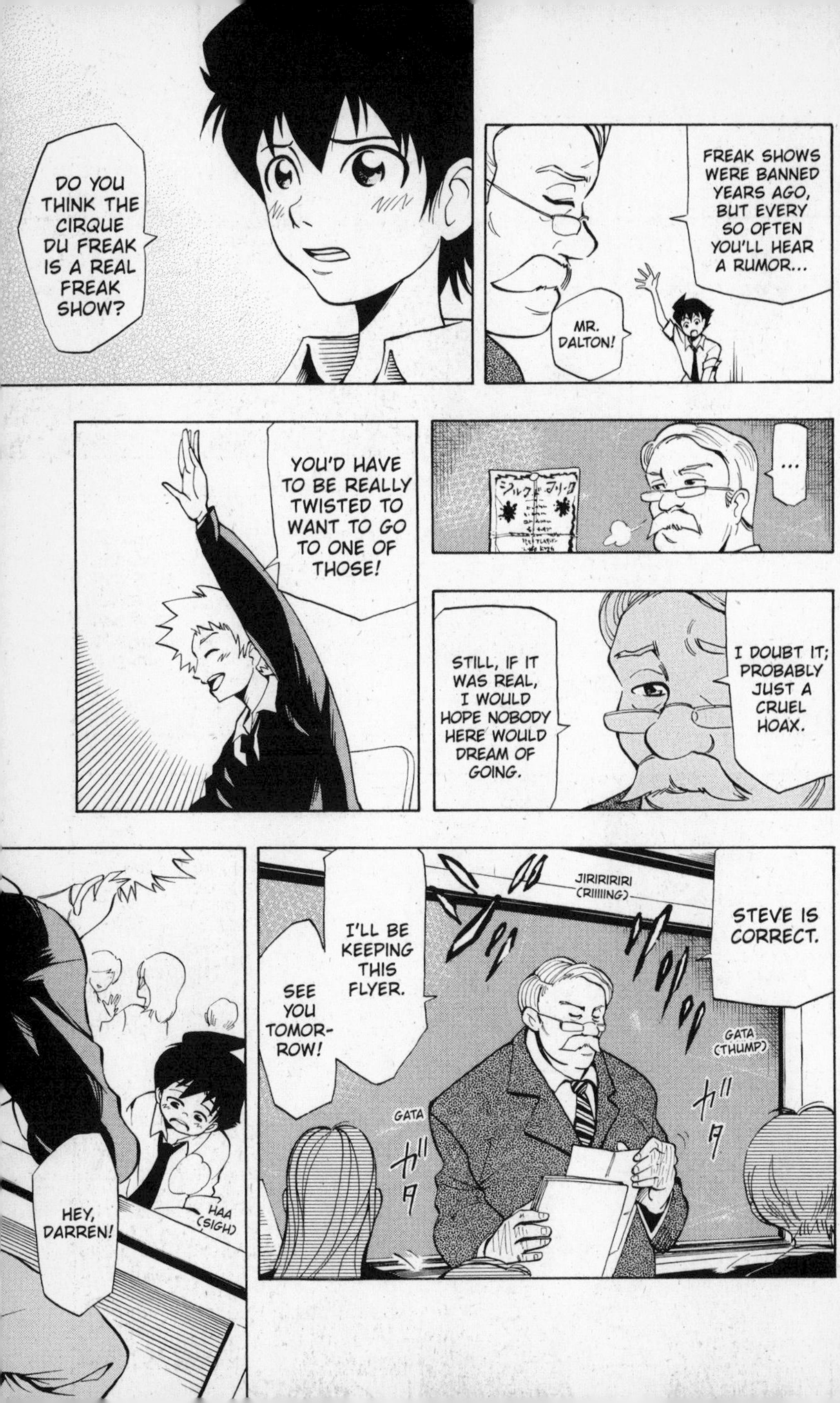
FREAK SHOWS WERE BANNED YEARS AGO, BUT EVERY SO OFTEN YOU'LL HEAR A RUMOR...
MR. DALTON!
DO YOU THINK THE CIRQUE DU FREAK IS A REAL FREAK SHOW?
...
I DOUBT IT; PROBABLY JUST A CRUEL HOAX.
STILL, IF IT WAS REAL, I WOULD HOPE NOBODY HERE WOULD DREAM OF GOING.
YOU'D HAVE TO BE REALLY TWISTED TO WANT TO GO TO ONE OF THOSE!
STEVE IS CORRECT.
JIRIRIRIRI (RIIIIING)
GATA (THUMP)
I'LL BE KEEPING THIS FLYER.
SEE YOU TOMOR-ROW!
GATA
HAA (SIGH)
HEY, DARREN!

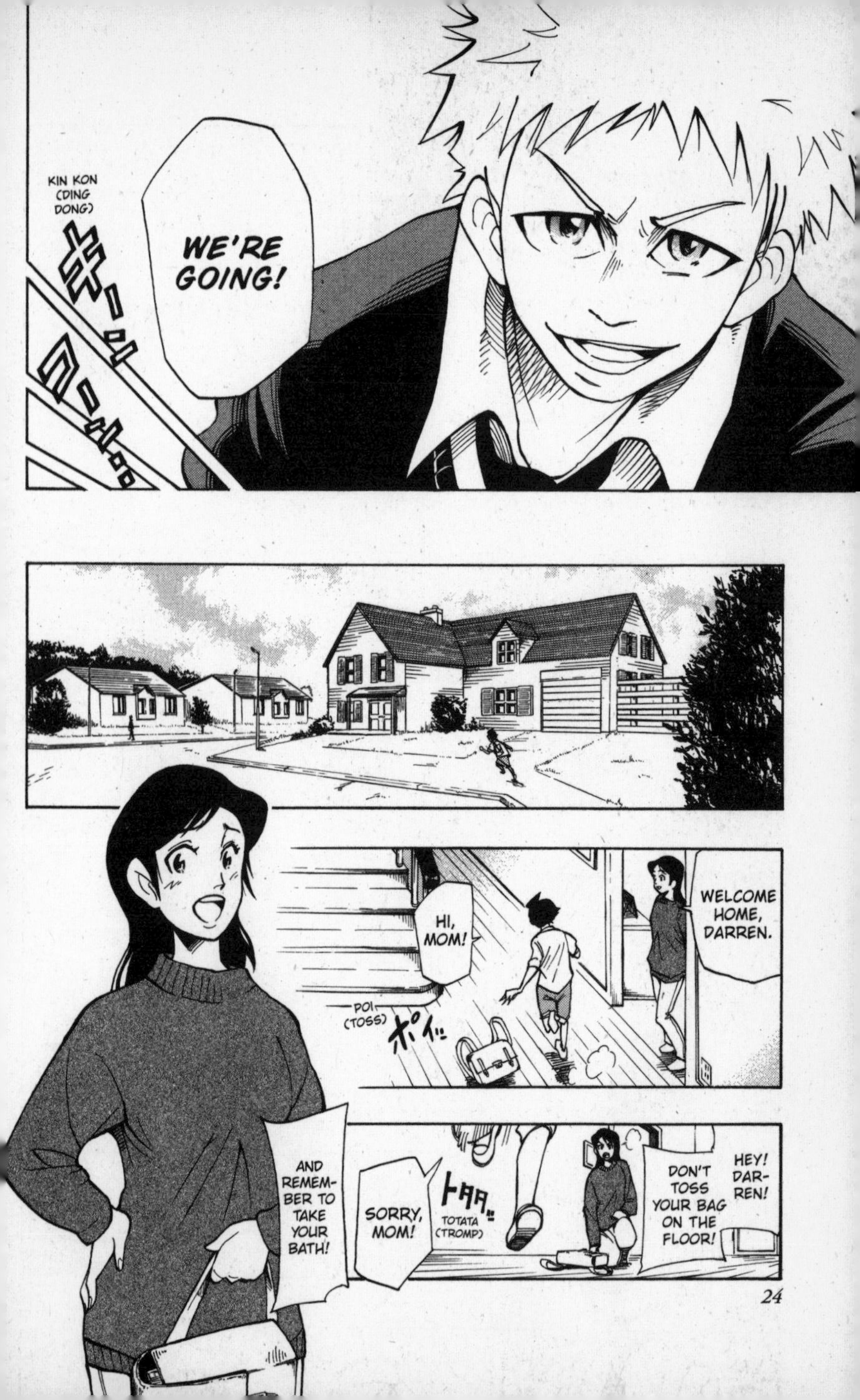
WE'RE GOING!
KIN KON (DING DONG)
WELCOME HOME, DARREN.
HI, MOM!
POI (TOSS)
HEY! DARREN!
DON'T TOSS YOUR BAG ON THE FLOOR!
TOTATA (TROMP)
SORRY, MOM!
AND REMEMBER TO TAKE YOUR BATH!

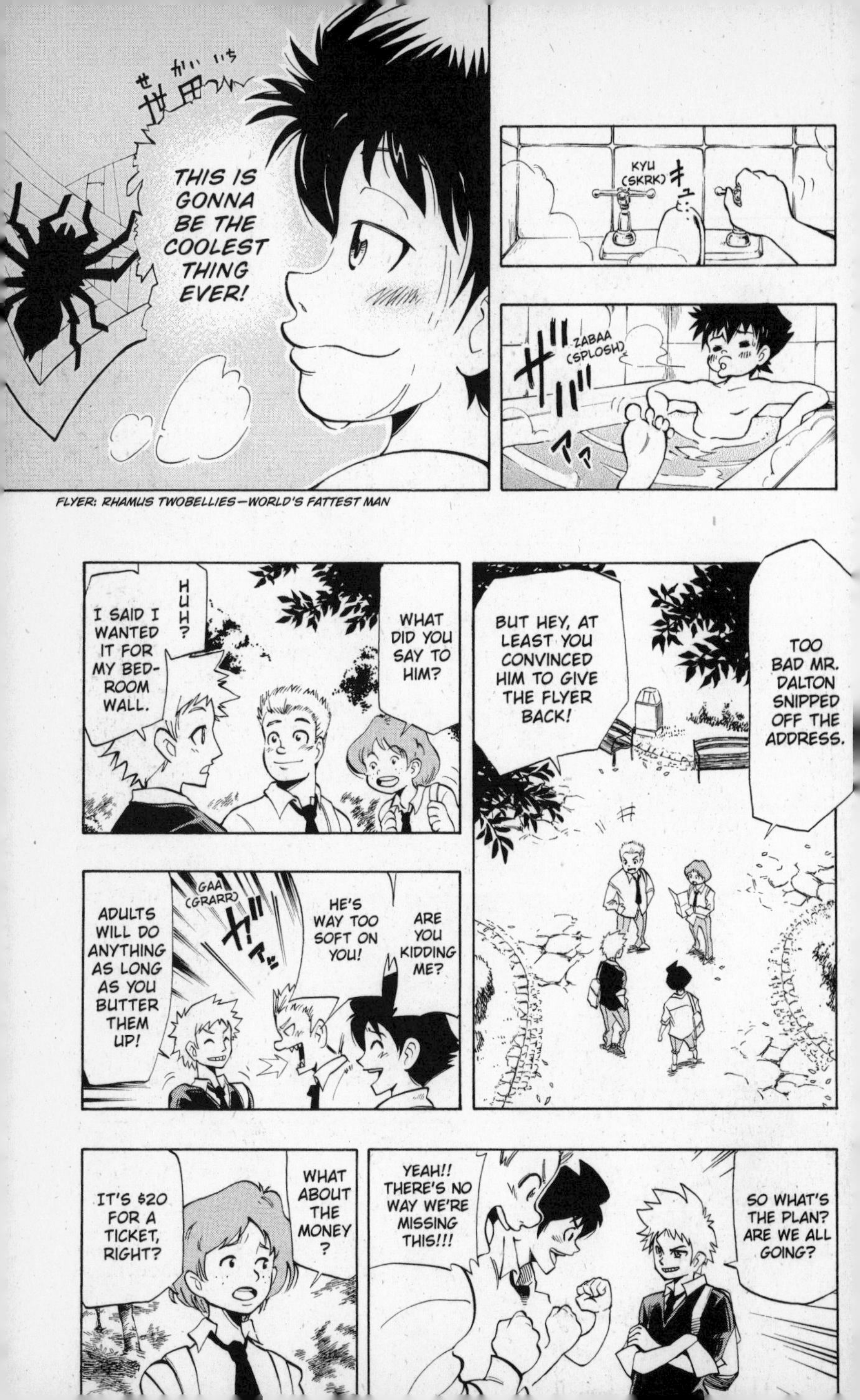
KYU (SKRK)
キュ
ZABAA (SPLOSH)
ザバァ
世界一
THIS IS GONNA BE THE COOLEST THING EVER!
FLYER: RHAMUS TWOBELLIES—WORLD'S FATTEST MAN
TOO BAD MR. DALTON SNIPPED OFF THE ADDRESS.
BUT HEY, AT LEAST YOU CONVINCED HIM TO GIVE THE FLYER BACK!
WHAT DID YOU SAY TO HIM?
HUH?
I SAID I WANTED IT FOR MY BEDROOM WALL.
ARE YOU KIDDING ME?
HE'S WAY TOO SOFT ON YOU!
GAA (GRARR)
ガァッ
ADULTS WILL DO ANYTHING AS LONG AS YOU BUTTER THEM UP!
SO WHAT'S THE PLAN? ARE WE ALL GOING?
YEAH!! THERE'S NO WAY WE'RE MISSING THIS!!!
WHAT ABOUT THE MONEY?
IT'S $20 FOR A TICKET, RIGHT?

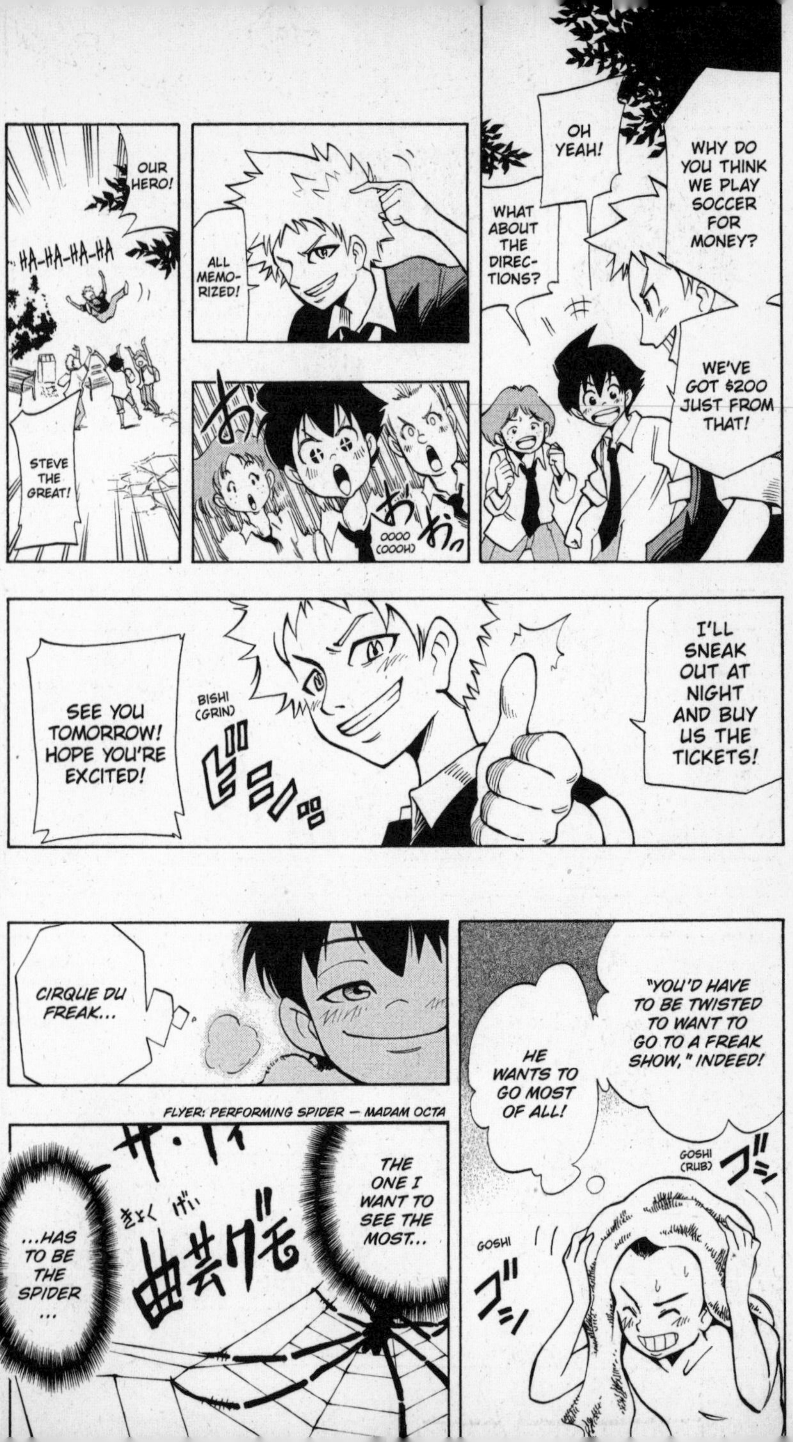
WHY DO YOU THINK WE PLAY SOCCER FOR MONEY?
OH YEAH!
WHAT ABOUT THE DIRECTIONS?
WE'VE GOT $200 JUST FROM THAT!
ALL MEMORIZED!
OOOO (OOOH)
OUR HERO!
HA-HA-HA-HA
STEVE THE GREAT!
I'LL SNEAK OUT AT NIGHT AND BUY US THE TICKETS!
BISHI (GRIN)
SEE YOU TOMORROW! HOPE YOU'RE EXCITED!
"YOU'D HAVE TO BE TWISTED TO WANT TO GO TO A FREAK SHOW," INDEED!
HE WANTS TO GO MOST OF ALL!
GOSHI (RUB)
GOSHI
CIRQUE DU FREAK...
FLYER: PERFORMING SPIDER — MADAM OCTA
THE ONE I WANT TO SEE THE MOST...
曲芸グモ
...HAS TO BE THE SPIDER ...

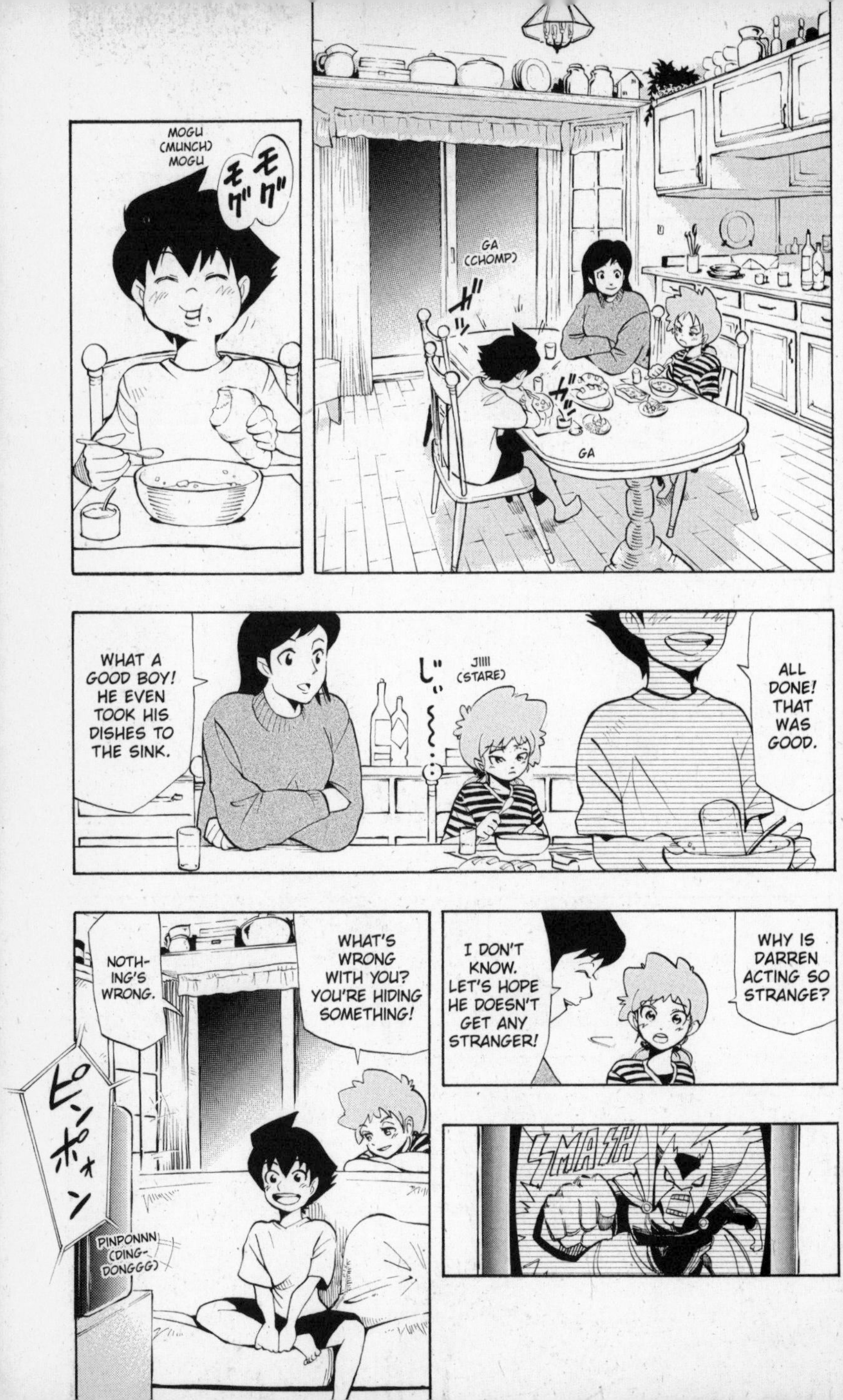
GA (CHOMP)
GA
MOGU (MUNCH) MOGU
モグ モグ
ALL DONE! THAT WAS GOOD.
JIIII (STARE)
じぃ～…
WHAT A GOOD BOY! HE EVEN TOOK HIS DISHES TO THE SINK.
WHY IS DARREN ACTING SO STRANGE?
I DON'T KNOW. LET'S HOPE HE DOESN'T GET ANY STRANGER!
SMASH
WHAT'S WRONG WITH YOU? YOU'RE HIDING SOMETHING!
NOTHING'S WRONG.
ピンポォン
PINPONNN (DING-DONGGG)

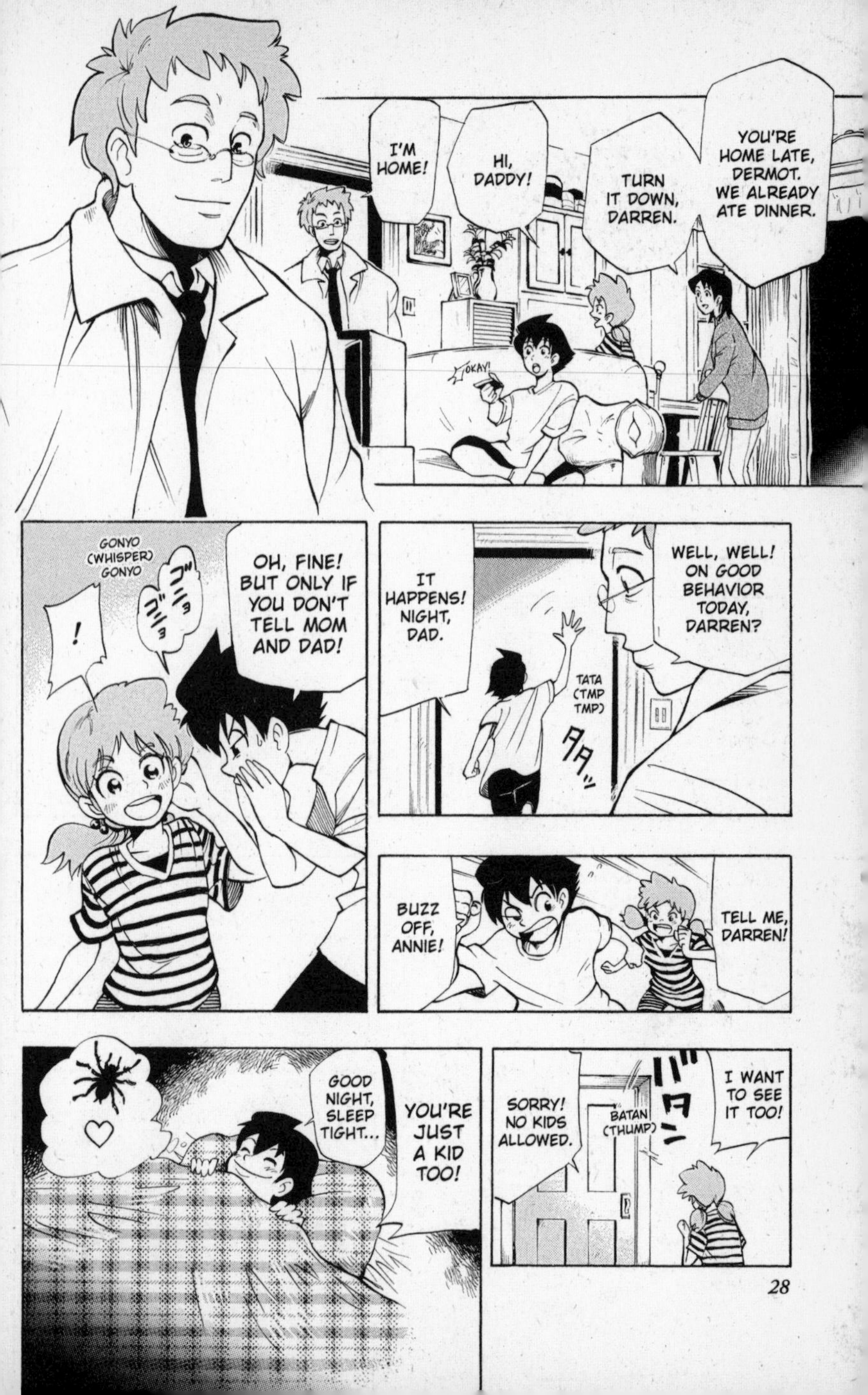
YOU'RE HOME LATE, DERMOT. WE ALREADY ATE DINNER.
TURN IT DOWN, DARREN.
HI, DADDY!
I'M HOME!
OKAY!
WELL, WELL! ON GOOD BEHAVIOR TODAY, DARREN?
TATA (TMP TMP)
IT HAPPENS! NIGHT, DAD.
TELL ME, DARREN!
BUZZ OFF, ANNIE!
OH, FINE! BUT ONLY IF YOU DON'T TELL MOM AND DAD!
GONYO (WHISPER) GONYO
!
I WANT TO SEE IT TOO!
BATAN (THUMP)
SORRY! NO KIDS ALLOWED.
YOU'RE JUST A KID TOO!
GOOD NIGHT, SLEEP TIGHT...

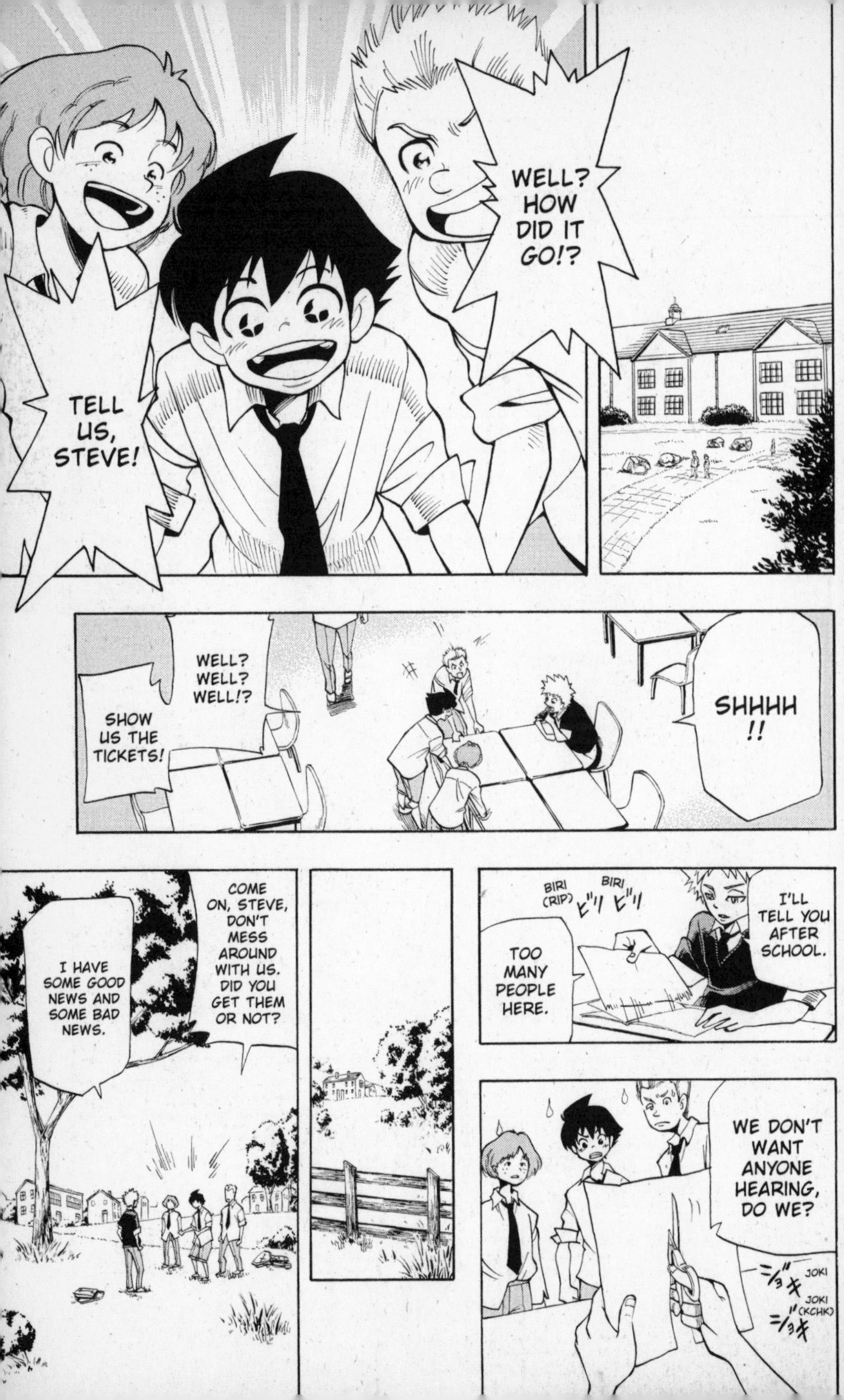

WELL? HOW DID IT GO!?
TELL US, STEVE!
SHHHH !!
WELL? WELL? WELL!?
SHOW US THE TICKETS!
I'LL TELL YOU AFTER SCHOOL.
BIRI (RIP) ビリ
BIRI ビリ
TOO MANY PEOPLE HERE.
WE DON'T WANT ANYONE HEARING, DO WE?
ジョキ JOKI
ジョキ JOKI (KCHK)
COME ON, STEVE, DON'T MESS AROUND WITH US. DID YOU GET THEM OR NOT?
I HAVE SOME GOOD NEWS AND SOME BAD NEWS.

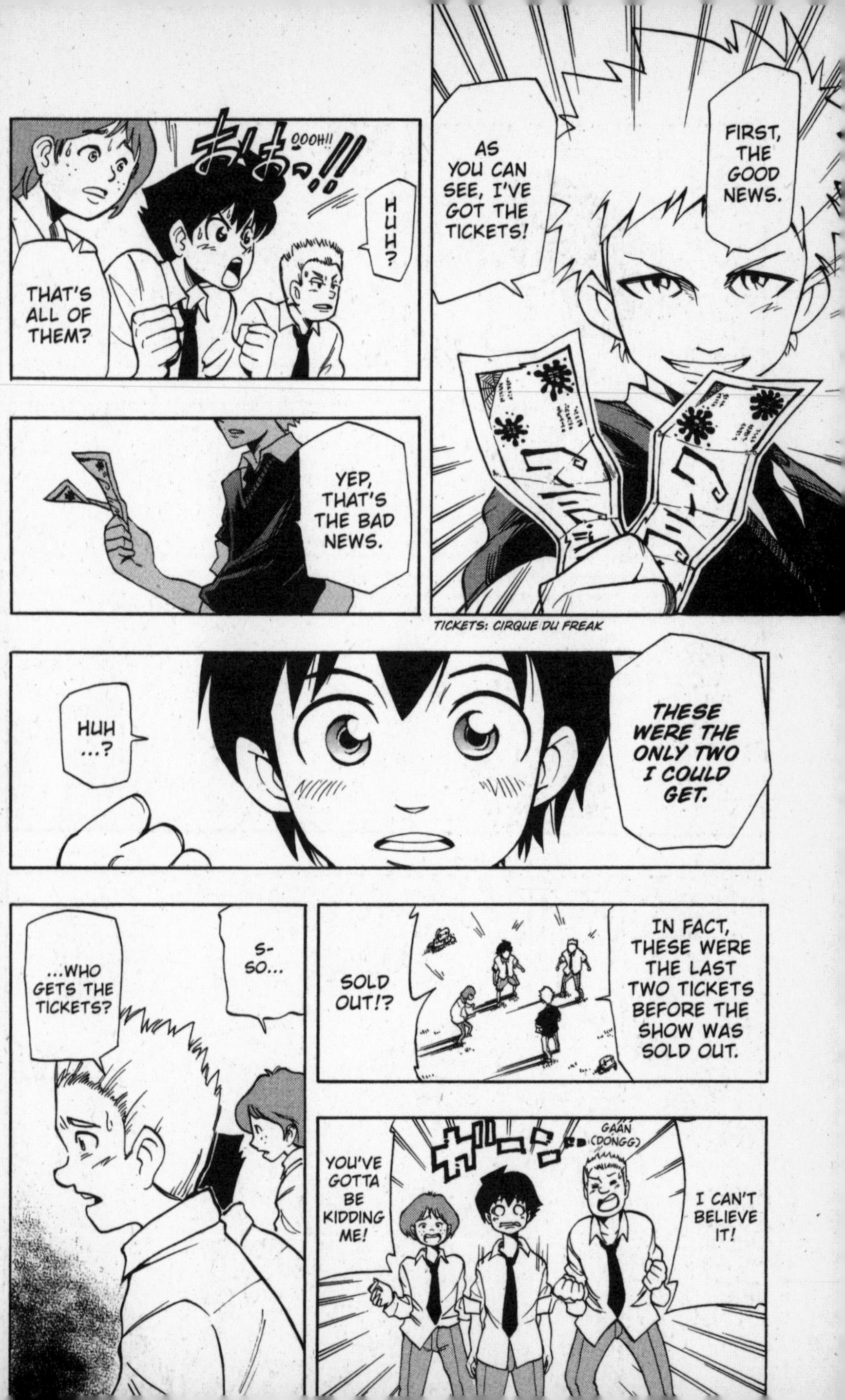
FIRST, THE GOOD NEWS.
AS YOU CAN SEE, I'VE GOT THE TICKETS!
OOOH!!
HUH?
THAT'S ALL OF THEM?
YEP, THAT'S THE BAD NEWS.
TICKETS: CIRQUE DU FREAK
THESE WERE THE ONLY TWO I COULD GET.
HUH ...?
IN FACT, THESE WERE THE LAST TWO TICKETS BEFORE THE SHOW WAS SOLD OUT.
SOLD OUT!?
GAAN (DONGG)
I CAN'T BELIEVE IT!
YOU'VE GOTTA BE KIDDING ME!
S-SO...
...WHO GETS THE TICKETS?

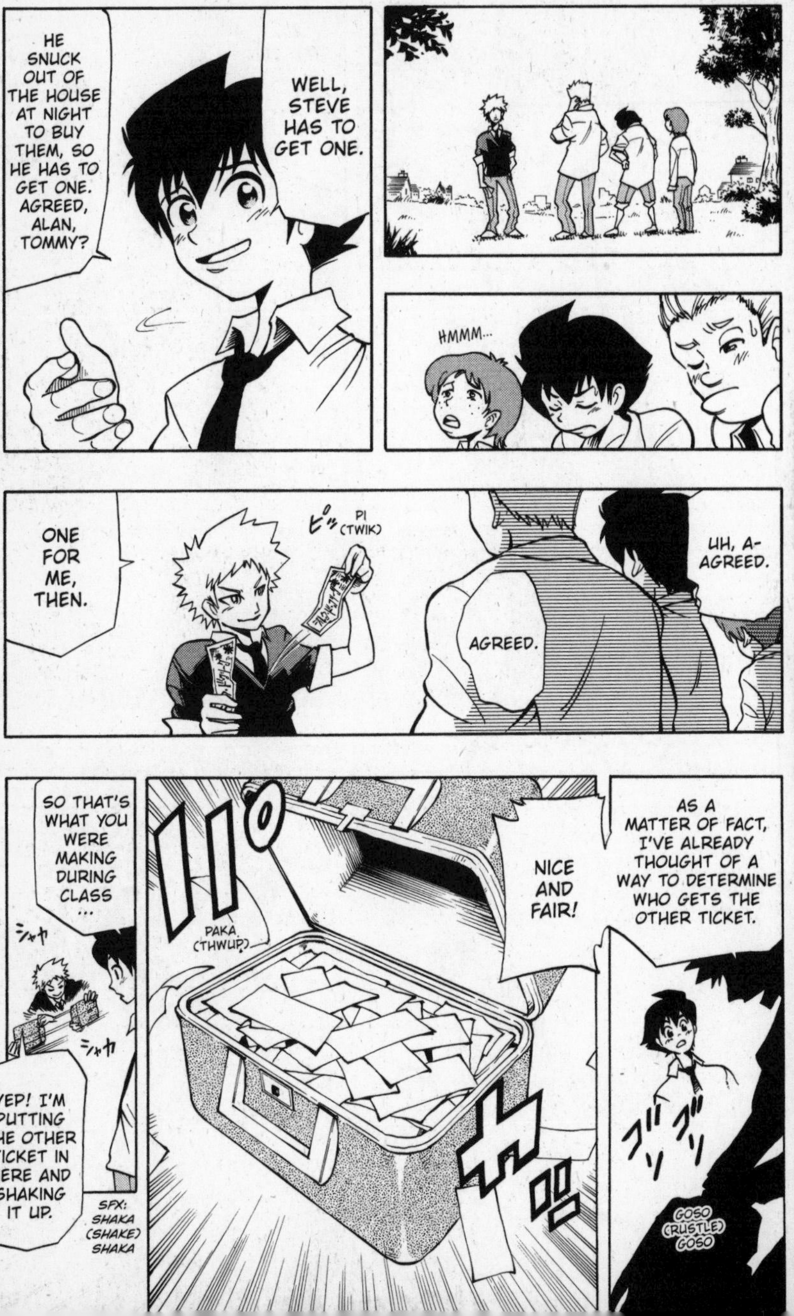
HMMM...
WELL, STEVE HAS TO GET ONE.
HE SNUCK OUT OF THE HOUSE AT NIGHT TO BUY THEM, SO HE HAS TO GET ONE. AGREED, ALAN, TOMMY?
UH, A- AGREED.
AGREED.
PI (TWIK)
ONE FOR ME, THEN.
AS A MATTER OF FACT, I'VE ALREADY THOUGHT OF A WAY TO DETERMINE WHO GETS THE OTHER TICKET.
GOSO (RUSTLE) GOSO
NICE AND FAIR!
PAKA (THWUP)
SO THAT'S WHAT YOU WERE MAKING DURING CLASS...
YEP! I'M PUTTING THE OTHER TICKET IN HERE AND SHAKING IT UP.
SFX: SHAKA (SHAKE) SHAKA

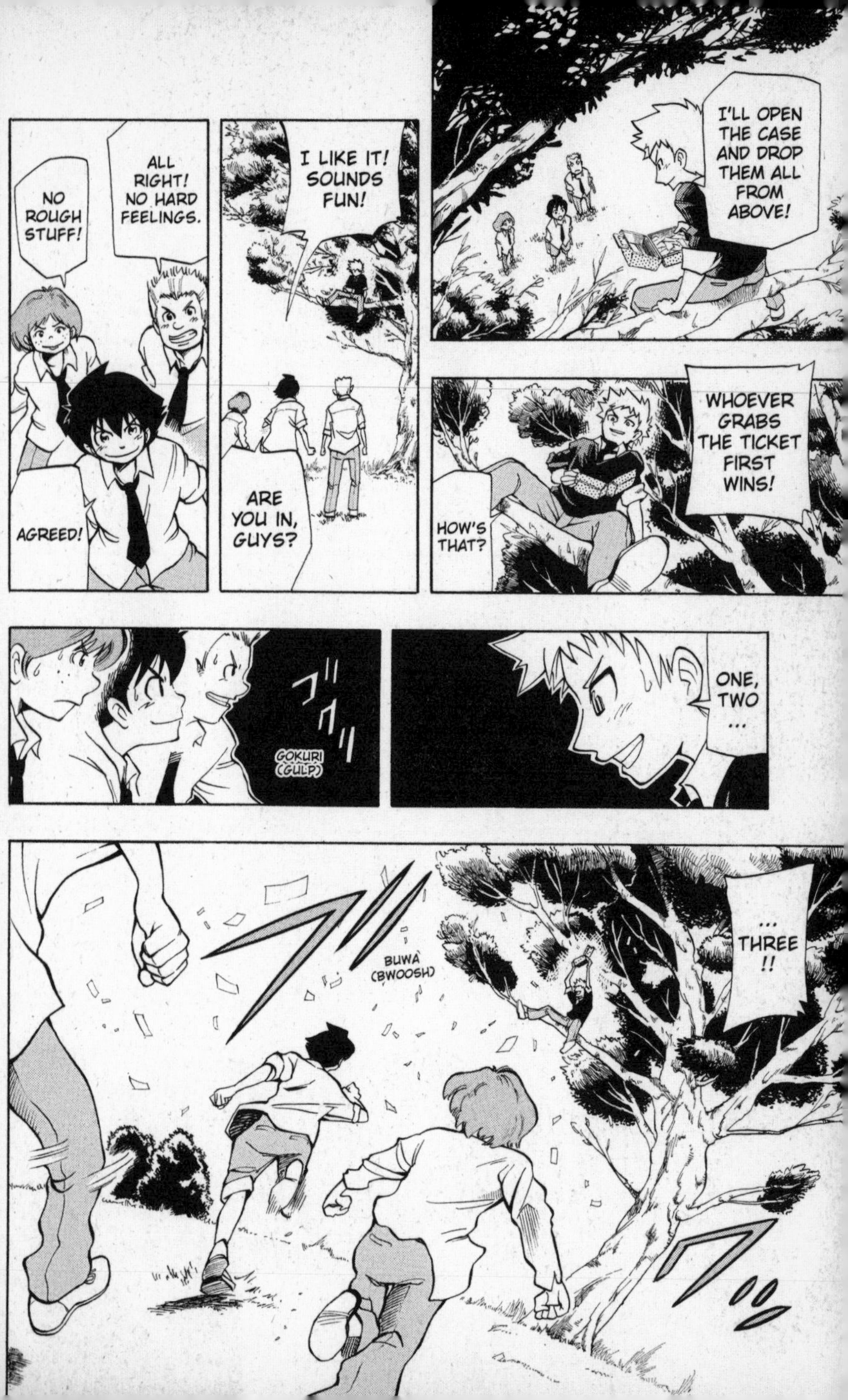
I'LL OPEN THE CASE AND DROP THEM ALL FROM ABOVE!
WHOEVER GRABS THE TICKET FIRST WINS!
HOW'S THAT?
I LIKE IT! SOUNDS FUN!
ARE YOU IN, GUYS?
ALL RIGHT! NO HARD FEELINGS.
NO ROUGH STUFF!
AGREED!
ONE, TWO ...
GOKURI (GULP)
... THREE !!
BUWA (BWOOSH)

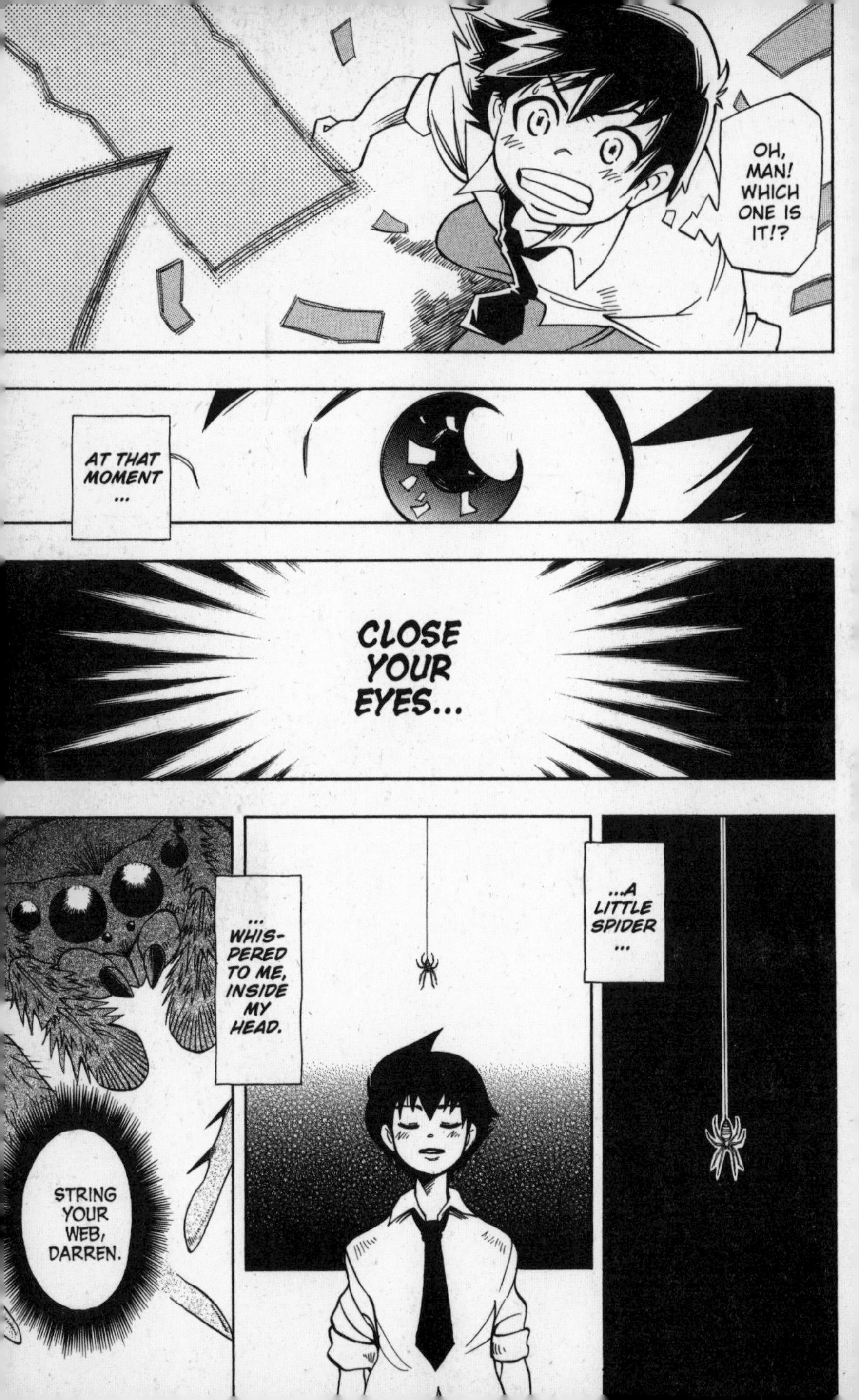
OH, MAN! WHICH ONE IS IT!?
AT THAT MOMENT ...
CLOSE YOUR EYES...
...A LITTLE SPIDER ...
... WHIS-PERED TO ME, INSIDE MY HEAD.
STRING YOUR WEB, DARREN.

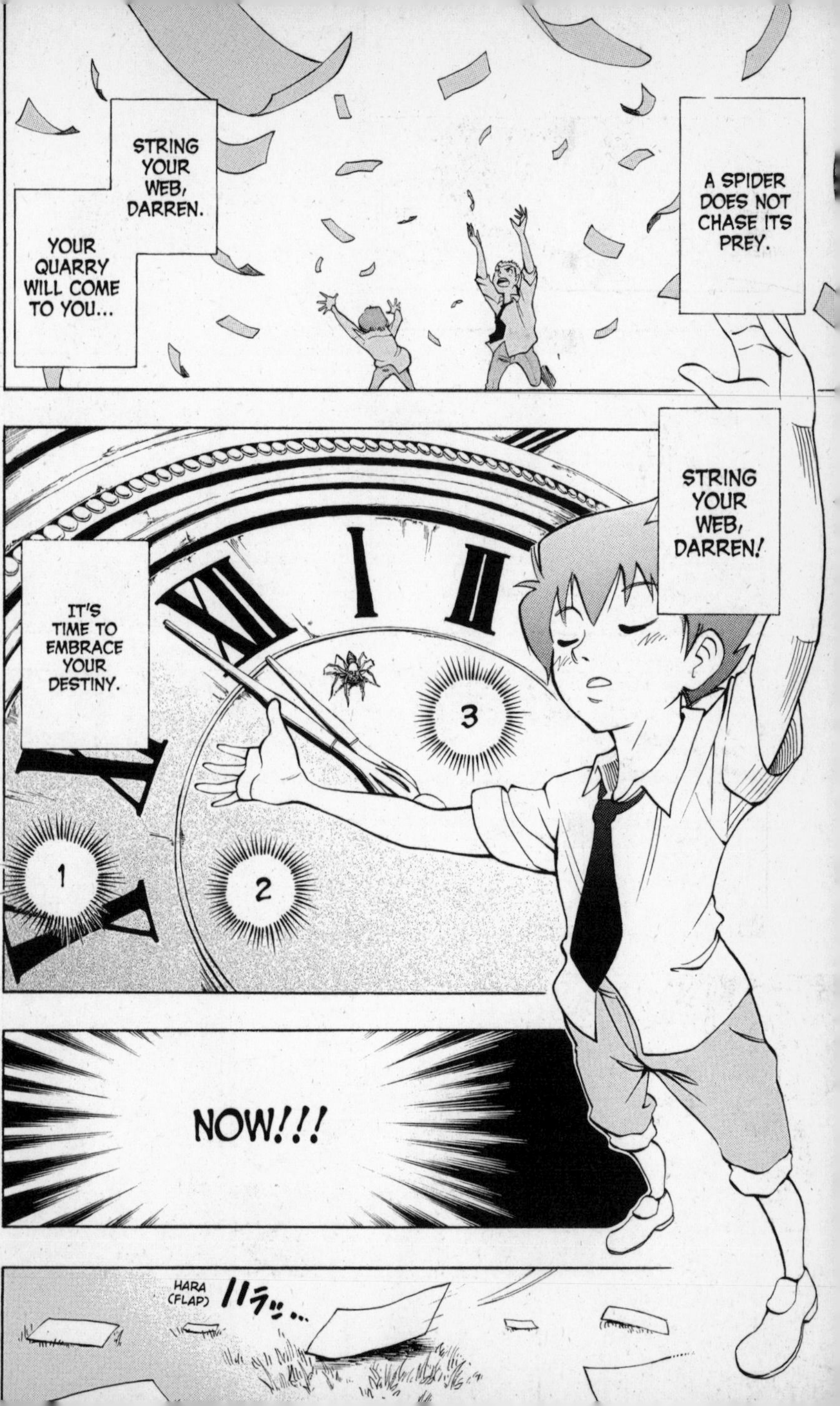
A SPIDER DOES NOT CHASE ITS PREY.
STRING YOUR WEB, DARREN.
YOUR QUARRY WILL COME TO YOU...
STRING YOUR WEB, DARREN!
IT'S TIME TO EMBRACE YOUR DESTINY.
3
2
1
NOW!!!
HARA (FLAP)
ハラッ...

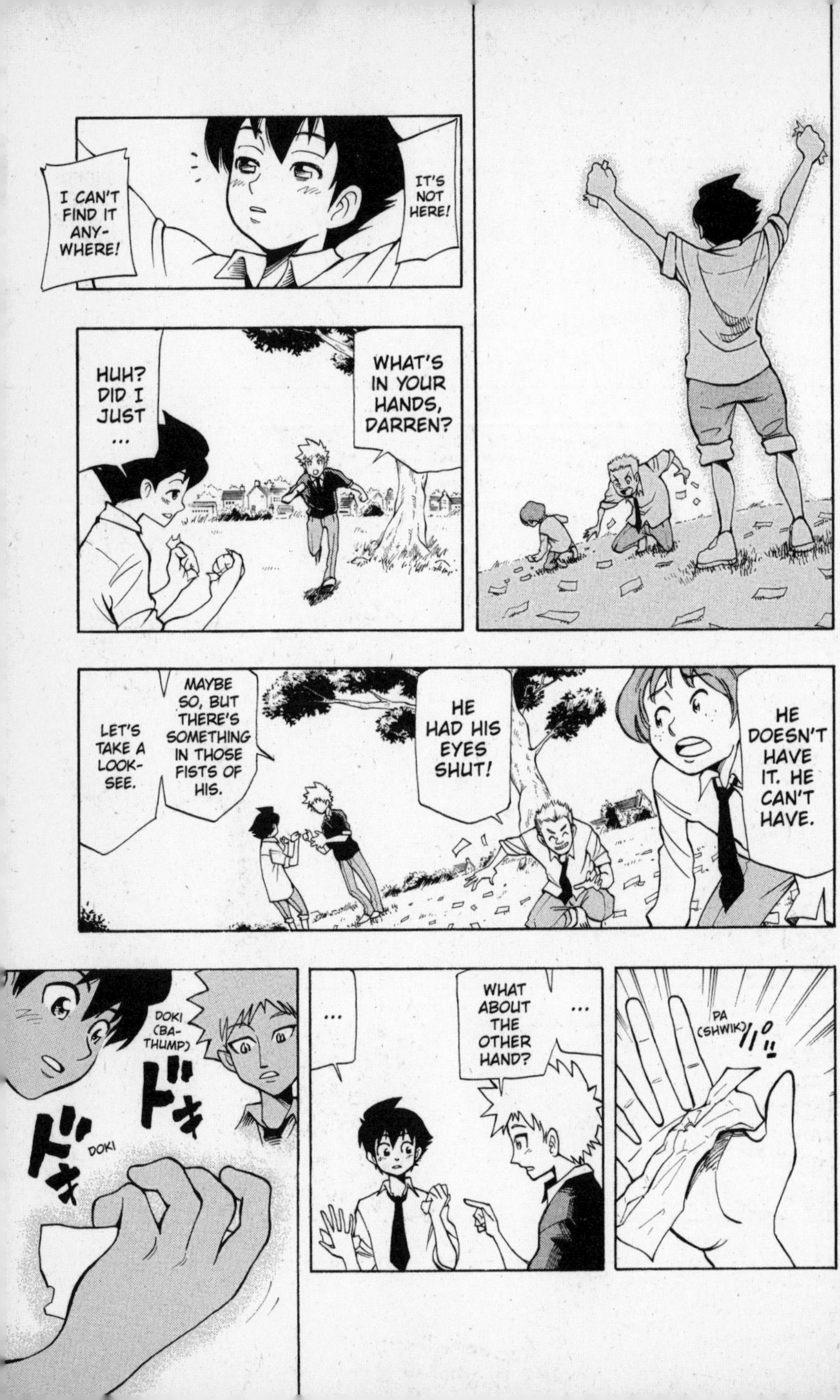
IT'S NOT HERE!
I CAN'T FIND IT ANY-WHERE!
WHAT'S IN YOUR HANDS, DARREN?
HUH? DID I JUST ...
HE DOESN'T HAVE IT. HE CAN'T HAVE.
HE HAD HIS EYES SHUT!
MAYBE SO, BUT THERE'S SOMETHING IN THOSE FISTS OF HIS.
LET'S TAKE A LOOK-SEE.
PA (SHWIK)
...
WHAT ABOUT THE OTHER HAND?
...
DOKI (BA-THUMP)
ドキ
ドキ
DOKI

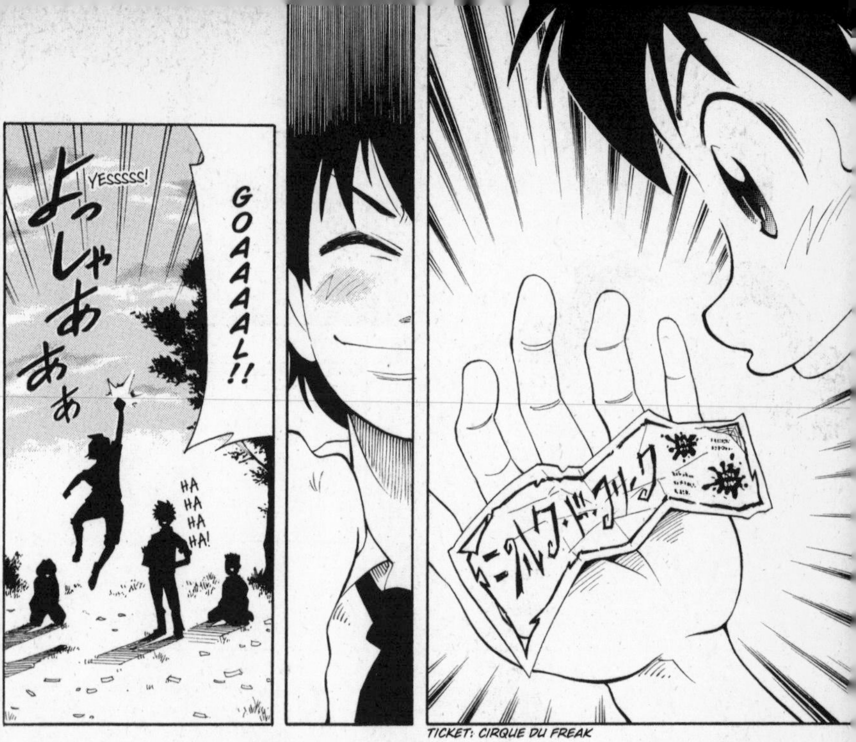
GOAAAAAL!!
よっしゃあぁぁ
YESSSSS!
HA HA HA HA!
TICKET: CIRQUE DU FREAK

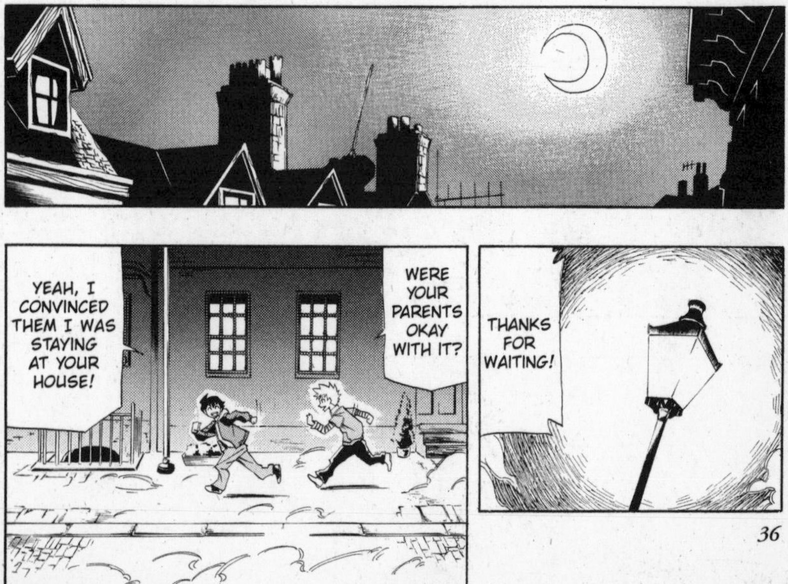
THANKS FOR WAITING!
WERE YOUR PARENTS OKAY WITH IT?
YEAH, I CONVINCED THEM I WAS STAYING AT YOUR HOUSE!

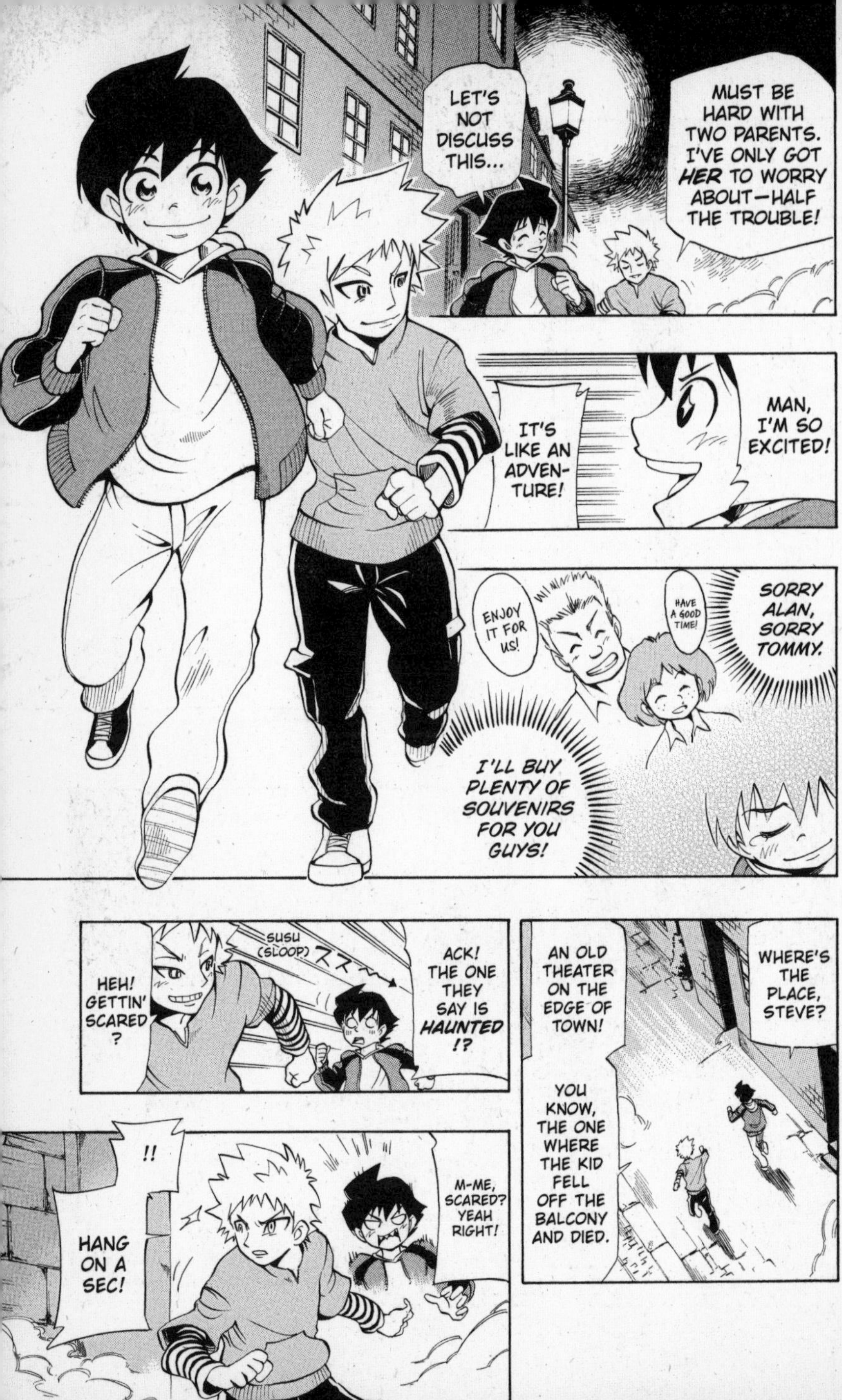
MUST BE HARD WITH TWO PARENTS. I'VE ONLY GOT HER TO WORRY ABOUT—HALF THE TROUBLE!
LET'S NOT DISCUSS THIS...
MAN, I'M SO EXCITED!
IT'S LIKE AN ADVENTURE!
SORRY ALAN, SORRY TOMMY.
HAVE A GOOD TIME!
ENJOY IT FOR US!
I'LL BUY PLENTY OF SOUVENIRS FOR YOU GUYS!
WHERE'S THE PLACE, STEVE?
AN OLD THEATER ON THE EDGE OF TOWN!
YOU KNOW, THE ONE WHERE THE KID FELL OFF THE BALCONY AND DIED.
ACK! THE ONE THEY SAY IS HAUNTED!?
スス
SUSU (SLOOP)
HEH! GETTIN' SCARED?
M-ME, SCARED? YEAH RIGHT!
!!
HANG ON A SEC!

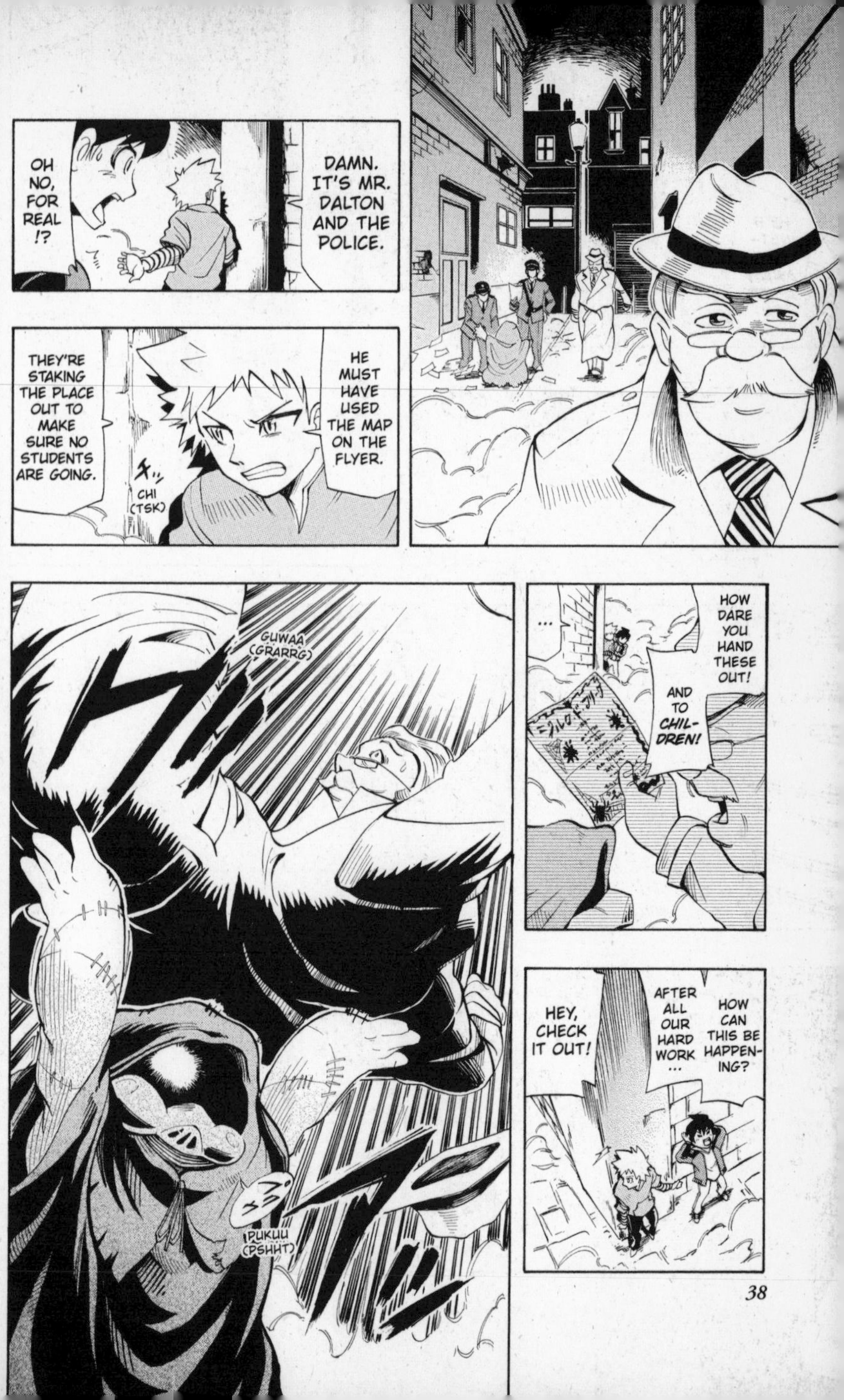
DAMN. IT'S MR. DALTON AND THE POLICE.
OH NO, FOR REAL!?
HE MUST HAVE USED THE MAP ON THE FLYER.
THEY'RE STAKING THE PLACE OUT TO MAKE SURE NO STUDENTS ARE GOING.
CHI (TSK)
HOW DARE YOU HAND THESE OUT!
AND TO CHILDREN!
...
HOW CAN THIS BE HAPPENING?
AFTER ALL OUR HARD WORK...
HEY, CHECK IT OUT!
GUWAA (GRARRG)
PUKUU (PSHHT)

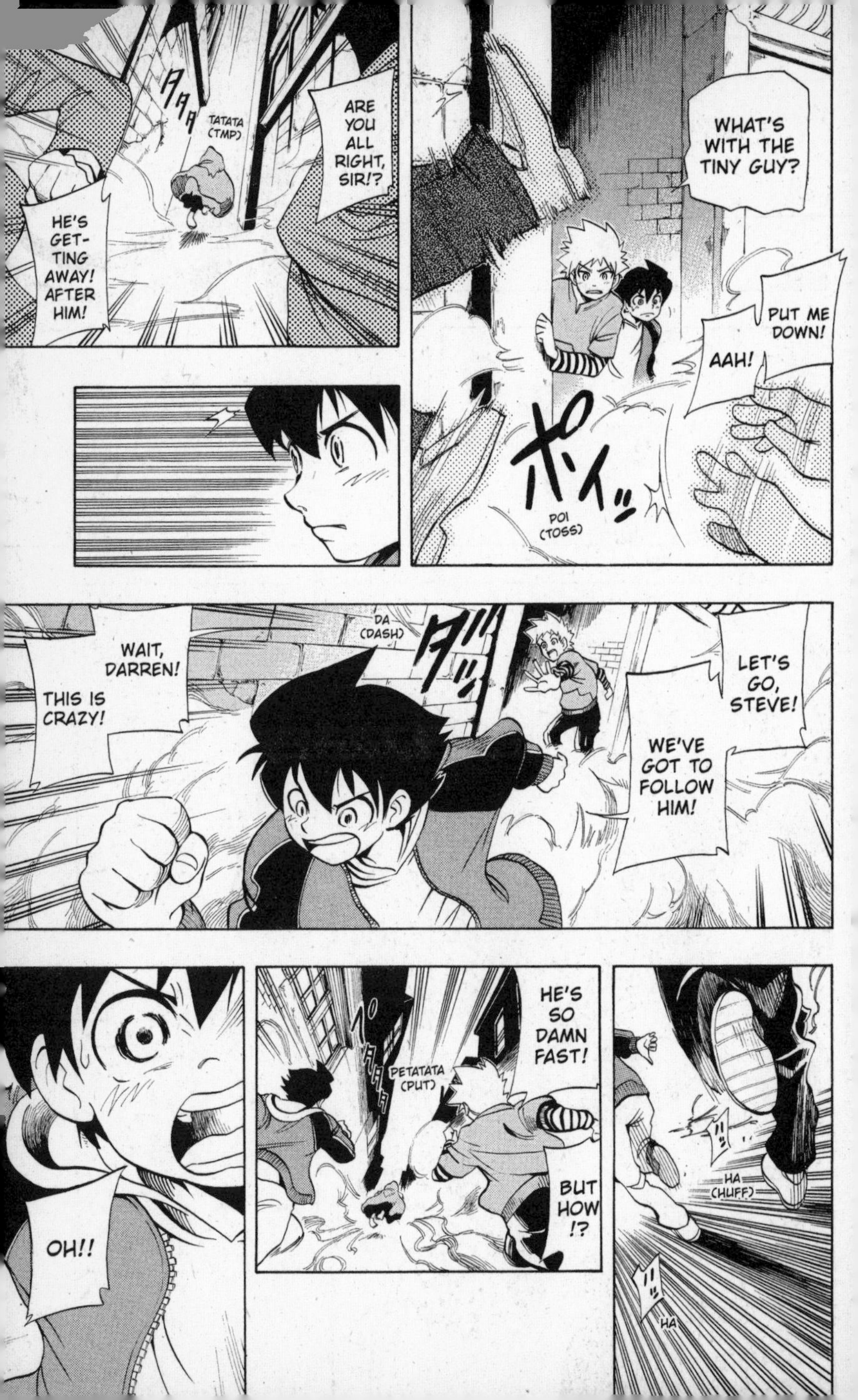
WHAT'S WITH THE TINY GUY?
PUT ME DOWN!
AAH!
POI (TOSS)
ARE YOU ALL RIGHT, SIR!?
TATATA (TMP)
HE'S GET-TING AWAY! AFTER HIM!
LET'S GO, STEVE!
WE'VE GOT TO FOLLOW HIM!
DA (DASH)
WAIT, DARREN!
THIS IS CRAZY!
HA (CHUFF)
HA
HE'S SO DAMN FAST!
BUT HOW !?
PETATATA (PUT)
OH!!

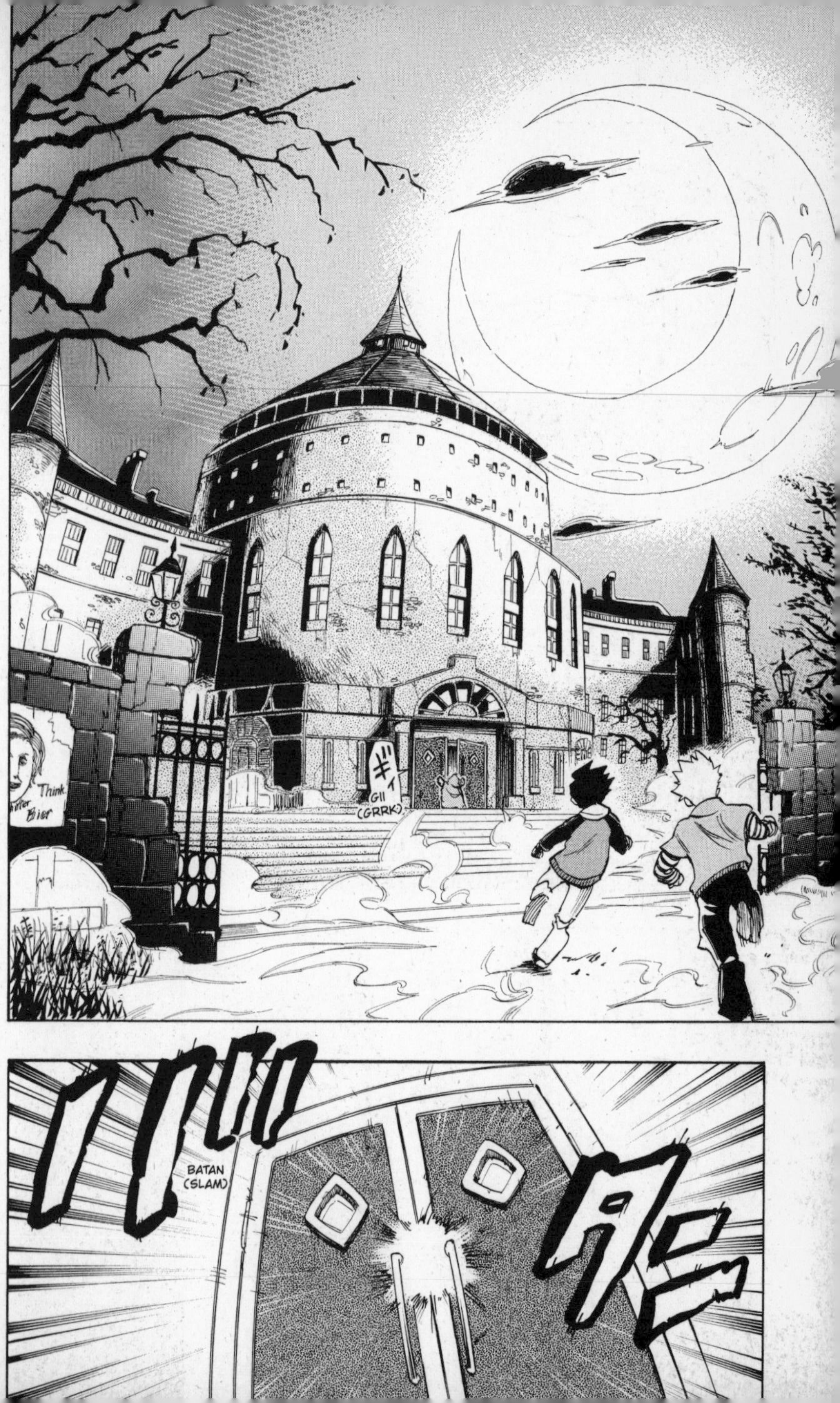
ギイ
GII
(GRRK-)
Think
BATAN
(SLAM)

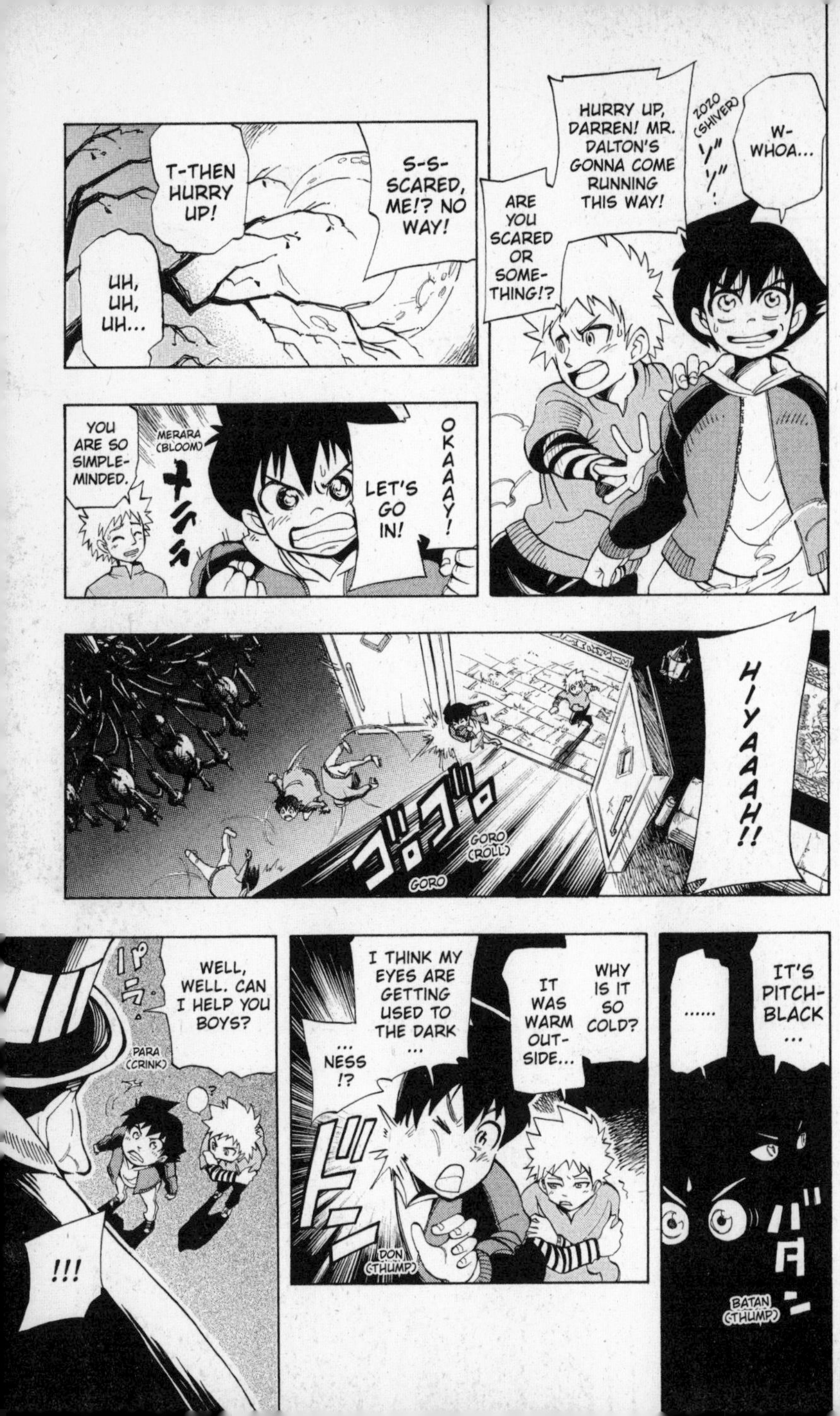
W-WHOA...
ZOZO (SHIVER)
HURRY UP, DARREN! MR. DALTON'S GONNA COME RUNNING THIS WAY!
ARE YOU SCARED OR SOMETHING!?
S-S-SCARED, ME!? NO WAY!
T-THEN HURRY UP!
UH, UH, UH...
OKAAAAY!
LET'S GO IN!
MERARA (BLOOM)
YOU ARE SO SIMPLE-MINDED.
HIYAAAAH!!
GORO (ROLL)
GORO
IT'S PITCH-BLACK...
......
BATAN (THUMP)
WHY IS IT SO COLD?
IT WAS WARM OUTSIDE...
I THINK MY EYES ARE GETTING USED TO THE DARK...
...NESS!?
DON (THUMP)
WELL, WELL. CAN I HELP YOU BOYS?
PARA (CRINK)
!!!

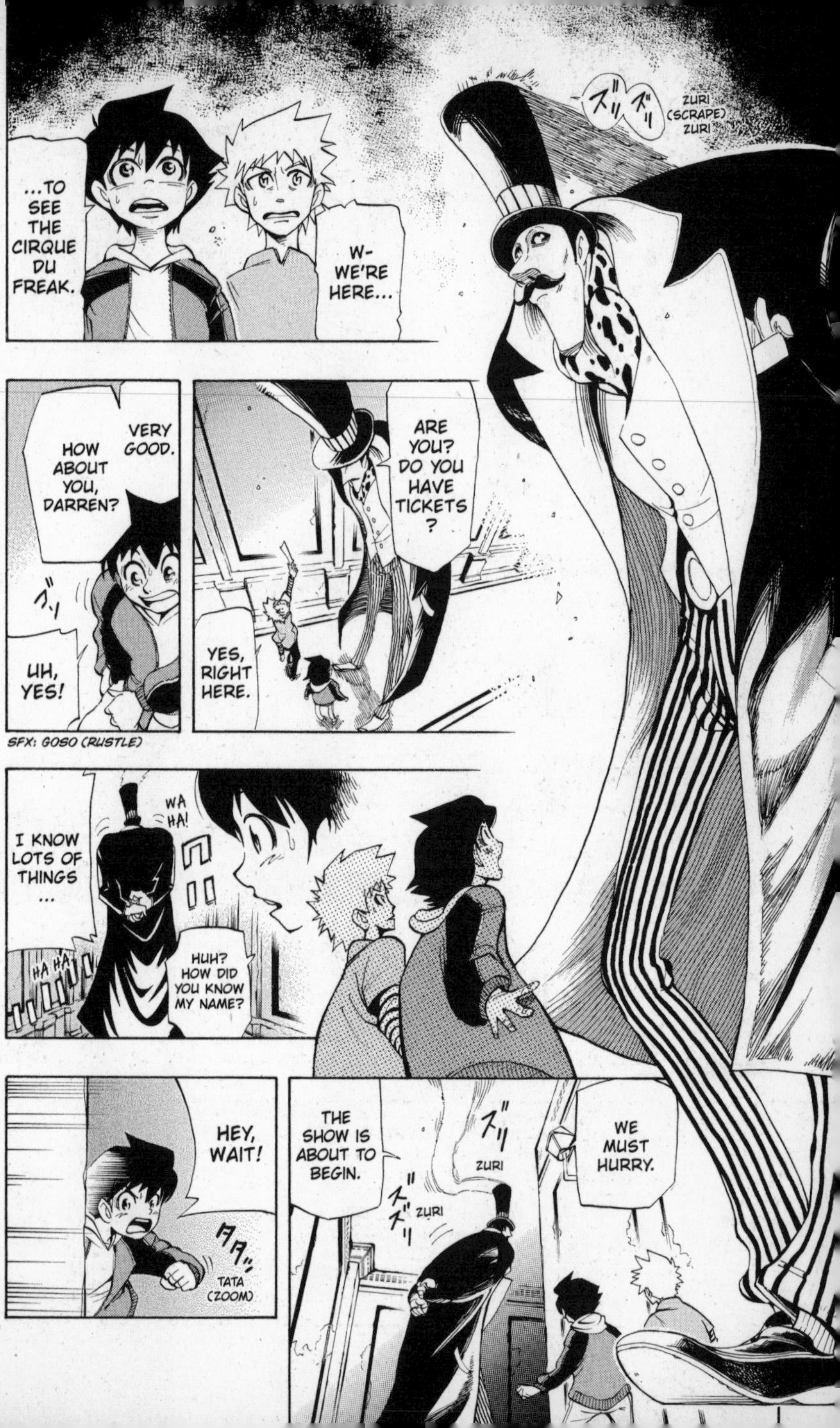

ZURI (SCRAPE) ZURI
W-WE'RE HERE...
...TO SEE THE CIRQUE DU FREAK.
ARE YOU? DO YOU HAVE TICKETS?
YES, RIGHT HERE.
VERY GOOD.
HOW ABOUT YOU, DARREN?
UH, YES!
SFX: GOSO (RUSTLE)
HUH? HOW DID YOU KNOW MY NAME?
WA HA!
I KNOW LOTS OF THINGS...
HA HA
WE MUST HURRY.
ZURI
THE SHOW IS ABOUT TO BEGIN.
ZURI
HEY, WAIT!
TATA (ZOOM)

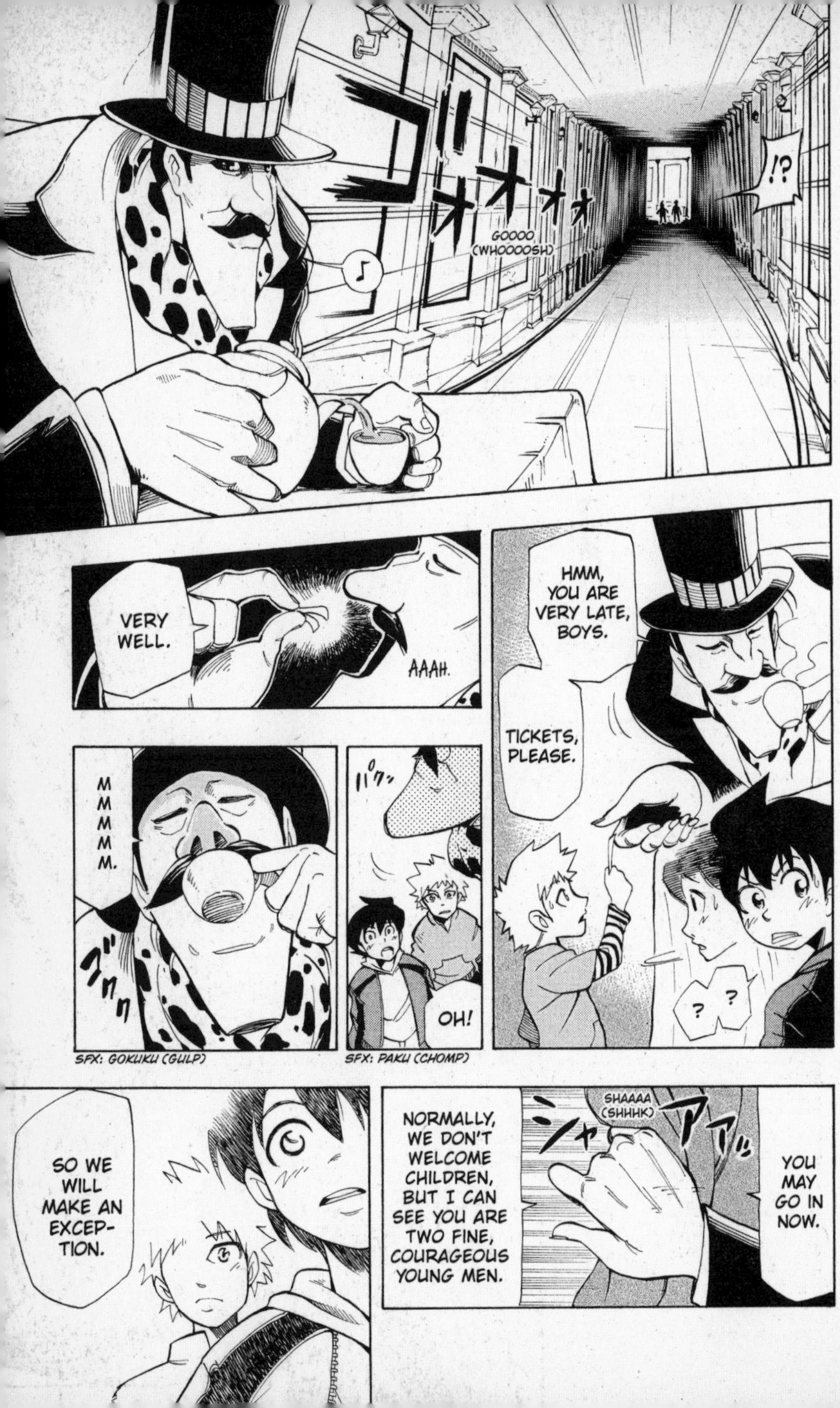
!?
GOOOO (WHOOOOSH)
HMM, YOU ARE VERY LATE, BOYS.
TICKETS, PLEASE.
? ?
VERY WELL.
AAAH.
OH!
SFX: PAKU (CHOMP)
MMMMMM.
SFX: GOKUKU (GULP)
SHAAAA (SHHHK)
YOU MAY GO IN NOW.
NORMALLY, WE DON'T WELCOME CHILDREN, BUT I CAN SEE YOU ARE TWO FINE, COURAGEOUS YOUNG MEN.
SO WE WILL MAKE AN EXCEPTION.

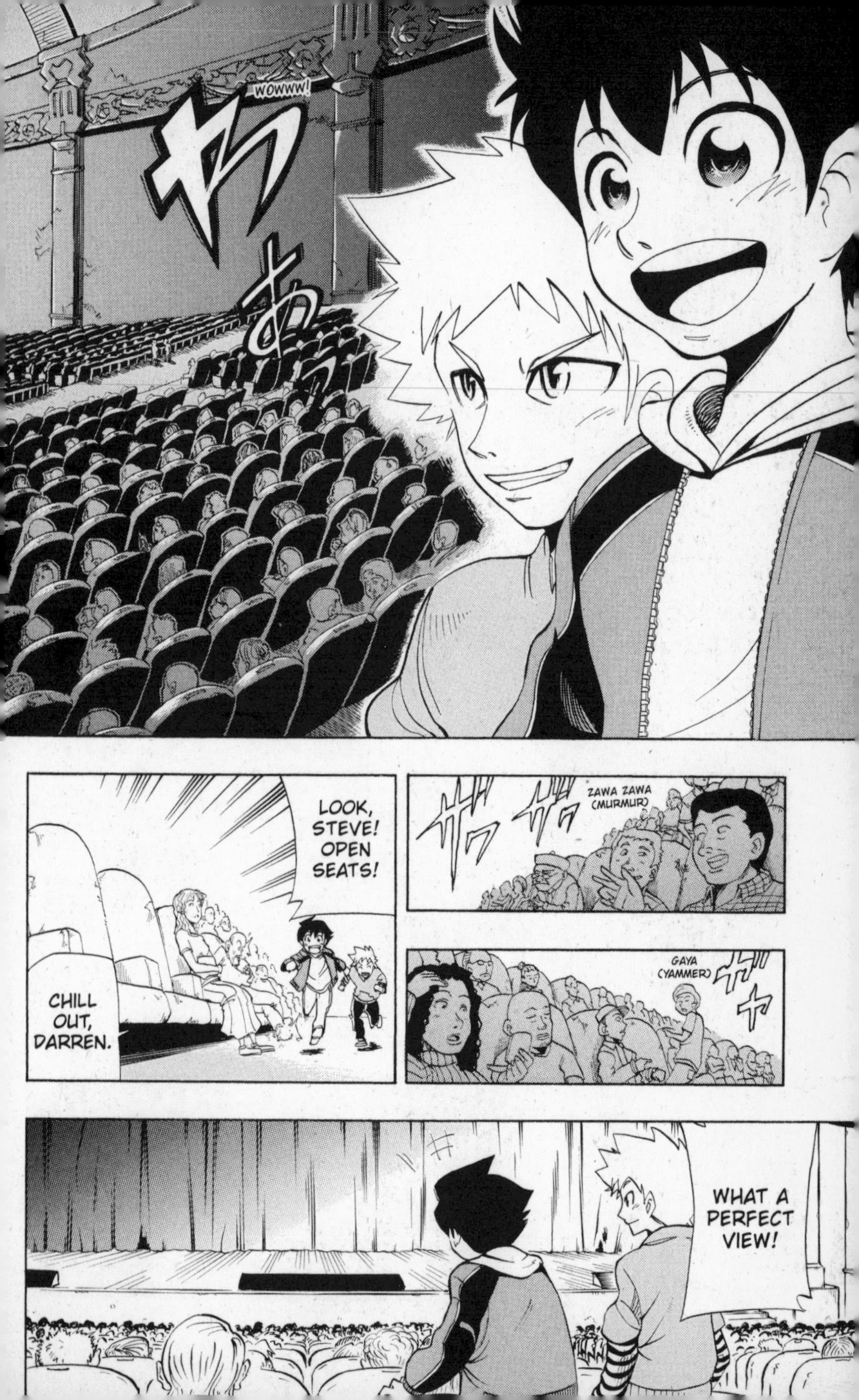
WOWWW!
ZAWA ZAWA (MURMUR)
GAYA (YAMMER)
LOOK, STEVE! OPEN SEATS!
CHILL OUT, DARREN.
WHAT A PERFECT VIEW!

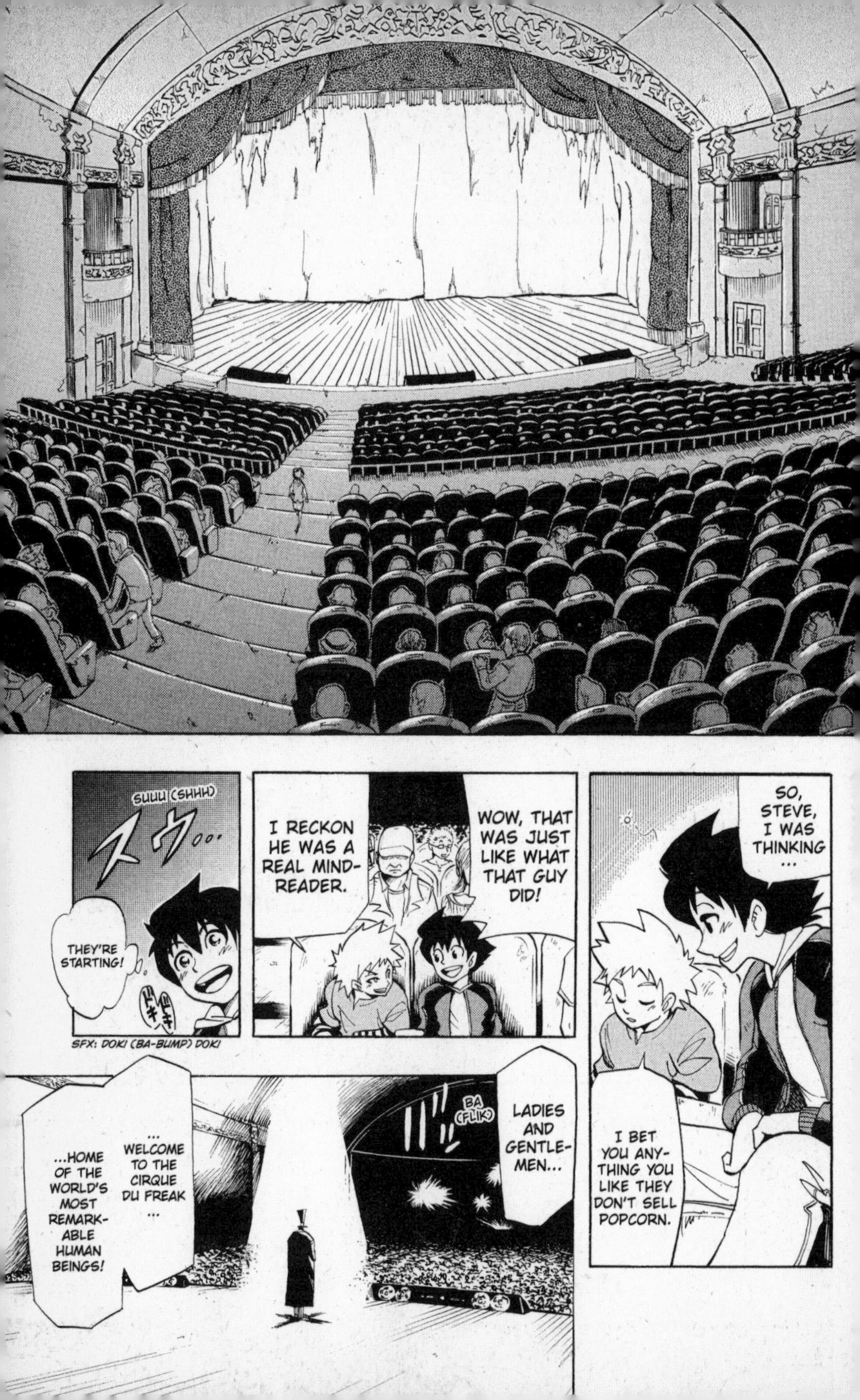
SO, STEVE, I WAS THINKING ...
I BET YOU ANYTHING YOU LIKE THEY DON'T SELL POPCORN.
WOW, THAT WAS JUST LIKE WHAT THAT GUY DID!
I RECKON HE WAS A REAL MIND-READER.
SUUU (SHHH)
THEY'RE STARTING!
SFX: DOKI (BA-BUMP) DOKI
BA (FLIK)
LADIES AND GENTLE-MEN...
... WELCOME TO THE CIRQUE DU FREAK ...
...HOME OF THE WORLD'S MOST REMARK-ABLE HUMAN BEINGS!

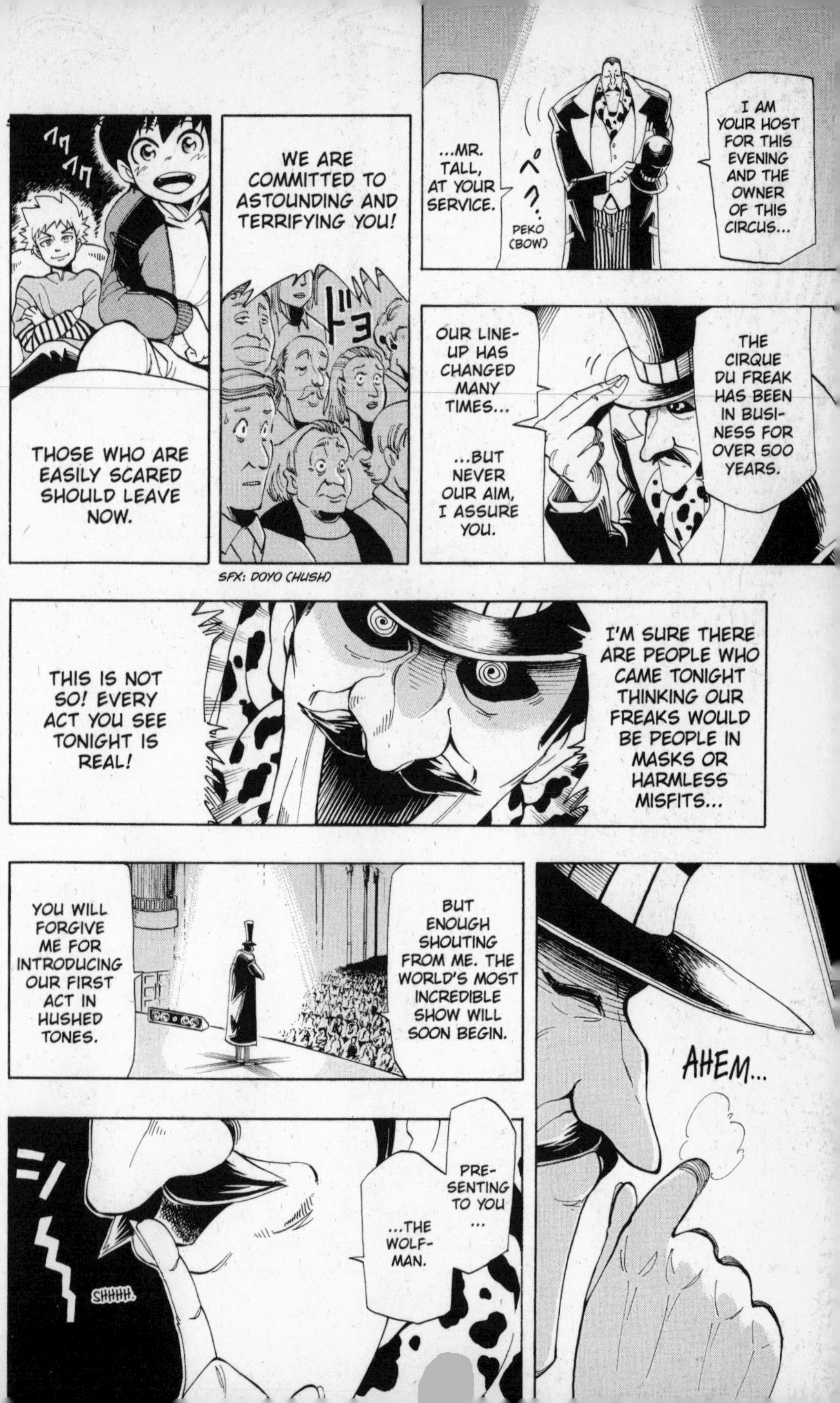
I AM YOUR HOST FOR THIS EVENING AND THE OWNER OF THIS CIRCUS...
...MR. TALL, AT YOUR SERVICE.
PEKO (BOW)
THE CIRQUE DU FREAK HAS BEEN IN BUSINESS FOR OVER 500 YEARS.
OUR LINE-UP HAS CHANGED MANY TIMES...
...BUT NEVER OUR AIM, I ASSURE YOU.
WE ARE COMMITTED TO ASTOUNDING AND TERRIFYING YOU!
SFX: DOYO (HUSH)
THOSE WHO ARE EASILY SCARED SHOULD LEAVE NOW.
I'M SURE THERE ARE PEOPLE WHO CAME TONIGHT THINKING OUR FREAKS WOULD BE PEOPLE IN MASKS OR HARMLESS MISFITS...
THIS IS NOT SO! EVERY ACT YOU SEE TONIGHT IS REAL!
AHEM...
BUT ENOUGH SHOUTING FROM ME. THE WORLD'S MOST INCREDIBLE SHOW WILL SOON BEGIN.
YOU WILL FORGIVE ME FOR INTRODUCING OUR FIRST ACT IN HUSHED TONES.
PRESENTING TO YOU ...
...THE WOLFMAN.
SHHHH.

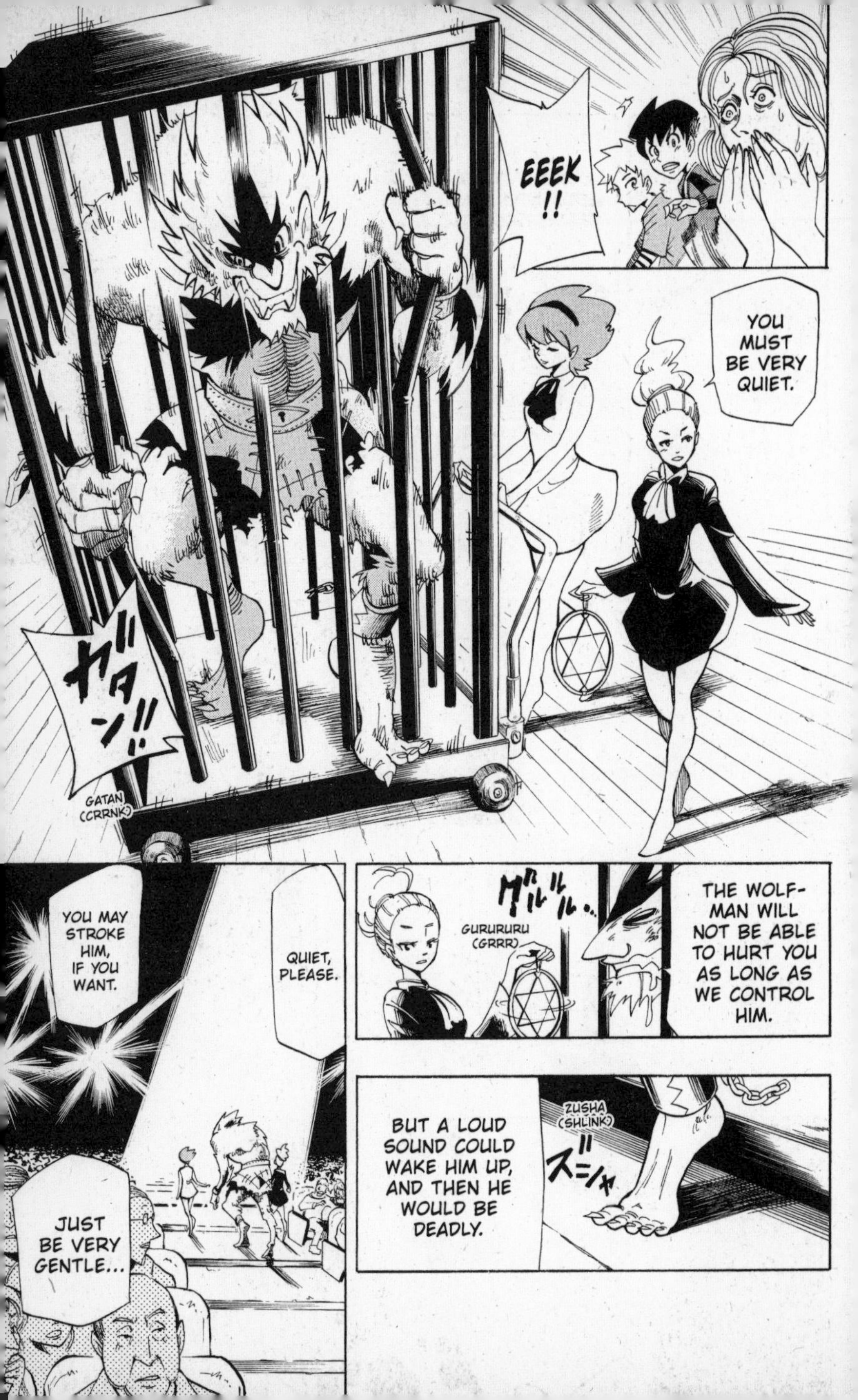
EEEK !!
YOU MUST BE VERY QUIET.
ガタン!!
GATAN (CRRNK)
THE WOLF-MAN WILL NOT BE ABLE TO HURT YOU AS LONG AS WE CONTROL HIM.
グルルル…
GURURURU (GRRR)
BUT A LOUD SOUND COULD WAKE HIM UP, AND THEN HE WOULD BE DEADLY.
ズシャ
ZUSHA (SHLINK)
QUIET, PLEASE.
YOU MAY STROKE HIM, IF YOU WANT.
JUST BE VERY GENTLE...

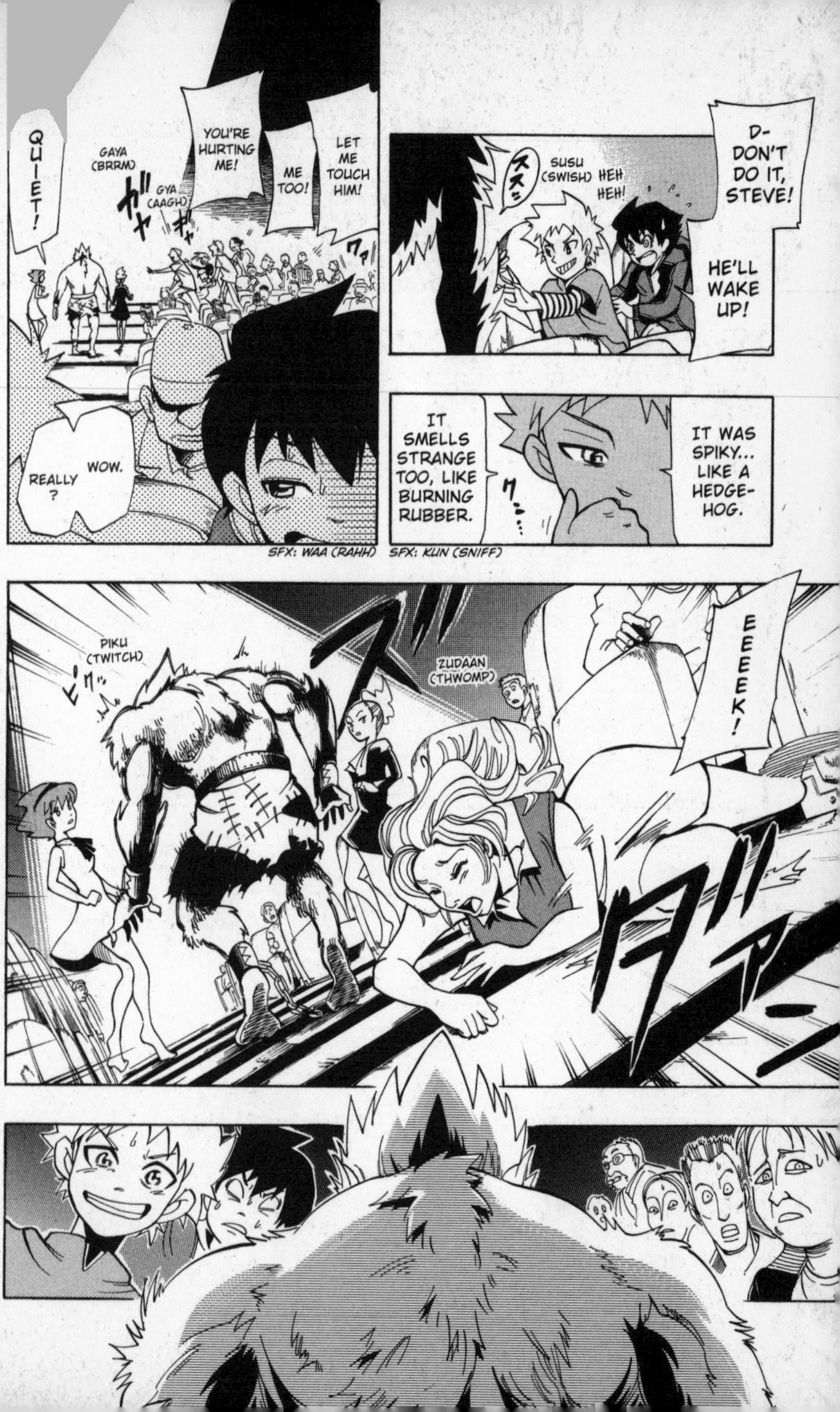
D-DON'T DO IT, STEVE!
HE'LL WAKE UP!
HEH HEH!
SUSU (SWISH)
IT WAS SPIKY... LIKE A HEDGEHOG.
IT SMELLS STRANGE TOO, LIKE BURNING RUBBER.
SFX: KUN (SNIFF)
LET ME TOUCH HIM!
ME TOO!
YOU'RE HURTING ME!
GYA (AAGH)
GAYA (BRRM)
QUIET!
WOW.
REALLY?
SFX: WAA (RAHH)
EEEEK!
ZUDAAN (THWOMP)
PIKU (TWITCH)

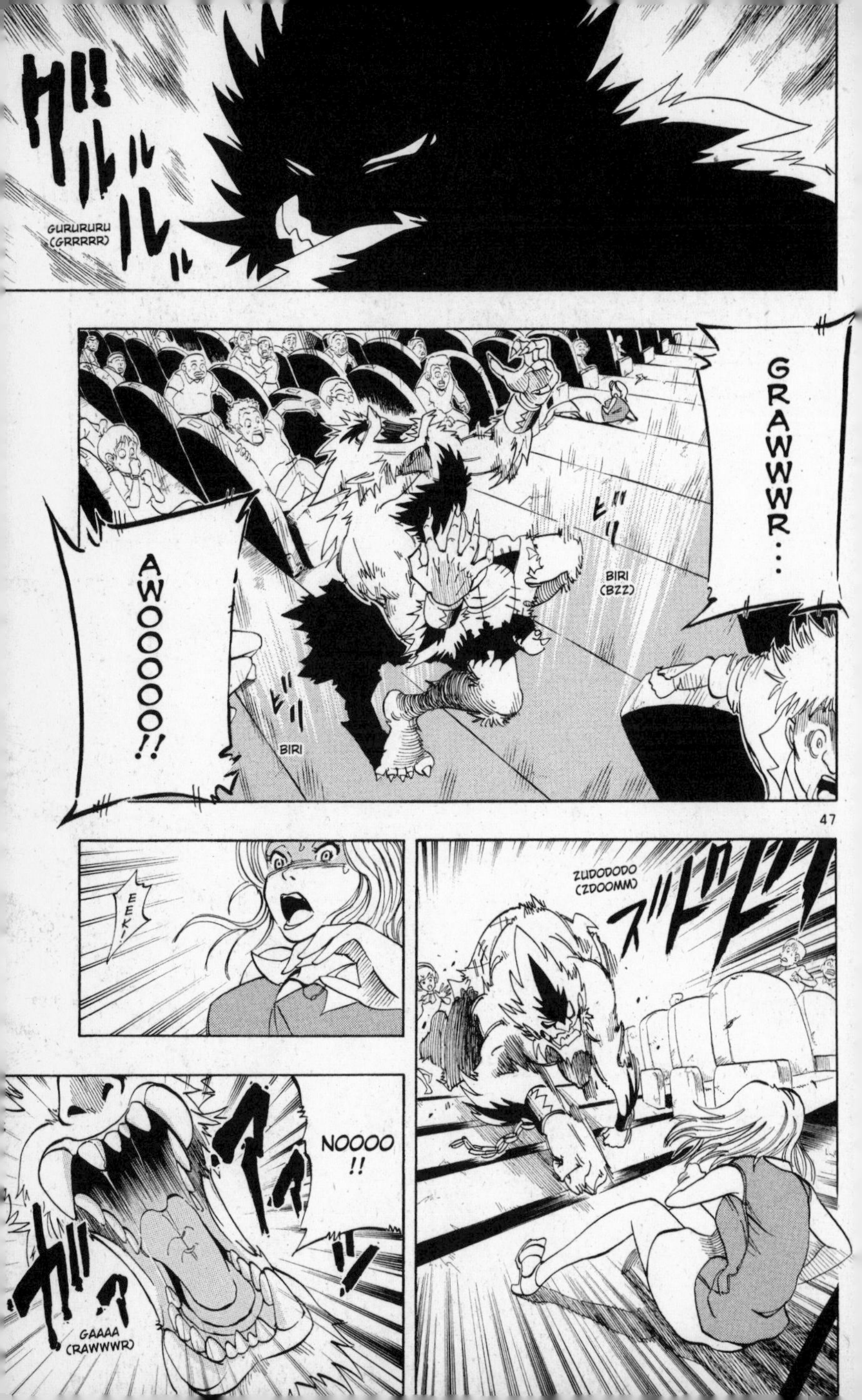
GURURURU
(GRRRRR)
GRAWWWR...
BIRI
(BZZ)
AWOOOOOOO!!
BIRI
ZUDODODO
(ZDOOMM)
EEK!
NOOOO!!
GAAAA
(RAWWWR)

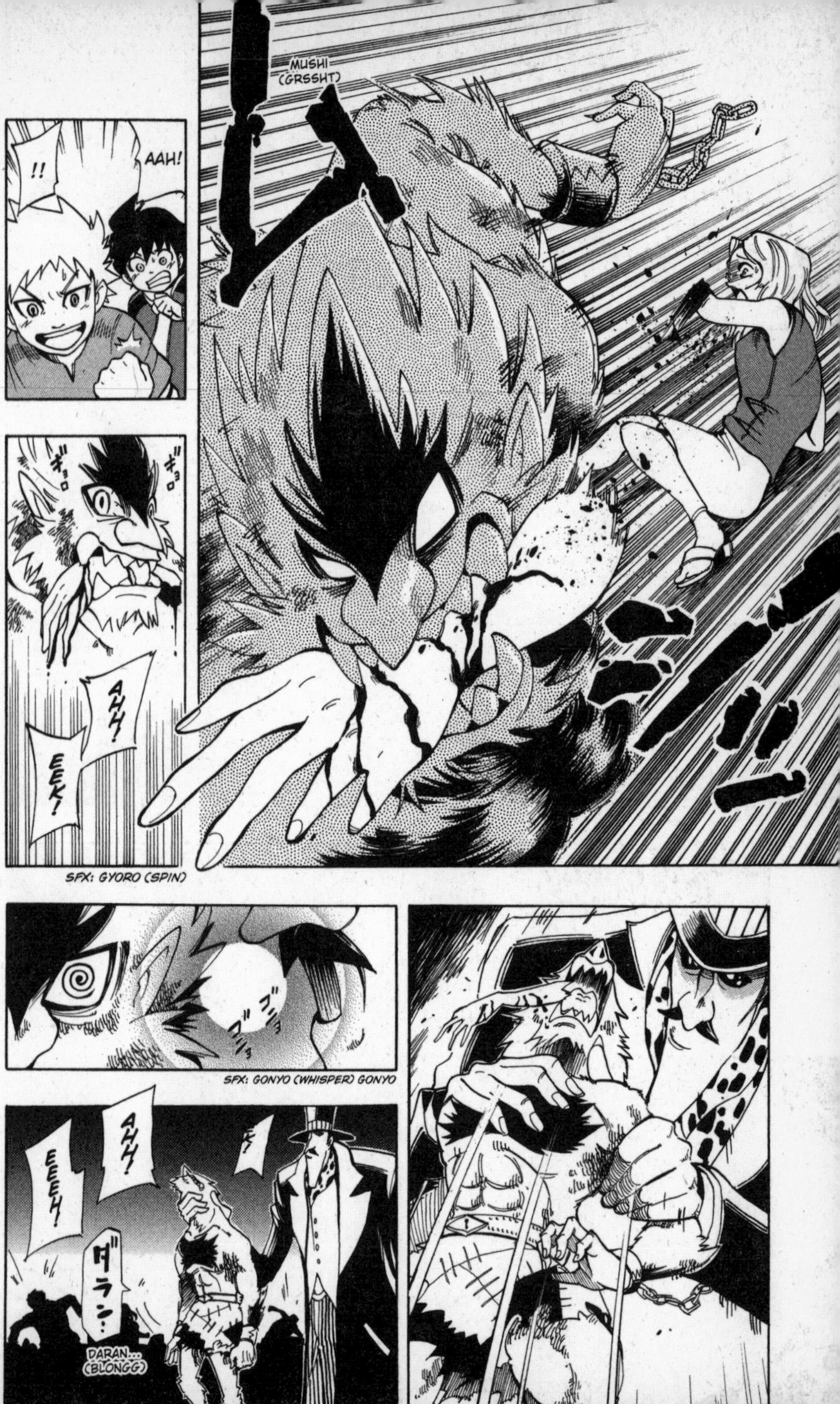
MUSHI (GRSSHT)
AAH!
!!
AHH!
EEEK!
SFX: GYORO (SPIN)
SFX: GONYO (WHISPER) GONYO
AHH!
EEEH!
DARAN... (BLONGG)

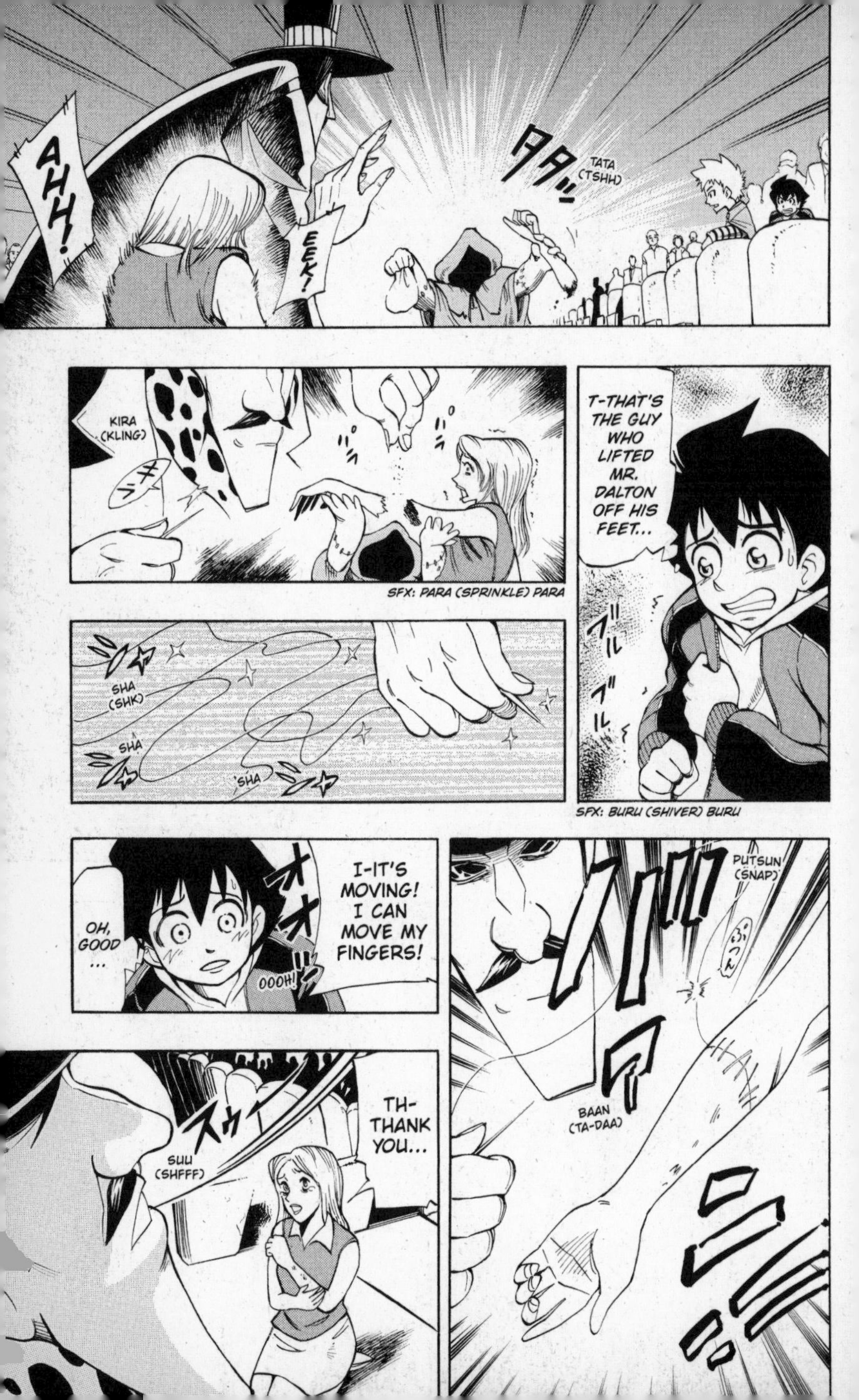
TATA (TSHH)
EEK!
AHH!
T-THAT'S THE GUY WHO LIFTED MR. DALTON OFF HIS FEET...
SFX: BURU (SHIVER) BURU
KIRA (KLING)
SFX: PARA (SPRINKLE) PARA
SHA (SHK)
SHA
SHA
PUTSUN (SNAP)
BAAN (TA-DAA)
I-IT'S MOVING! I CAN MOVE MY FINGERS!
OOOH!
OH, GOOD ...
TH-THANK YOU...
SUU (SHFFF)

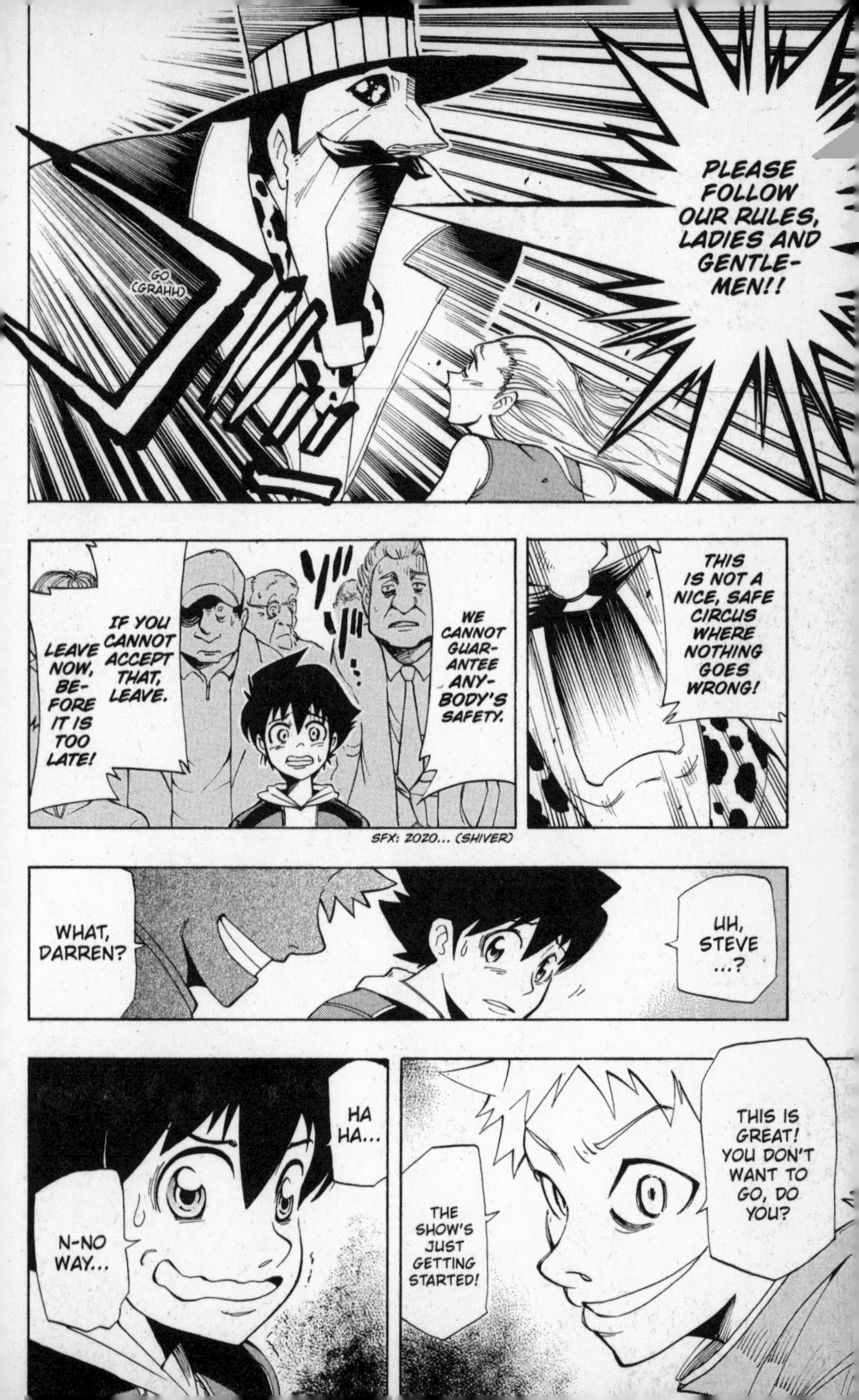
PLEASE FOLLOW OUR RULES, LADIES AND GENTLEMEN!!
GO (GRAHH)
THIS IS NOT A NICE, SAFE CIRCUS WHERE NOTHING GOES WRONG!
WE CANNOT GUARANTEE ANYBODY'S SAFETY.
IF YOU CANNOT ACCEPT THAT, LEAVE.
LEAVE NOW, BEFORE IT IS TOO LATE!
SFX: ZOZO... (SHIVER)
UH, STEVE ...?
WHAT, DARREN?
THIS IS GREAT! YOU DON'T WANT TO GO, DO YOU?
THE SHOW'S JUST GETTING STARTED!
HA HA...
N-NO WAY...

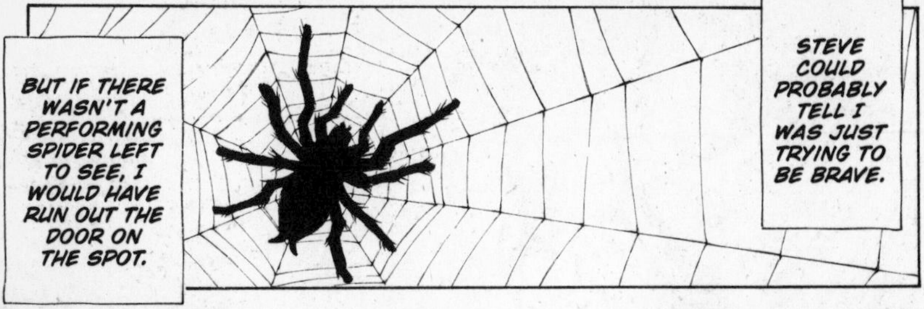
STEVE COULD PROBABLY TELL I WAS JUST TRYING TO BE BRAVE.
BUT IF THERE WASN'T A PERFORMING SPIDER LEFT TO SEE, I WOULD HAVE RUN OUT THE DOOR ON THE SPOT.

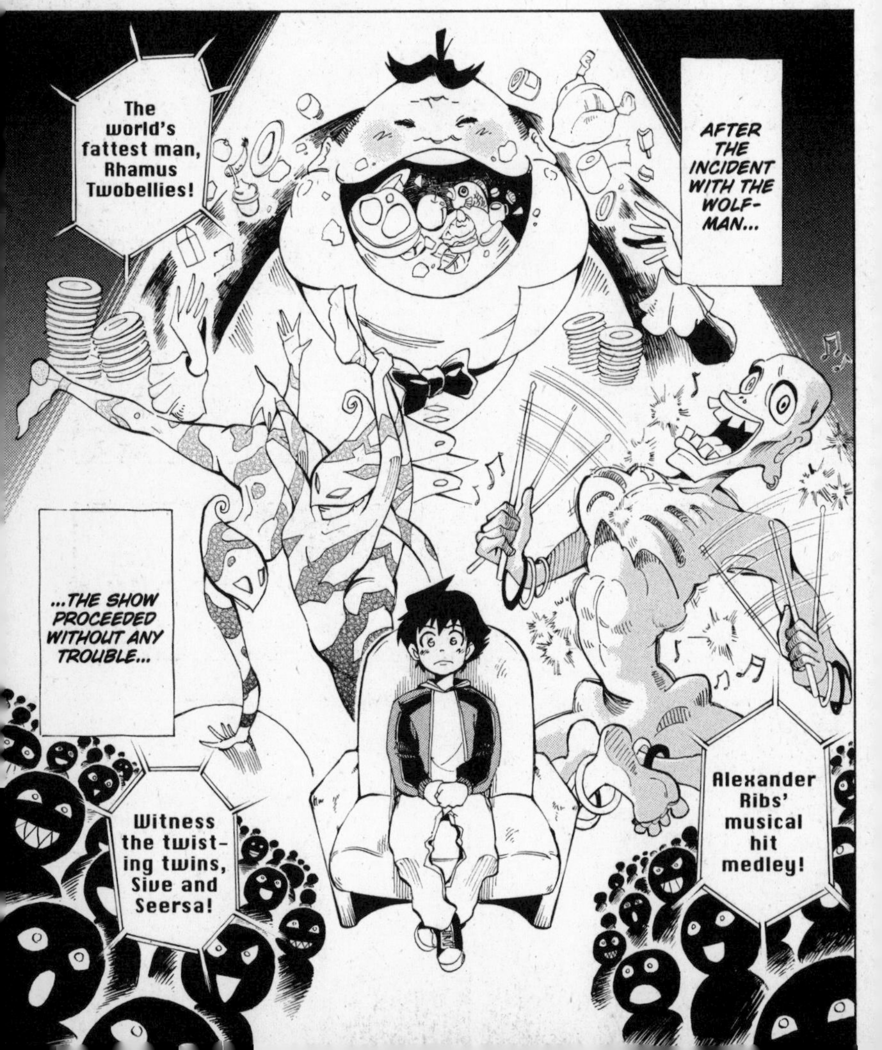
AFTER THE INCIDENT WITH THE WOLF-MAN...
The world's fattest man, Rhamus Twobellies!
...THE SHOW PROCEEDED WITHOUT ANY TROUBLE...
Alexander Ribs' musical hit medley!
Witness the twist-ing twins, Sive and Seersa!

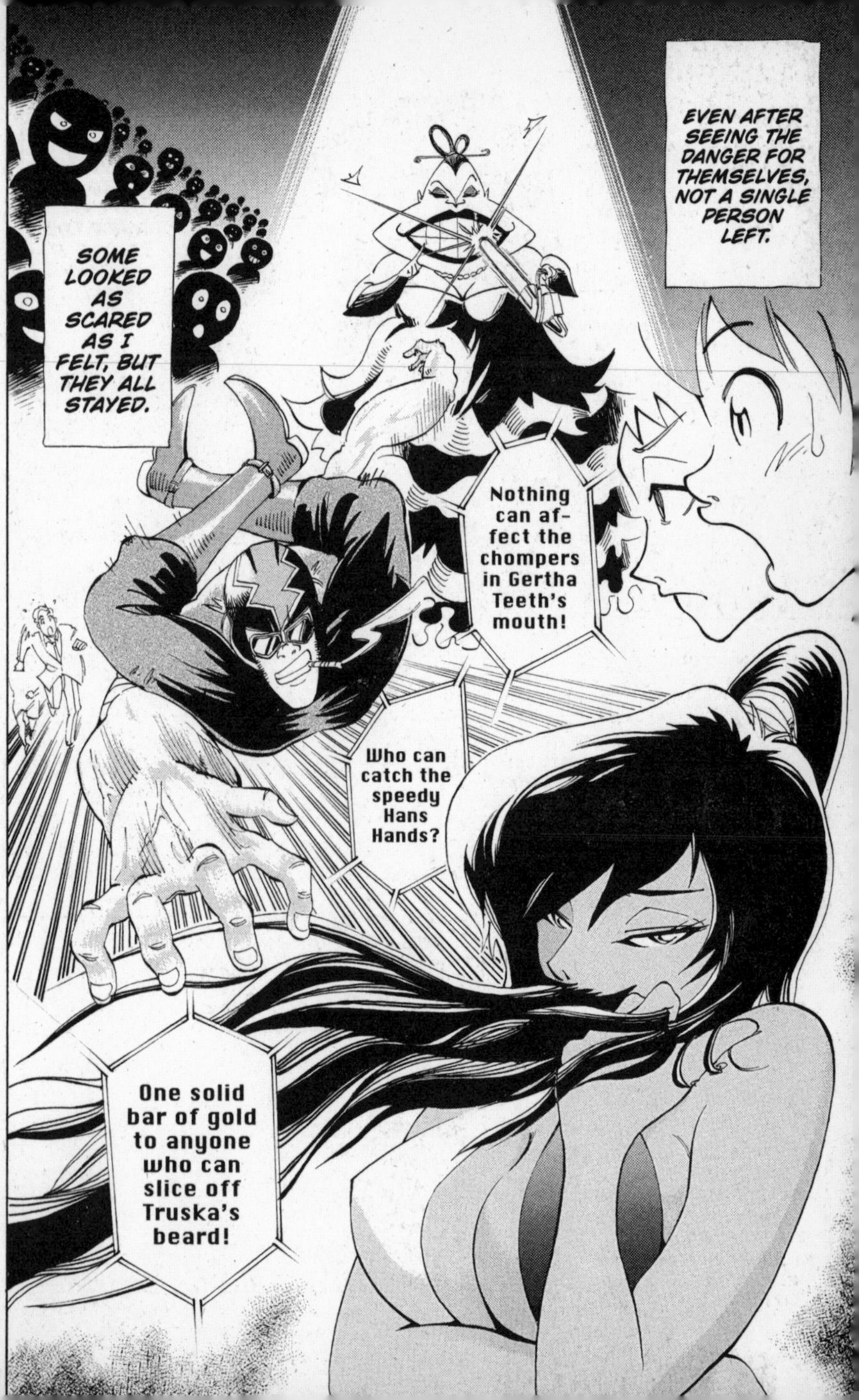
EVEN AFTER SEEING THE DANGER FOR THEMSELVES, NOT A SINGLE PERSON LEFT.
SOME LOOKED AS SCARED AS I FELT, BUT THEY ALL STAYED.
Nothing can af- fect the chompers in Gertha Teeth's mouth!
Who can catch the speedy Hans Hands?
One solid bar of gold to anyone who can slice off Truska's beard!

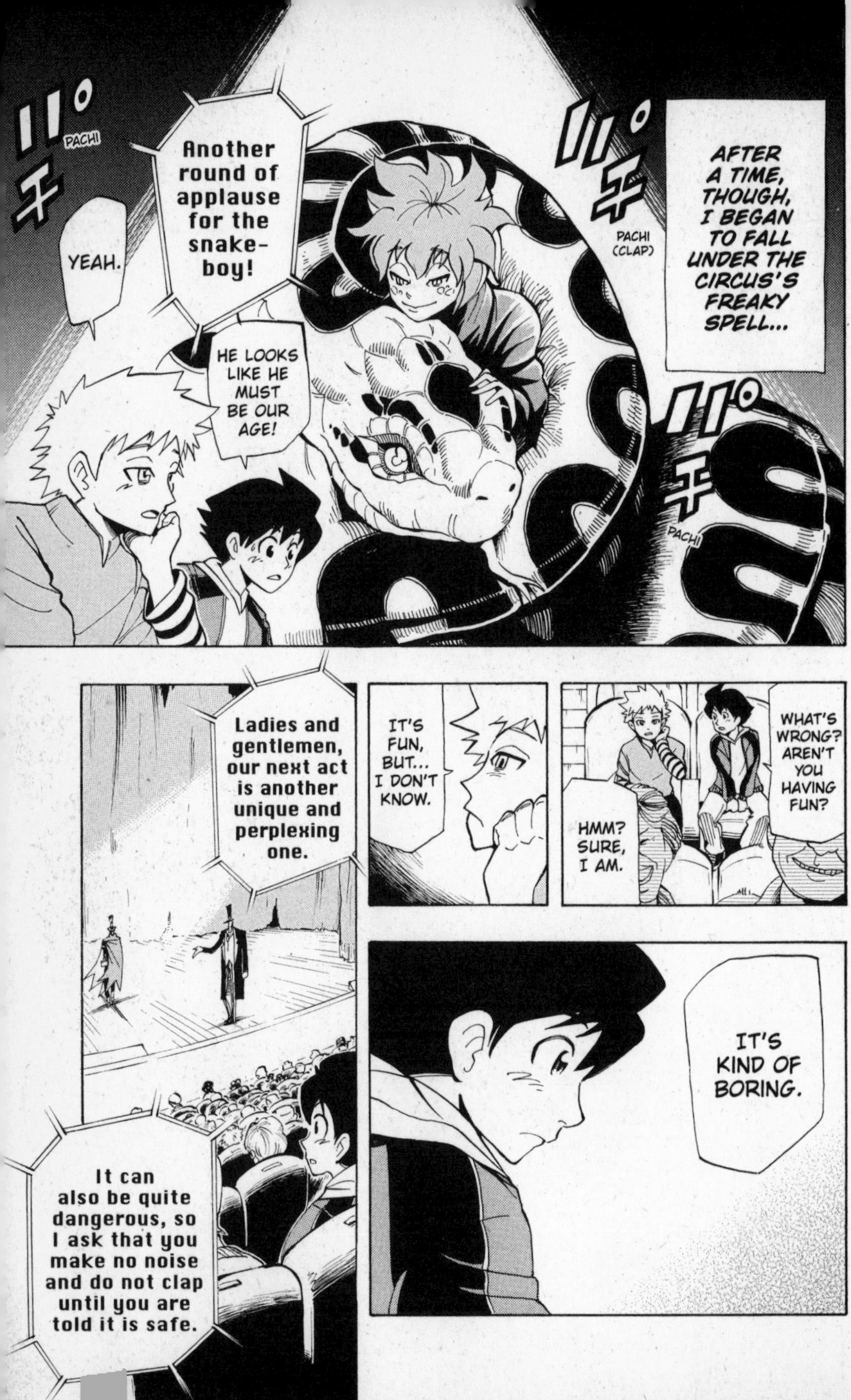
AFTER A TIME, THOUGH, I BEGAN TO FALL UNDER THE CIRCUS'S FREAKY SPELL...
PACHI (CLAP)
Another round of applause for the snake-boy!
PACHI
YEAH.
PACHI
HE LOOKS LIKE HE MUST BE OUR AGE!
WHAT'S WRONG? AREN'T YOU HAVING FUN?
HMM? SURE, I AM.
IT'S FUN, BUT... I DON'T KNOW.
IT'S KIND OF BORING.
Ladies and gentlemen, our next act is another unique and perplexing one.
It can also be quite dangerous, so I ask that you make no noise and do not clap until you are told it is safe.

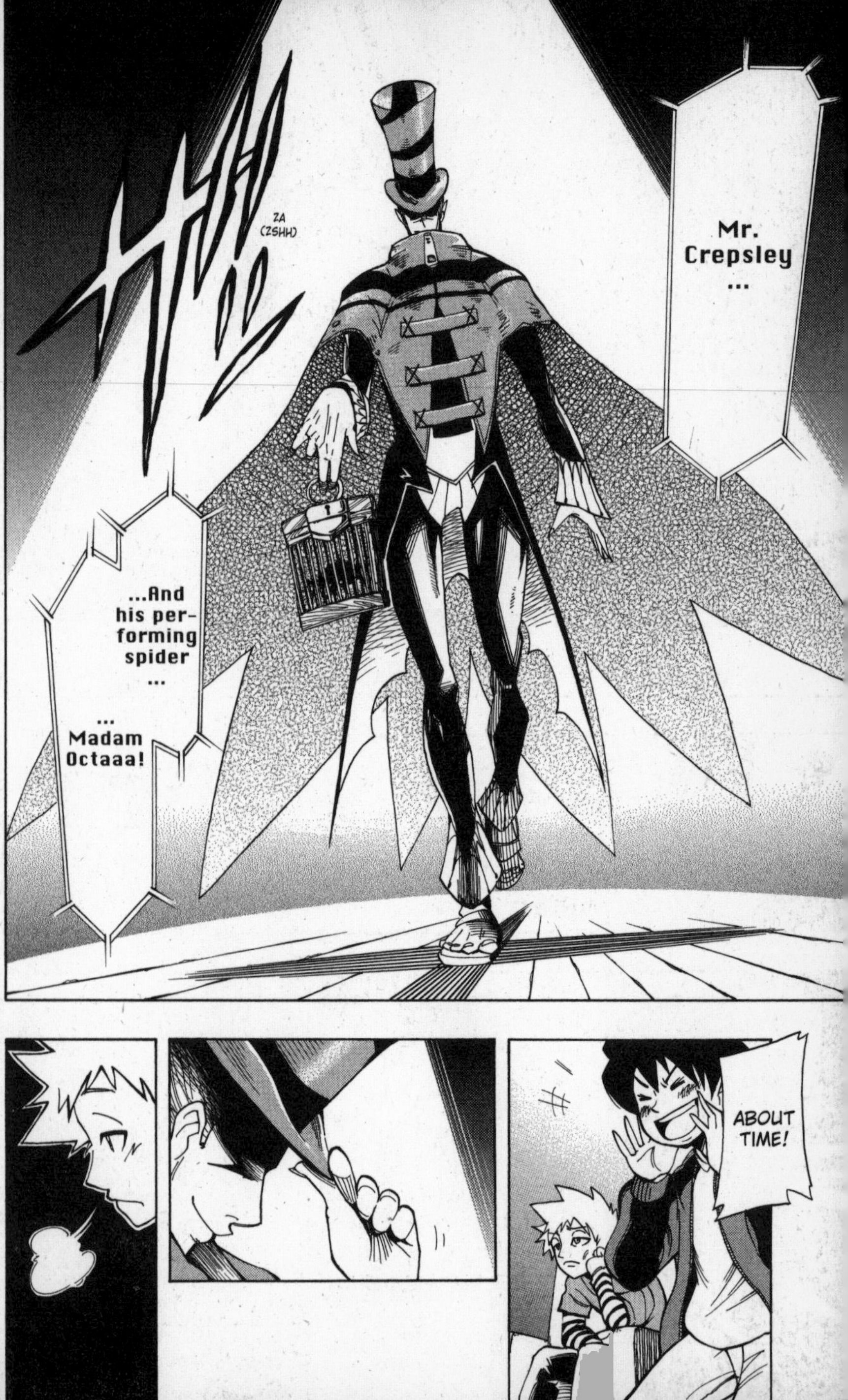
Mr. Crepsley ...
ZA (ZSHH)
...And his per-forming spider ...
... Madam Octaaa!
ABOUT TIME!

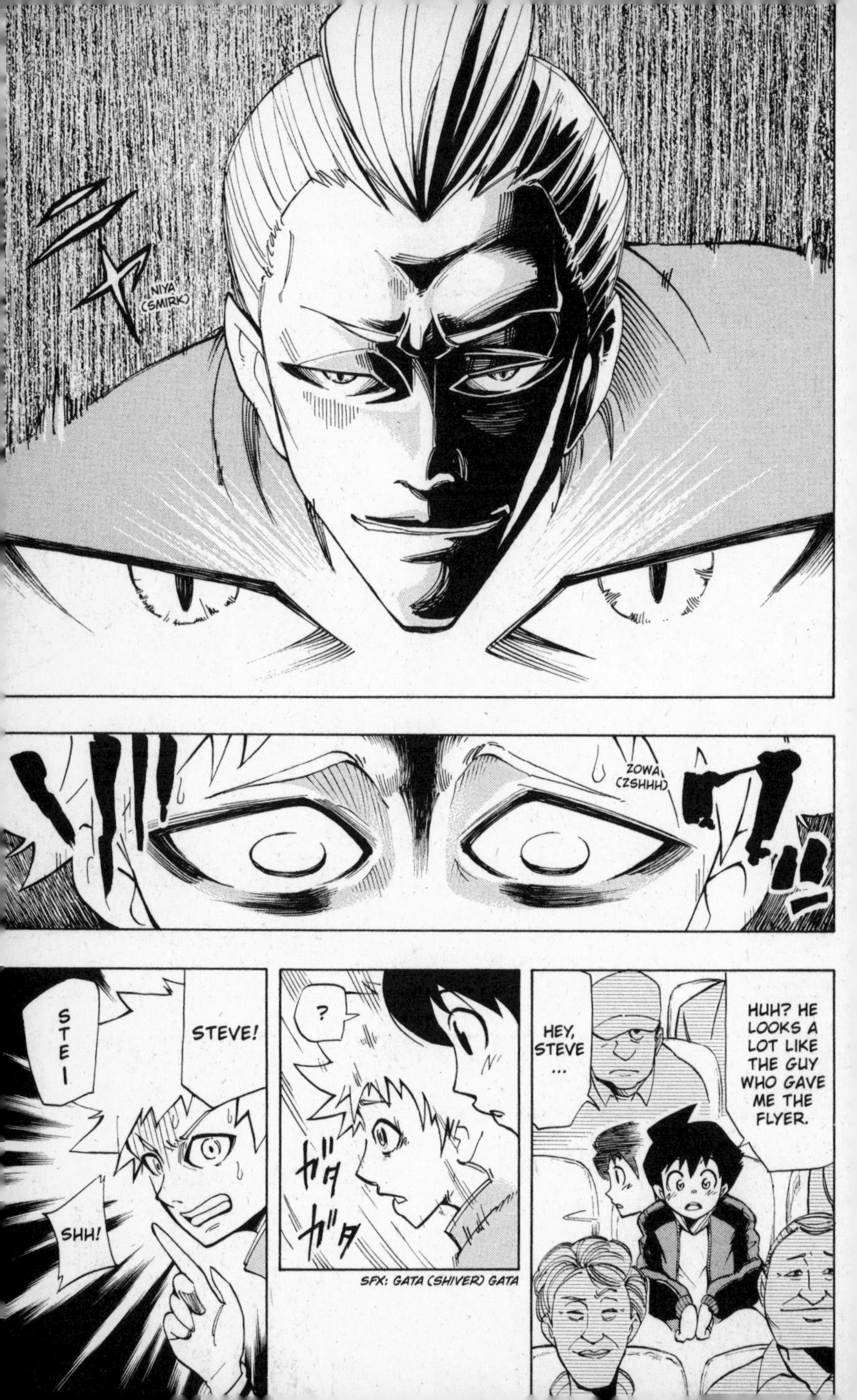
NIYA (SMIRK)
ZOWA (ZSHHH)
HUH? HE LOOKS A LOT LIKE THE GUY WHO GAVE ME THE FLYER.
HEY, STEVE ...
?
SFX: GATA (SHIVER) GATA
STEVE!
STE I
SHH!

COME ON OUT.

MADAM OCTA IS TRULY AN INCREDIBLE SPIDER.

SHE IS BOTH POISONOUS AND INTELLIGENT.

WHAT'S WITH HIM?

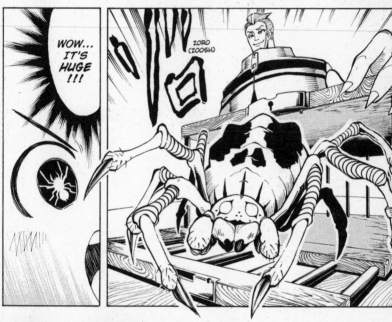

WOW... IT'S HUGE !!!

ZORO (ZOOSH)

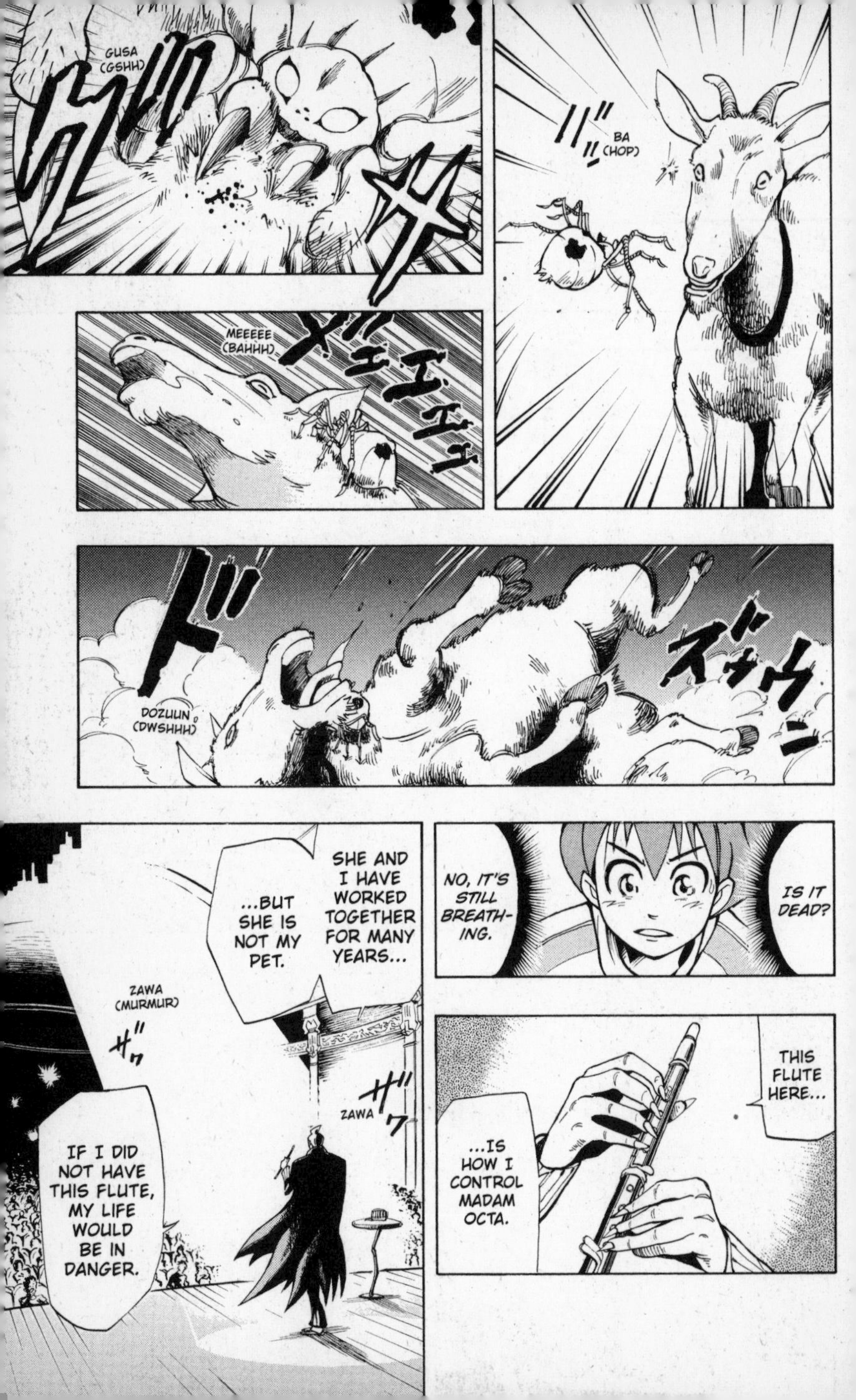
BA
(HOP)
GUSA
(GSHH)
MEEEEE
(BAHHH)
DOZUUN
(DWSHHH)
IS IT DEAD?
NO, IT'S STILL BREATHING.
THIS FLUTE HERE...
...IS HOW I CONTROL MADAM OCTA.
SHE AND I HAVE WORKED TOGETHER FOR MANY YEARS...
...BUT SHE IS NOT MY PET.
ZAWA
(MURMUR)
ZAWA
IF I DID NOT HAVE THIS FLUTE, MY LIFE WOULD BE IN DANGER.

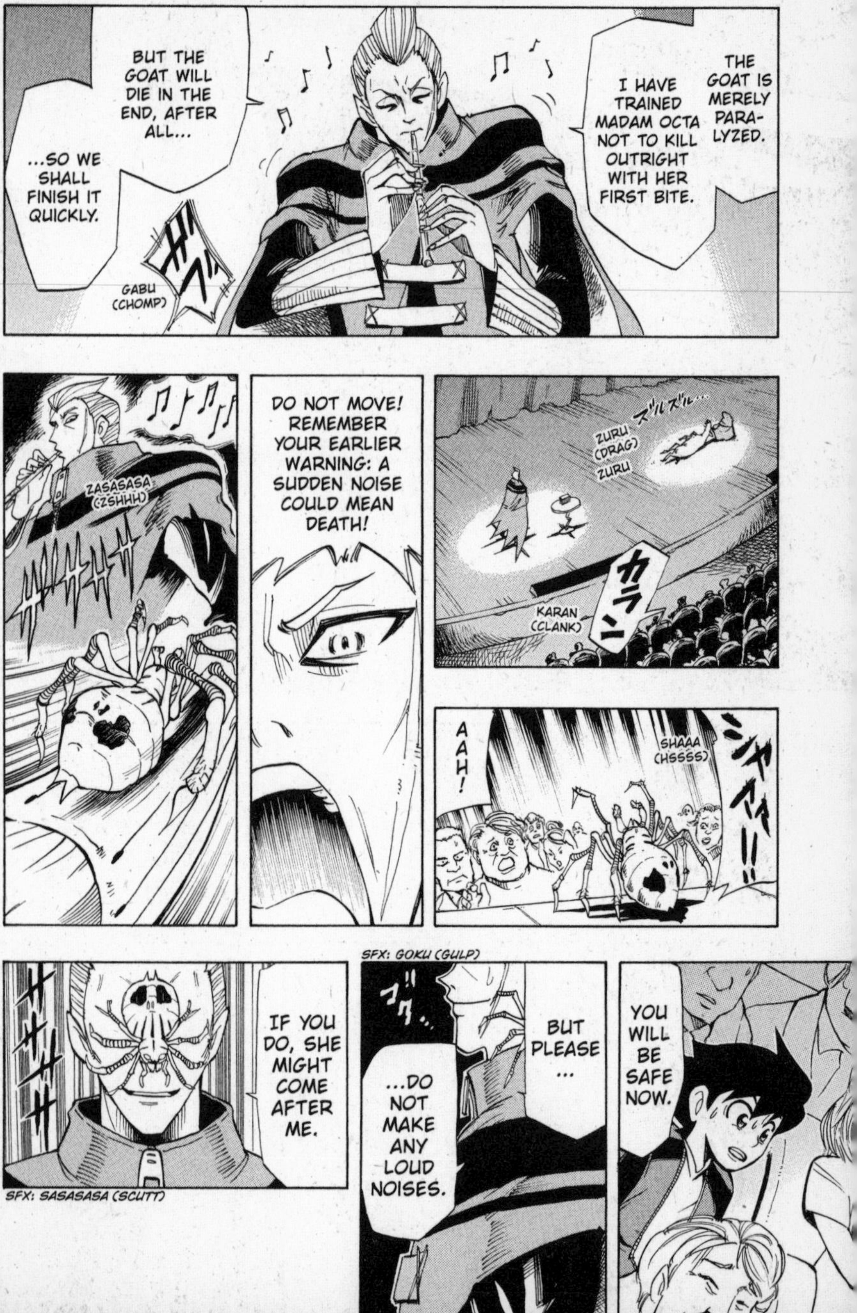
THE GOAT IS MERELY PARALYZED.
I HAVE TRAINED MADAM OCTA NOT TO KILL OUTRIGHT WITH HER FIRST BITE.
BUT THE GOAT WILL DIE IN THE END, AFTER ALL...
...SO WE SHALL FINISH IT QUICKLY.
GABU (CHOMP)
ZURU (DRAG) ZURU
KARAN (CLANK)
SHAAA (HSSSS)
AAH!
DO NOT MOVE! REMEMBER YOUR EARLIER WARNING: A SUDDEN NOISE COULD MEAN DEATH!
ZASASASA (ZSHHH)
SFX: GOKU (GULP)
YOU WILL BE SAFE NOW.
BUT PLEASE ...
...DO NOT MAKE ANY LOUD NOISES.
IF YOU DO, SHE MIGHT COME AFTER ME.
SFX: SASASASA (SCUTT)

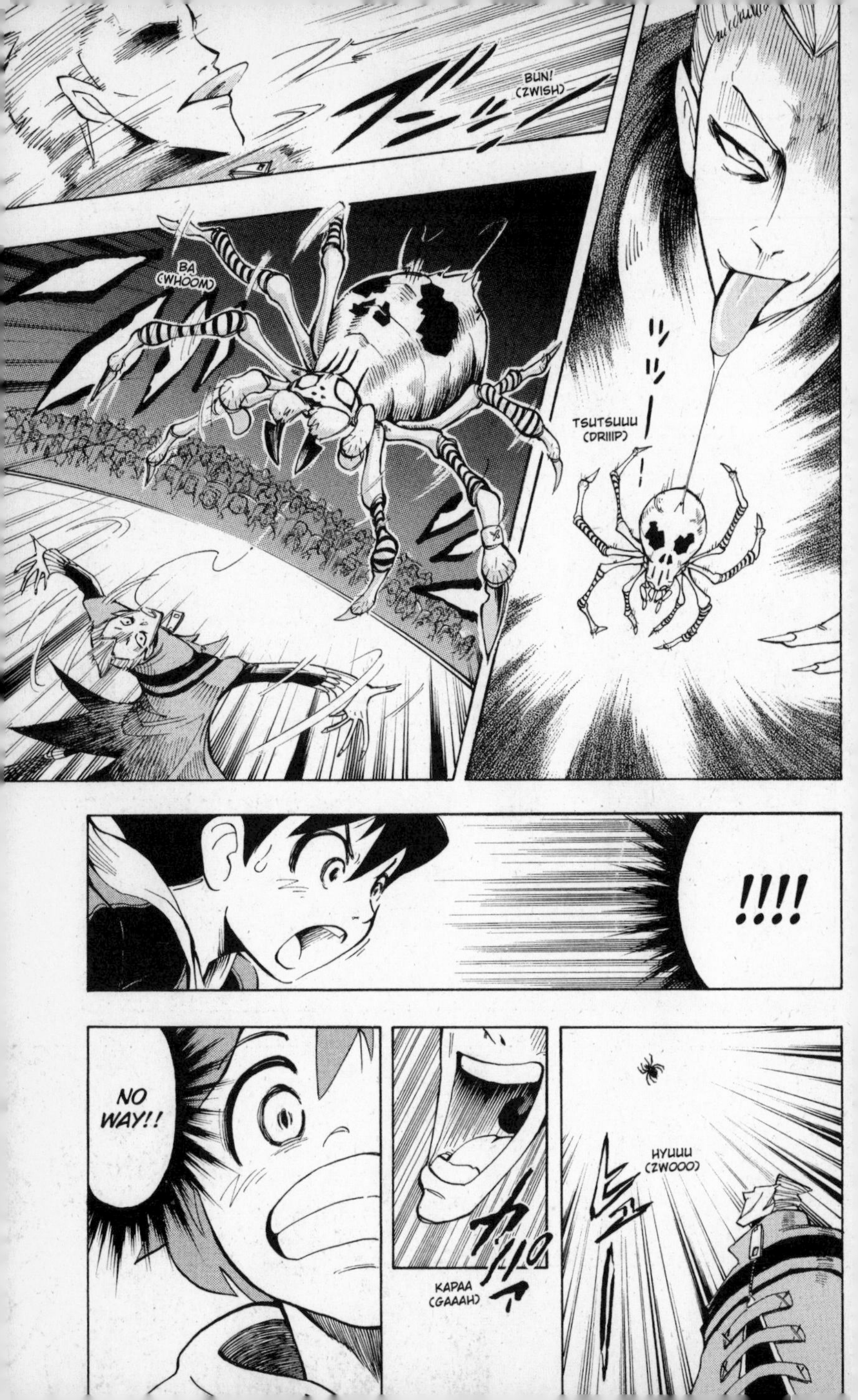
TSUTSUUU (DRIIIP)
BUN! (ZWISH)
BA (WHOOM)
!!!!
HYUUU (ZWOOO)
KAPAA (GAAAH)
NO WAY!!

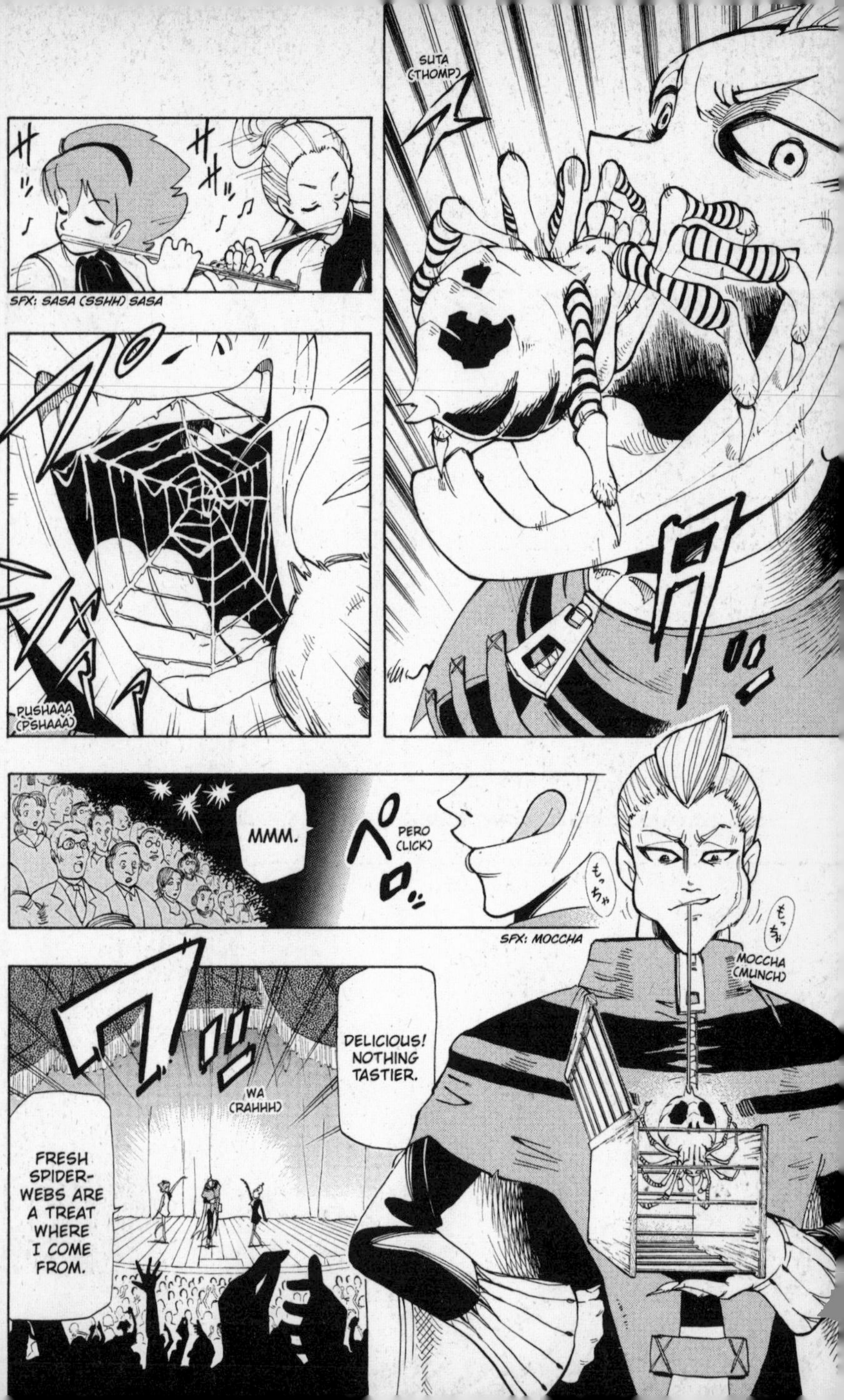
SUTA (THOMP)
SFX: SASA (SSHH) SASA
PUSHAAA (PSHAAA)
MOCCHA (MUNCH)
SFX: MOCCHA
PERO (LICK)
MMM.
DELICIOUS! NOTHING TASTIER.
WA (RAHHH)
FRESH SPIDER-WEBS ARE A TREAT WHERE I COME FROM.

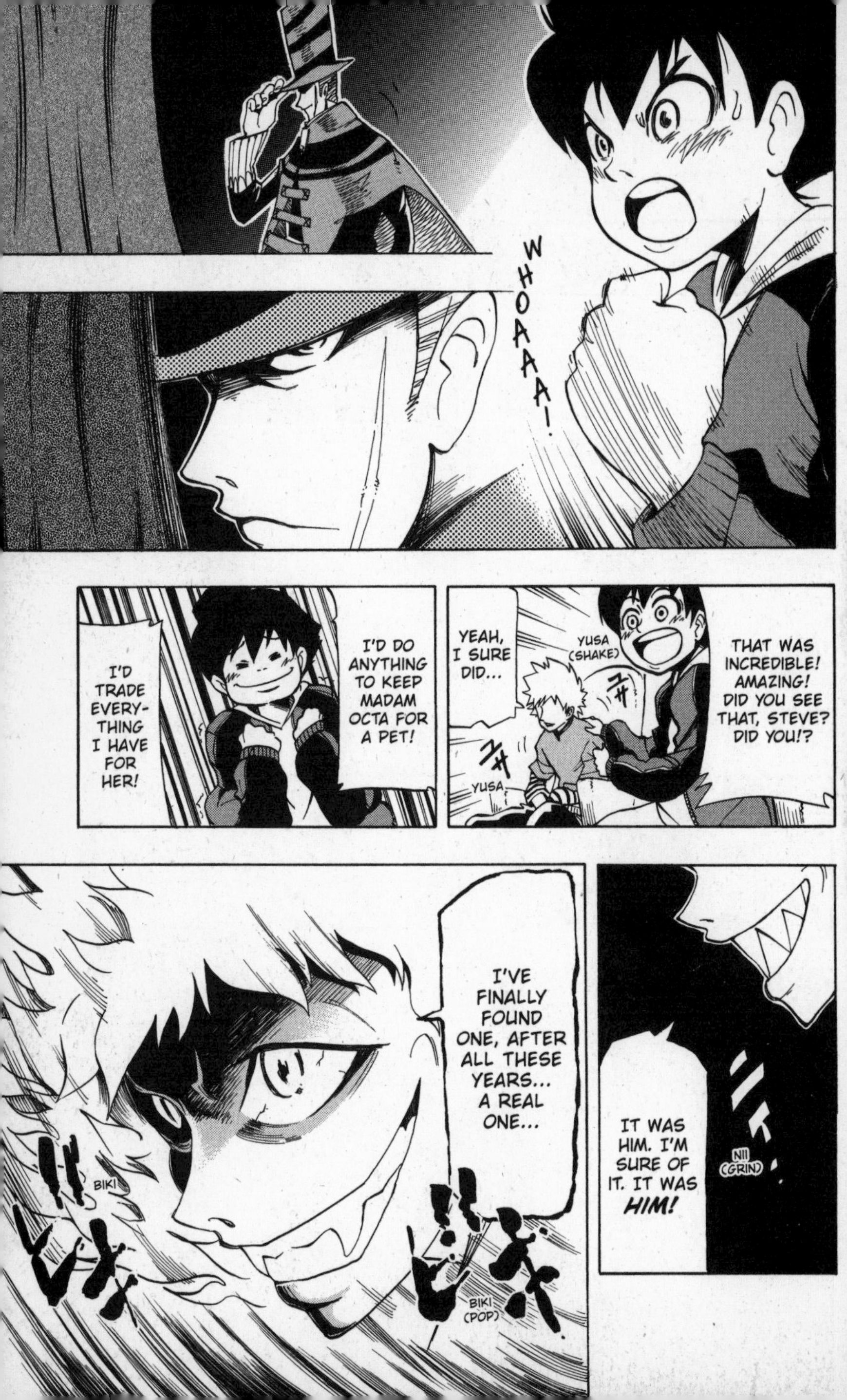
WHOAAAAI!
THAT WAS INCREDIBLE! AMAZING! DID YOU SEE THAT, STEVE? DID YOU!?
YUSA (SHAKE)
YUSA
YEAH, I SURE DID...
I'D DO ANYTHING TO KEEP MADAM OCTA FOR A PET!
I'D TRADE EVERY-THING I HAVE FOR HER!
IT WAS HIM. I'M SURE OF IT. IT WAS ***HIM!***
NII (GRIN)
I'VE FINALLY FOUND ONE, AFTER ALL THESE YEARS... A REAL ONE...
BIKI
BIKI (POP)

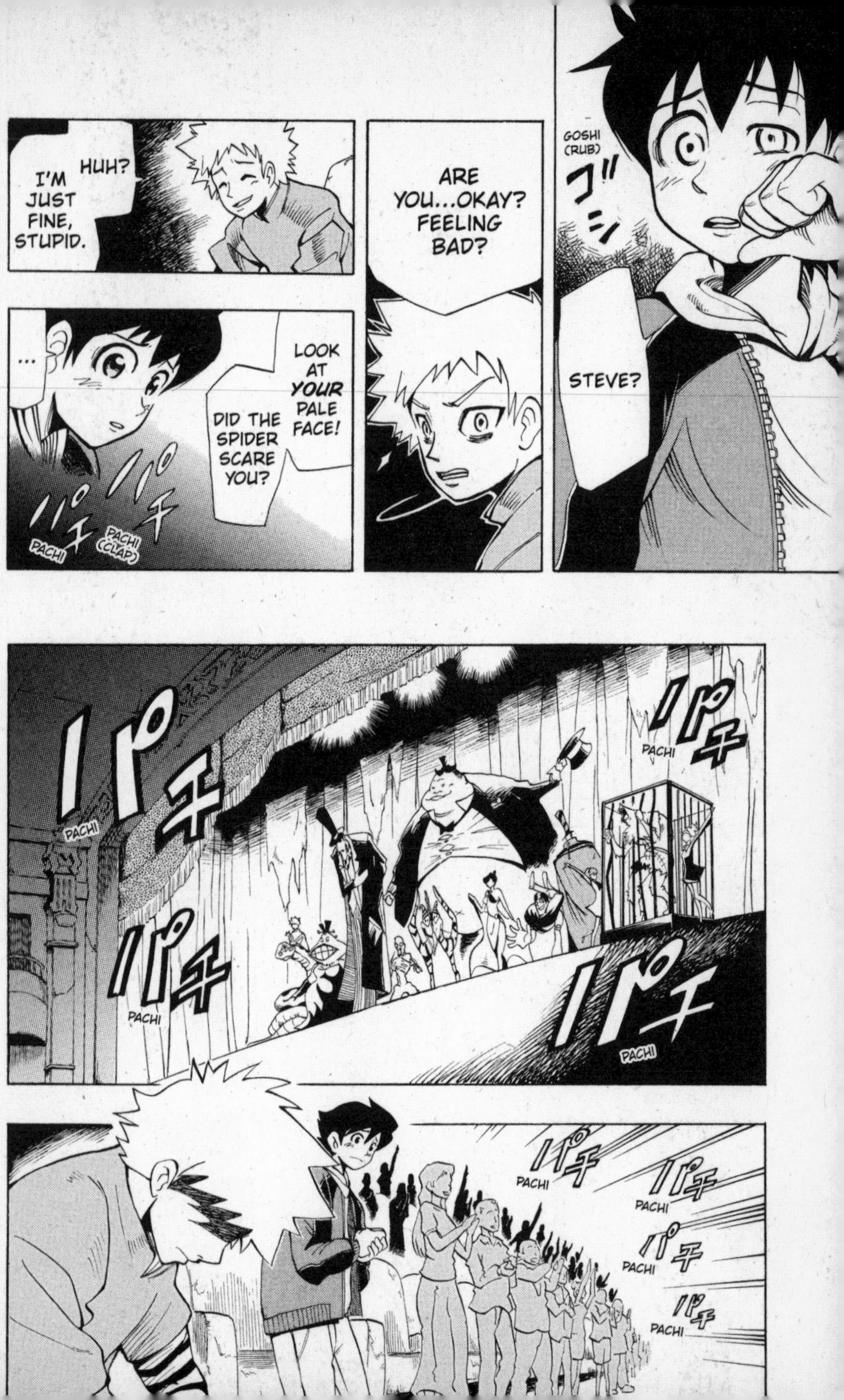

GOSHI (RUB)
STEVE?
ARE YOU...OKAY? FEELING BAD?
HUH?
I'M JUST FINE, STUPID.
...
LOOK AT YOUR PALE FACE!
DID THE SPIDER SCARE YOU?
PACHI (CLAP)
PACHI
PACHI
PACHI
PACHI
PACHI
PACHI
PACHI
PACHI
PACHI

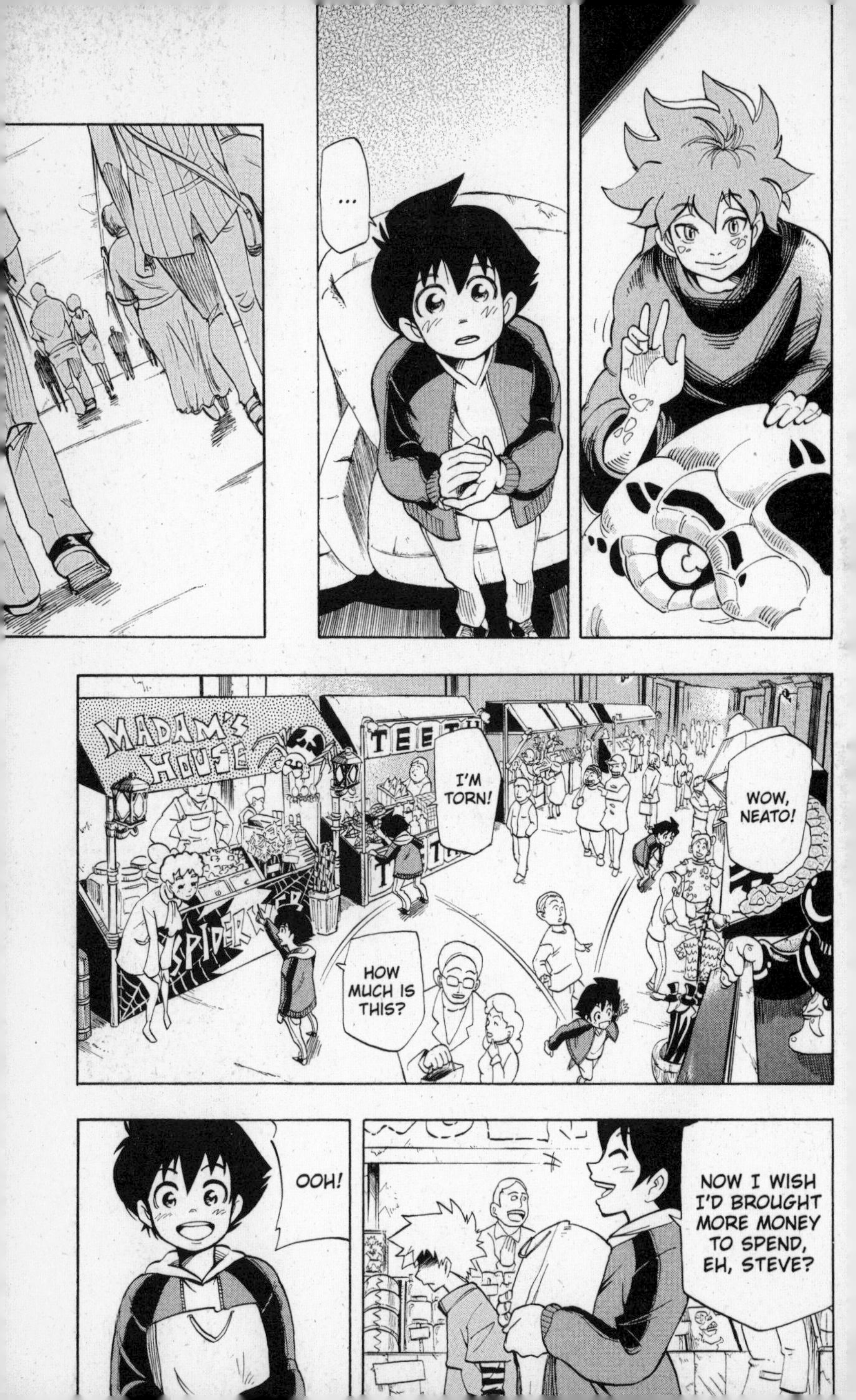

...
WOW, NEATO!
I'M TORN!
MADAM'S HOUSE
HOW MUCH IS THIS?
NOW I WISH I'D BROUGHT MORE MONEY TO SPEND, EH, STEVE?
OOH!

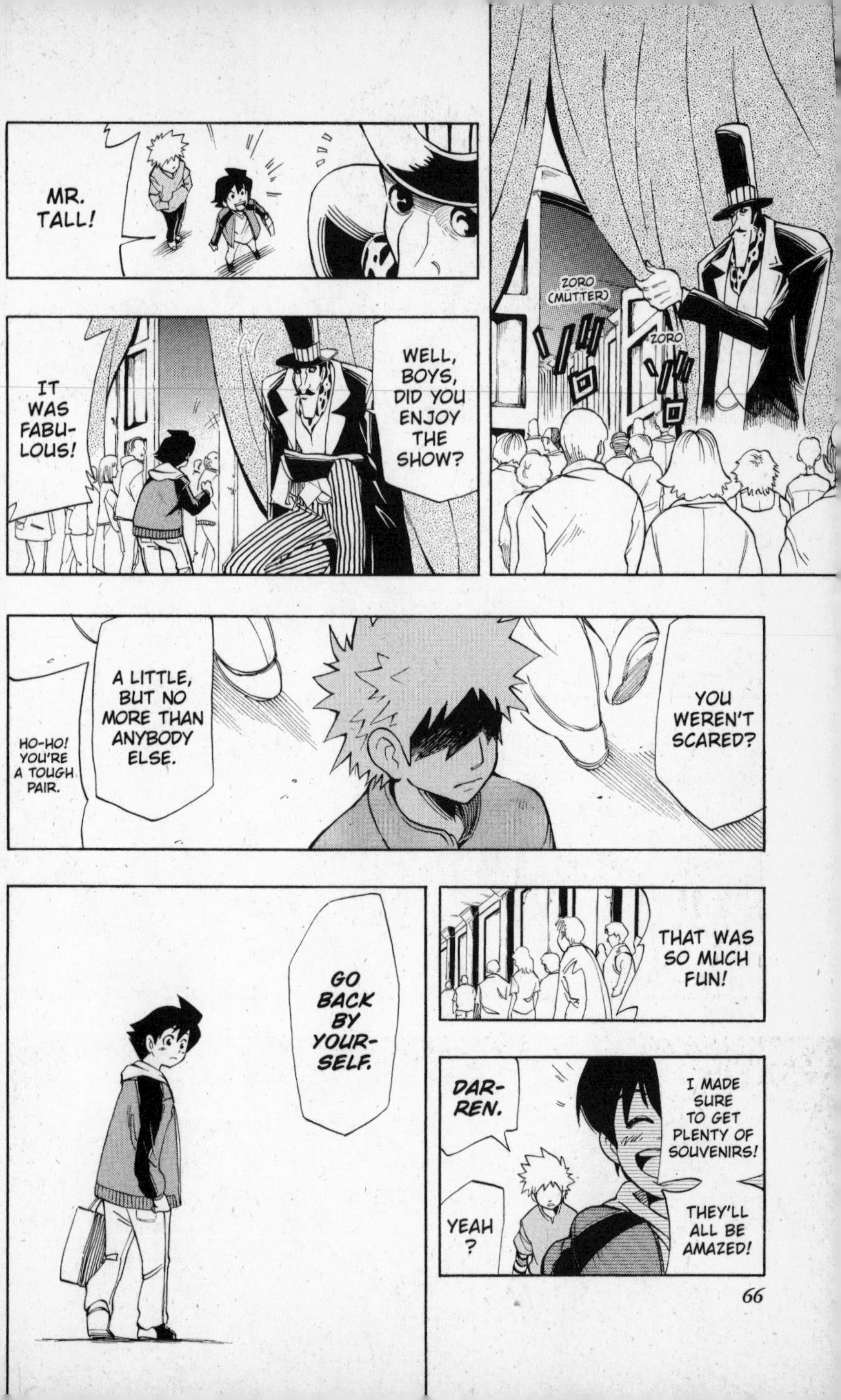

ZORO (MUTTER)
ZORO
MR. TALL!
WELL, BOYS, DID YOU ENJOY THE SHOW?
IT WAS FABULOUS!
YOU WEREN'T SCARED?
A LITTLE, BUT NO MORE THAN ANYBODY ELSE.
HO-HO! YOU'RE A TOUGH PAIR.
THAT WAS SO MUCH FUN!
I MADE SURE TO GET PLENTY OF SOUVENIRS!
DAR-REN.
THEY'LL ALL BE AMAZED!
YEAH?
GO BACK BY YOUR-SELF.

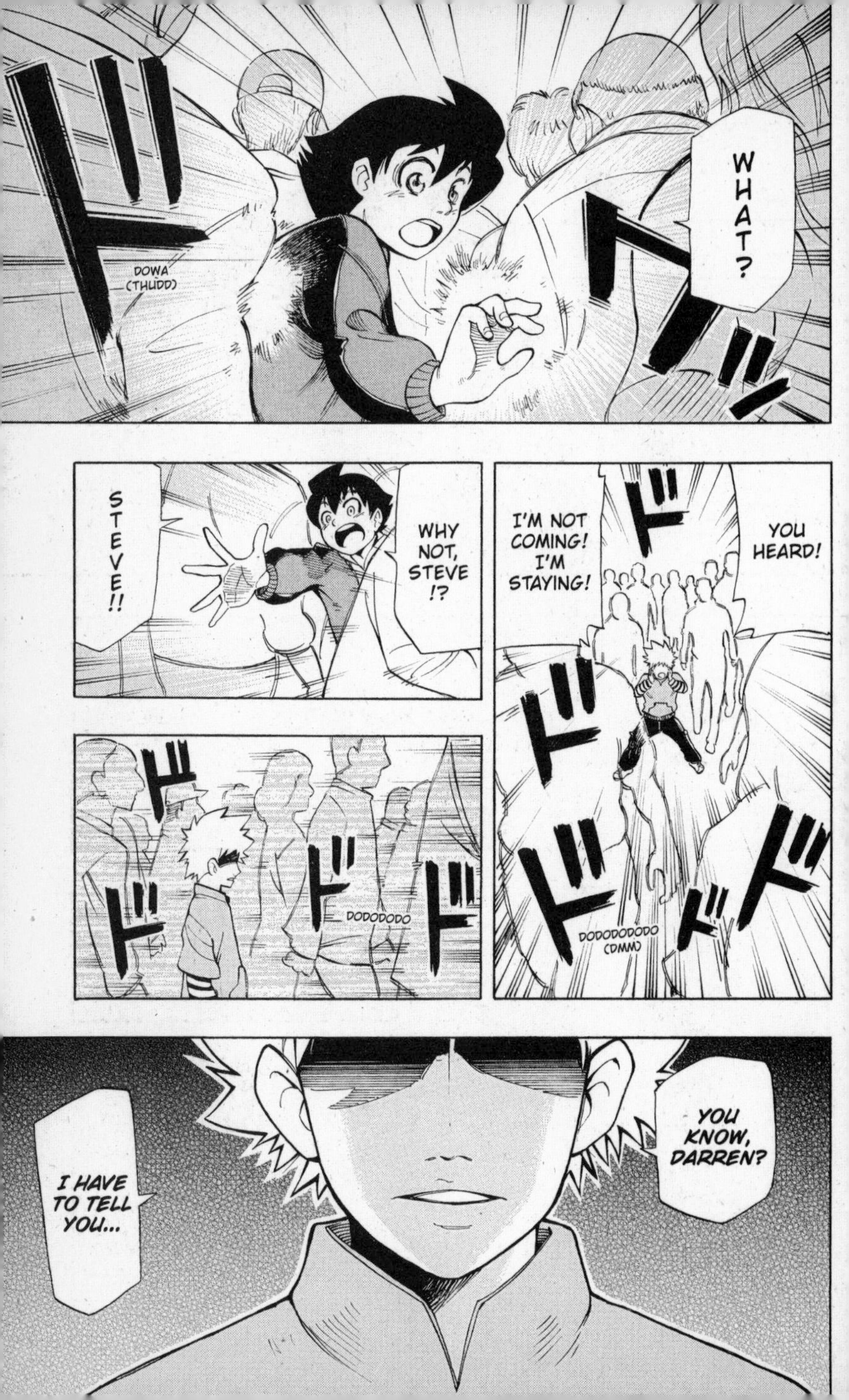
WHAT?
DOWA
(THUDD)
YOU HEARD!
I'M NOT COMING! I'M STAYING!
DODODODODO
(DMM)
WHY NOT, STEVE!?
STEVE!!
DODODODO
YOU KNOW, DARREN?
I HAVE TO TELL YOU...

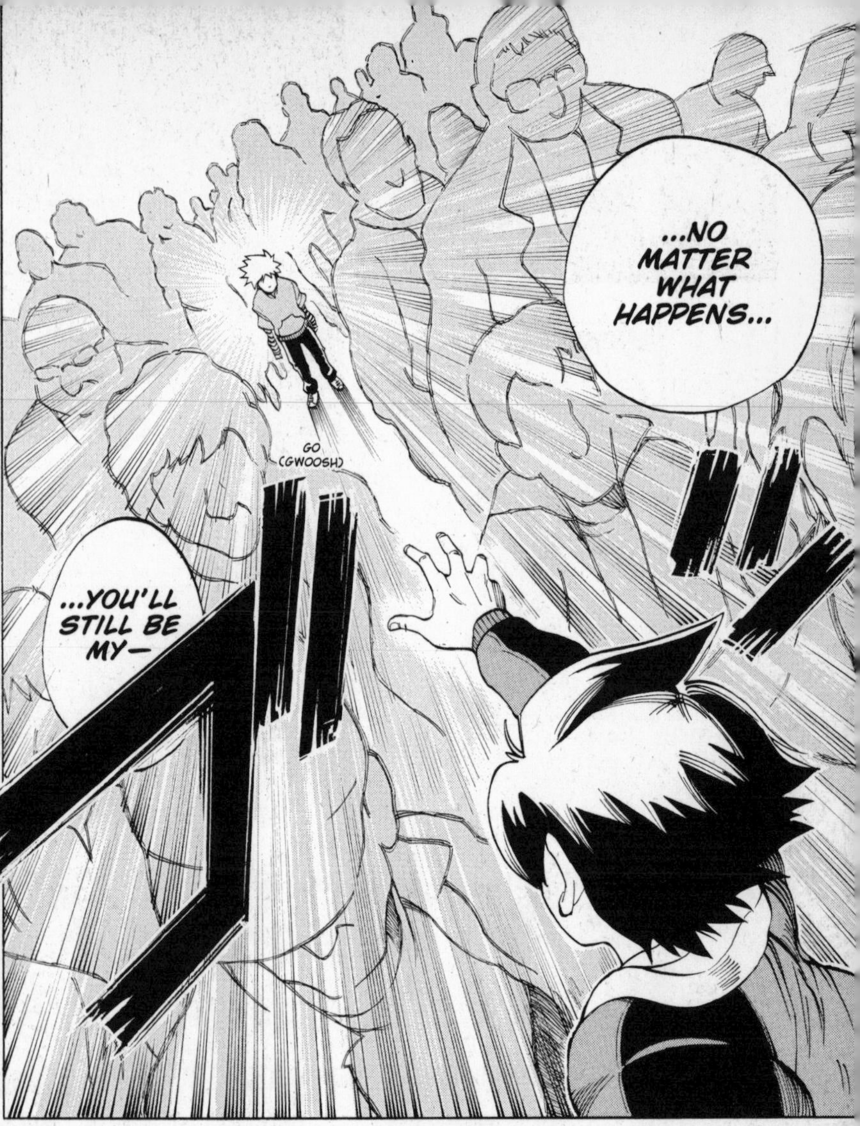
...NO MATTER WHAT HAPPENS...
GO (GWOOSH)
...YOU'LL STILL BE MY—

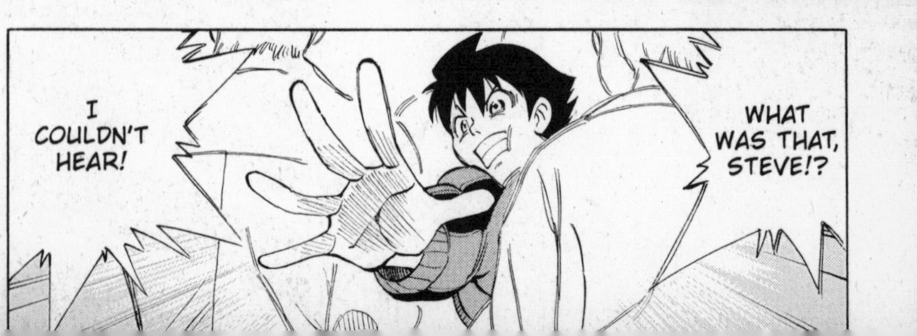
WHAT WAS THAT, STEVE!?
I COULDN'T HEAR!

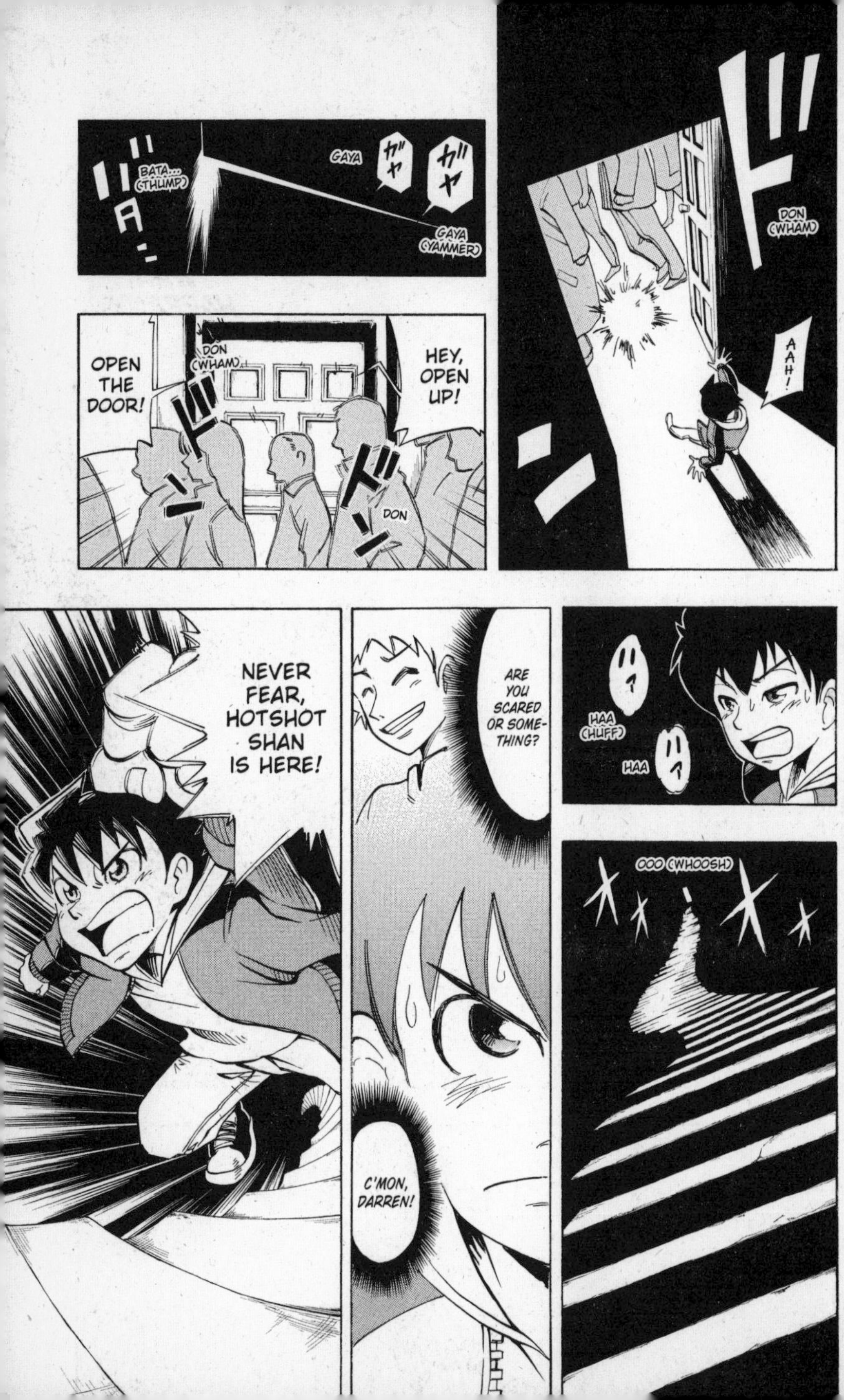
DON (WHAM)
AAH!
GAYA
GAYA (YAMMER)
BATA... (THUMP)
HEY, OPEN UP!
DON (WHAM)
OPEN THE DOOR!
DON
HAA (HUFF)
HAA
OOO (WHOOSH)
ARE YOU SCARED OR SOME-THING?
C'MON, DARREN!
NEVER FEAR, HOTSHOT SHAN IS HERE!

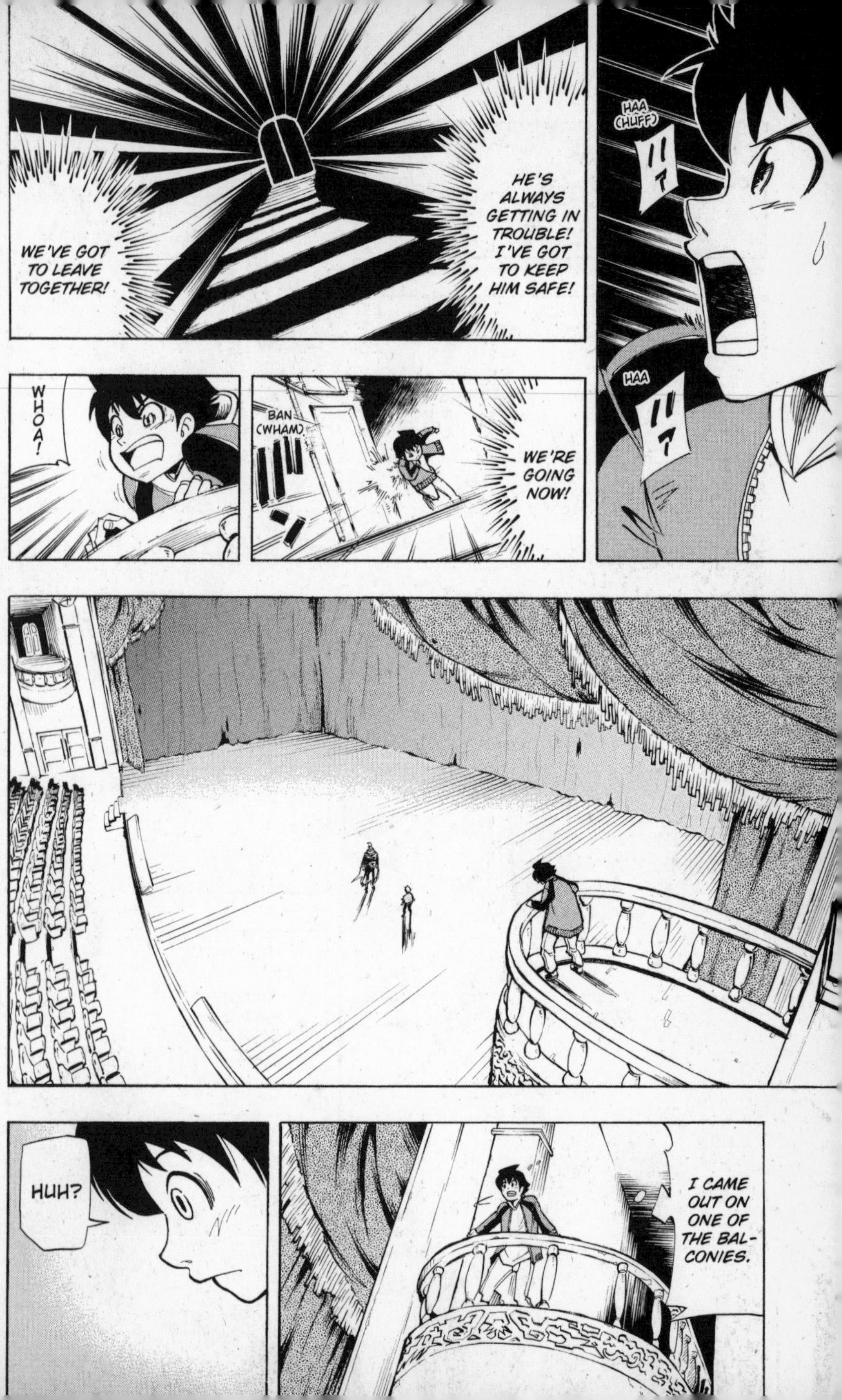
HAA (HUFF)
ハァ
HAA
ハァ
HE'S ALWAYS GETTING IN TROUBLE! I'VE GOT TO KEEP HIM SAFE!
WE'VE GOT TO LEAVE TOGETHER!
BAN (WHAM)
WE'RE GOING NOW!
WHOA!
I CAME OUT ON ONE OF THE BAL- CONIES.
HUH?

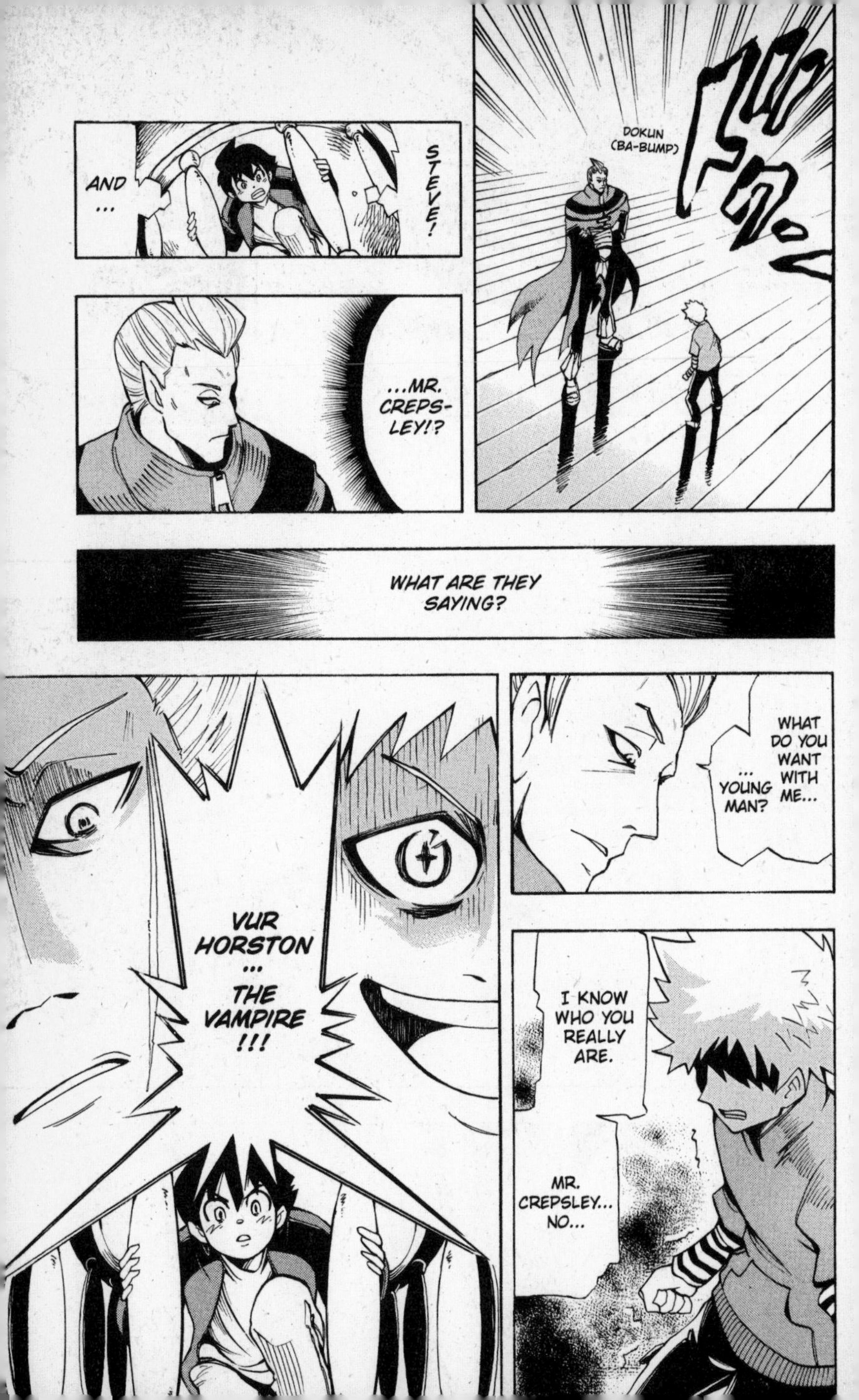
DOKUN (BA-BUMP)
STEVE!
AND ...
...MR. CREPSLEY!?
WHAT ARE THEY SAYING?
WHAT DO YOU WANT WITH ME...
... YOUNG MAN?
I KNOW WHO YOU REALLY ARE.
MR. CREPSLEY... NO...
VUR HORSTON ... THE VAMPIRE !!!

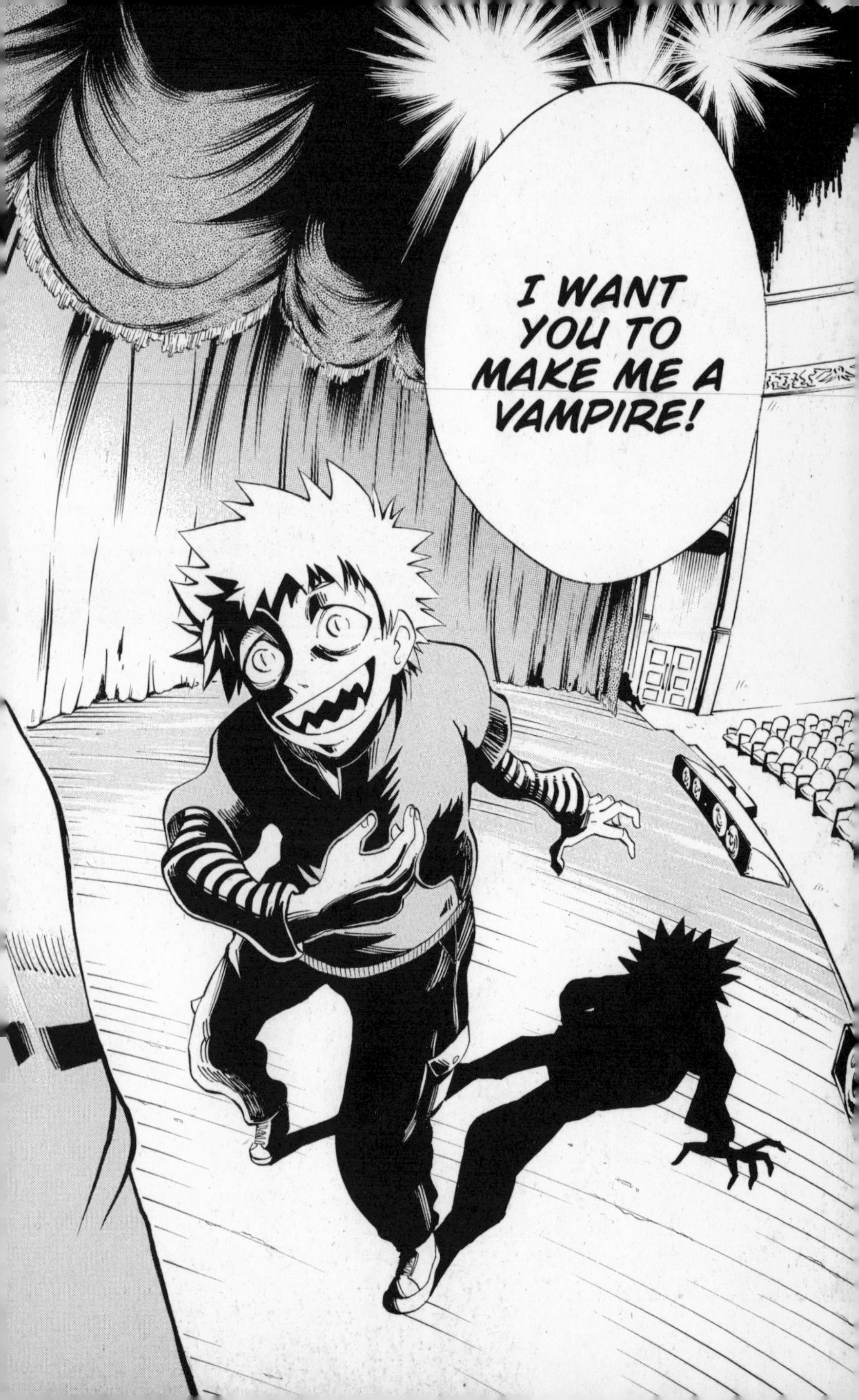
I WANT YOU TO MAKE ME A VAMPIRE!

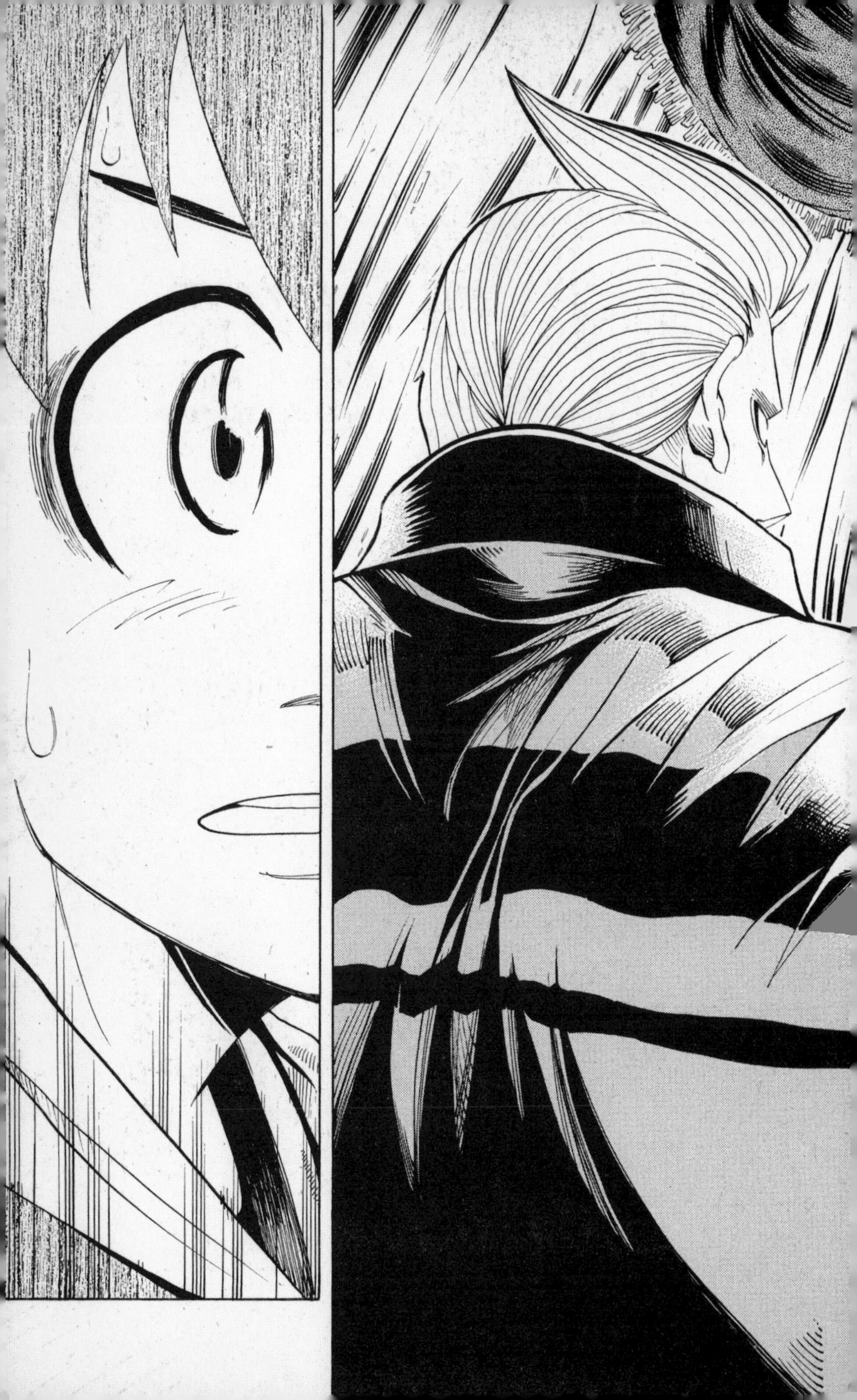

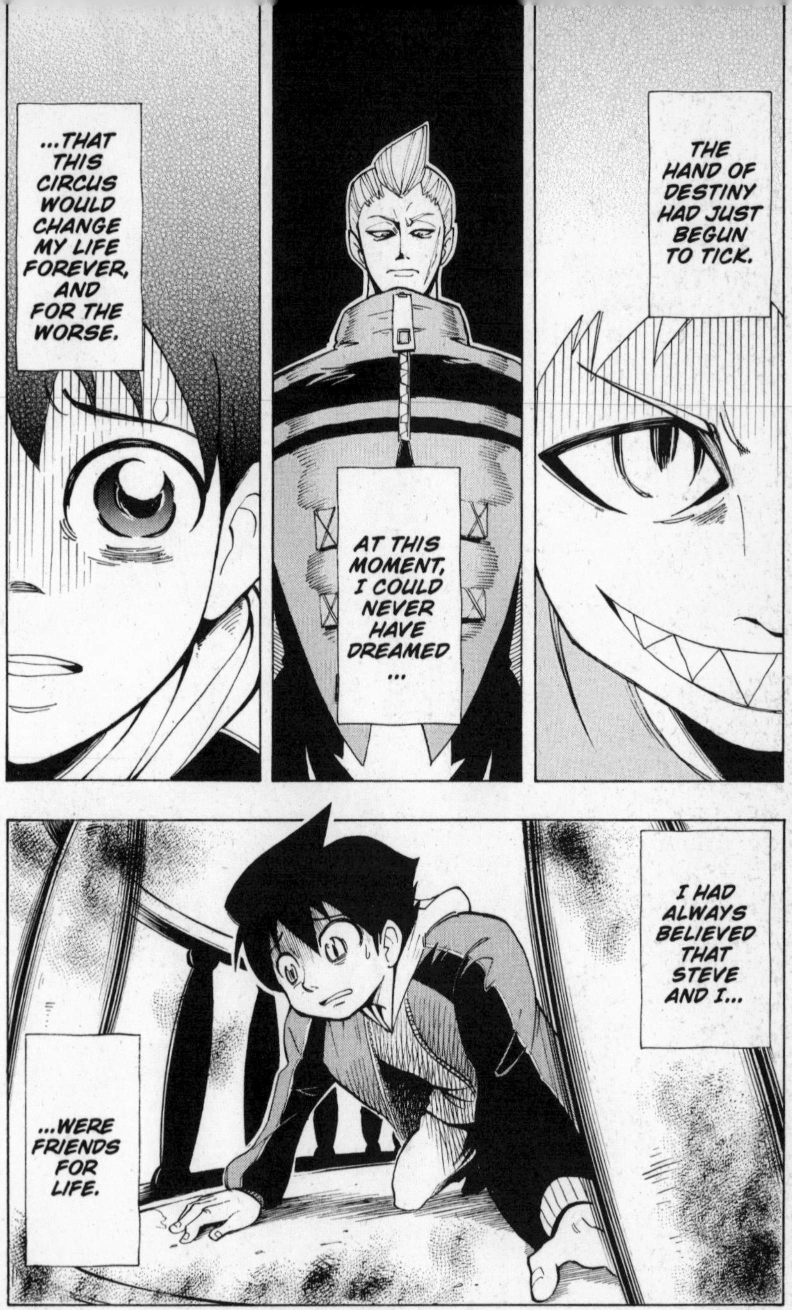

THE HAND OF DESTINY HAD JUST BEGUN TO TICK.
AT THIS MOMENT, I COULD NEVER HAVE DREAMED ...
...THAT THIS CIRCUS WOULD CHANGE MY LIFE FOREVER, AND FOR THE WORSE.
I HAD ALWAYS BELIEVED THAT STEVE AND I...
...WERE FRIENDS FOR LIFE.

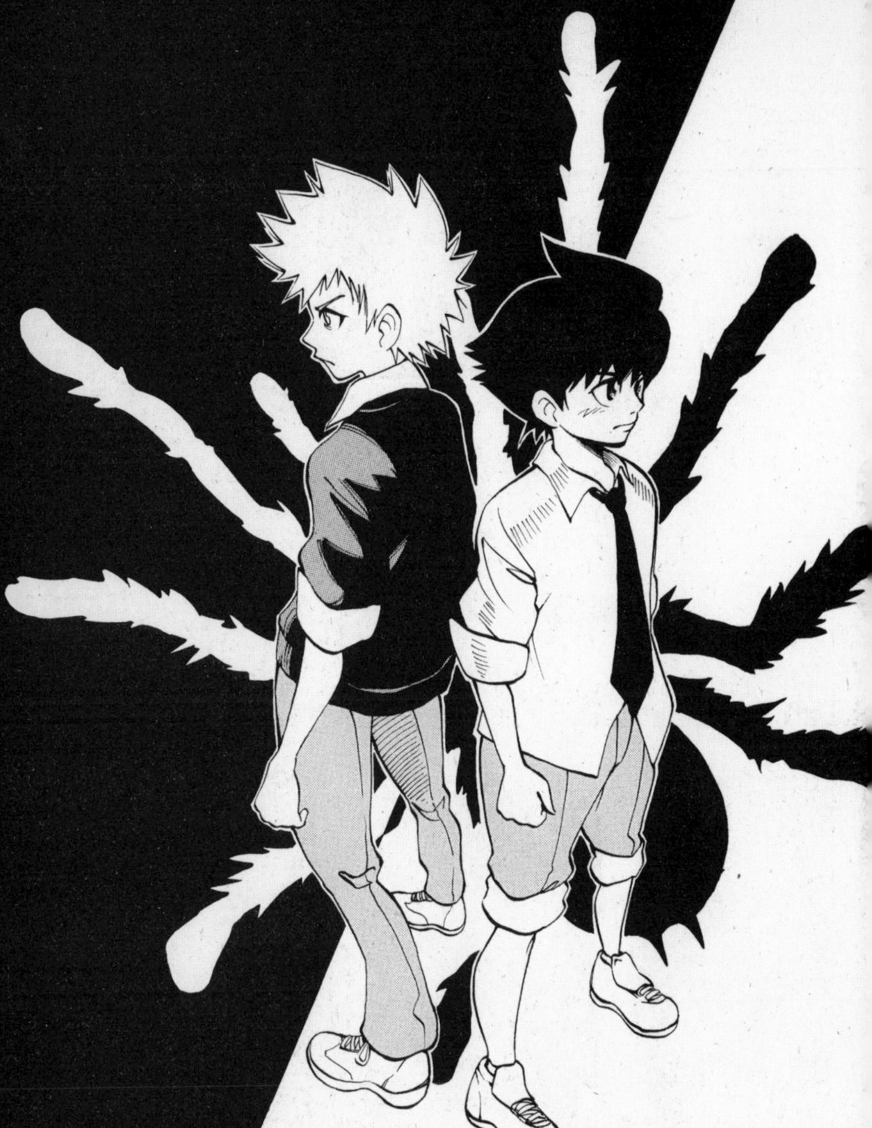

CHAPTER 2:
A DANGEROUS GAME

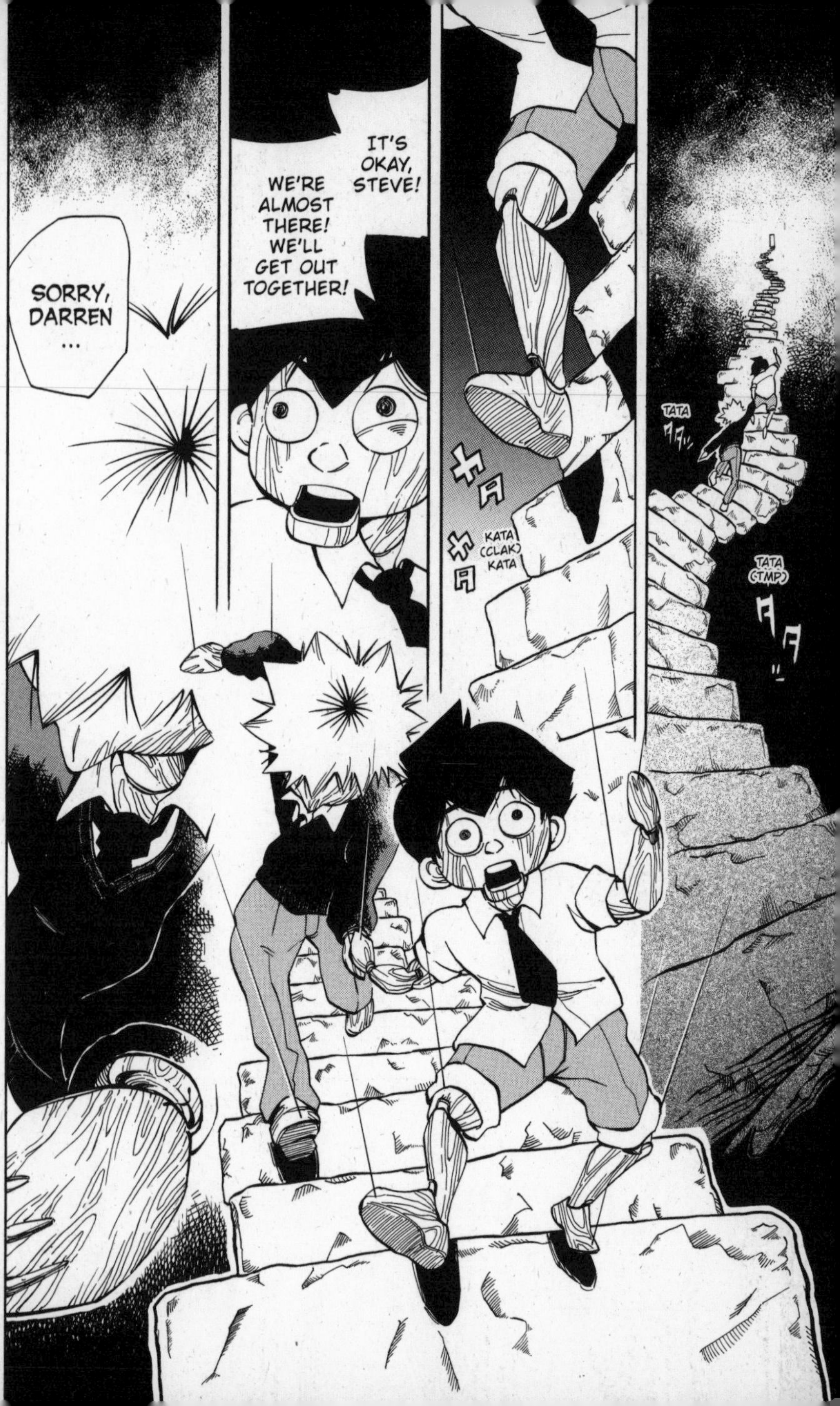
TATA
TATA (TMP)
KATA (CLAK) KATA
IT'S OKAY, STEVE!
WE'RE ALMOST THERE! WE'LL GET OUT TOGETHER!
SORRY, DARREN ...

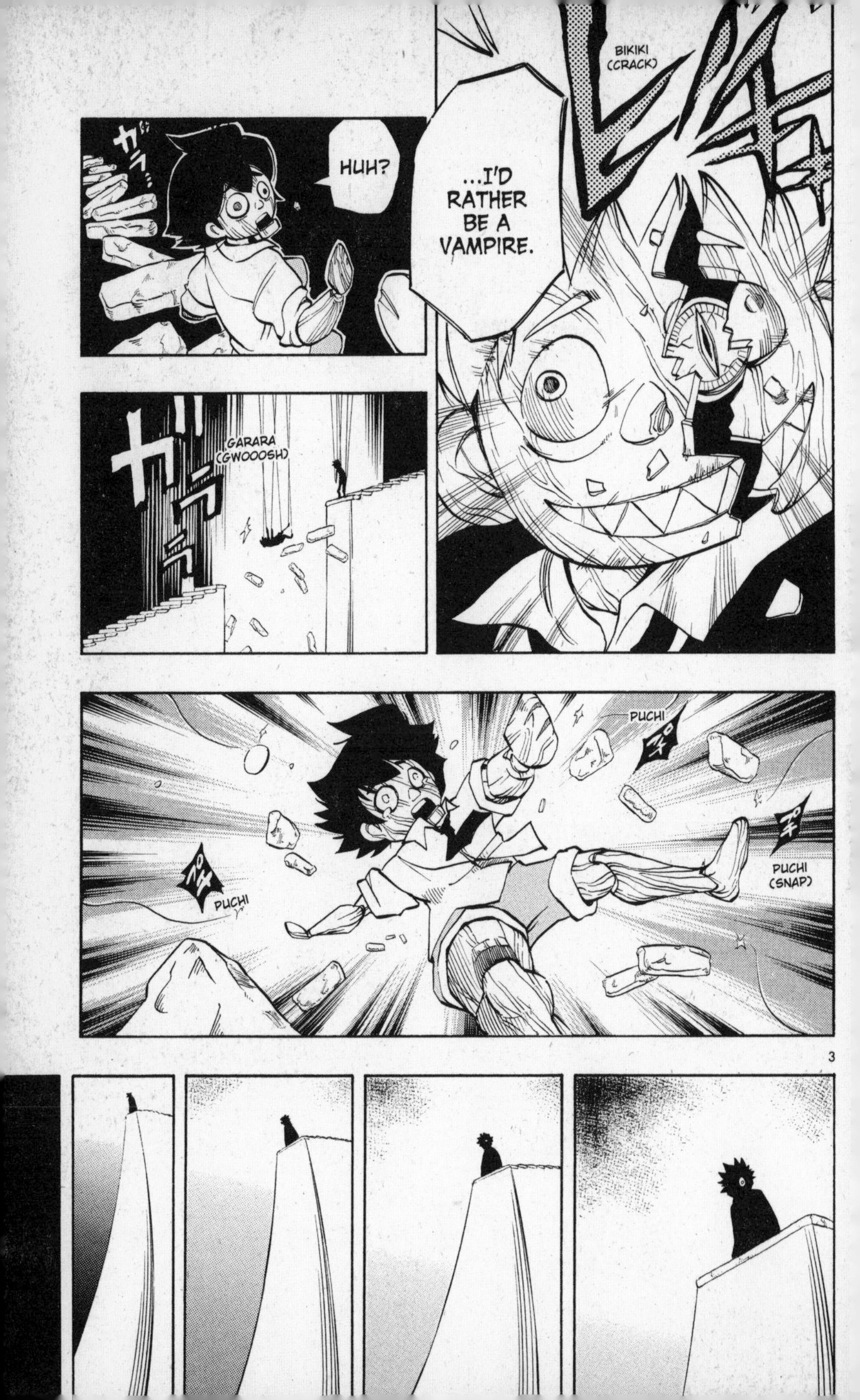
BIKIKI (CRACK)
...I'D RATHER BE A VAMPIRE.
HUH?
GARARA (GWOOOSH)
PUCHI
PUCHI (SNAP)
PUCHI
3

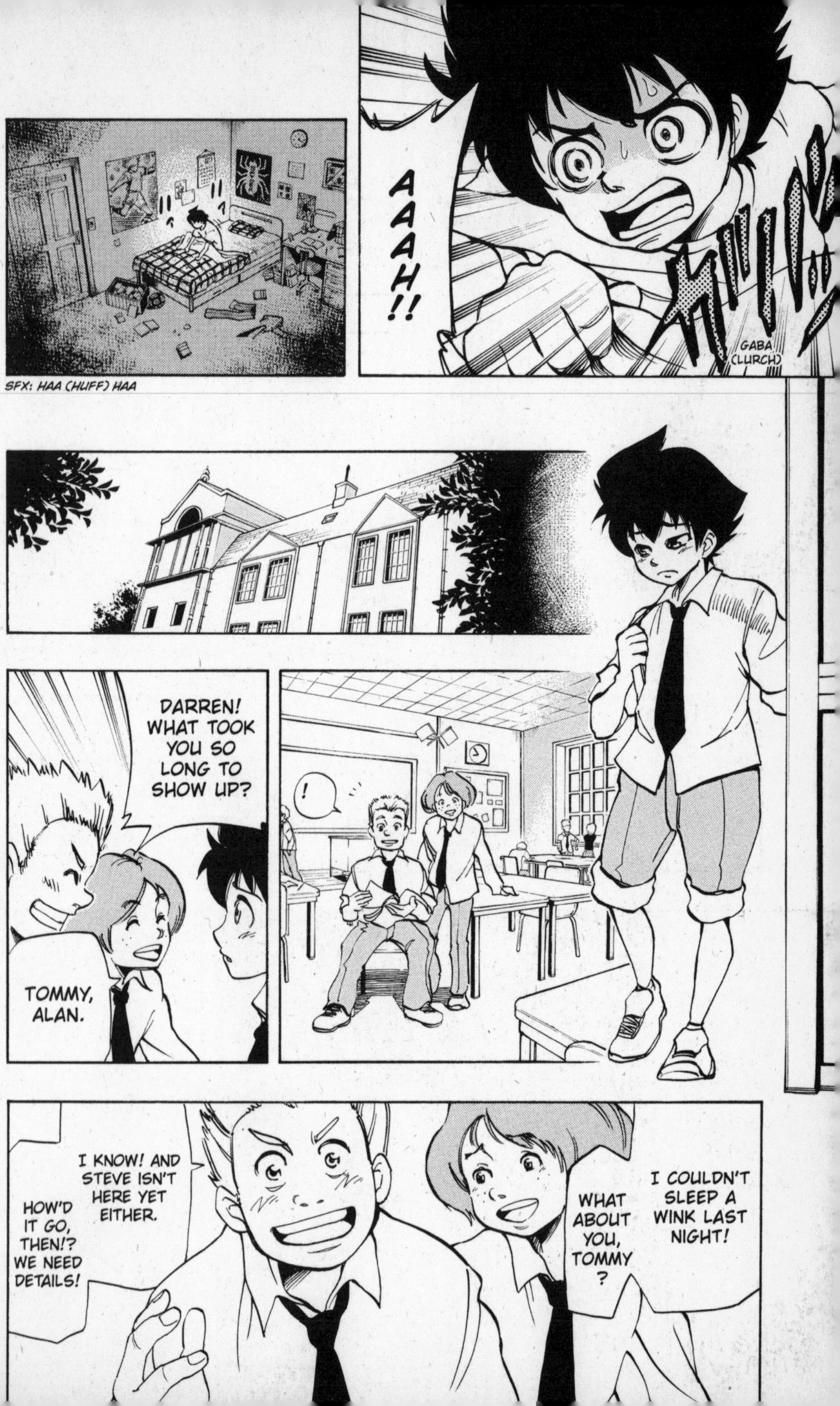
AAAAH!!
GABA (LURCH)
SFX: HAA (HUFF) HAA
!
DARREN! WHAT TOOK YOU SO LONG TO SHOW UP?
TOMMY, ALAN.
I COULDN'T SLEEP A WINK LAST NIGHT!
WHAT ABOUT YOU, TOMMY?
I KNOW! AND STEVE ISN'T HERE YET EITHER.
HOW'D IT GO, THEN!? WE NEED DETAILS!

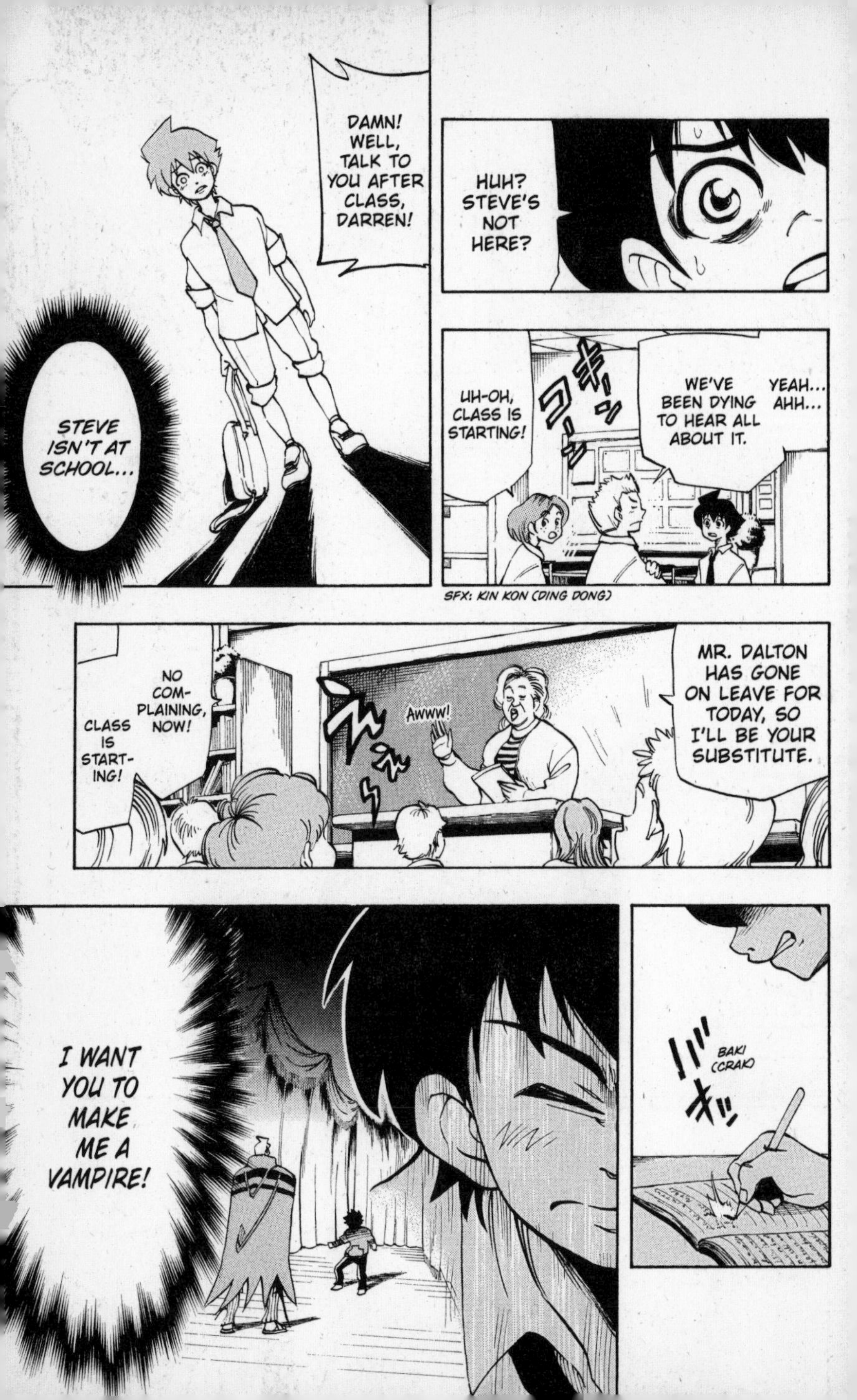
HUH? STEVE'S NOT HERE?
YEAH... AHH...
WE'VE BEEN DYING TO HEAR ALL ABOUT IT.
UH-OH, CLASS IS STARTING!
SFX: KIN KON (DING DONG)
DAMN! WELL, TALK TO YOU AFTER CLASS, DARREN!
STEVE ISN'T AT SCHOOL...
MR. DALTON HAS GONE ON LEAVE FOR TODAY, SO I'LL BE YOUR SUBSTITUTE.
AWWW!
NO COM-PLAINING, NOW!
CLASS IS START-ING!
BAKI (CRAK)
I WANT YOU TO MAKE ME A VAMPIRE!

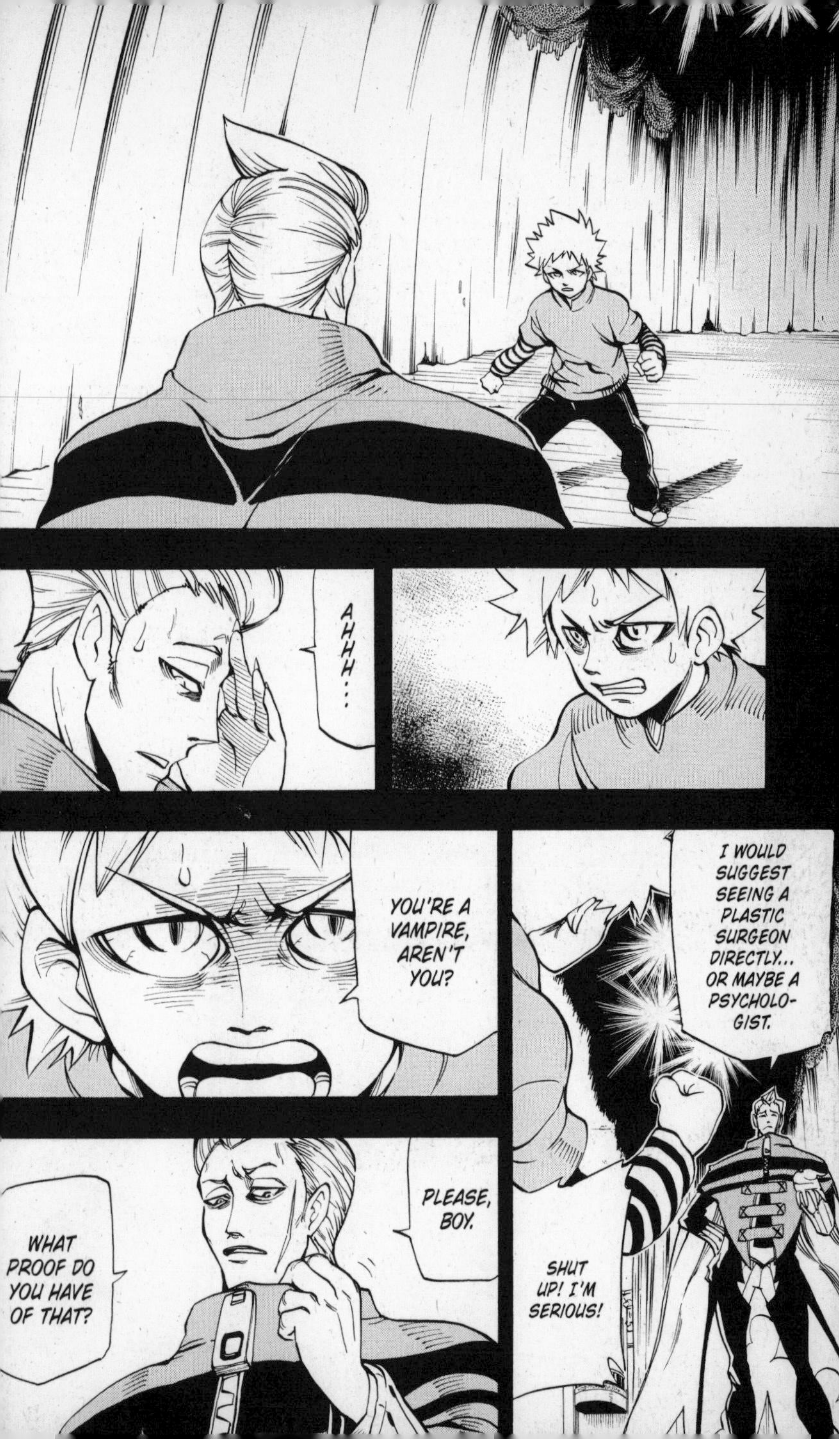
AHHH...
I WOULD SUGGEST SEEING A PLASTIC SURGEON DIRECTLY... OR MAYBE A PSYCHOLOGIST.
SHUT UP! I'M SERIOUS!
YOU'RE A VAMPIRE, AREN'T YOU?
PLEASE, BOY.
WHAT PROOF DO YOU HAVE OF THAT?

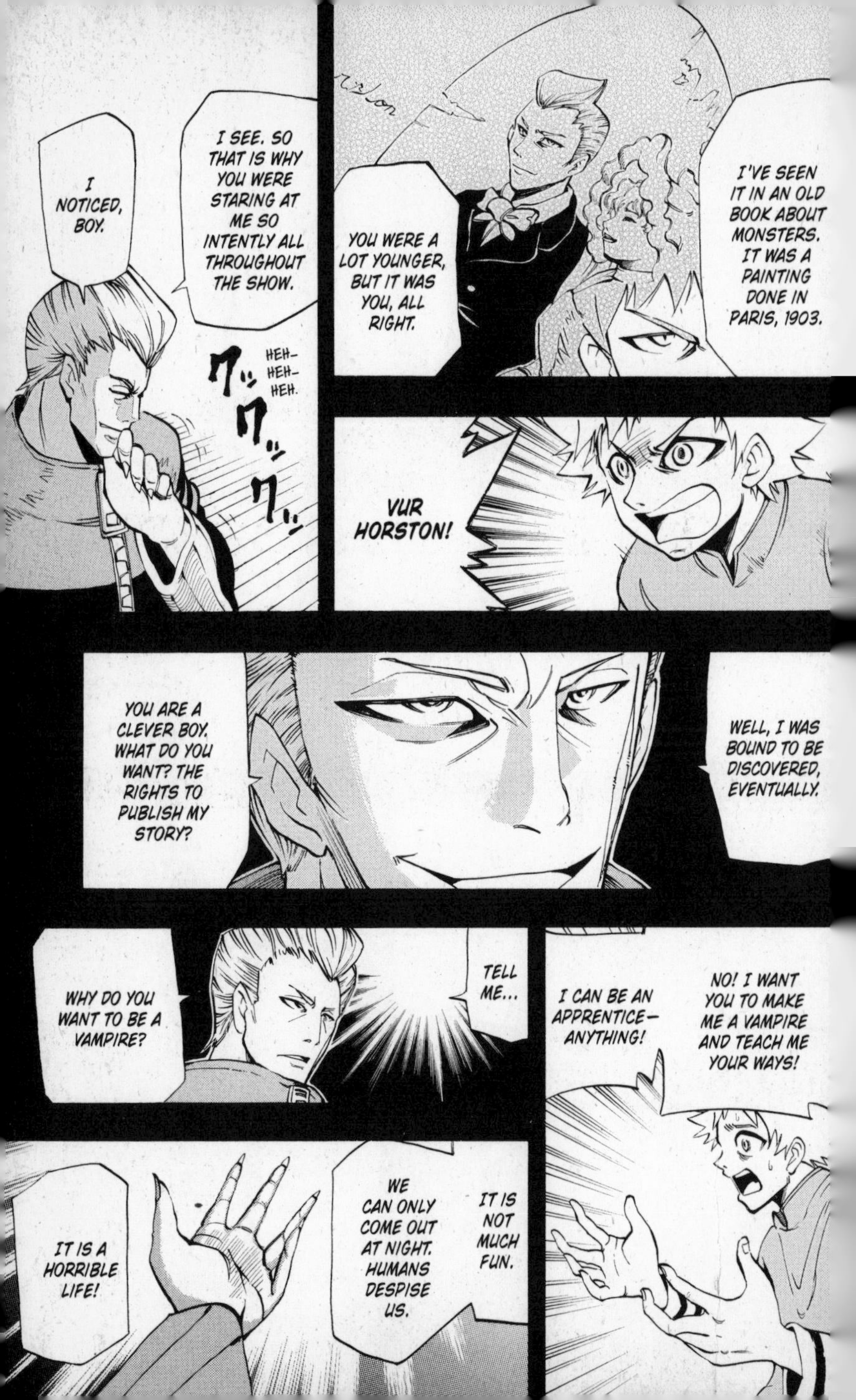
I'VE SEEN IT IN AN OLD BOOK ABOUT MONSTERS. IT WAS A PAINTING DONE IN PARIS, 1903.
YOU WERE A LOT YOUNGER, BUT IT WAS YOU, ALL RIGHT.
VUR HORSTON!
I SEE. SO THAT IS WHY YOU WERE STARING AT ME SO INTENTLY ALL THROUGHOUT THE SHOW.
I NOTICED, BOY.
HEH-HEH-HEH.
WELL, I WAS BOUND TO BE DISCOVERED, EVENTUALLY.
YOU ARE A CLEVER BOY. WHAT DO YOU WANT? THE RIGHTS TO PUBLISH MY STORY?
NO! I WANT YOU TO MAKE ME A VAMPIRE AND TEACH ME YOUR WAYS!
I CAN BE AN APPRENTICE—ANYTHING!
TELL ME...
WHY DO YOU WANT TO BE A VAMPIRE?
IT IS NOT MUCH FUN.
WE CAN ONLY COME OUT AT NIGHT. HUMANS DESPISE US.
IT IS A HORRIBLE LIFE!

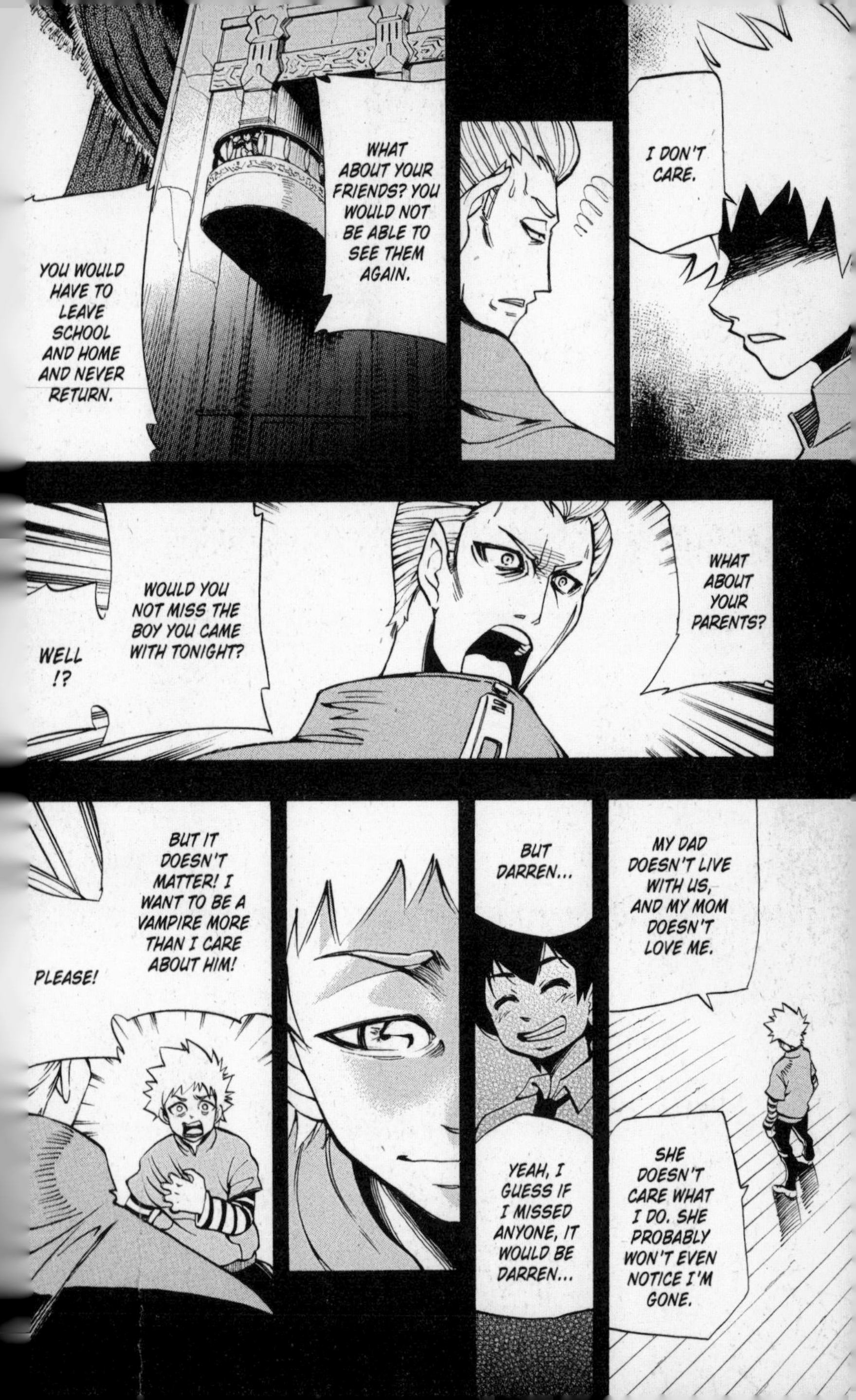
I DON'T CARE.
WHAT ABOUT YOUR FRIENDS? YOU WOULD NOT BE ABLE TO SEE THEM AGAIN.
YOU WOULD HAVE TO LEAVE SCHOOL AND HOME AND NEVER RETURN.
WHAT ABOUT YOUR PARENTS?
WOULD YOU NOT MISS THE BOY YOU CAME WITH TONIGHT?
WELL !?
MY DAD DOESN'T LIVE WITH US, AND MY MOM DOESN'T LOVE ME.
SHE DOESN'T CARE WHAT I DO. SHE PROBABLY WON'T EVEN NOTICE I'M GONE.
BUT DARREN...
YEAH, I GUESS IF I MISSED ANYONE, IT WOULD BE DARREN...
BUT IT DOESN'T MATTER! I WANT TO BE A VAMPIRE MORE THAN I CARE ABOUT HIM!
PLEASE!

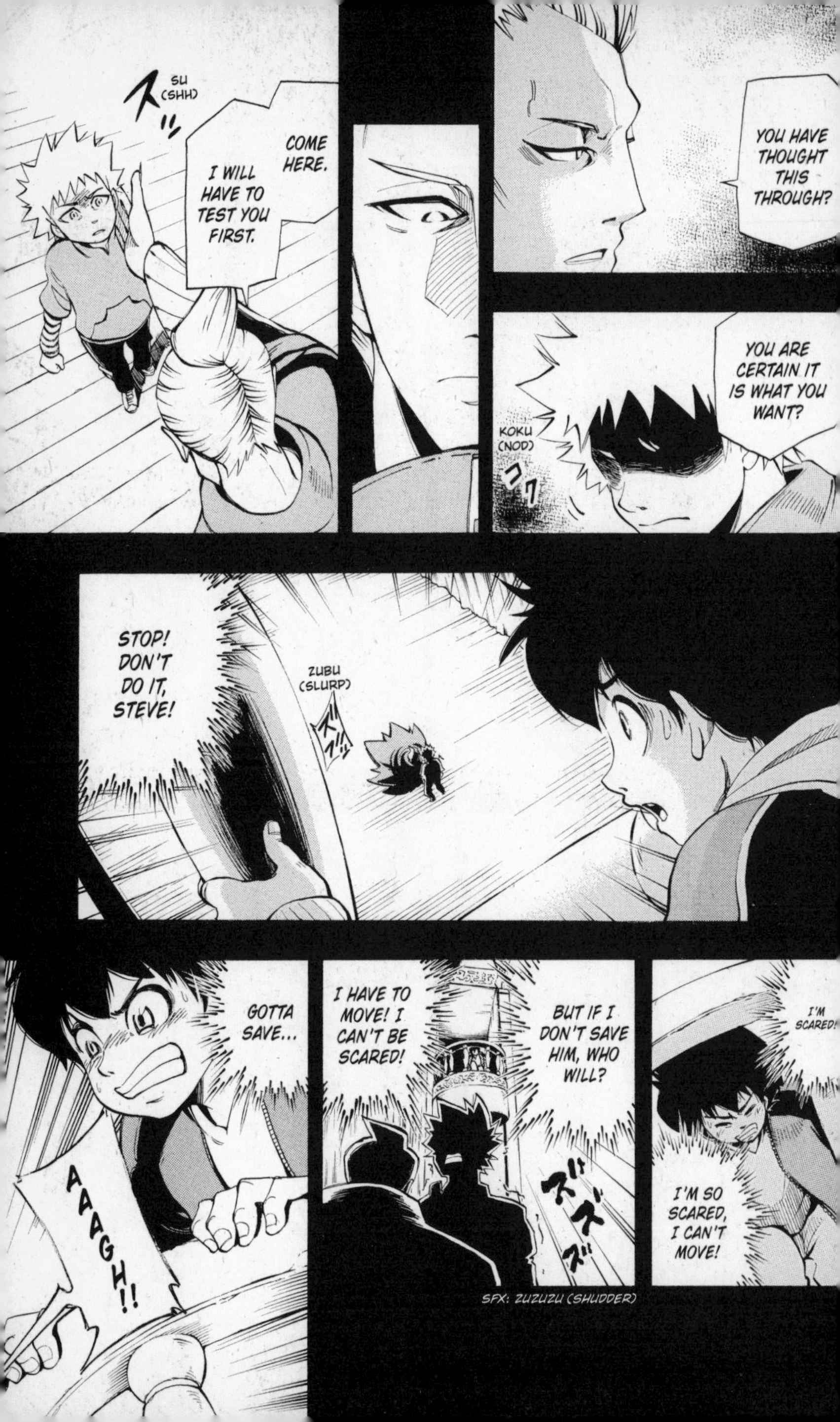
YOU HAVE THOUGHT THIS THROUGH?
YOU ARE CERTAIN IT IS WHAT YOU WANT?
KOKU (NOD)
COME HERE.
I WILL HAVE TO TEST YOU FIRST.
SU (SHH)
STOP! DON'T DO IT, STEVE!
ZUBU (SLURP)
I'M SCARED!
I'M SO SCARED, I CAN'T MOVE!
BUT IF I DON'T SAVE HIM, WHO WILL?
I HAVE TO MOVE! I CAN'T BE SCARED!
SFX: ZUZUZU (SHUDDER)
GOTTA SAVE...
AAAGH!!

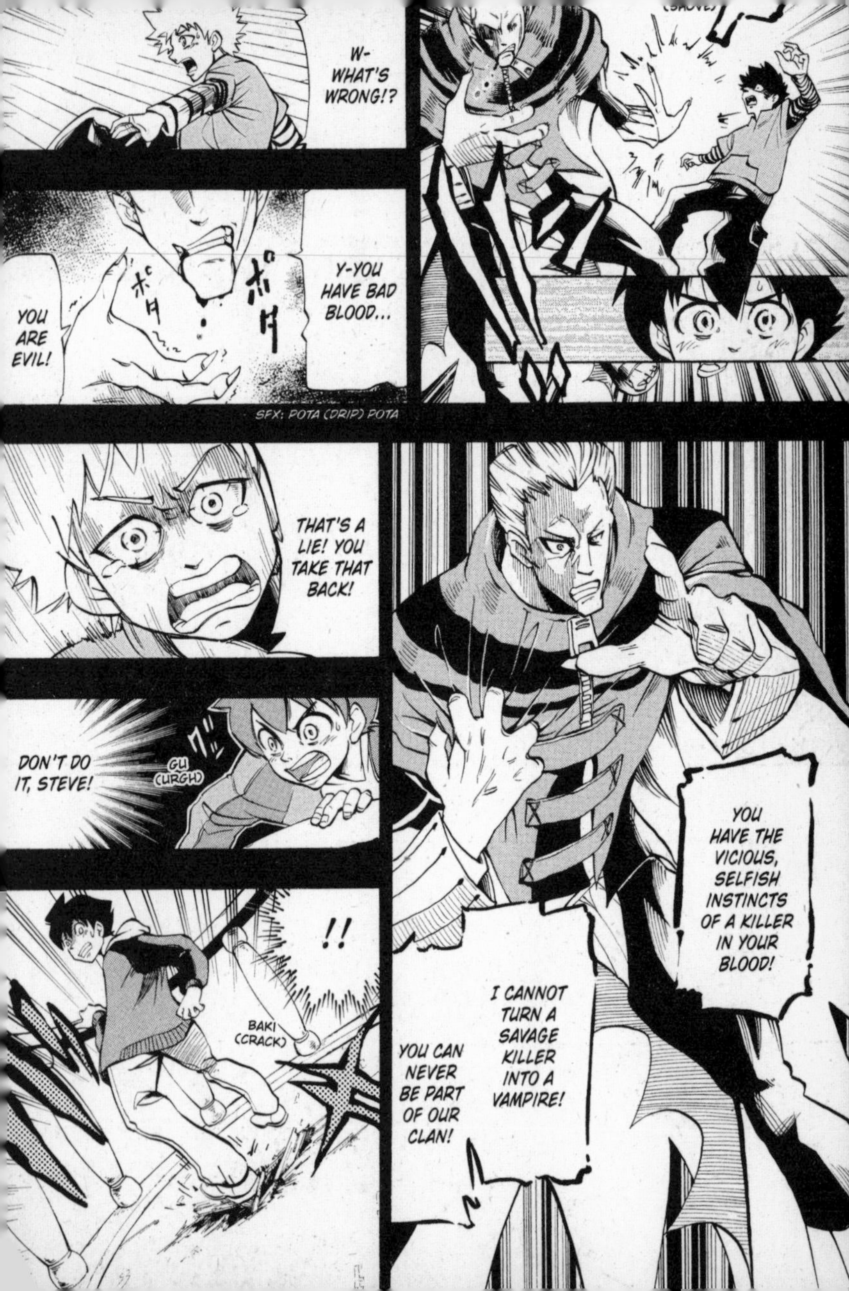
W-WHAT'S WRONG!?
Y-YOU HAVE BAD BLOOD...
YOU ARE EVIL!
SFX: POTA (DRIP) POTA
YOU HAVE THE VICIOUS, SELFISH INSTINCTS OF A KILLER IN YOUR BLOOD!
I CANNOT TURN A SAVAGE KILLER INTO A VAMPIRE!
YOU CAN NEVER BE PART OF OUR CLAN!
THAT'S A LIE! YOU TAKE THAT BACK!
GU (URGH)
DON'T DO IT, STEVE!
!!
BAKI (CRACK)

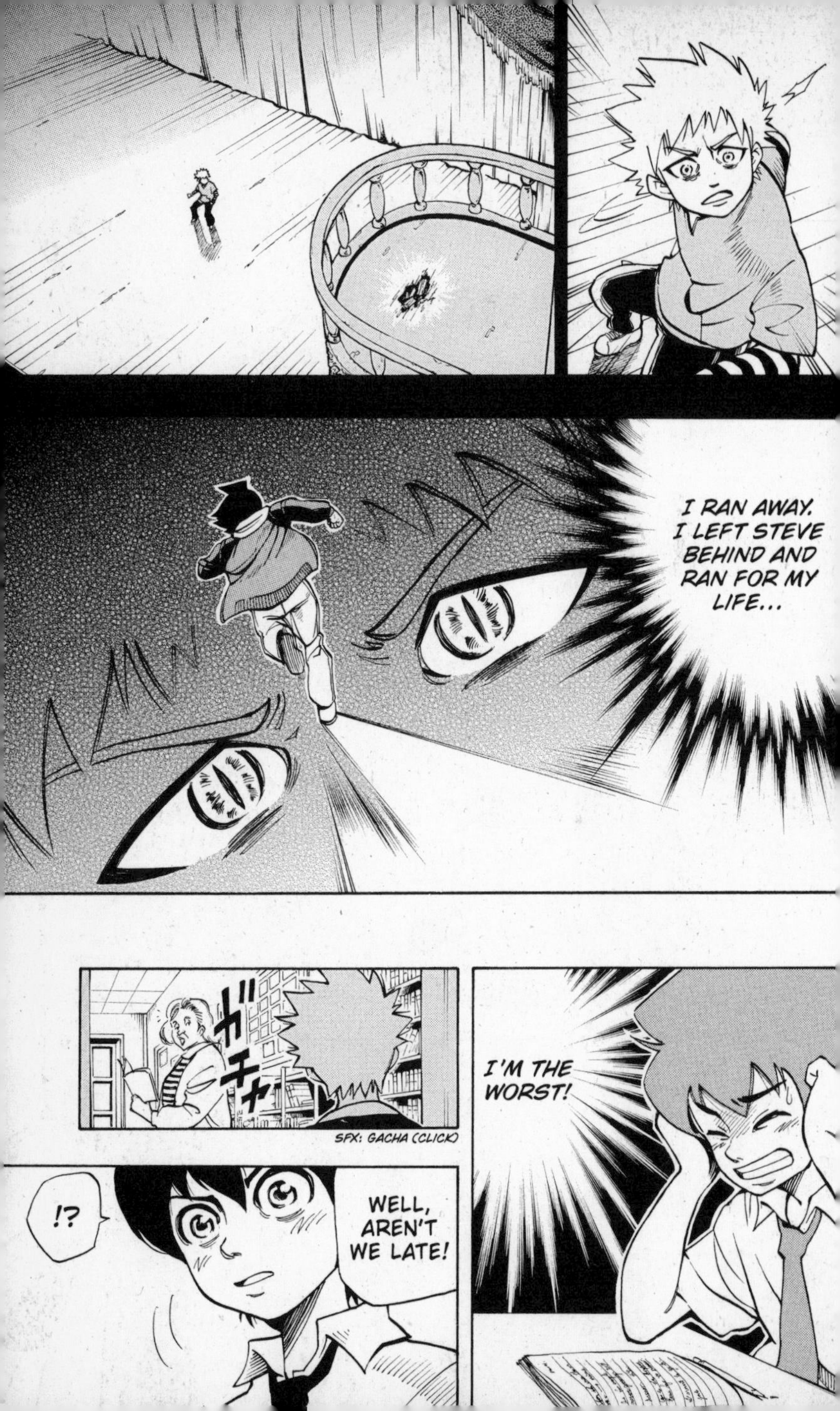
I RAN AWAY. I LEFT STEVE BEHIND AND RAN FOR MY LIFE...
I'M THE WORST!
ガチャ
SFX: GACHA (CLICK)
WELL, AREN'T WE LATE!
!?

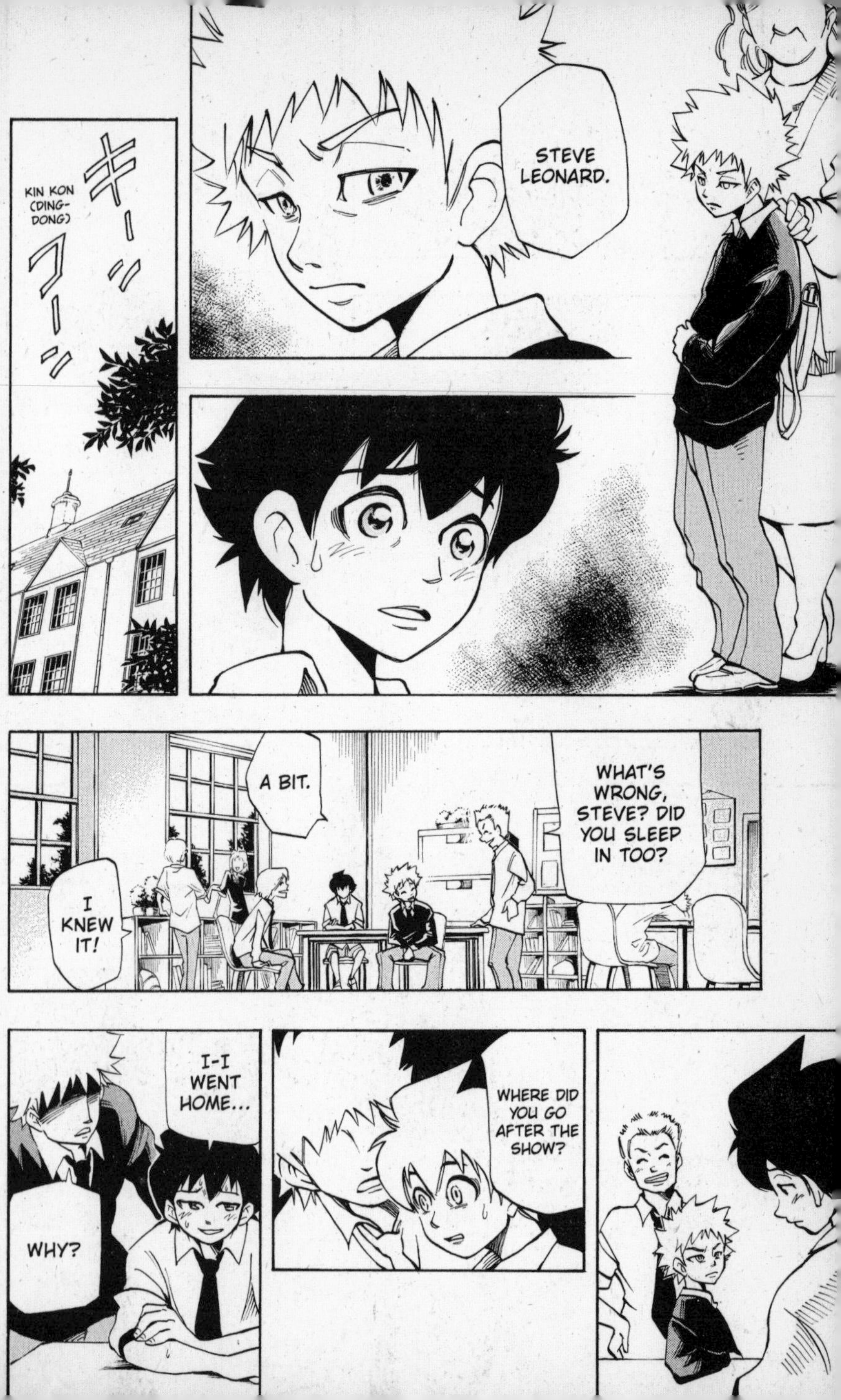
STEVE LEONARD.
キーン コーン
KIN KON (DING-DONG)
WHAT'S WRONG, STEVE? DID YOU SLEEP IN TOO?
A BIT.
I KNEW IT!
WHERE DID YOU GO AFTER THE SHOW?
I-I WENT HOME...
WHY?

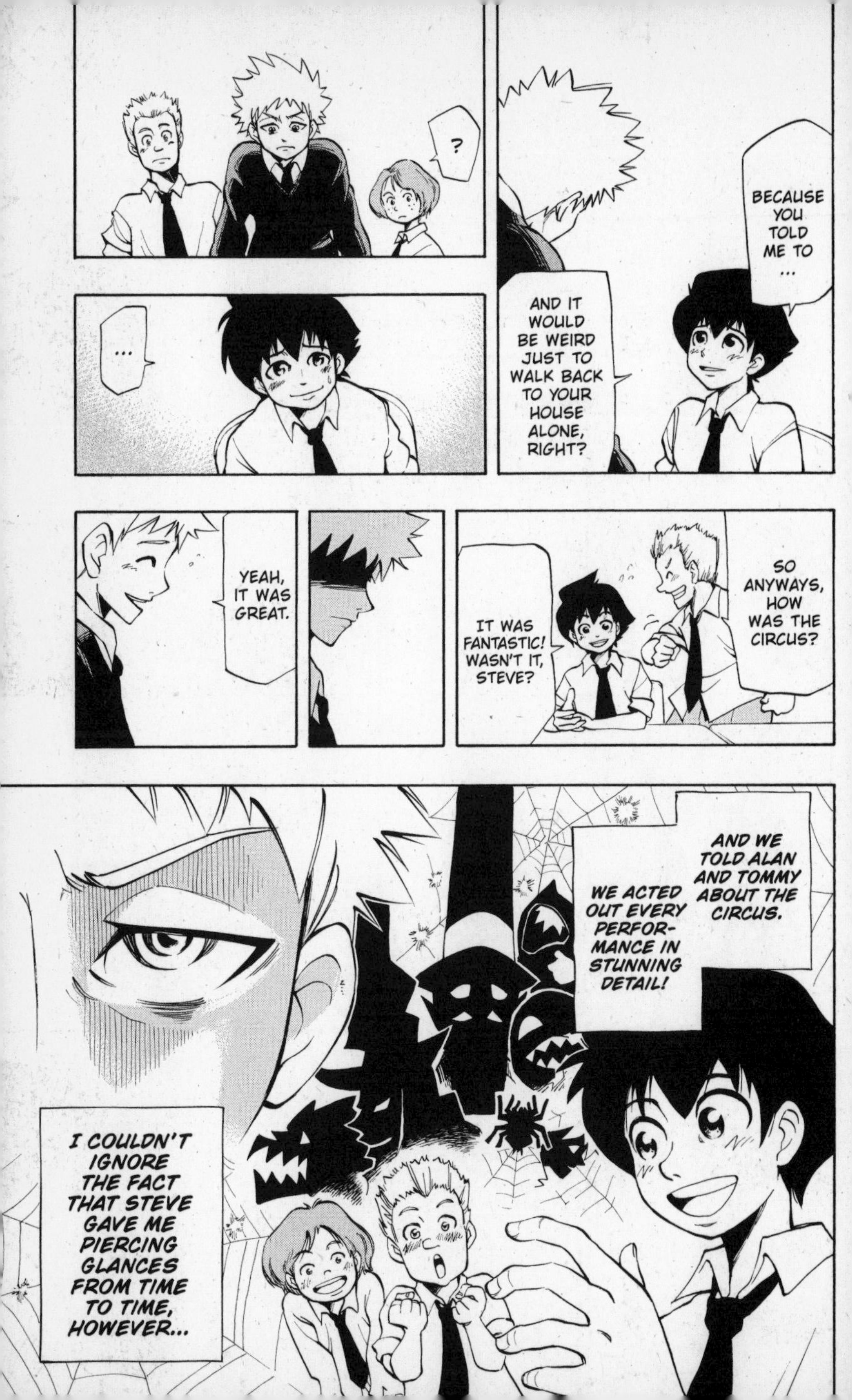
BECAUSE YOU TOLD ME TO ...
AND IT WOULD BE WEIRD JUST TO WALK BACK TO YOUR HOUSE ALONE, RIGHT?
?
...
SO ANYWAYS, HOW WAS THE CIRCUS?
IT WAS FANTASTIC! WASN'T IT, STEVE?
YEAH, IT WAS GREAT.
AND WE TOLD ALAN AND TOMMY ABOUT THE CIRCUS.
WE ACTED OUT EVERY PERFORMANCE IN STUNNING DETAIL!
I COULDN'T IGNORE THE FACT THAT STEVE GAVE ME PIERCING GLANCES FROM TIME TO TIME, HOWEVER...

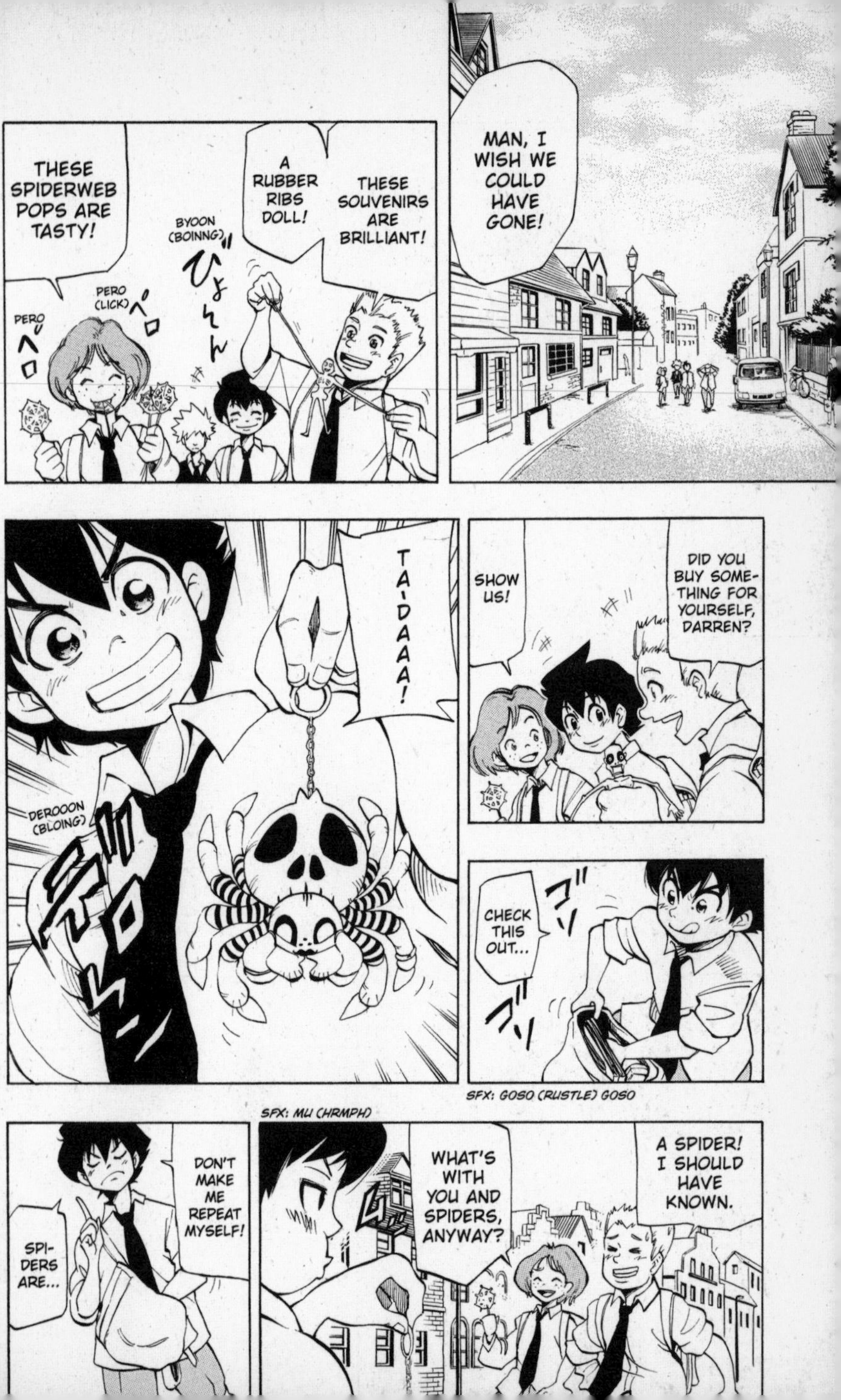

MAN, I WISH WE COULD HAVE GONE!
THESE SOUVENIRS ARE BRILLIANT!
A RUBBER RIBS DOLL!
BYOON (BOINNG)
THESE SPIDERWEB POPS ARE TASTY!
PERO (LICK)
PERO
DID YOU BUY SOME-THING FOR YOURSELF, DARREN?
SHOW US!
CHECK THIS OUT...
SFX: GOSO (RUSTLE) GOSO
TA-DAAAA!
DEROOON (BLOING)
A SPIDER! I SHOULD HAVE KNOWN.
WHAT'S WITH YOU AND SPIDERS, ANYWAY?
SFX: MU (HRMPH)
DON'T MAKE ME REPEAT MYSELF!
SPI-DERS ARE...

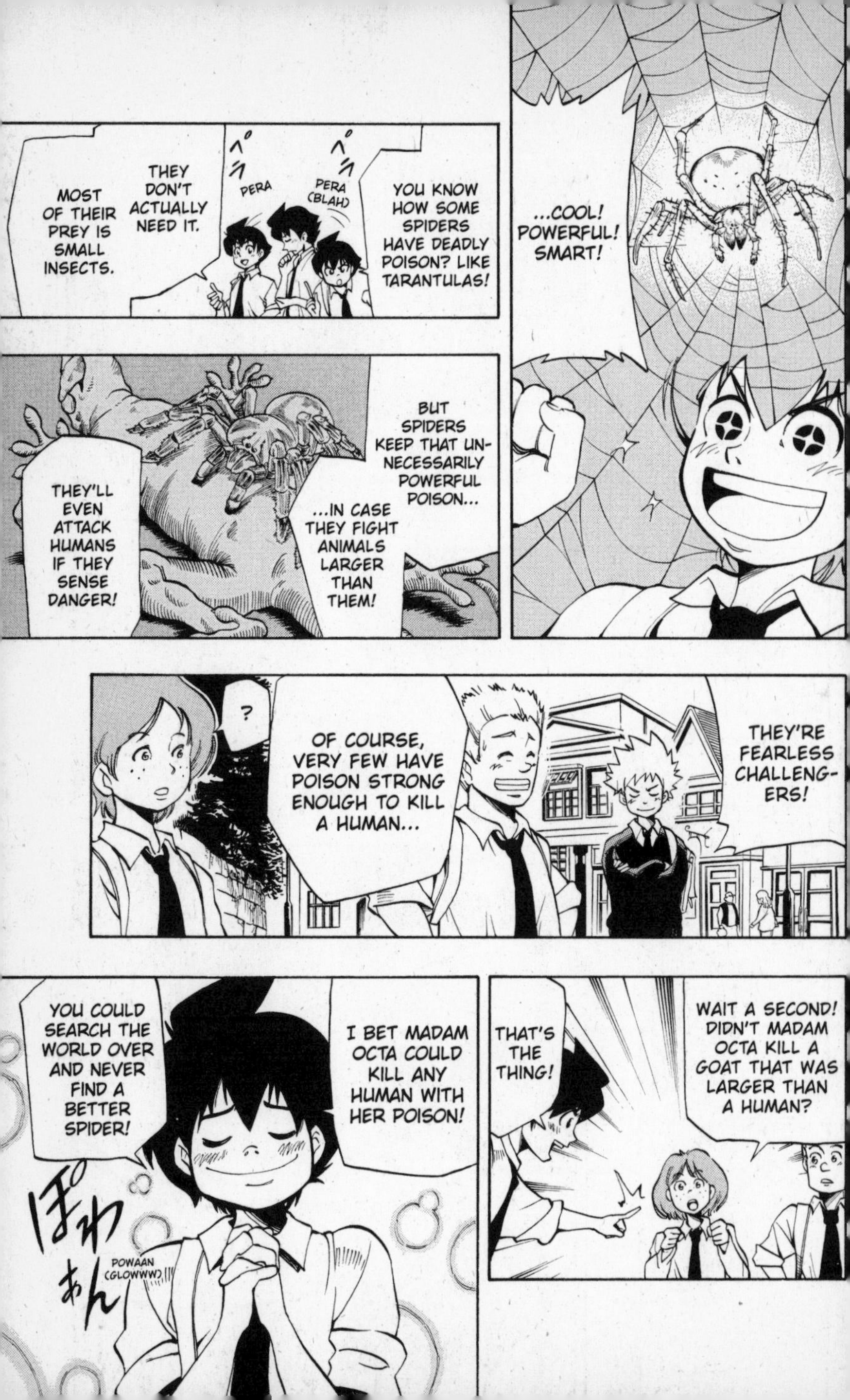
...COOL! POWERFUL! SMART!
YOU KNOW HOW SOME SPIDERS HAVE DEADLY POISON? LIKE TARANTULAS!
ペラ PERA (BLAH)
ペラ PERA
THEY DON'T ACTUALLY NEED IT.
MOST OF THEIR PREY IS SMALL INSECTS.
BUT SPIDERS KEEP THAT UN-NECESSARILY POWERFUL POISON...
...IN CASE THEY FIGHT ANIMALS LARGER THAN THEM!
THEY'LL EVEN ATTACK HUMANS IF THEY SENSE DANGER!
THEY'RE FEARLESS CHALLENG-ERS!
OF COURSE, VERY FEW HAVE POISON STRONG ENOUGH TO KILL A HUMAN...
?
WAIT A SECOND! DIDN'T MADAM OCTA KILL A GOAT THAT WAS LARGER THAN A HUMAN?
THAT'S THE THING!
I BET MADAM OCTA COULD KILL ANY HUMAN WITH HER POISON!
YOU COULD SEARCH THE WORLD OVER AND NEVER FIND A BETTER SPIDER!
ぽわあん POWAAN (GLOWWW)

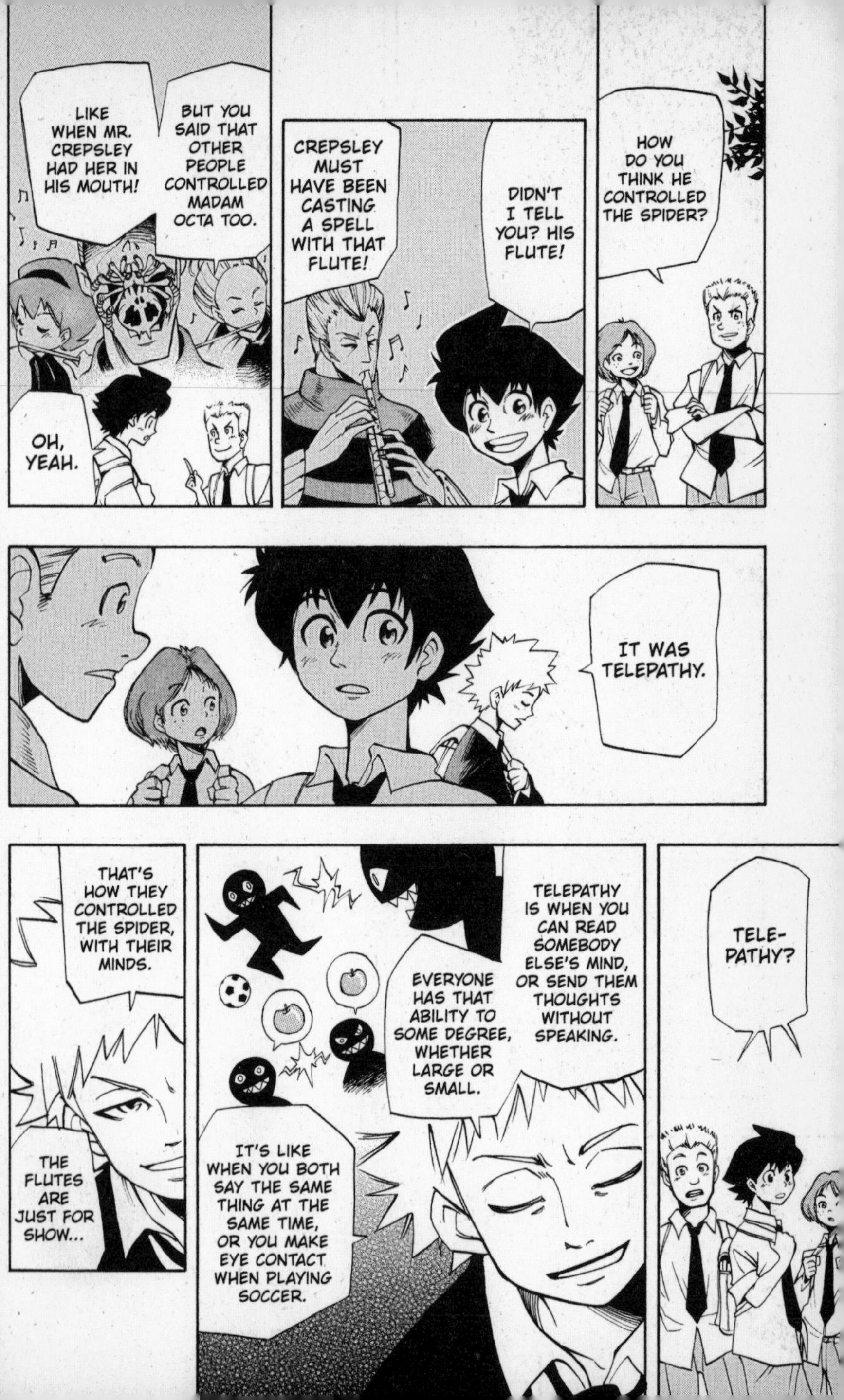
HOW DO YOU THINK HE CONTROLLED THE SPIDER?
DIDN'T I TELL YOU? HIS FLUTE!
CREPSLEY MUST HAVE BEEN CASTING A SPELL WITH THAT FLUTE!
BUT YOU SAID THAT OTHER PEOPLE CONTROLLED MADAM OCTA TOO.
LIKE WHEN MR. CREPSLEY HAD HER IN HIS MOUTH!
OH, YEAH.
IT WAS TELEPATHY.
TELE-PATHY?
TELEPATHY IS WHEN YOU CAN READ SOMEBODY ELSE'S MIND, OR SEND THEM THOUGHTS WITHOUT SPEAKING.
EVERYONE HAS THAT ABILITY TO SOME DEGREE, WHETHER LARGE OR SMALL.
IT'S LIKE WHEN YOU BOTH SAY THE SAME THING AT THE SAME TIME, OR YOU MAKE EYE CONTACT WHEN PLAYING SOCCER.
THAT'S HOW THEY CONTROLLED THE SPIDER, WITH THEIR MINDS.
THE FLUTES ARE JUST FOR SHOW...

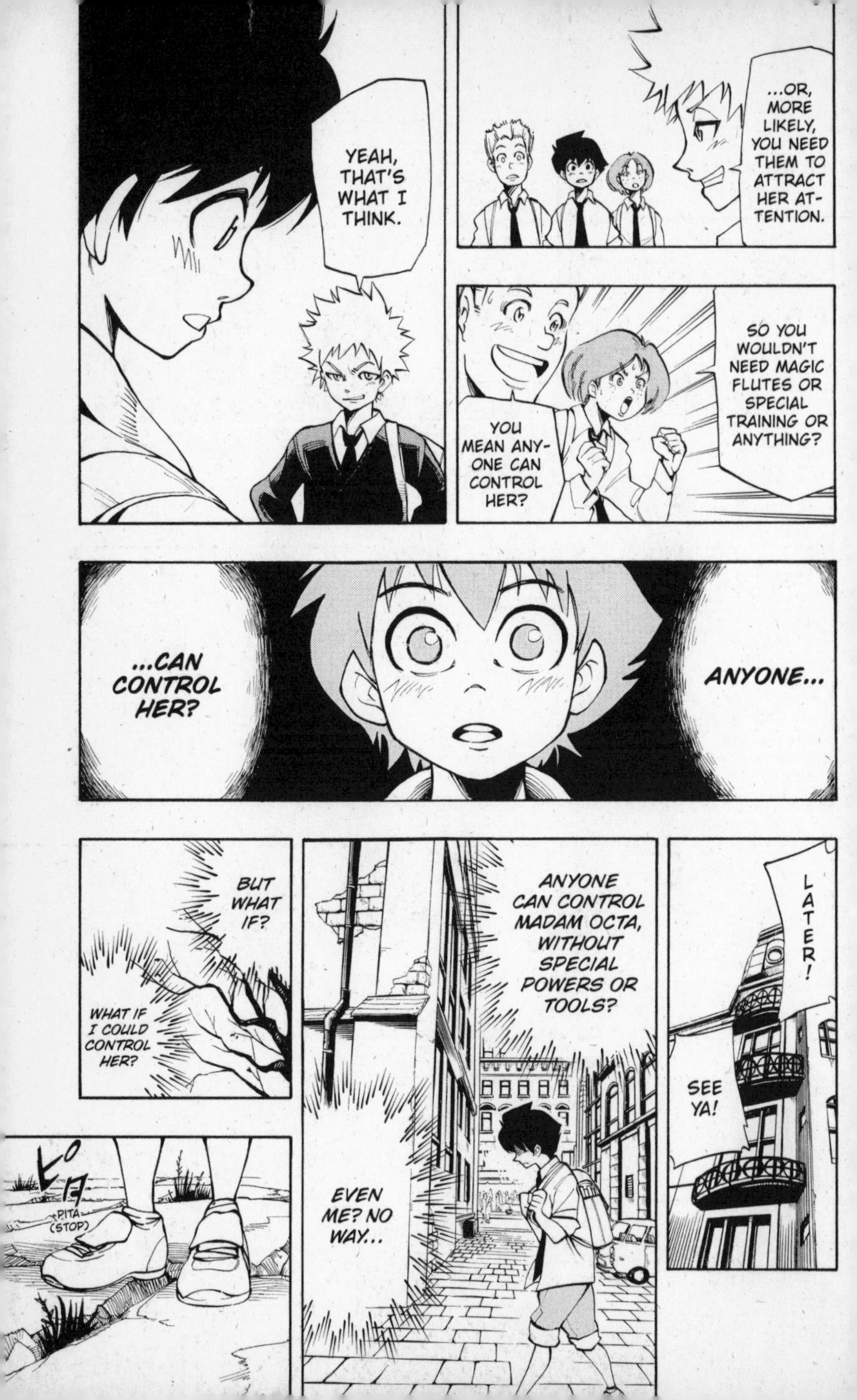
...OR, MORE LIKELY, YOU NEED THEM TO ATTRACT HER AT-TENTION.
SO YOU WOULDN'T NEED MAGIC FLUTES OR SPECIAL TRAINING OR ANYTHING?
YOU MEAN ANY-ONE CAN CONTROL HER?
YEAH, THAT'S WHAT I THINK.
ANYONE...
...CAN CONTROL HER?
LATER!
SEE YA!
ANYONE CAN CONTROL MADAM OCTA, WITHOUT SPECIAL POWERS OR TOOLS?
EVEN ME? NO WAY...
BUT WHAT IF?
WHAT IF I COULD CONTROL HER?
PITA (STOP)

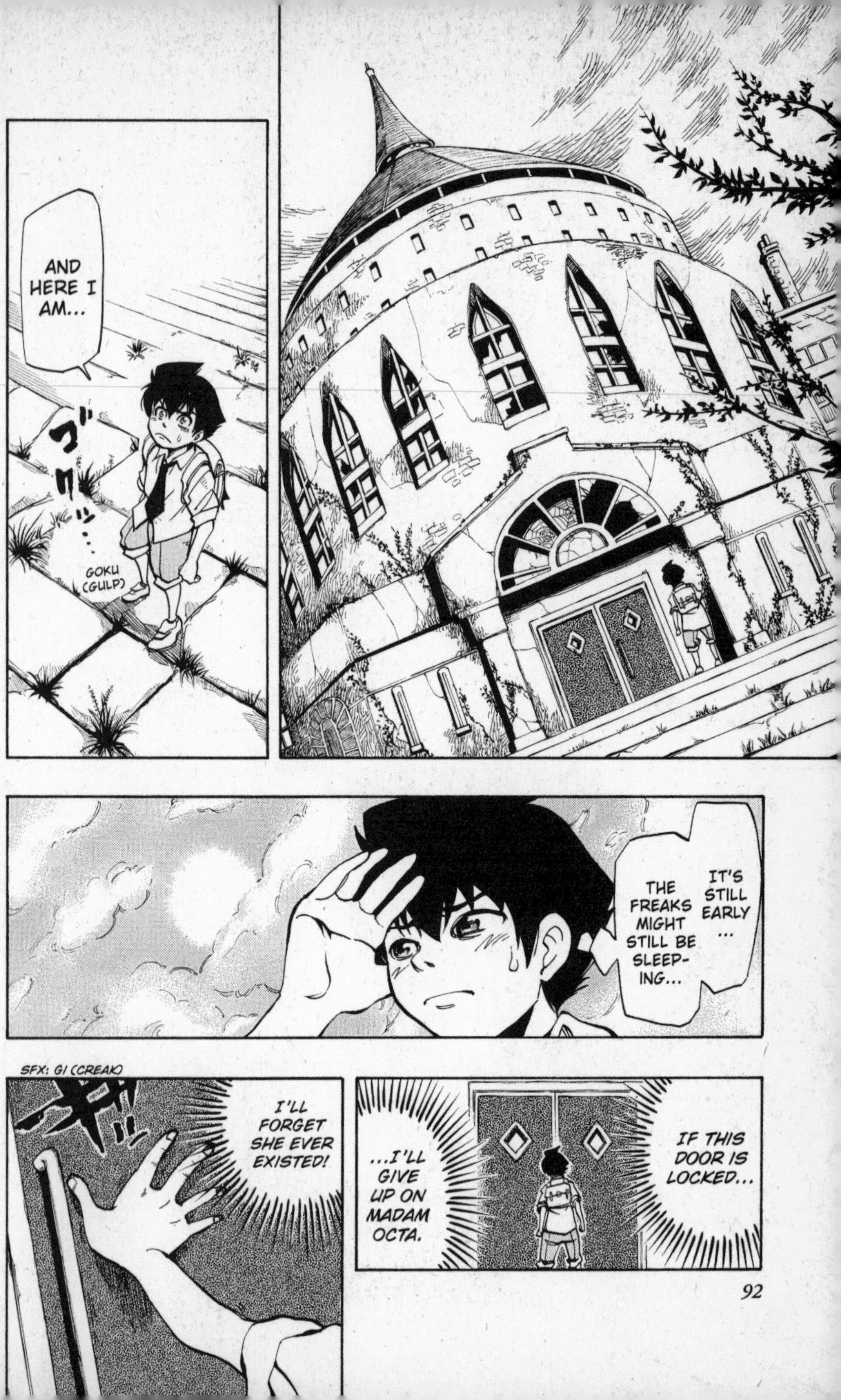
AND HERE I AM...
GOKU (GULP)
IT'S STILL EARLY...
THE FREAKS MIGHT STILL BE SLEEPING...
IF THIS DOOR IS LOCKED...
...I'LL GIVE UP ON MADAM OCTA.
SFX: GI (CREAK)
I'LL FORGET SHE EVER EXISTED!

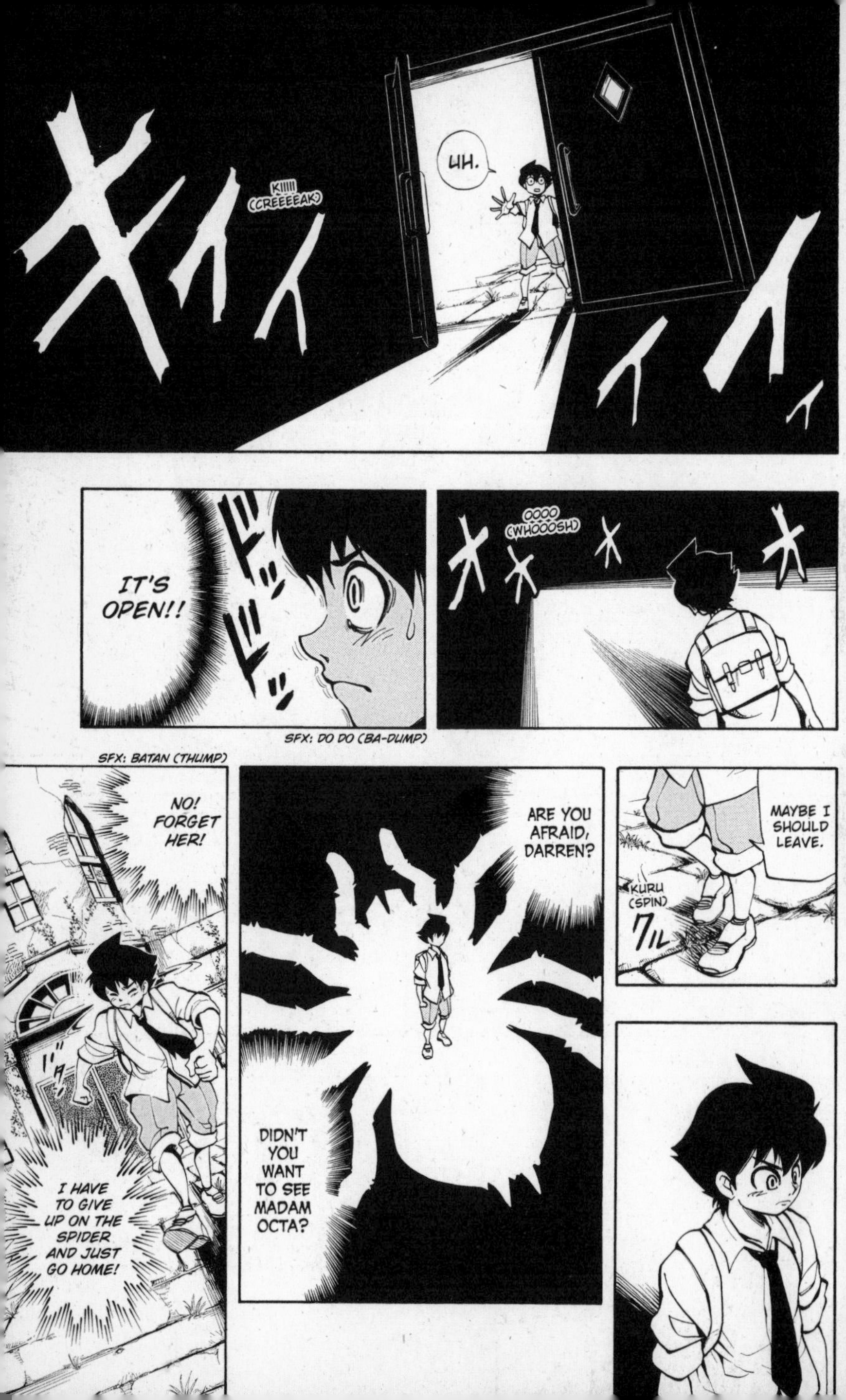
UH.
KIIIII (CREEEEAK)
OOOO (WHOOOSH)
IT'S OPEN!!
SFX: DO DO (BA-DUMP)
MAYBE I SHOULD LEAVE.
KURU (SPIN)
ARE YOU AFRAID, DARREN?
DIDN'T YOU WANT TO SEE MADAM OCTA?
SFX: BATAN (THUMP)
NO! FORGET HER!
I HAVE TO GIVE UP ON THE SPIDER AND JUST GO HOME!

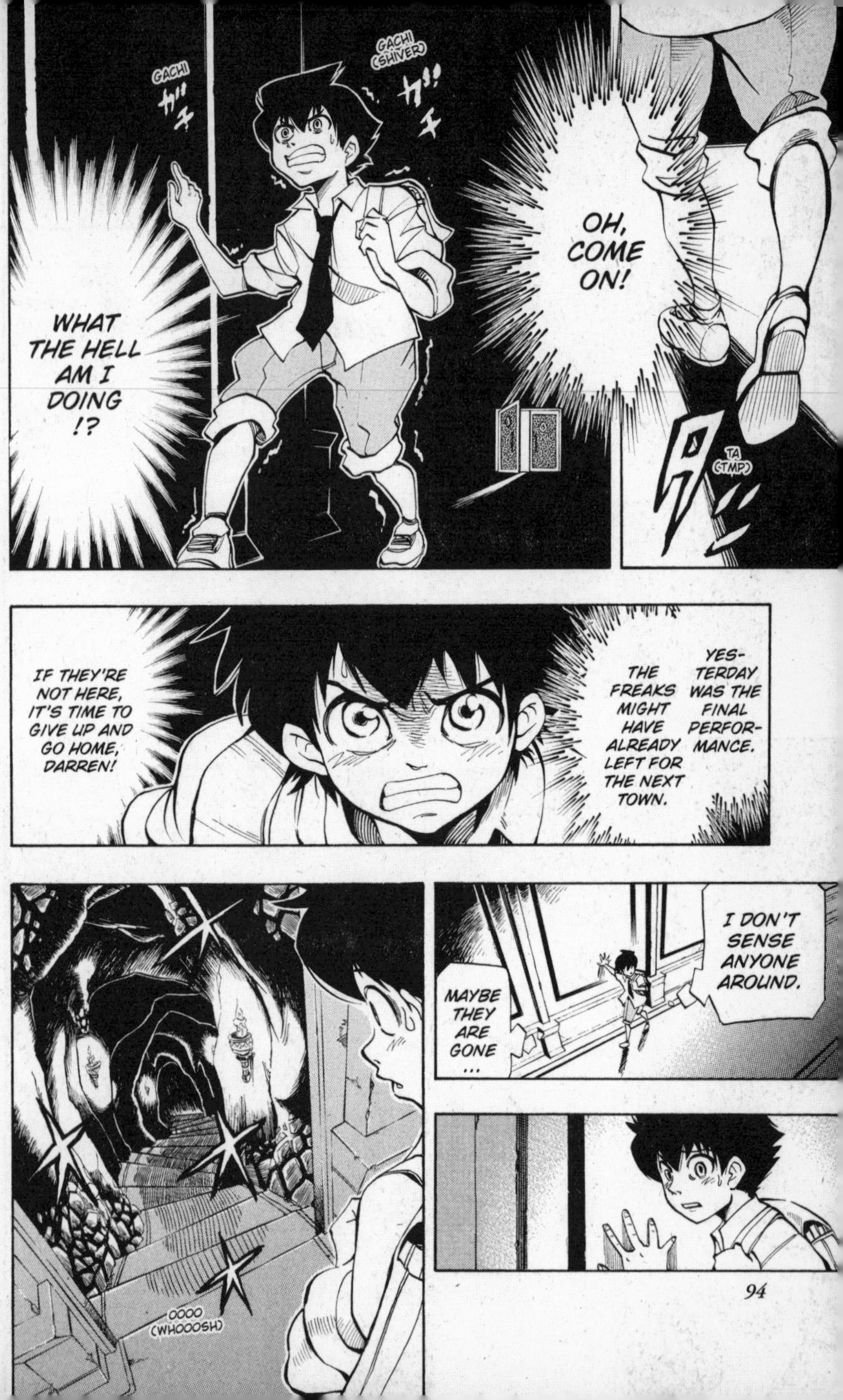
OH, COME ON!
TA (TMP)
GACHI (SHIVER)
GACHI
WHAT THE HELL AM I DOING !?
YES-TERDAY WAS THE FINAL PERFOR-MANCE.
THE FREAKS MIGHT HAVE ALREADY LEFT FOR THE NEXT TOWN.
IF THEY'RE NOT HERE, IT'S TIME TO GIVE UP AND GO HOME, DARREN!
I DON'T SENSE ANYONE AROUND.
MAYBE THEY ARE GONE ...
OOOO (WHOOOSH)

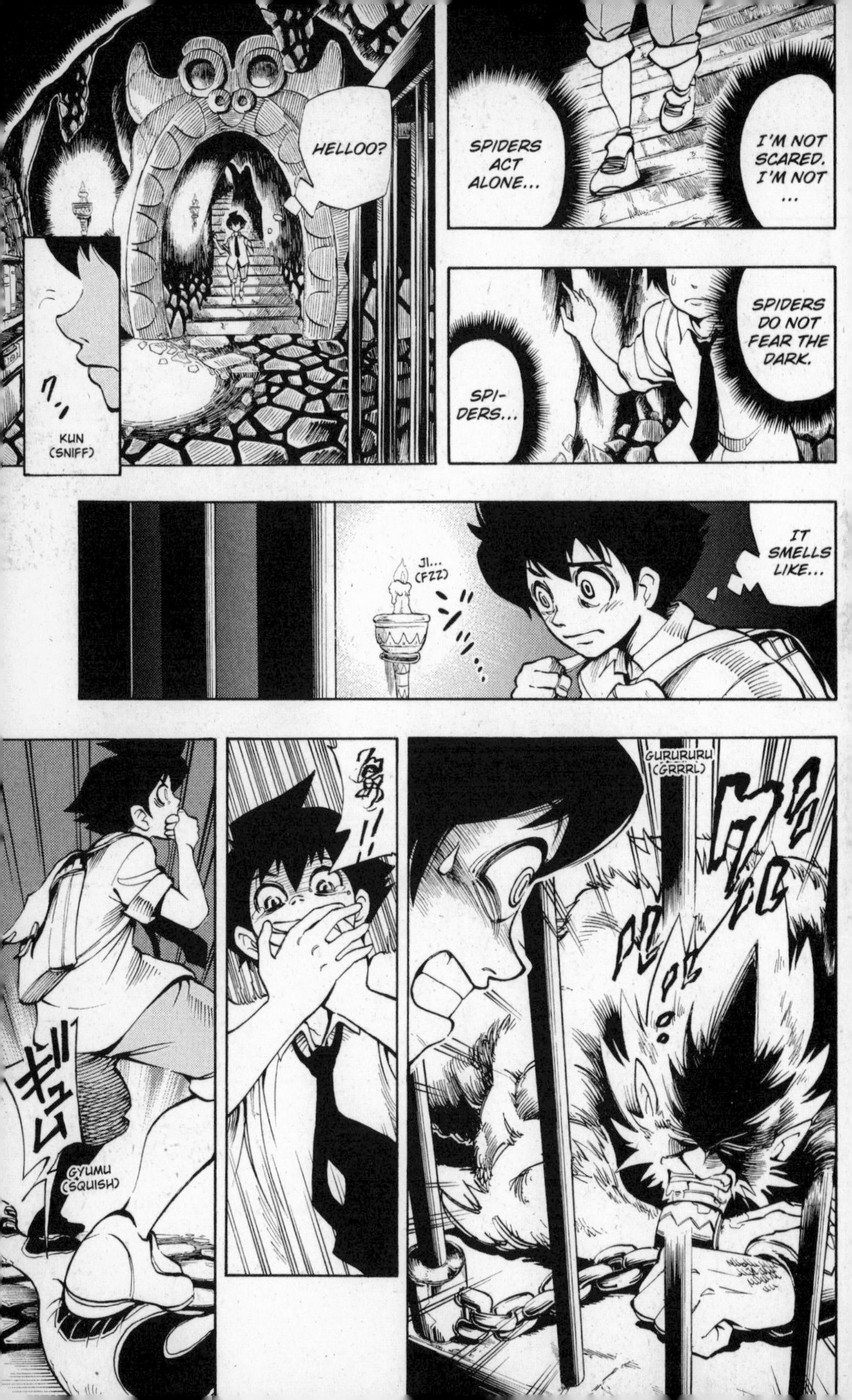
I'M NOT SCARED. I'M NOT ...
SPIDERS ACT ALONE...
SPIDERS DO NOT FEAR THE DARK.
SPI- DERS...
HELLOO?
KUN (SNIFF)
IT SMELLS LIKE...
JI... (FZZ)
GURURURU (GRRRL)
GYUMU (SQUISH)

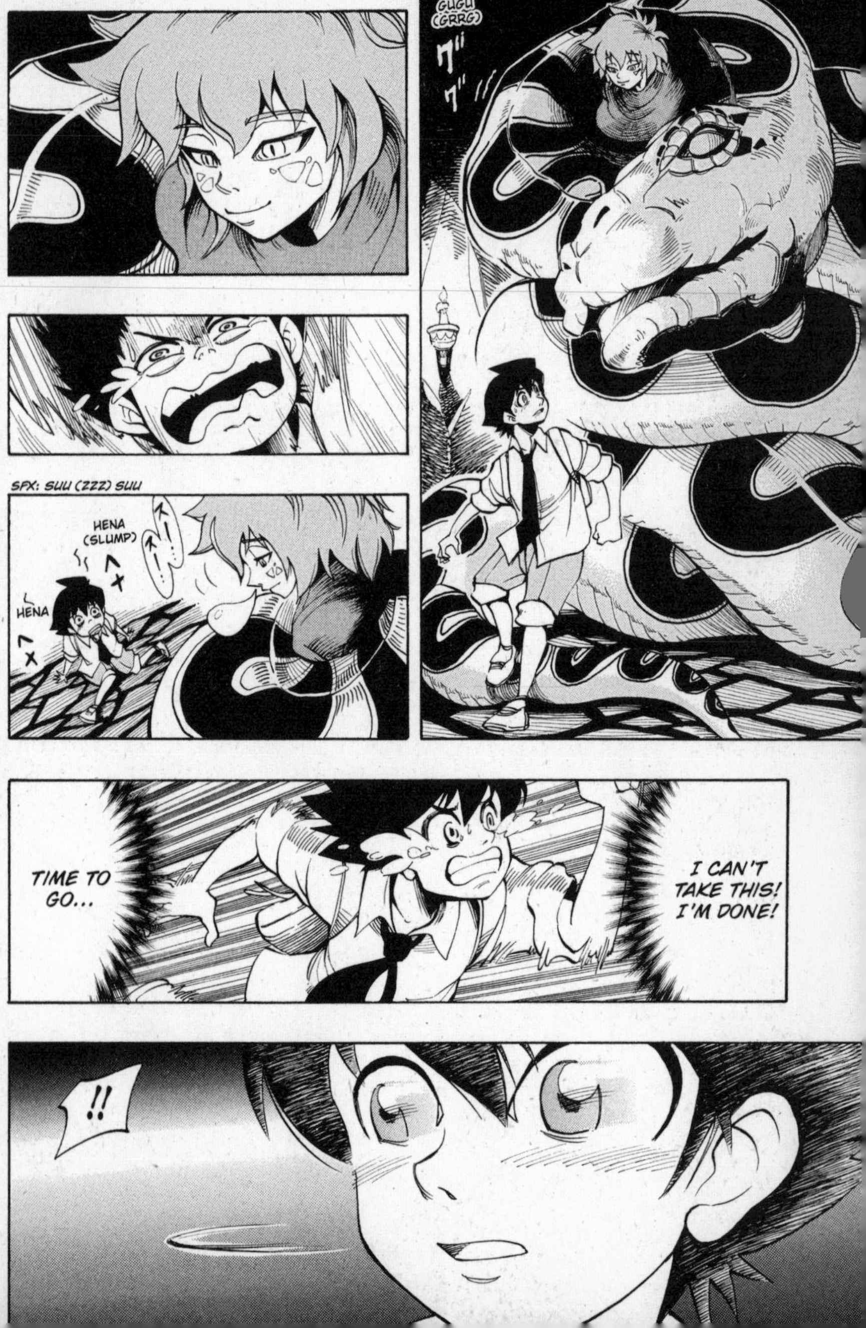
GUGU (GRRG)
SFX: SUU (ZZZ) SUU
HENA (SLUMP)
HENA
I CAN'T TAKE THIS! I'M DONE!
TIME TO GO...
!!

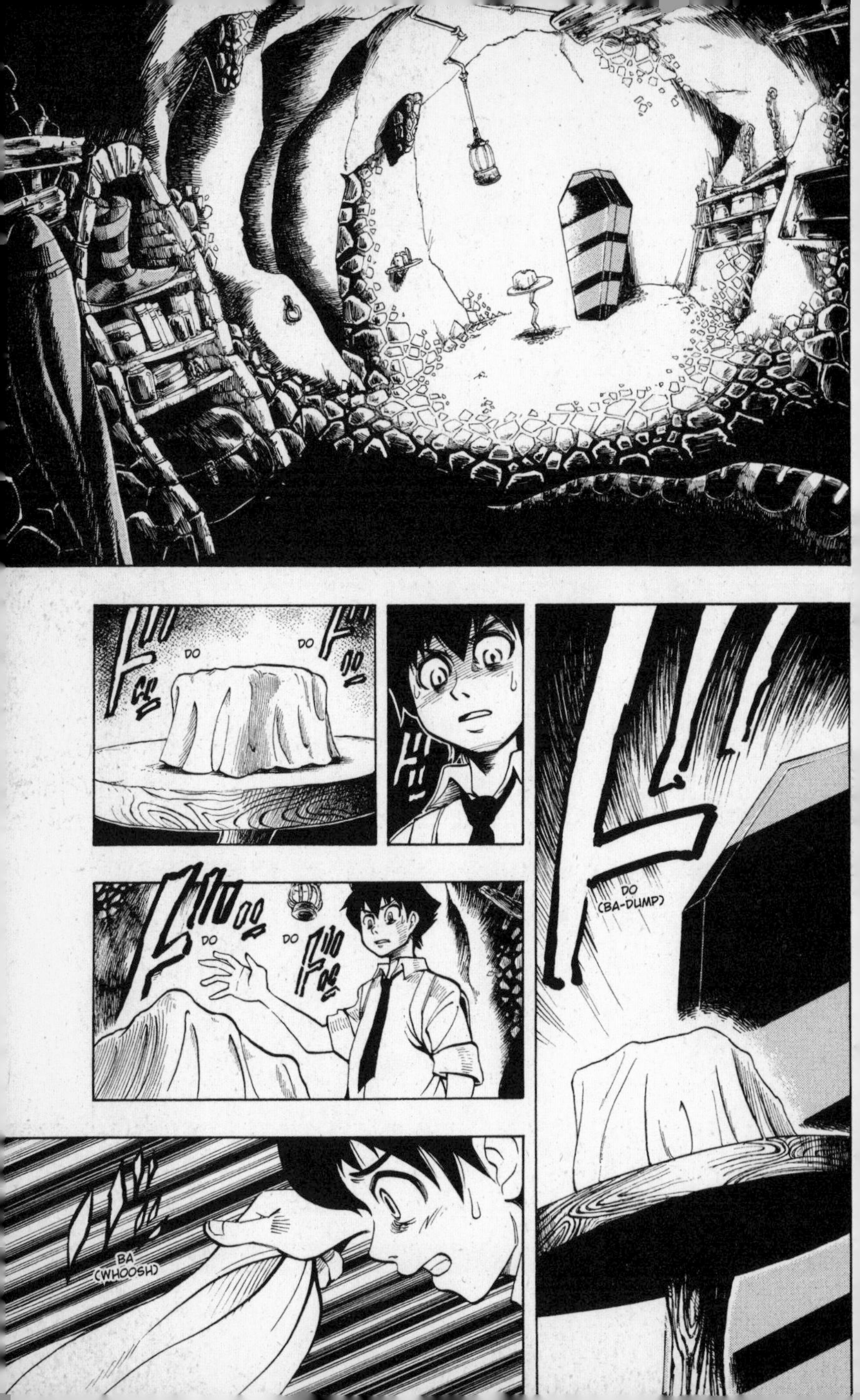
DO
(BA-DUMP)
DO
DO
DO
DO
BA
(WHOOSH)

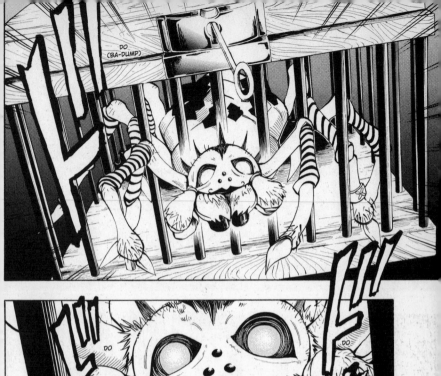

DO (BA-DUMP)
DO
DO
ARE YOU SATIS-FIED YET?
LET'S JUST GO...
ARE YOU SCARED OR SOME-THING?
C'MON, DARREN!
SFX: MOZO (RUSTLE) MOZO

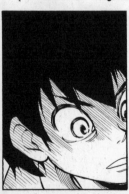

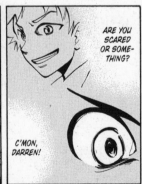

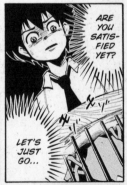

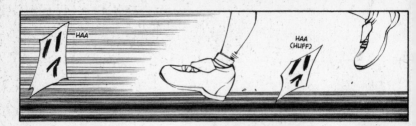

HAA

HAA
(HUFF)

BATAN
(SLAM)

GOGO
(BRRRRMMMM)

GOGO

GOGO

GOGO

DO

MOZO

MOZO

MOZO

DO

DO

DO

HAA

HAA

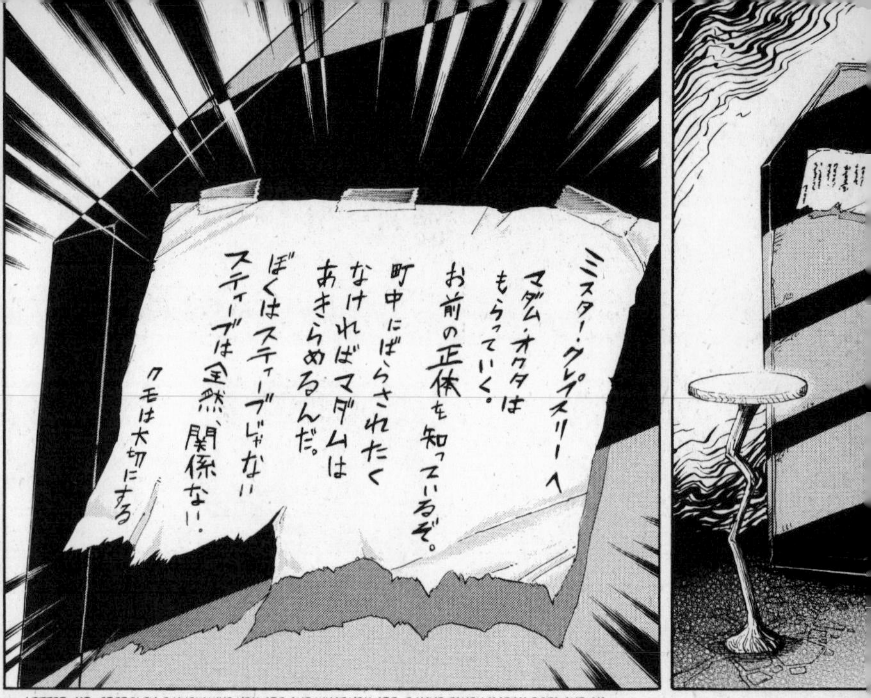
ミスター・クレプスリーへ
マダム・オクタは
もらっていく。
お前の正体を知っているぞ。
町中にばらされたく
なければマダムは
あきらめるんだ。
ぼくはスティーブじゃない
スティーブは全然、関係ない。
クモは大切にする

LETTER: MR. CREPSLEY, I KNOW WHO YOU ARE AND WHAT YOU ARE. I HAVE TAKEN MADAM OCTA AND AM KEEPING HER. DO NOT COME LOOKING FOR HER. DO NOT COME BACK TO THIS TOWN. IF YOU DO, I WILL TELL EVERYONE THAT YOU ARE A VAMPIRE AND YOU WILL BE HUNTED DOWN AND KILLED. I AM NOT STEVE. STEVE KNOWS NOTHING ABOUT THIS. I WILL TAKE GOOD CARE OF THE SPIDER.

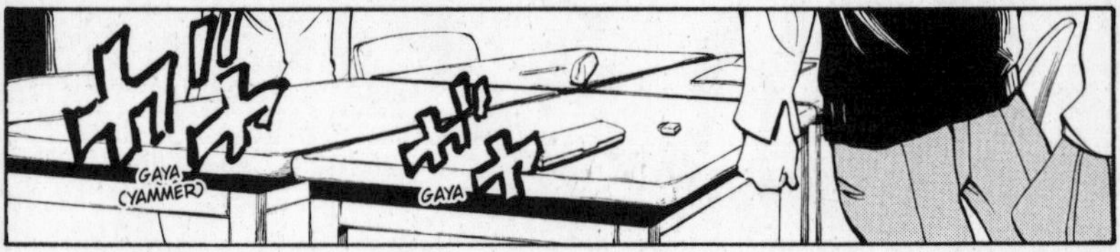
GAYA
GAYA (YAMMER)

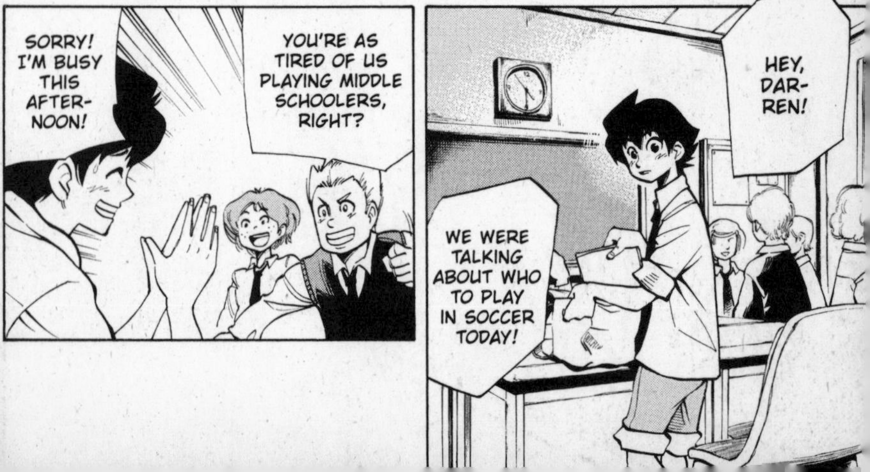
HEY, DAR-REN!
WE WERE TALKING ABOUT WHO TO PLAY IN SOCCER TODAY!
YOU'RE AS TIRED OF US PLAYING MIDDLE SCHOOLERS, RIGHT?
SORRY! I'M BUSY THIS AFTER-NOON!

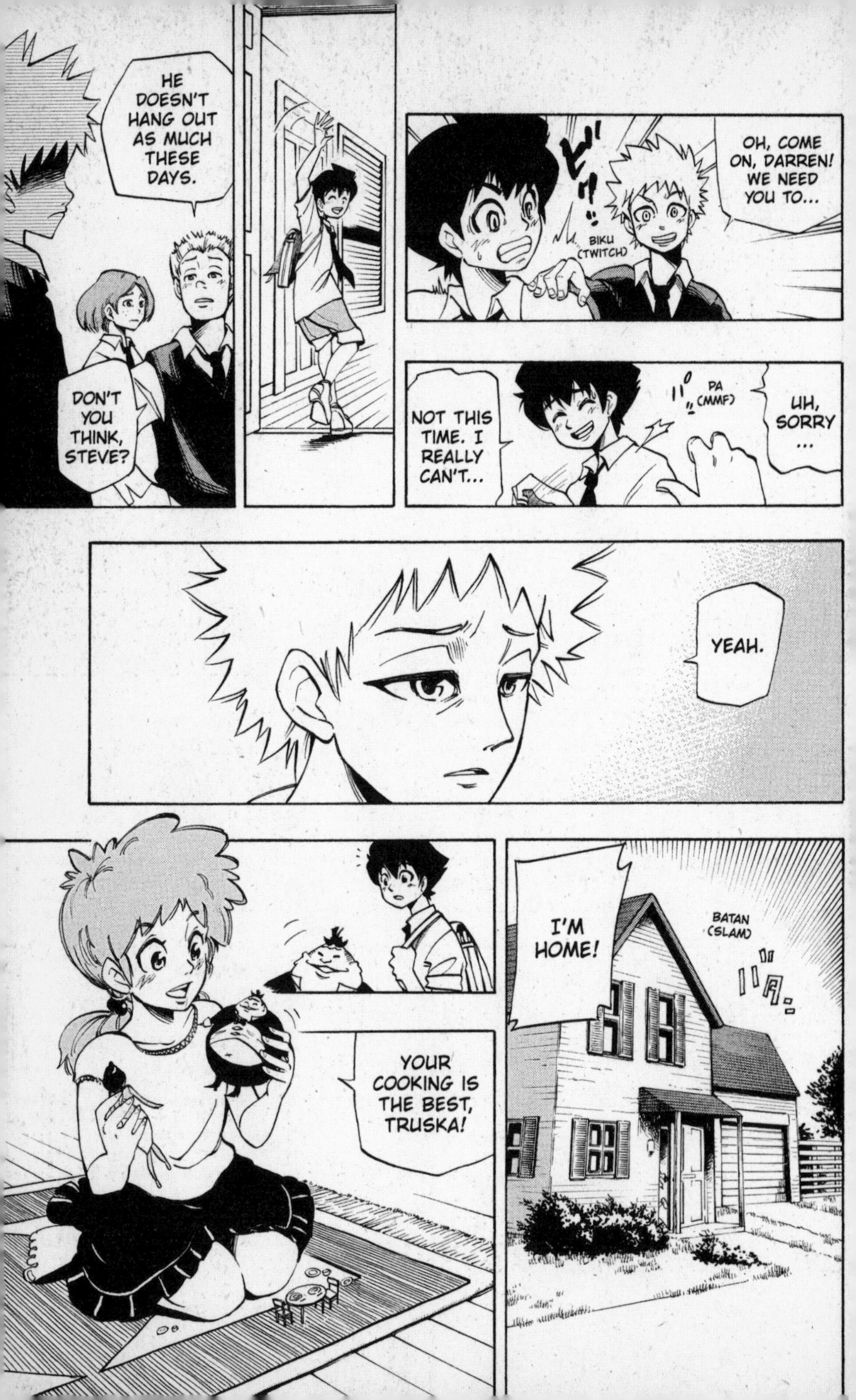
OH, COME ON, DARREN! WE NEED YOU TO...
BIKU (TWITCH)
UH, SORRY ...
PA (MMF)
NOT THIS TIME. I REALLY CAN'T...
HE DOESN'T HANG OUT AS MUCH THESE DAYS.
DON'T YOU THINK, STEVE?
YEAH.
BATAN (SLAM)
I'M HOME!
YOUR COOKING IS THE BEST, TRUSKA!

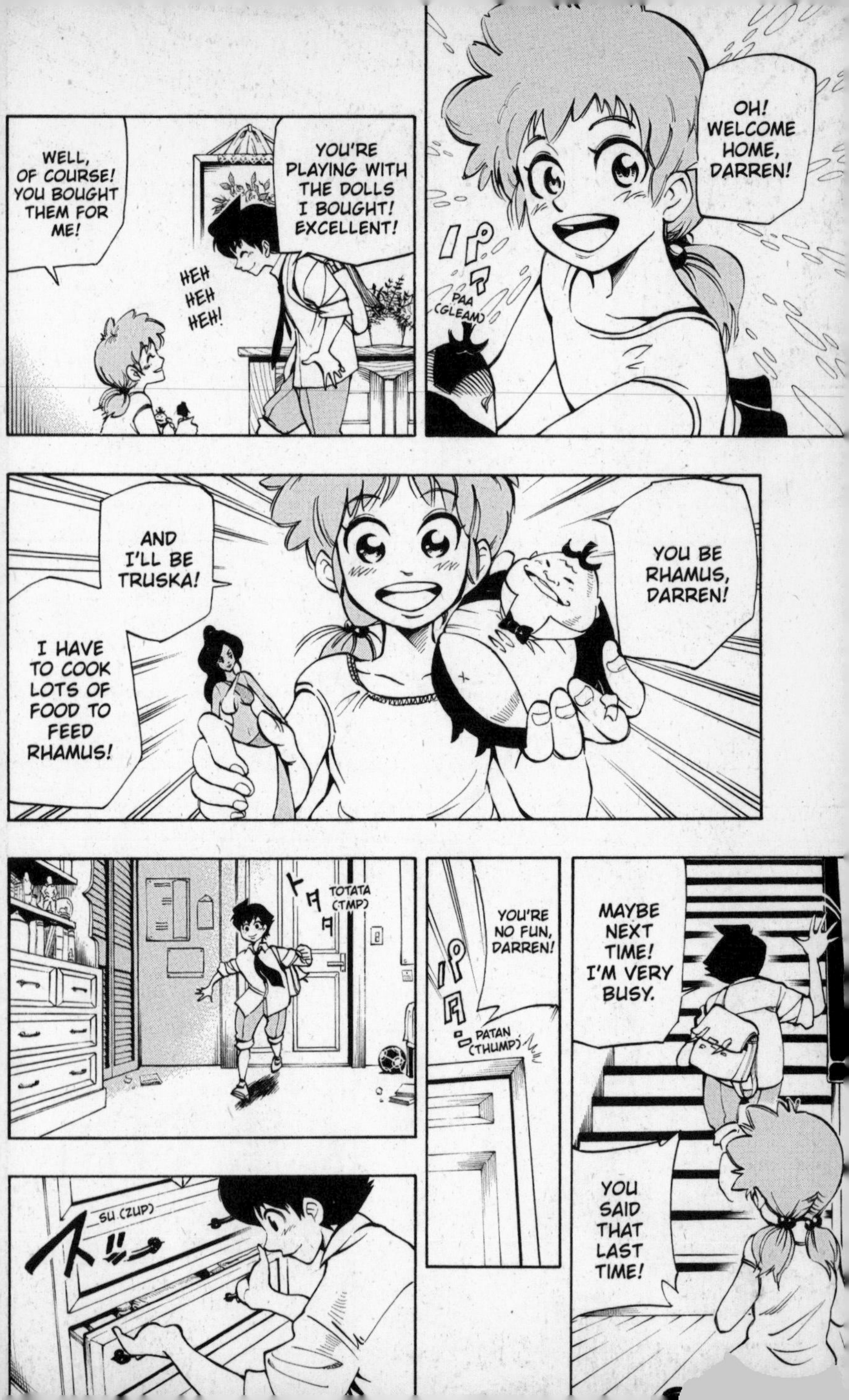
OH! WELCOME HOME, DARREN!
PAA (GLEAM)
YOU'RE PLAYING WITH THE DOLLS I BOUGHT! EXCELLENT!
HEH HEH HEH!
WELL, OF COURSE! YOU BOUGHT THEM FOR ME!
YOU BE RHAMUS, DARREN!
AND I'LL BE TRUSKA!
I HAVE TO COOK LOTS OF FOOD TO FEED RHAMUS!
MAYBE NEXT TIME! I'M VERY BUSY.
YOU SAID THAT LAST TIME!
YOU'RE NO FUN, DARREN!
PATAN (THUMP)
TOTATA (TMP)
SU (ZUP)

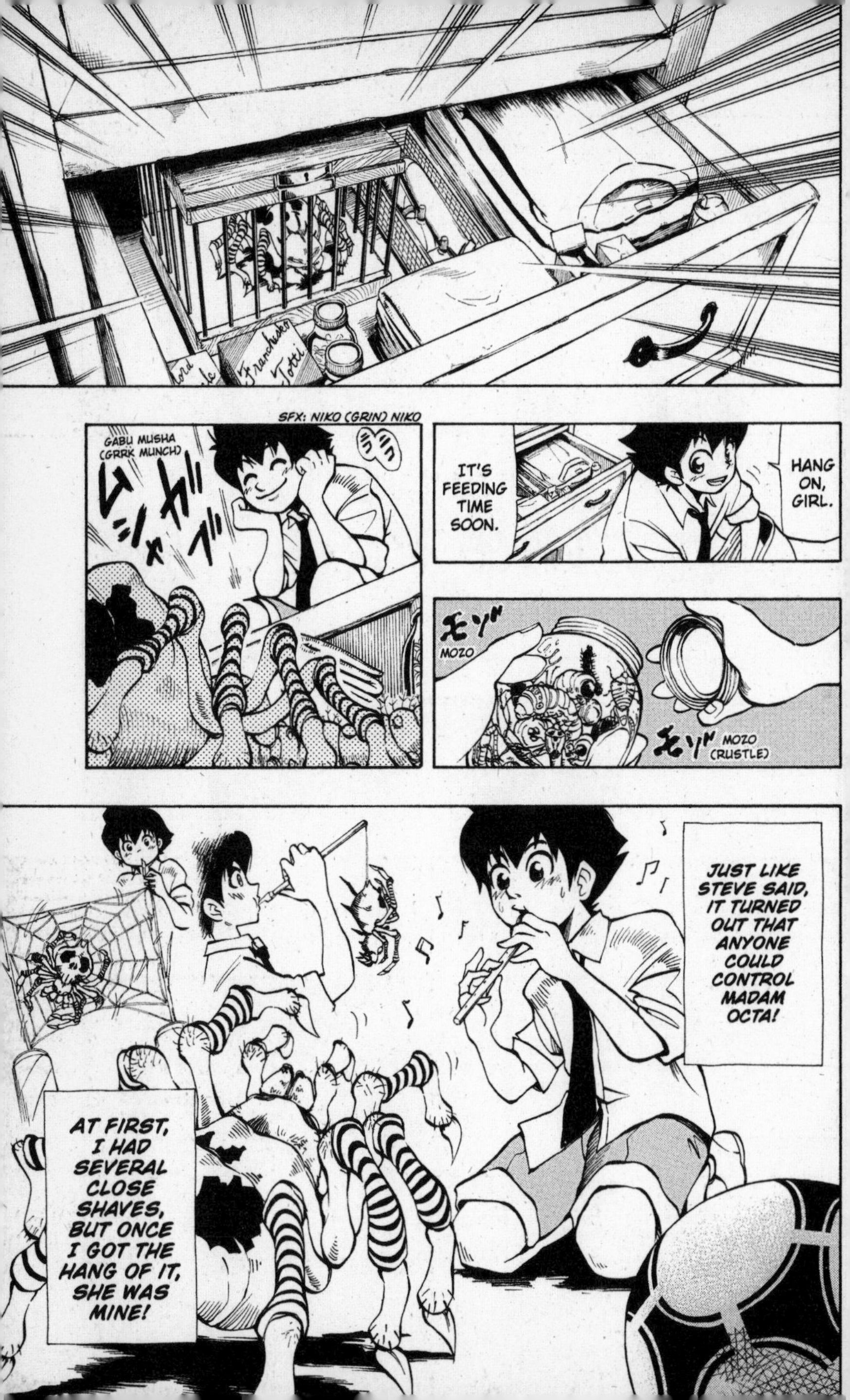
HANG ON, GIRL.
IT'S FEEDING TIME SOON.
MOZO
MOZO (RUSTLE)
SFX: NIKO (GRIN) NIKO
GABU MUSHA (GRRK MUNCH)
JUST LIKE STEVE SAID, IT TURNED OUT THAT ANYONE COULD CONTROL MADAM OCTA!
AT FIRST, I HAD SEVERAL CLOSE SHAVES, BUT ONCE I GOT THE HANG OF IT, SHE WAS MINE!

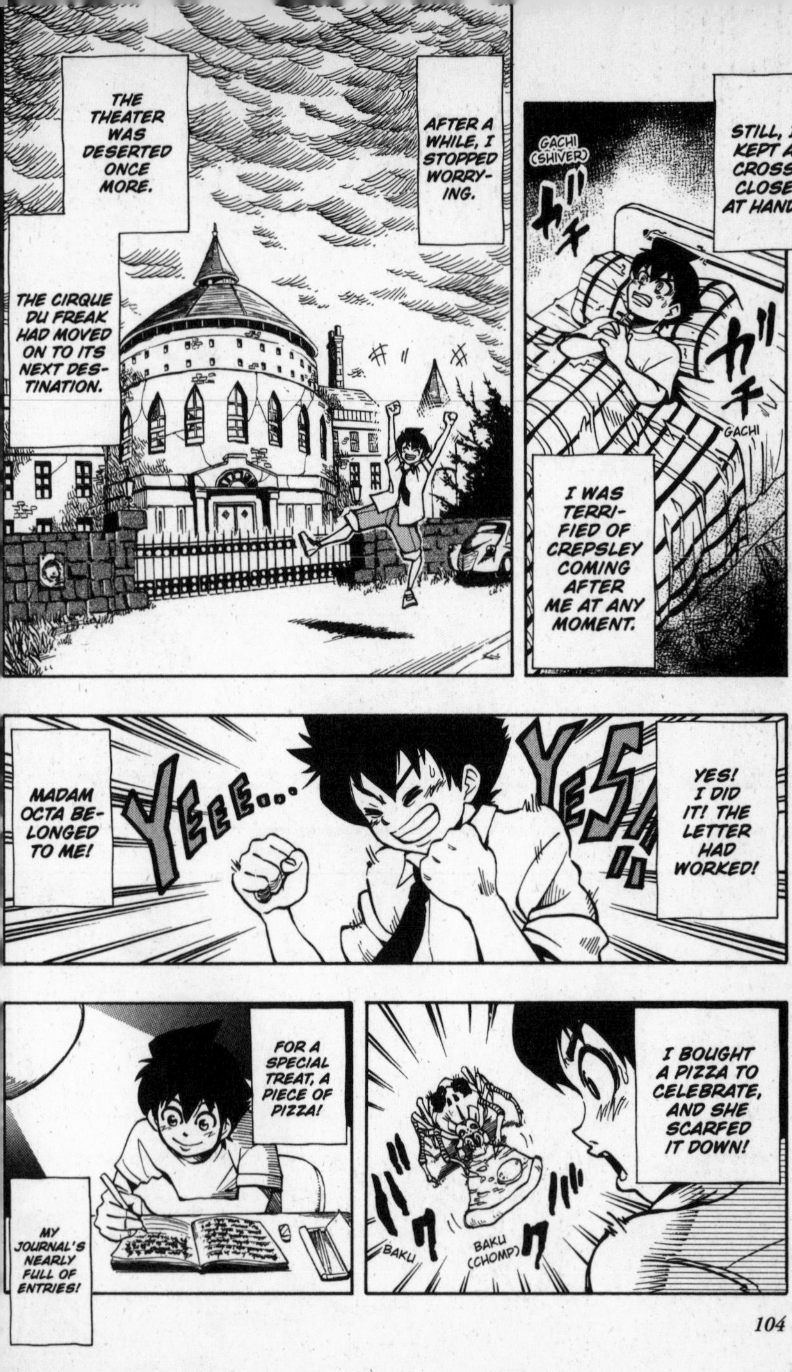
STILL, I KEPT A CROSS CLOSE AT HAND!
GACHI (SHIVER)
GACHI
I WAS TERRIFIED OF CREPSLEY COMING AFTER ME AT ANY MOMENT.
AFTER A WHILE, I STOPPED WORRYING.
THE THEATER WAS DESERTED ONCE MORE.
THE CIRQUE DU FREAK HAD MOVED ON TO ITS NEXT DESTINATION.
YES! I DID IT! THE LETTER HAD WORKED!
YESS
YEEE...
MADAM OCTA BELONGED TO ME!
I BOUGHT A PIZZA TO CELEBRATE, AND SHE SCARFED IT DOWN!
BAKU (CHOMP)
BAKU
FOR A SPECIAL TREAT, A PIECE OF PIZZA!
MY JOURNAL'S NEARLY FULL OF ENTRIES!

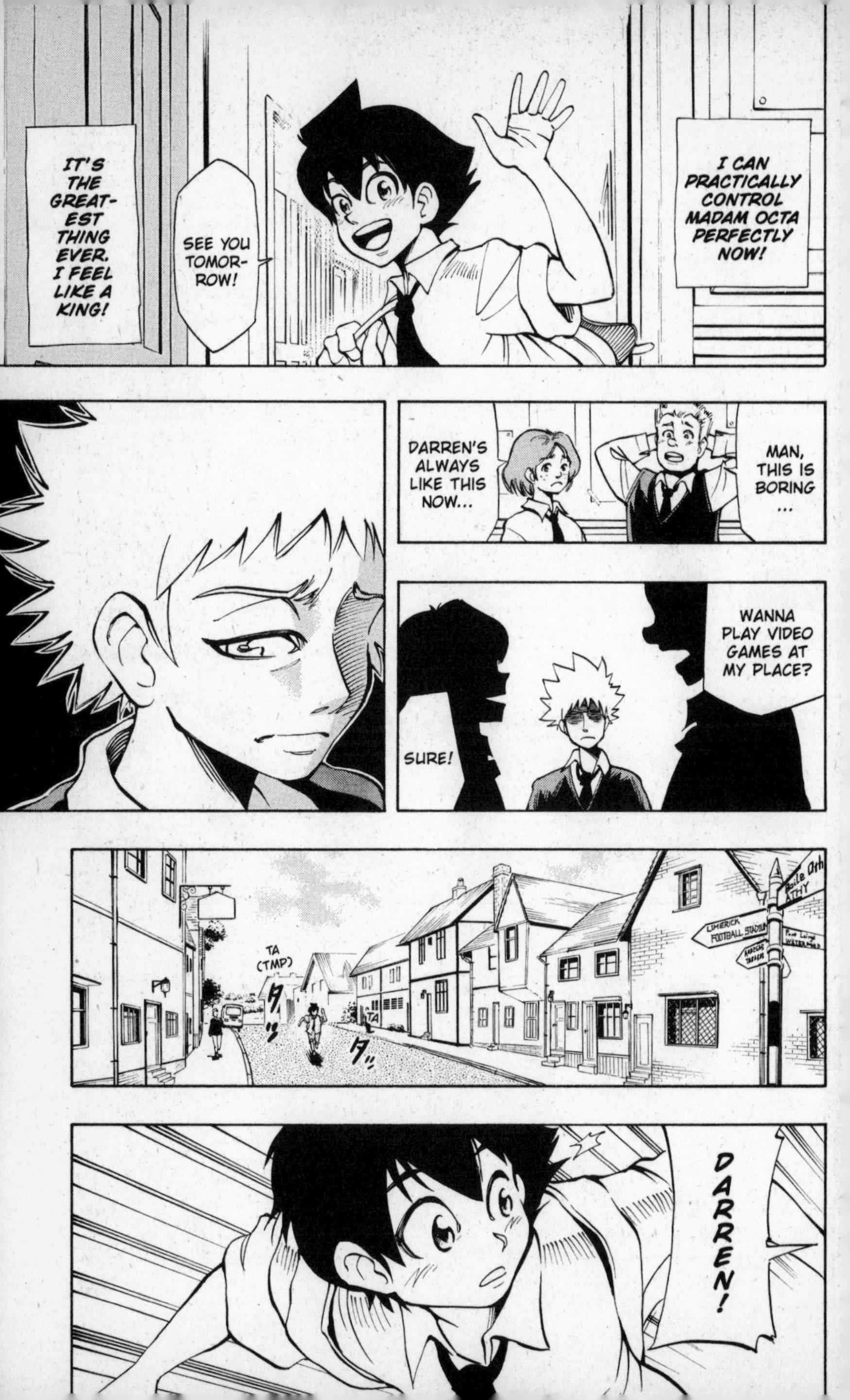
I CAN PRACTICALLY CONTROL MADAM OCTA PERFECTLY NOW!
SEE YOU TOMORROW!
IT'S THE GREATEST THING EVER. I FEEL LIKE A KING!
MAN, THIS IS BORING ...
DARREN'S ALWAYS LIKE THIS NOW...
WANNA PLAY VIDEO GAMES AT MY PLACE?
SURE!
LIMERICK FOOTBALL STADIUM
TA (TMP)
TA
DARREN!

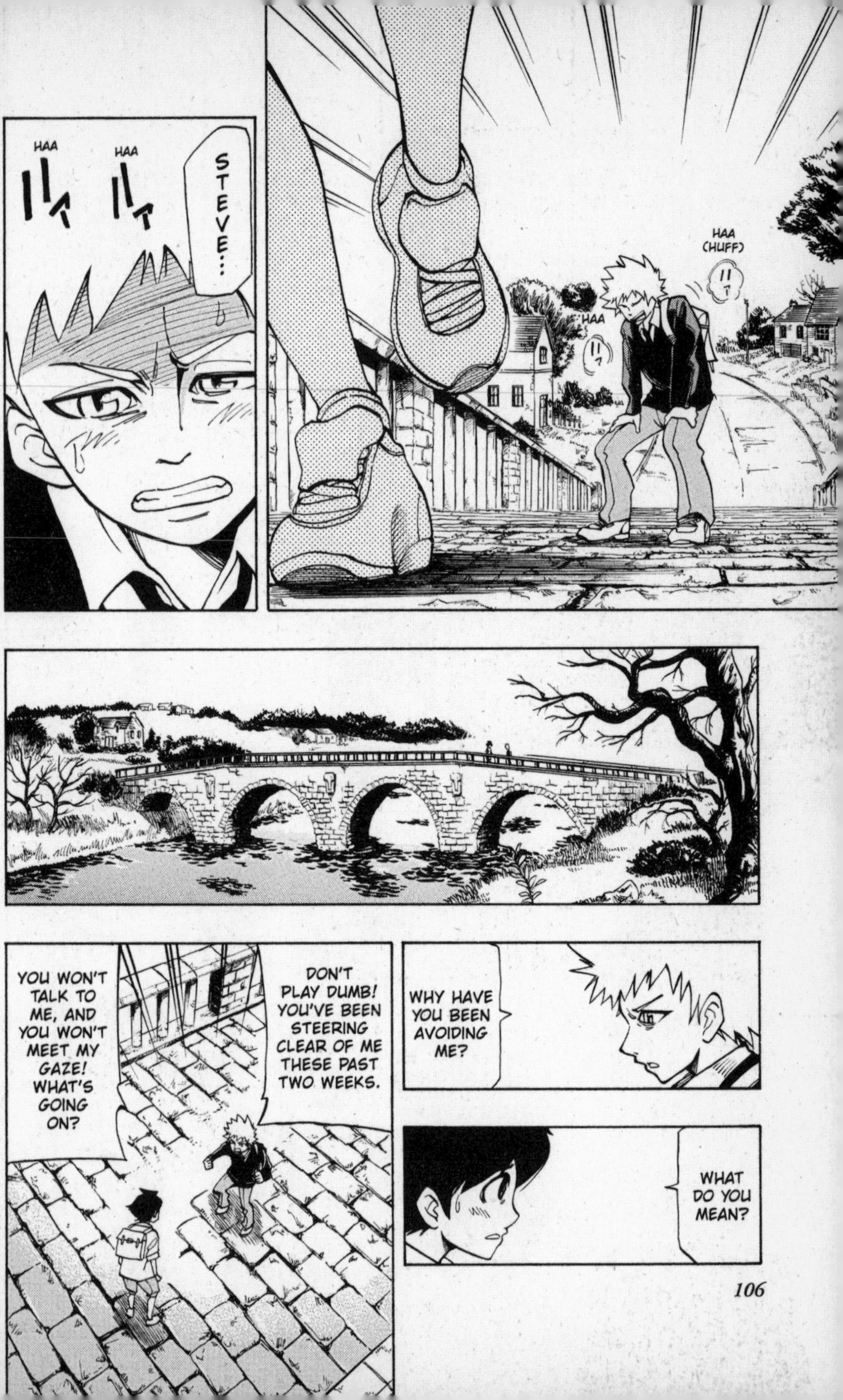

HAA (HUFF)
ハァ
HAA
ハァ
HAA
ハァ
HAA
ハァ
STEVE...
WHY HAVE YOU BEEN AVOIDING ME?
WHAT DO YOU MEAN?
DON'T PLAY DUMB! YOU'VE BEEN STEERING CLEAR OF ME THESE PAST TWO WEEKS.
YOU WON'T TALK TO ME, AND YOU WON'T MEET MY GAZE! WHAT'S GOING ON?

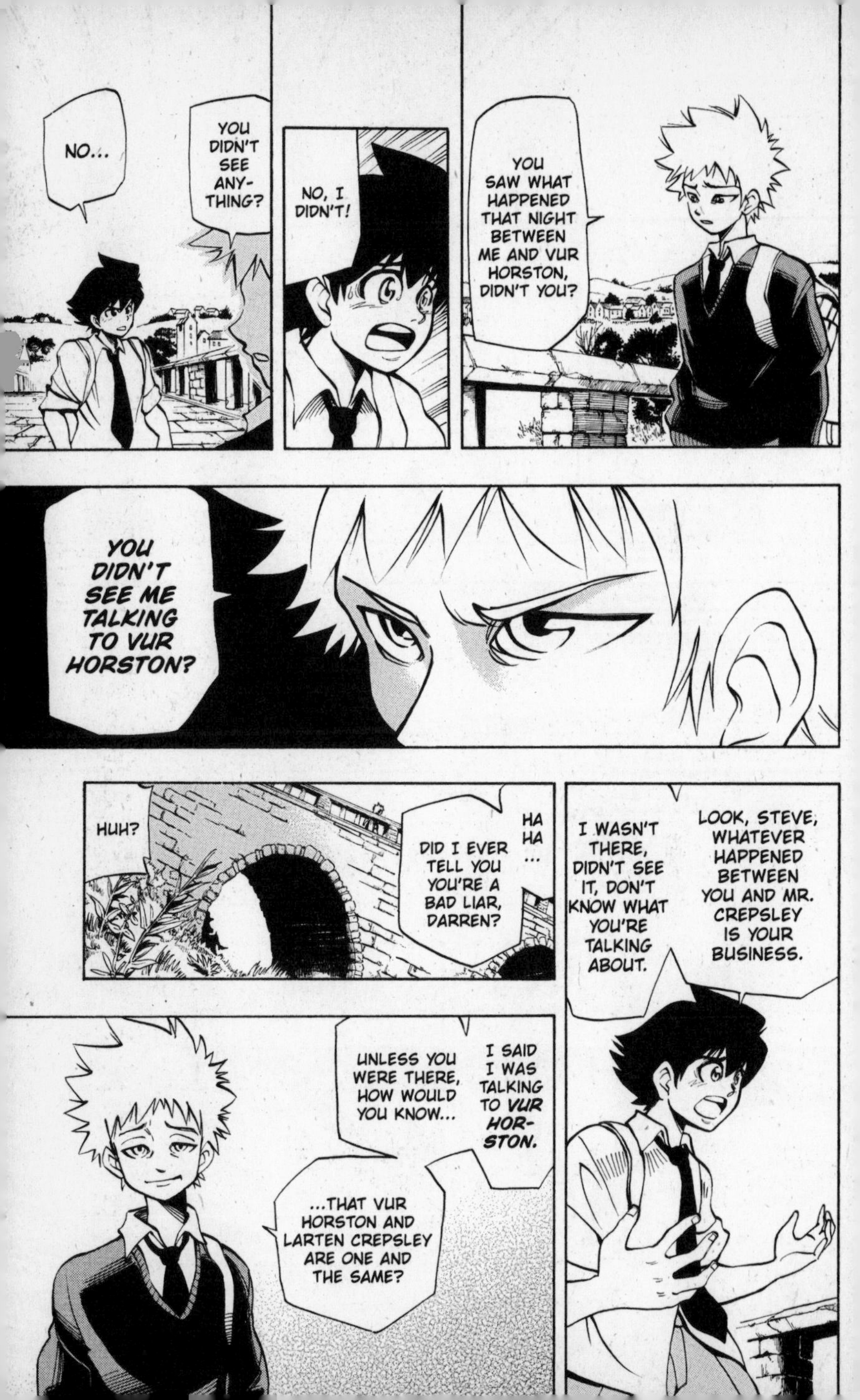
YOU SAW WHAT HAPPENED THAT NIGHT BETWEEN ME AND VUR HORSTON, DIDN'T YOU?
NO, I DIDN'T!
YOU DIDN'T SEE ANY-THING?
NO...
YOU DIDN'T SEE ME TALKING TO VUR HORSTON?
LOOK, STEVE, WHATEVER HAPPENED BETWEEN YOU AND MR. CREPSLEY IS YOUR BUSINESS.
I WASN'T THERE, DIDN'T SEE IT, DON'T KNOW WHAT YOU'RE TALKING ABOUT.
HA HA ...
DID I EVER TELL YOU YOU'RE A BAD LIAR, DARREN?
HUH?
I SAID I WAS TALKING TO VUR HOR-STON.
UNLESS YOU WERE THERE, HOW WOULD YOU KNOW...
...THAT VUR HORSTON AND LARTEN CREPSLEY ARE ONE AND THE SAME?

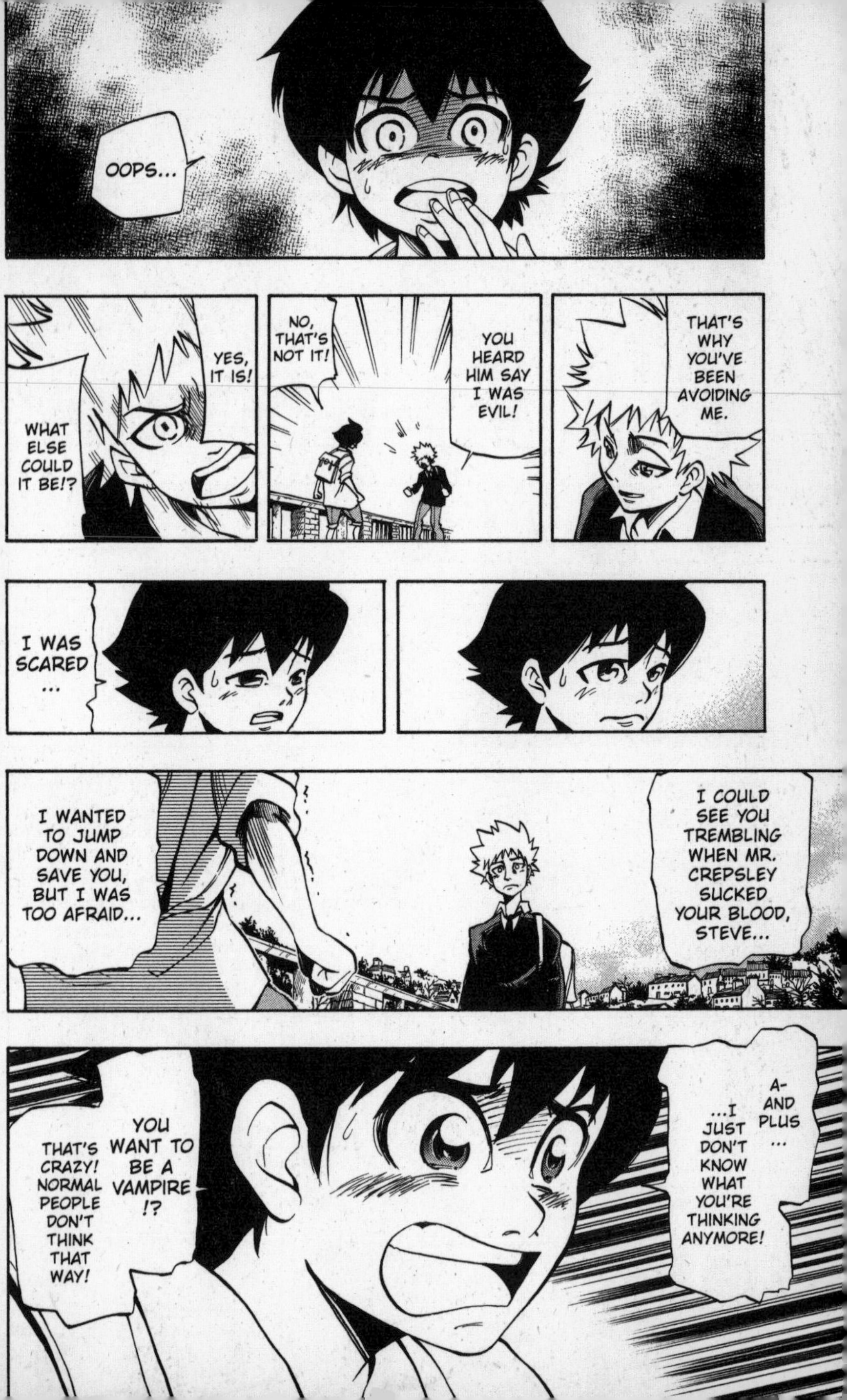
OOPS...
THAT'S WHY YOU'VE BEEN AVOIDING ME.
YOU HEARD HIM SAY I WAS EVIL!
NO, THAT'S NOT IT!
YES, IT IS!
WHAT ELSE COULD IT BE!?
I WAS SCARED...
I COULD SEE YOU TREMBLING WHEN MR. CREPSLEY SUCKED YOUR BLOOD, STEVE...
I WANTED TO JUMP DOWN AND SAVE YOU, BUT I WAS TOO AFRAID...
A-AND PLUS...
...I JUST DON'T KNOW WHAT YOU'RE THINKING ANYMORE!
YOU WANT TO BE A VAMPIRE!?
THAT'S CRAZY! NORMAL PEOPLE DON'T THINK THAT WAY!

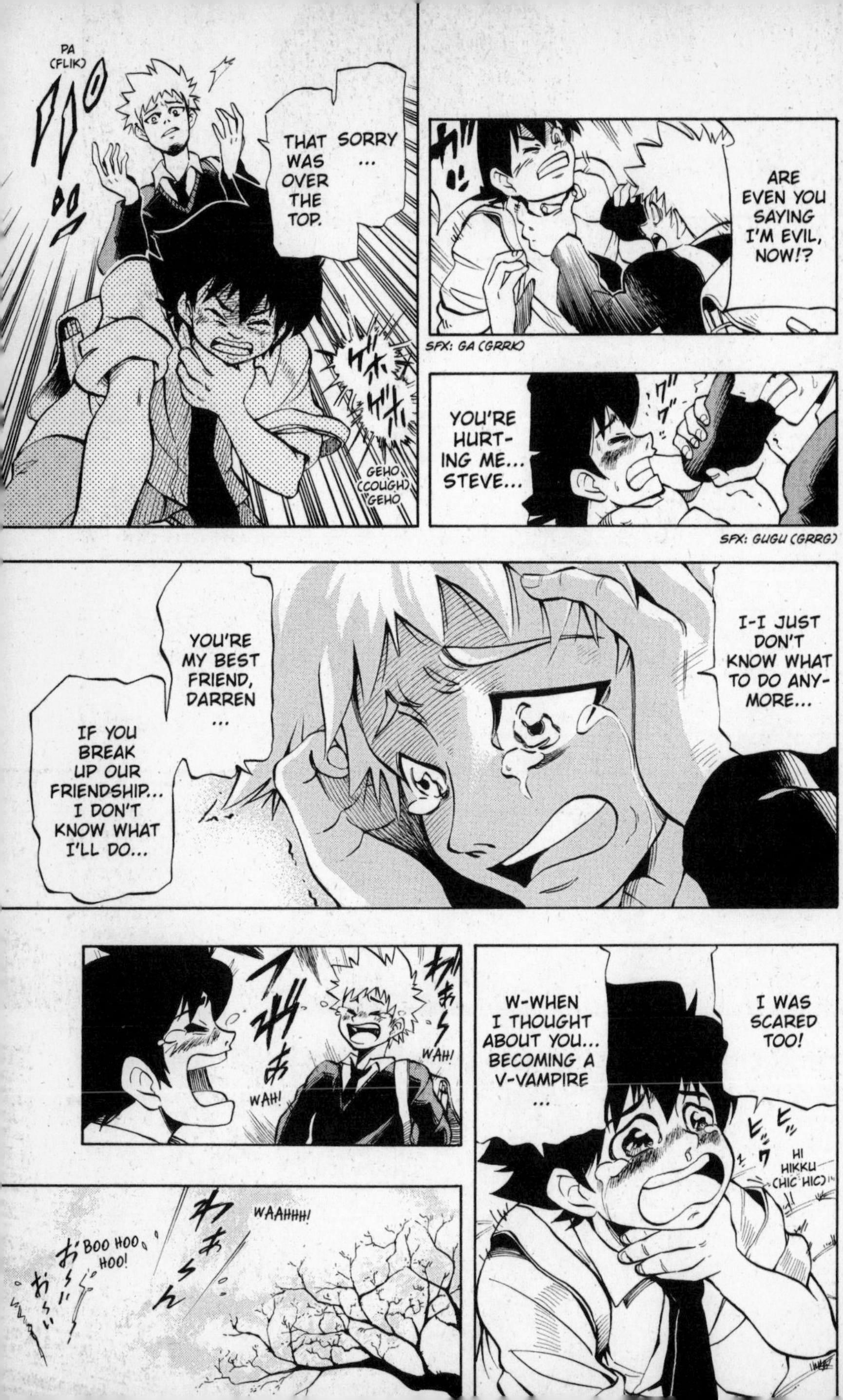
ARE EVEN YOU SAYING I'M EVIL, NOW!?
SFX: GA (GRRK)
YOU'RE HURT-ING ME... STEVE...
SFX: GUGU (GRRG)
PA (FLIK)
SORRY ...
THAT WAS OVER THE TOP.
GEHO (COUGH) GEHO
I-I JUST DON'T KNOW WHAT TO DO ANY-MORE...
YOU'RE MY BEST FRIEND, DARREN ...
IF YOU BREAK UP OUR FRIENDSHIP... I DON'T KNOW WHAT I'LL DO...
I WAS SCARED TOO!
W-WHEN I THOUGHT ABOUT YOU... BECOMING A V-VAMPIRE ...
HI HIKKU (CHIC HIC)
WAH!
WAH!
WAAHHH!
BOO HOO HOO!

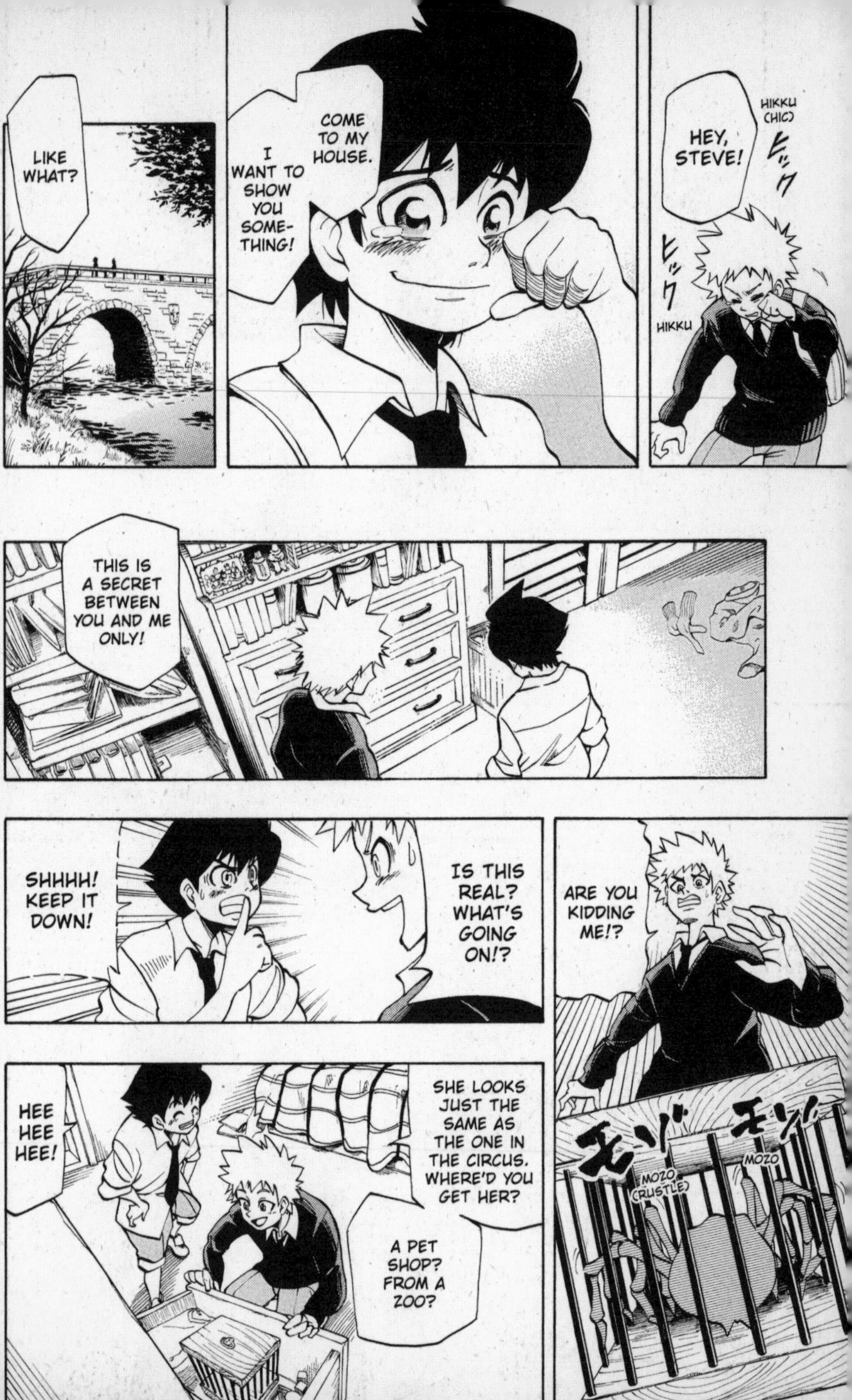
HIKKU (HIC)
HEY, STEVE!
HIKKU
COME TO MY HOUSE.
I WANT TO SHOW YOU SOME-THING!
LIKE WHAT?
THIS IS A SECRET BETWEEN YOU AND ME ONLY!
ARE YOU KIDDING ME!?
MOZO
MOZO (RUSTLE)
IS THIS REAL? WHAT'S GOING ON!?
SHHHH! KEEP IT DOWN!
SHE LOOKS JUST THE SAME AS THE ONE IN THE CIRCUS. WHERE'D YOU GET HER?
A PET SHOP? FROM A ZOO?
HEE HEE HEE!

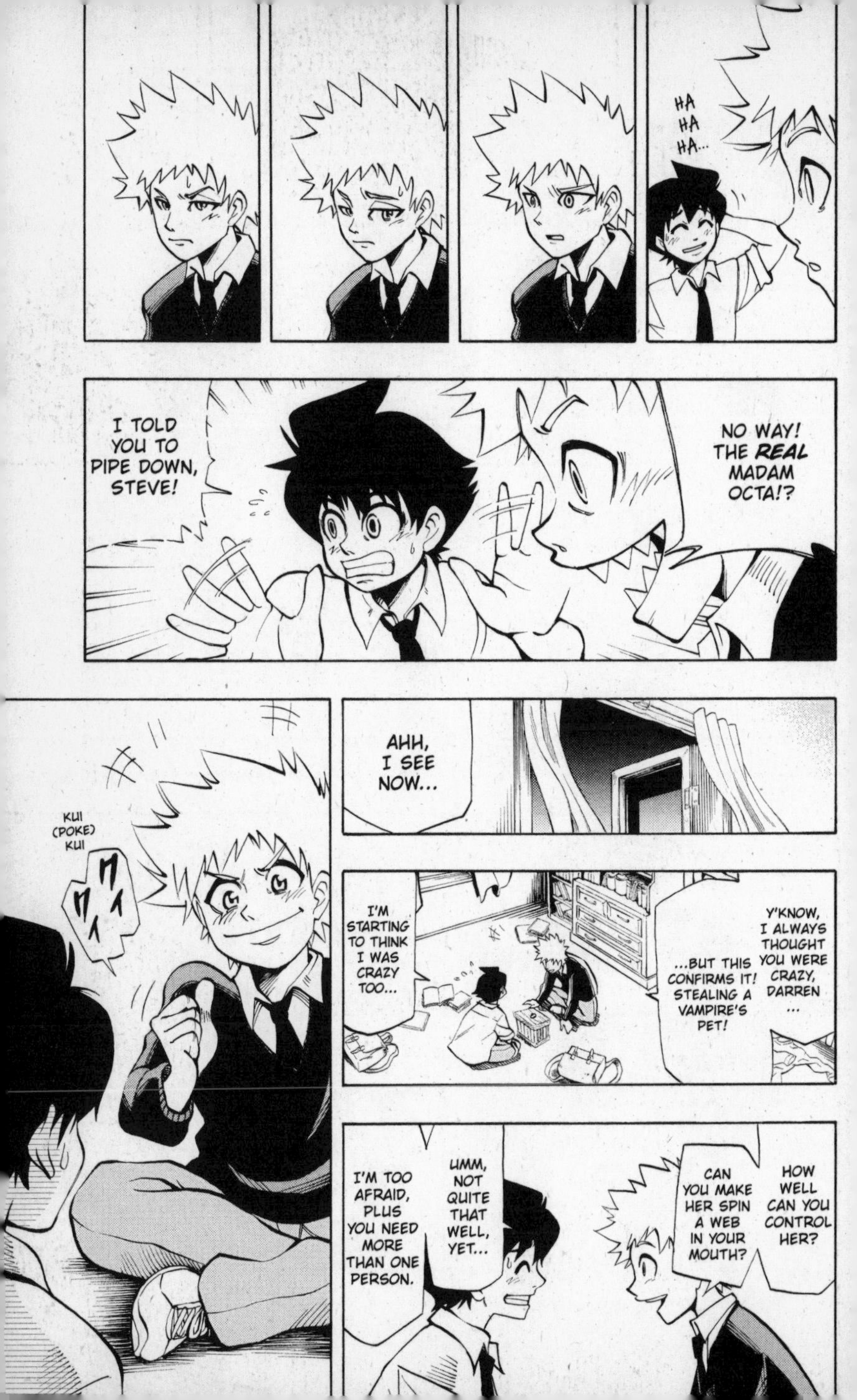
HA HA HA...
NO WAY! THE *REAL* MADAM OCTA!?
I TOLD YOU TO PIPE DOWN, STEVE!
AHH, I SEE NOW...
Y'KNOW, I ALWAYS THOUGHT YOU WERE CRAZY, DARREN...
...BUT THIS CONFIRMS IT! STEALING A VAMPIRE'S PET!
I'M STARTING TO THINK I WAS CRAZY TOO...
HOW WELL CAN YOU CONTROL HER?
CAN YOU MAKE HER SPIN A WEB IN YOUR MOUTH?
UMM, NOT QUITE THAT WELL, YET...
I'M TOO AFRAID, PLUS YOU NEED MORE THAN ONE PERSON.
KUI (POKE) KUI

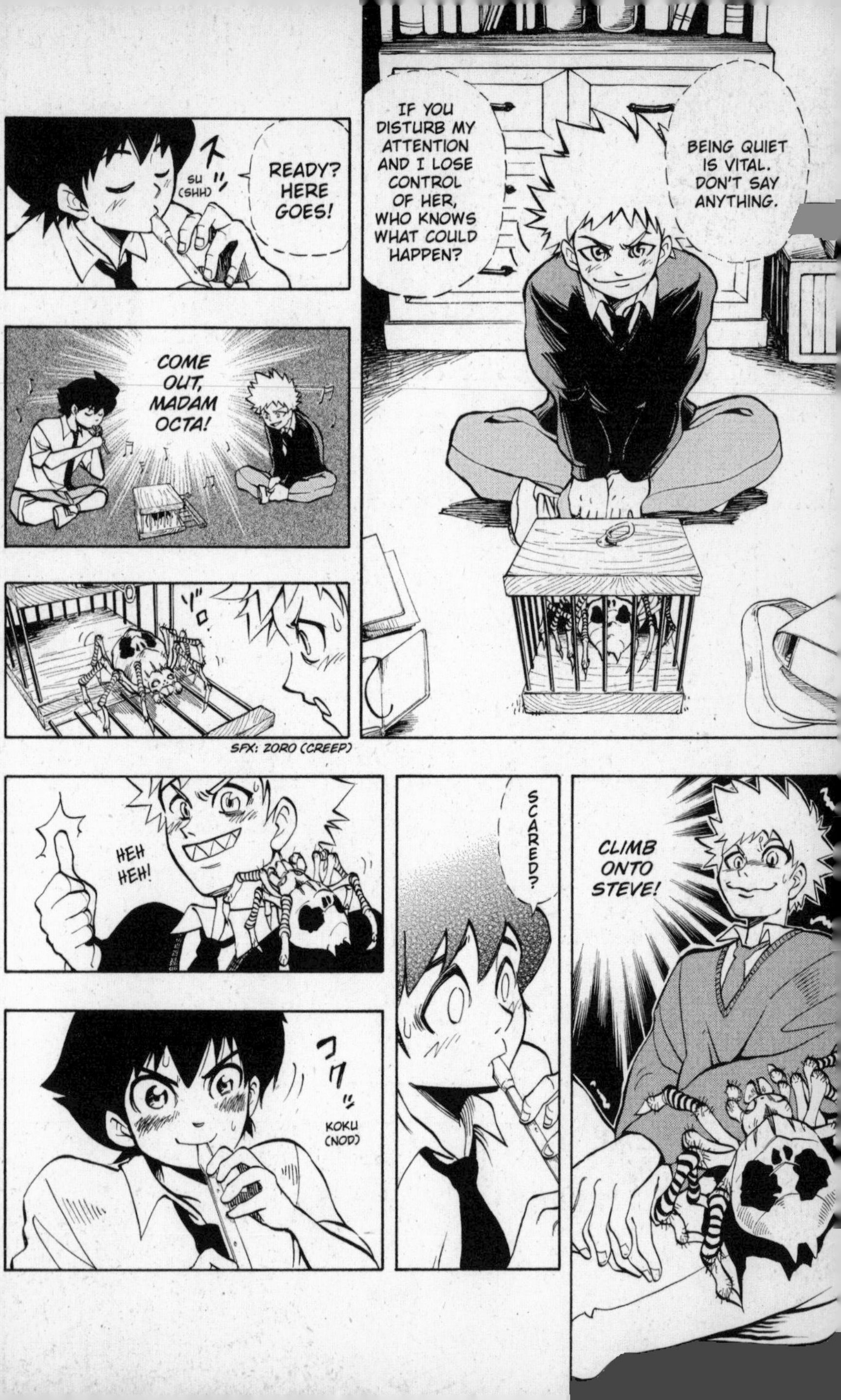
BEING QUIET IS VITAL. DON'T SAY ANYTHING.
IF YOU DISTURB MY ATTENTION AND I LOSE CONTROL OF HER, WHO KNOWS WHAT COULD HAPPEN?
SU (SHH)
READY? HERE GOES!
COME OUT, MADAM OCTA!
SFX: ZORO (CREEP)
CLIMB ONTO STEVE!
SCARED?
HEH HEH!
KOKU (NOD)

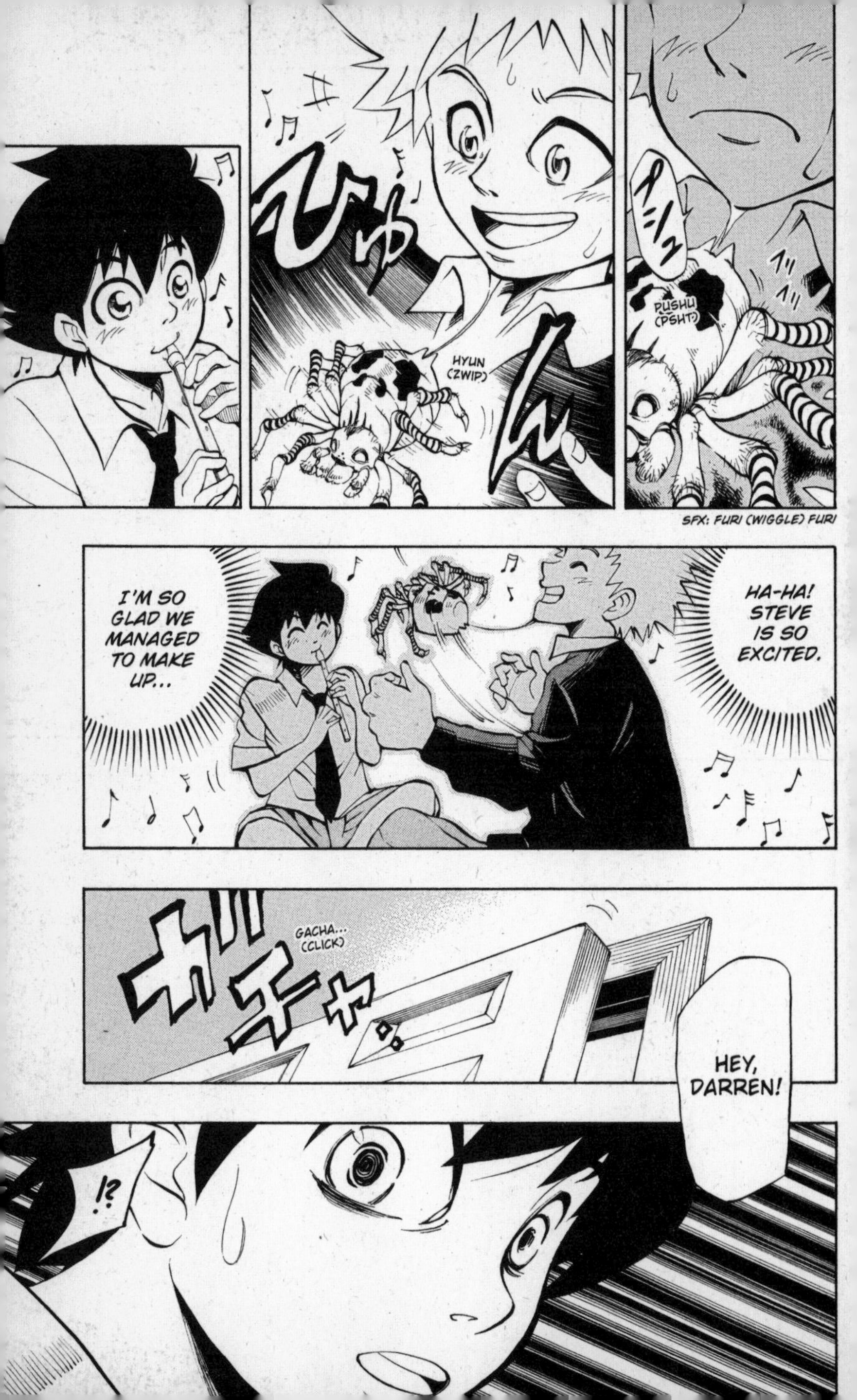
PUSHU (PSHT)
HYUN (ZWIP)
SFX: FURI (WIGGLE) FURI
HA-HA! STEVE IS SO EXCITED.
I'M SO GLAD WE MANAGED TO MAKE UP...
GACHA... (CLICK)
HEY, DARREN!
!?

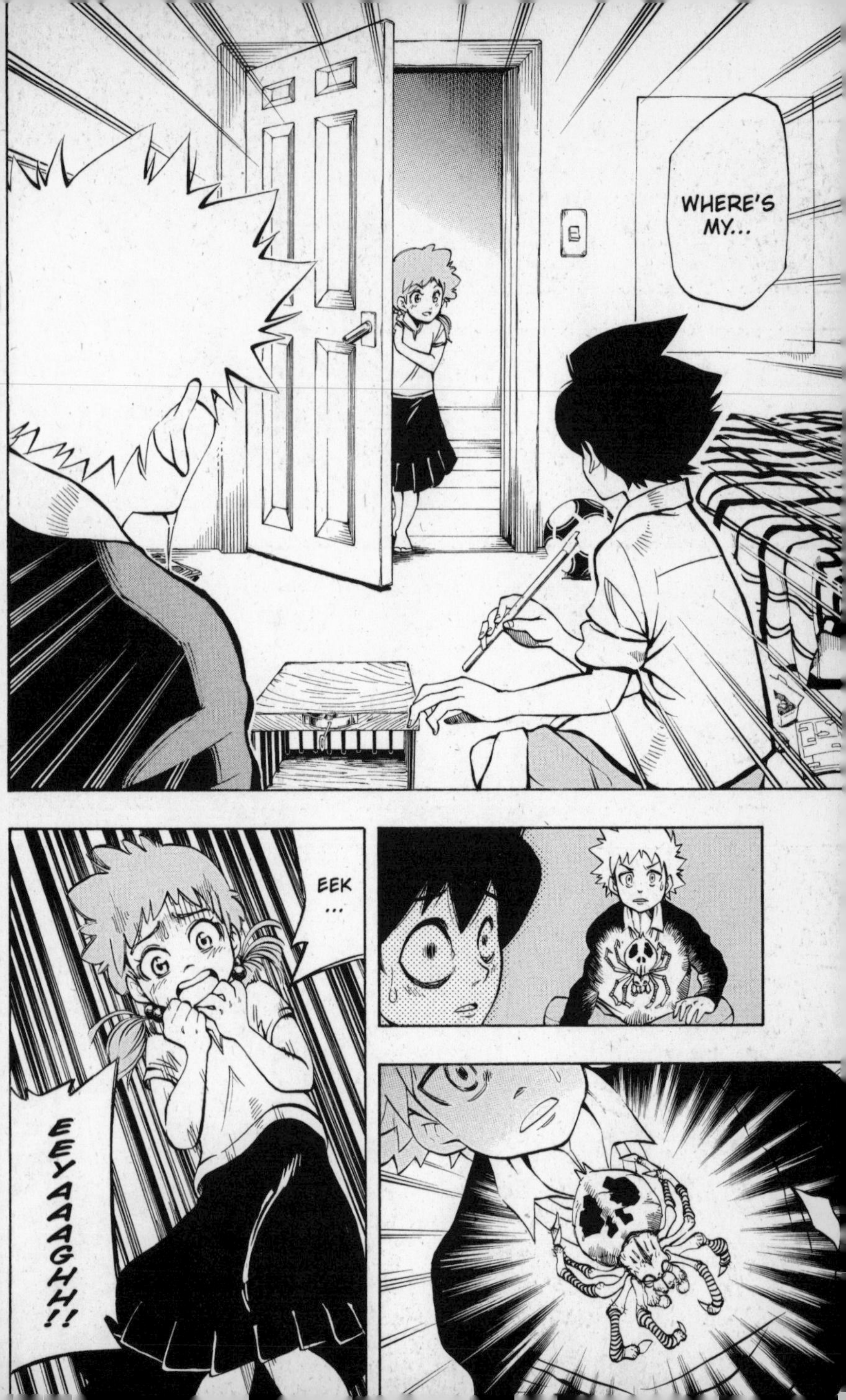
WHERE'S MY...
EEK ...
EEYAAAGHH!!

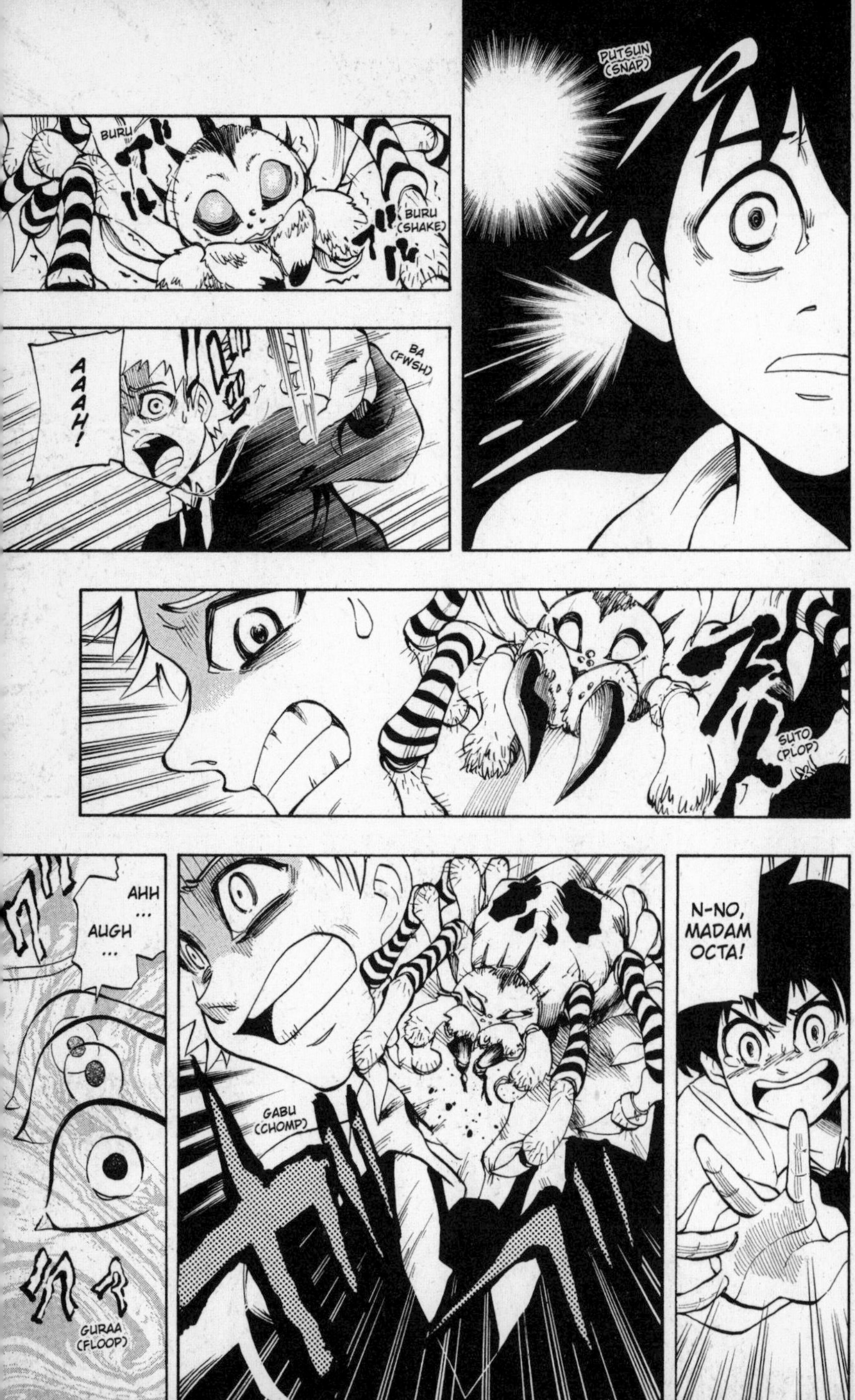
PUTSUN (SNAP)
BURU
BURU (SHAKE)
BA (FWSH)
AAAH!
SUTO (PLOP)
N-NO, MADAM OCTA!
GABU (CHOMP)
AHH ... AUGH ...
GURAA (FLOOP)

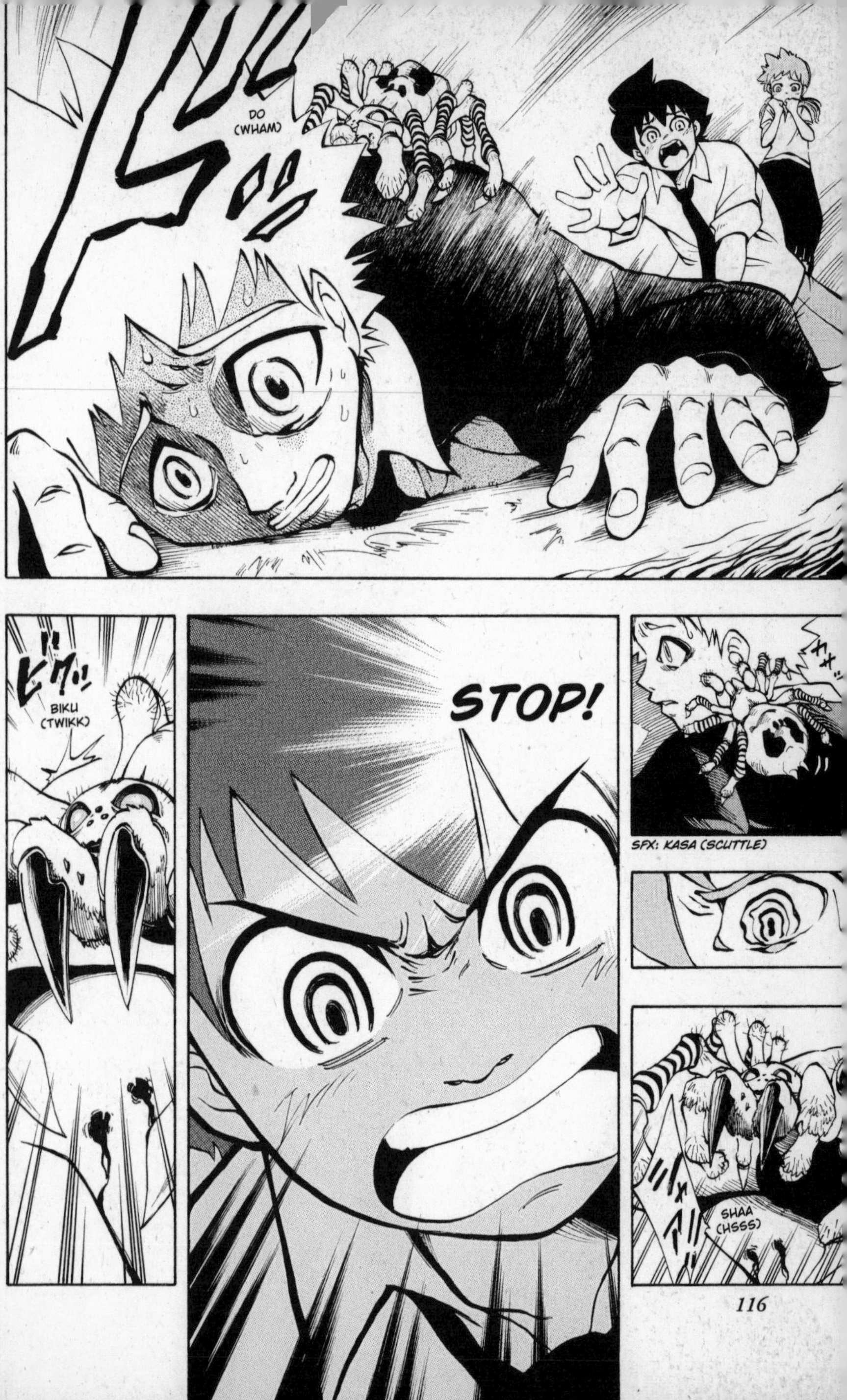
DO
(WHAM)
SFX: KASA (SCUTTLE)
SHAA
(HSSS)
STOP!
BIKU
(TWIKK)

BACK INSIDE THE CAGE!!!

HAA (HUFF)

HAA

KASA (SKITTER)

KASA

ARE YOU OKAY? STEVE?

STEVE?

AAAAHH...

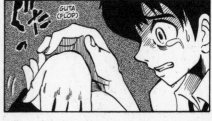

GUTA (FLOP)

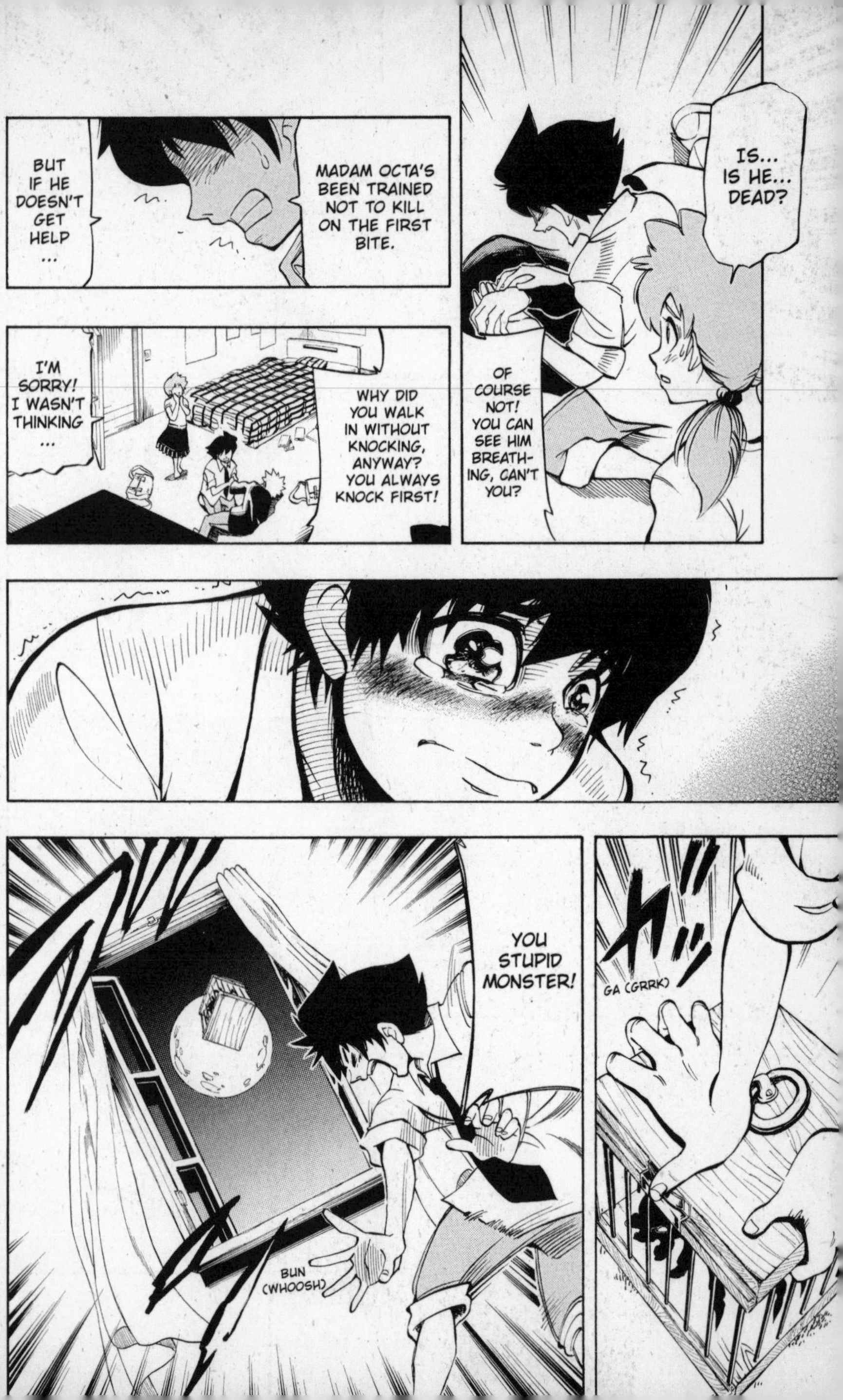
IS... IS HE... DEAD?
OF COURSE NOT! YOU CAN SEE HIM BREATHING, CAN'T YOU?
MADAM OCTA'S BEEN TRAINED NOT TO KILL ON THE FIRST BITE.
BUT IF HE DOESN'T GET HELP ...
WHY DID YOU WALK IN WITHOUT KNOCKING, ANYWAY? YOU ALWAYS KNOCK FIRST!
I'M SORRY! I WASN'T THINKING ...
GA (GRRK)
YOU STUPID MONSTER!
BUN (WHOOSH)

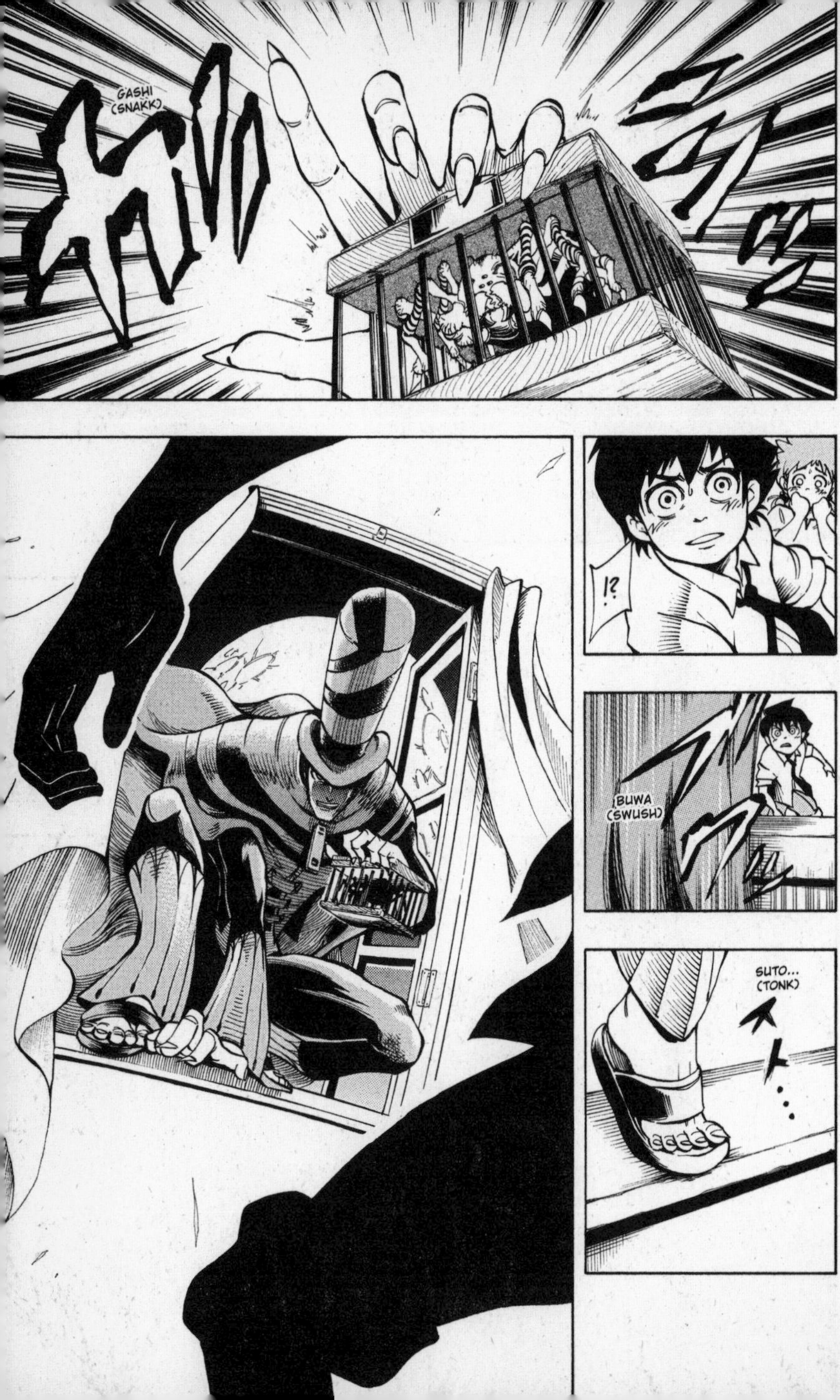
GASHI (SNAKK)
!?
BUWA (SWUSH)
SUTO... (TONK)

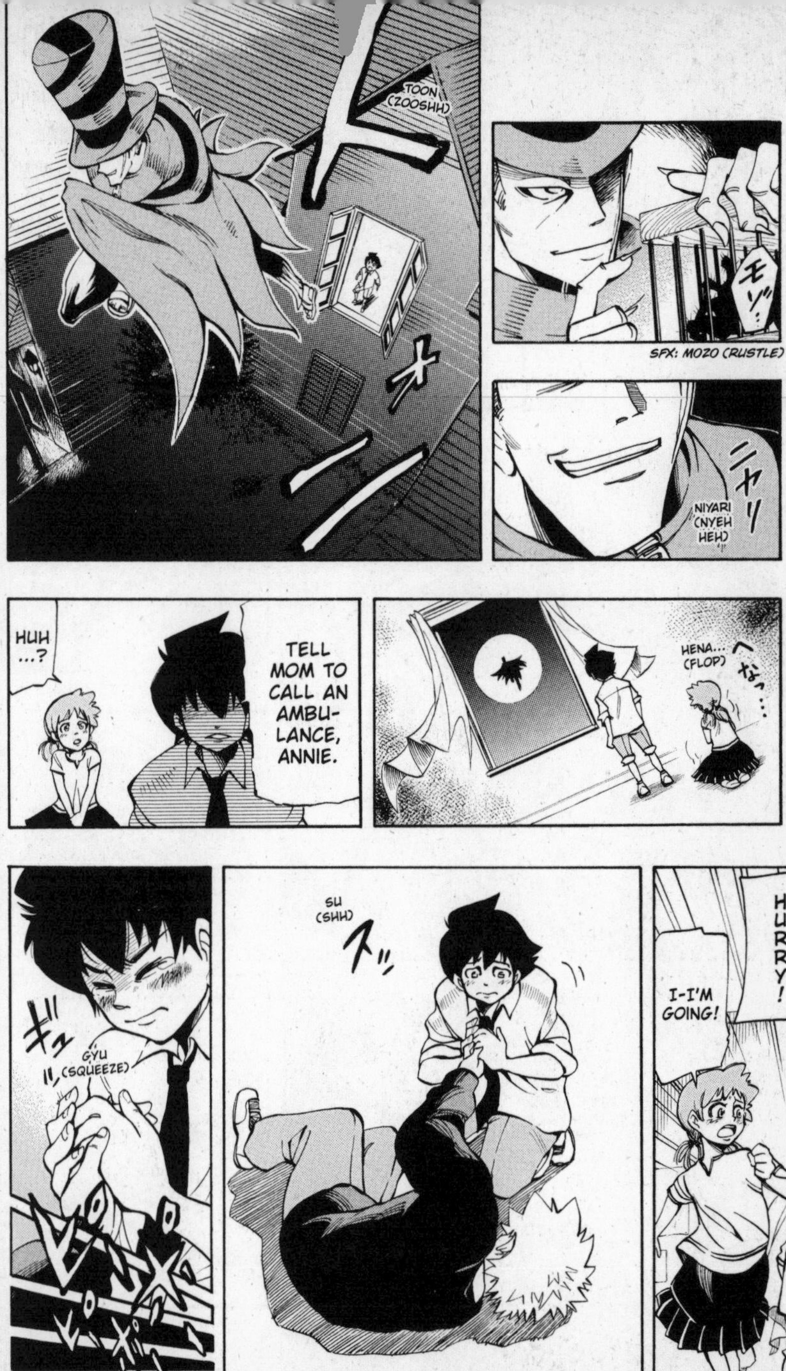
SFX: MOZO (RUSTLE)
NIYARI (NYEH HEH)
TOON (ZOOSHH)
HENA... (FLOP)
TELL MOM TO CALL AN AMBU-LANCE, ANNIE.
HUH ...?
HURRY!
I-I'M GOING!
SU (SHH)
GYU (SQUEEZE)
SFX: PIIPOO (WEE-OOH) PIIPOO

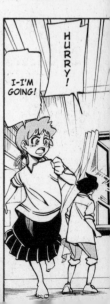

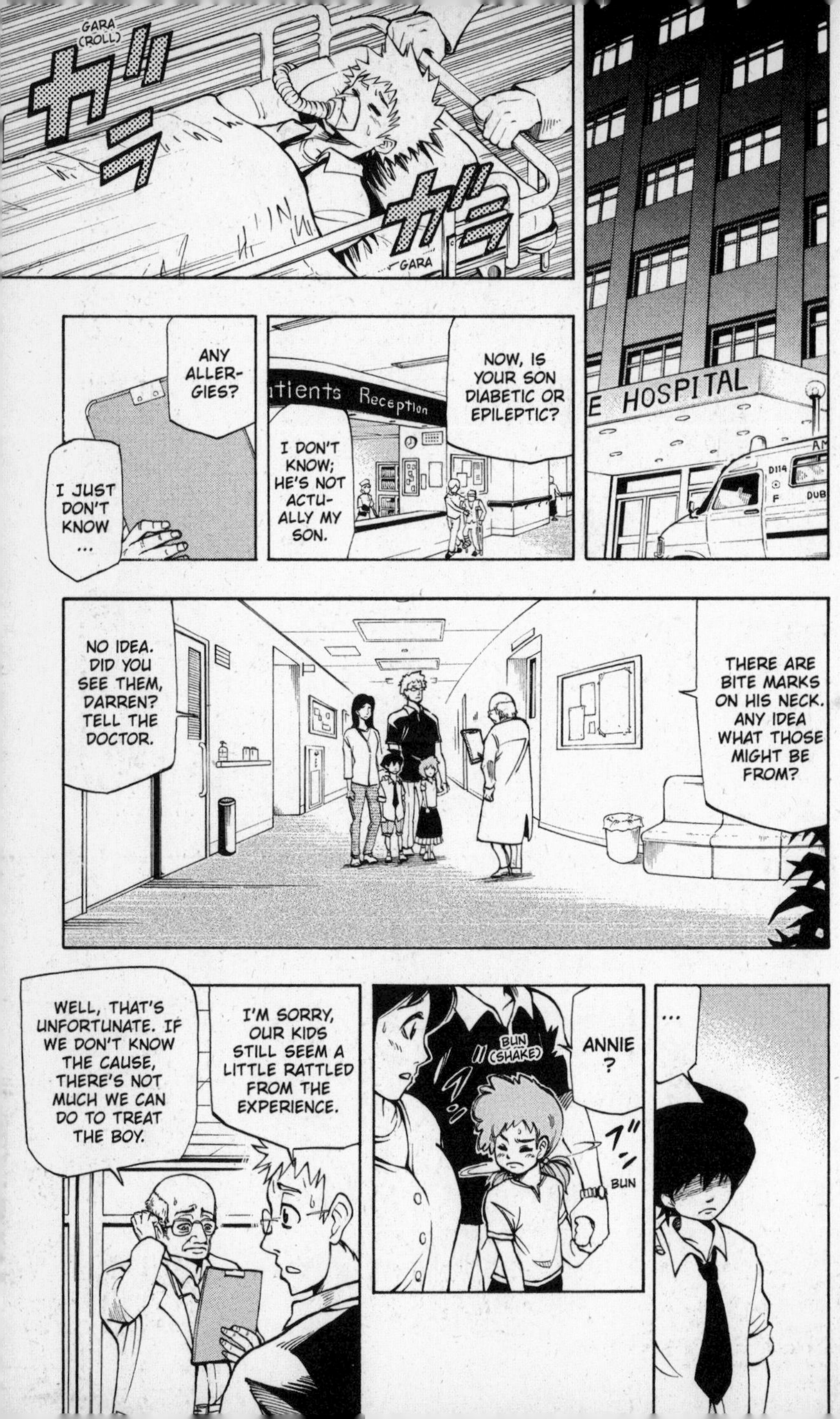
E HOSPITAL
GARA (ROLL)
ガラ
ガラ
GARA
NOW, IS YOUR SON DIABETIC OR EPILEPTIC?
I DON'T KNOW; HE'S NOT ACTUALLY MY SON.
tients Reception
ANY ALLERGIES?
I JUST DON'T KNOW ...
THERE ARE BITE MARKS ON HIS NECK. ANY IDEA WHAT THOSE MIGHT BE FROM?
NO IDEA. DID YOU SEE THEM, DARREN? TELL THE DOCTOR.
...
ANNIE ?
BUN (SHAKE)
ブン
BUN
I'M SORRY, OUR KIDS STILL SEEM A LITTLE RATTLED FROM THE EXPERIENCE.
WELL, THAT'S UNFORTUNATE. IF WE DON'T KNOW THE CAUSE, THERE'S NOT MUCH WE CAN DO TO TREAT THE BOY.

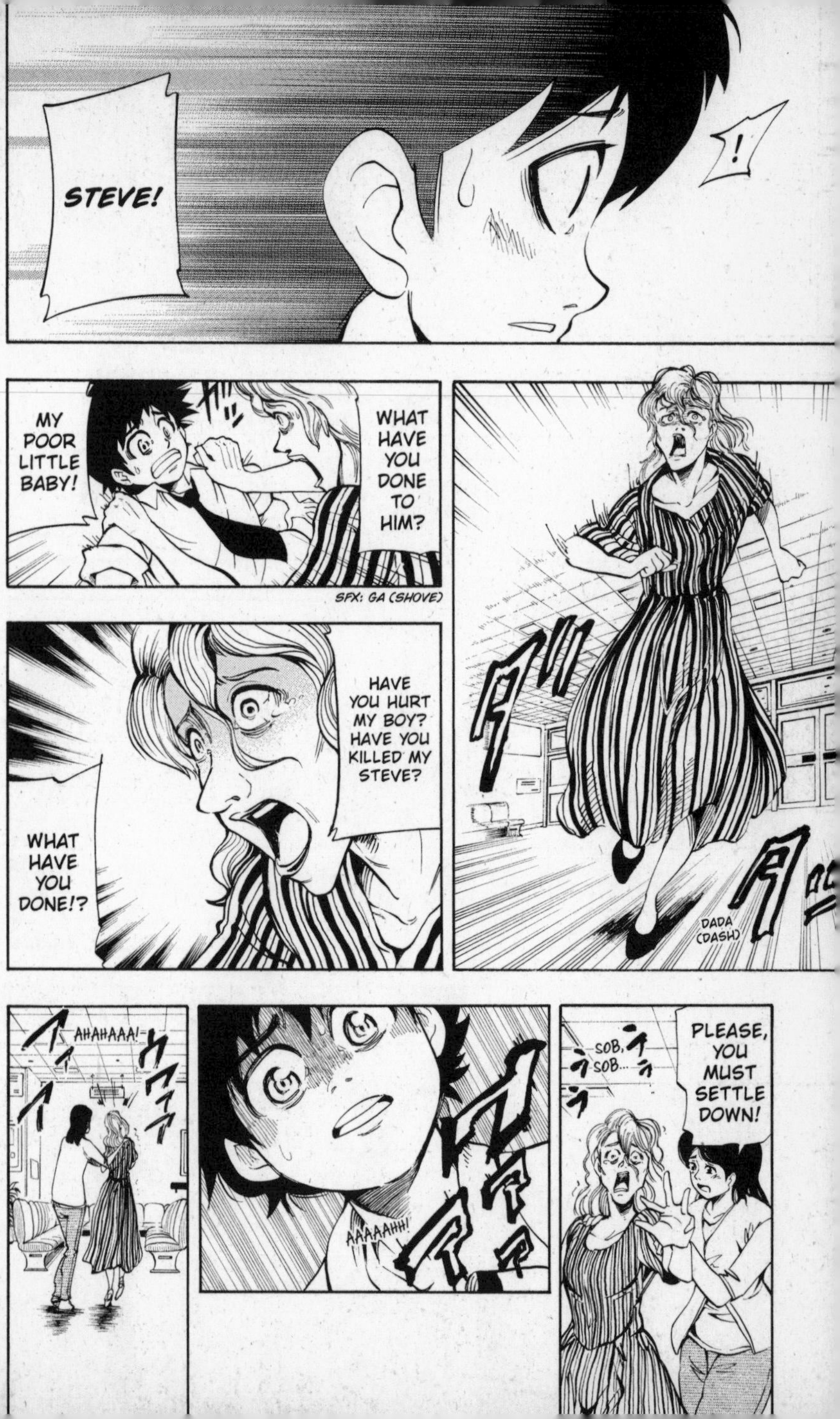
!
STEVE!
DADA (DASH)
WHAT HAVE YOU DONE TO HIM?
MY POOR LITTLE BABY!
SFX: GA (SHOVE)
HAVE YOU HURT MY BOY? HAVE YOU KILLED MY STEVE?
WHAT HAVE YOU DONE!?
PLEASE, YOU MUST SETTLE DOWN!
SOB, SOB...
AAAAAHH!
AHAHAAA!

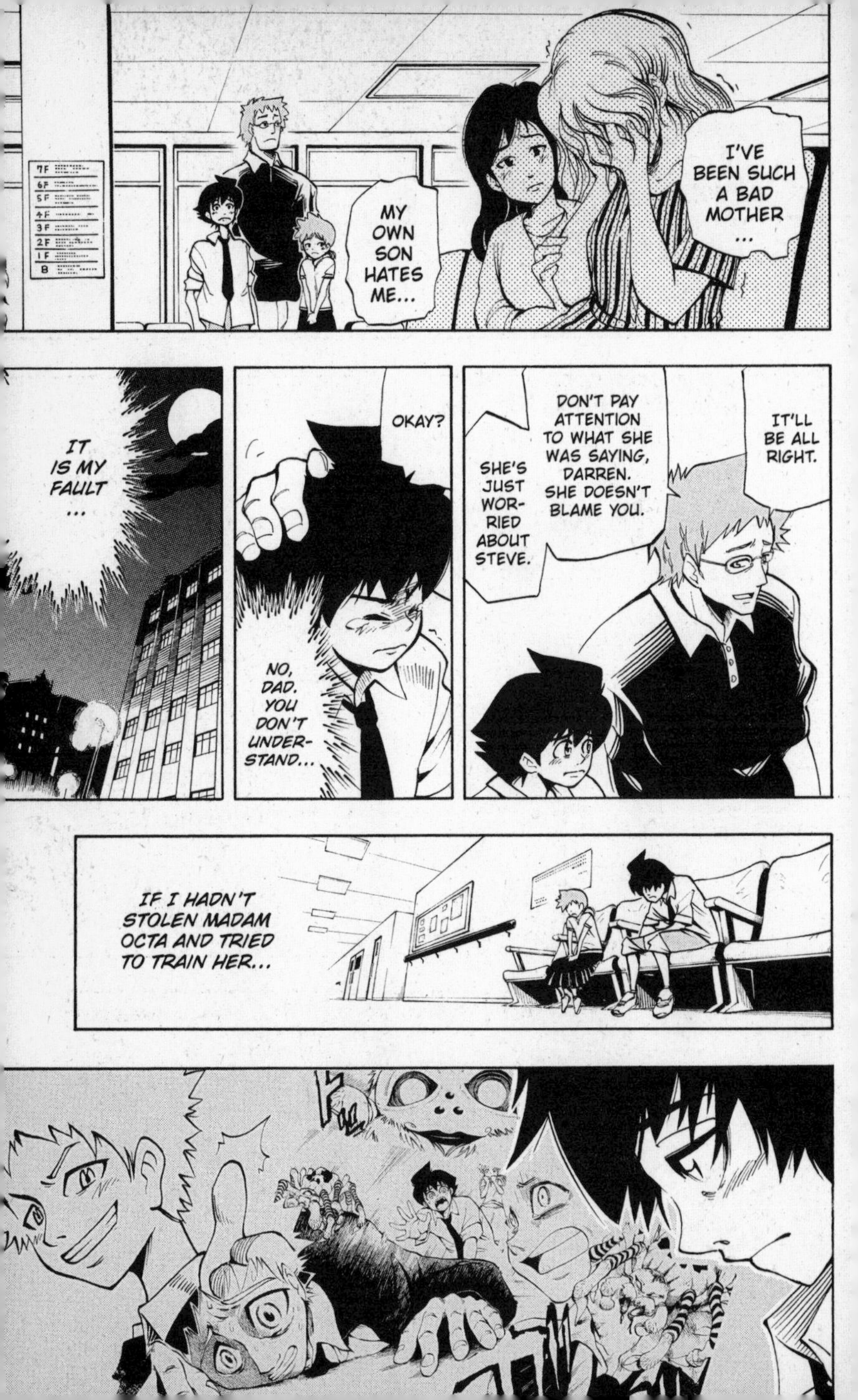
I'VE BEEN SUCH A BAD MOTHER...
MY OWN SON HATES ME...
7F 6F 5F 4F 3F 2F 1F B
IT'LL BE ALL RIGHT.
DON'T PAY ATTENTION TO WHAT SHE WAS SAYING, DARREN. SHE DOESN'T BLAME YOU.
SHE'S JUST WOR-RIED ABOUT STEVE.
OKAY?
NO, DAD. YOU DON'T UNDER-STAND...
IT IS MY FAULT...
IF I HADN'T STOLEN MADAM OCTA AND TRIED TO TRAIN HER...

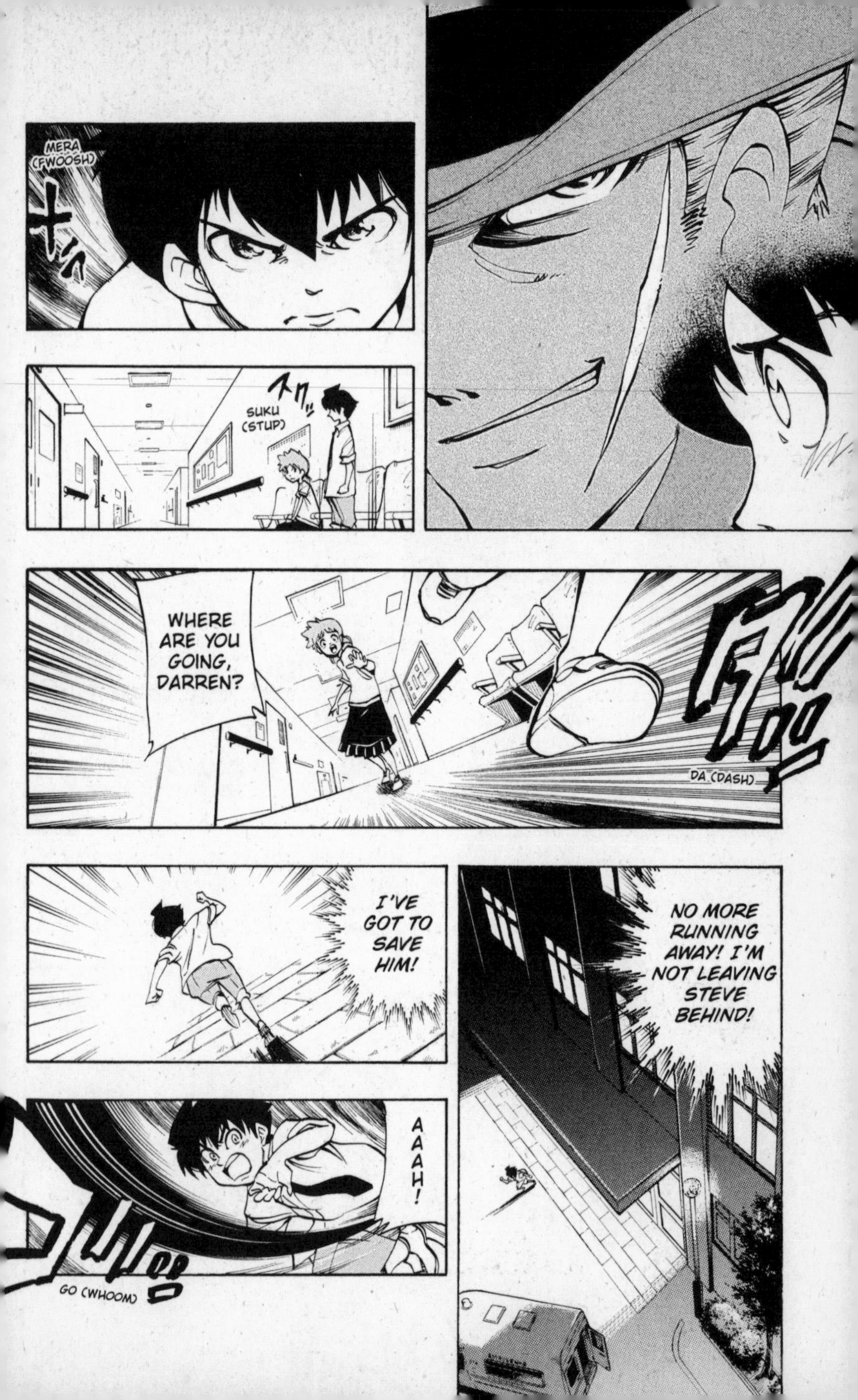
MERA (FWOOSH)
SUKU (STUP)
DA (DASH)
WHERE ARE YOU GOING, DARREN?
NO MORE RUNNING AWAY! I'M NOT LEAVING STEVE BEHIND!
I'VE GOT TO SAVE HIM!
AAAH!
GO (WHOOM)

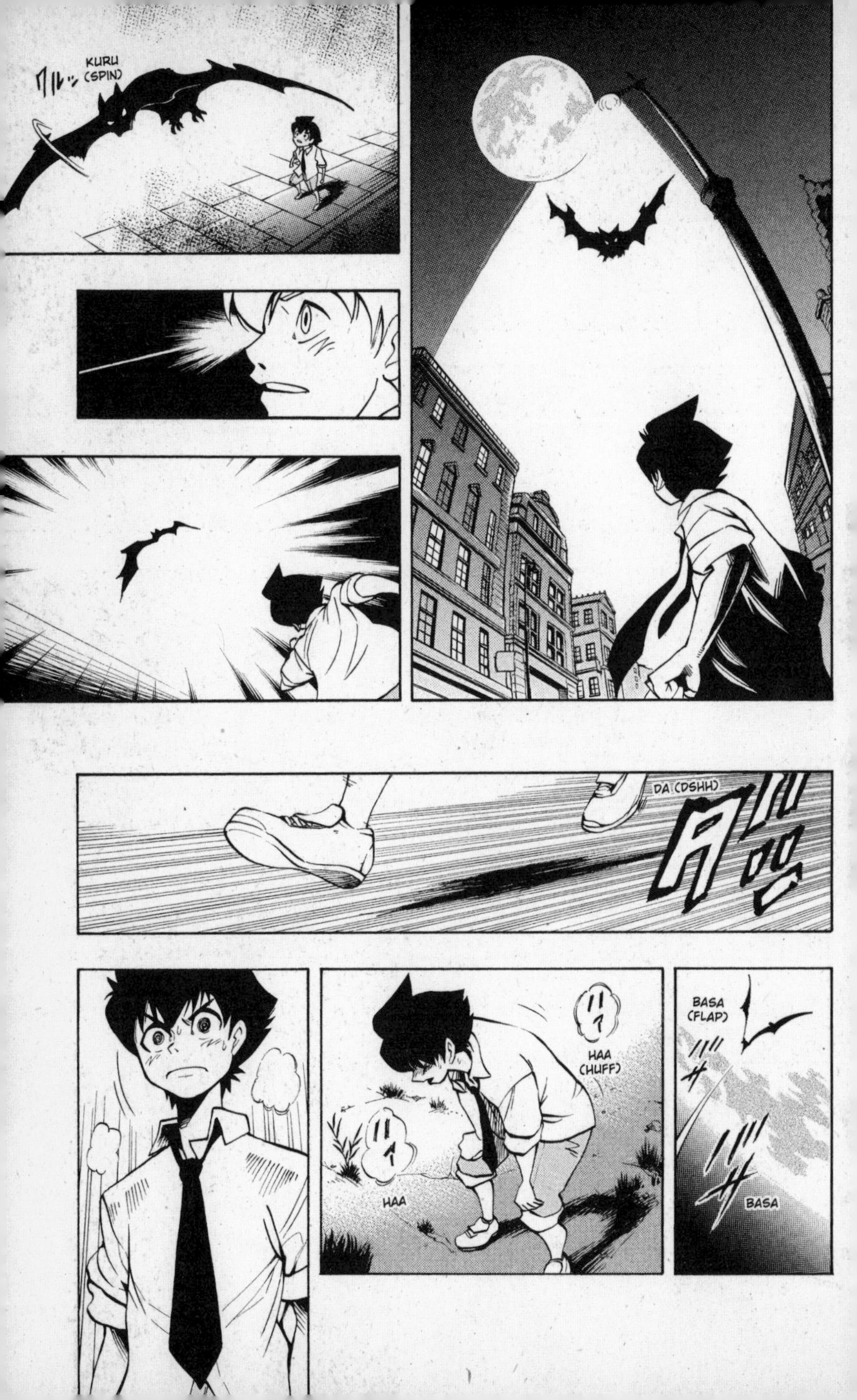
クルッ
KURU (SPIN)
DA (DSHH)
BASA (FLAP)
BASA
HAA (HUFF)
HAA

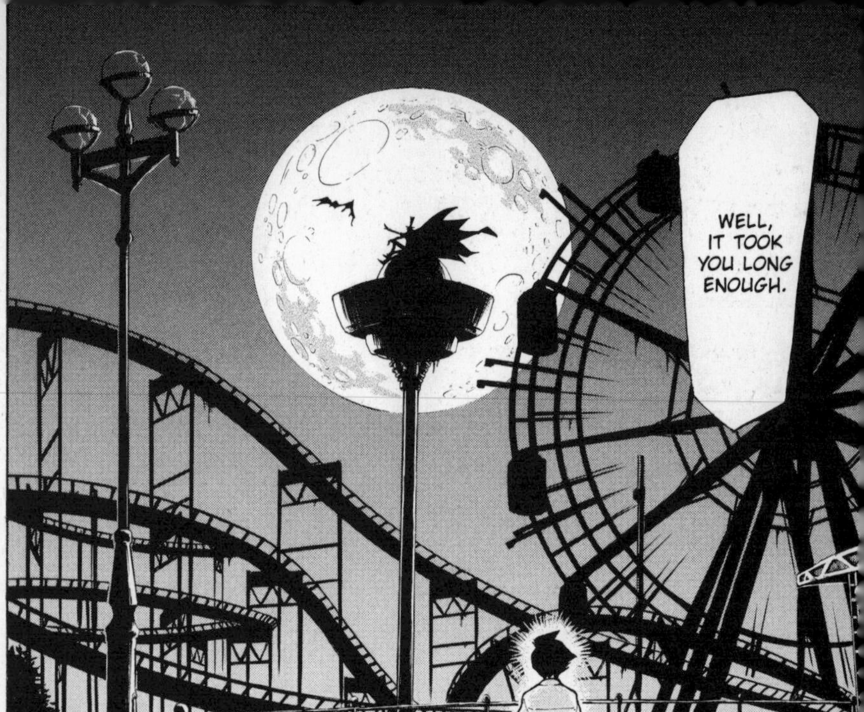
WELL, IT TOOK YOU LONG ENOUGH.

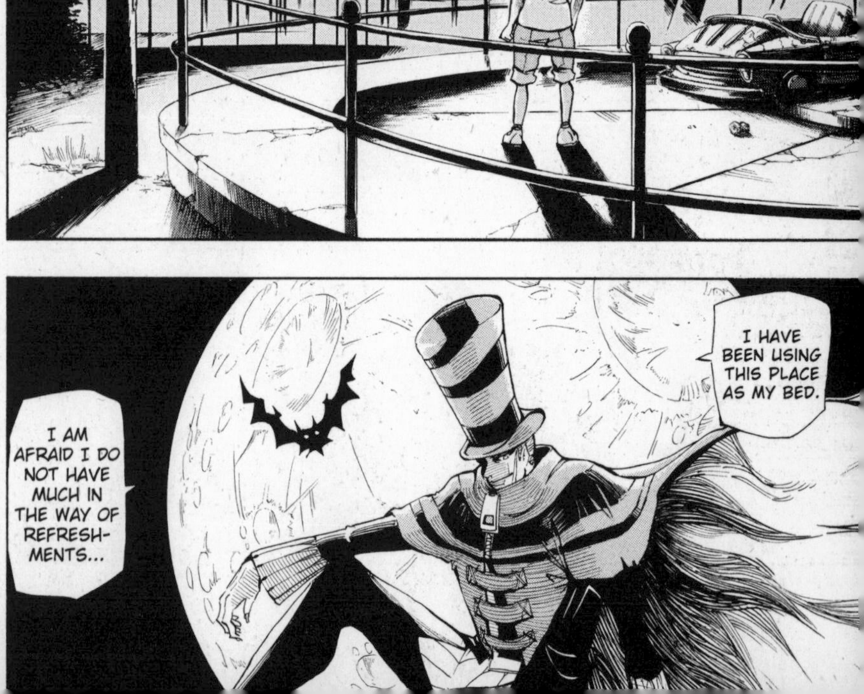
I HAVE BEEN USING THIS PLACE AS MY BED.
I AM AFRAID I DO NOT HAVE MUCH IN THE WAY OF REFRESH-MENTS...

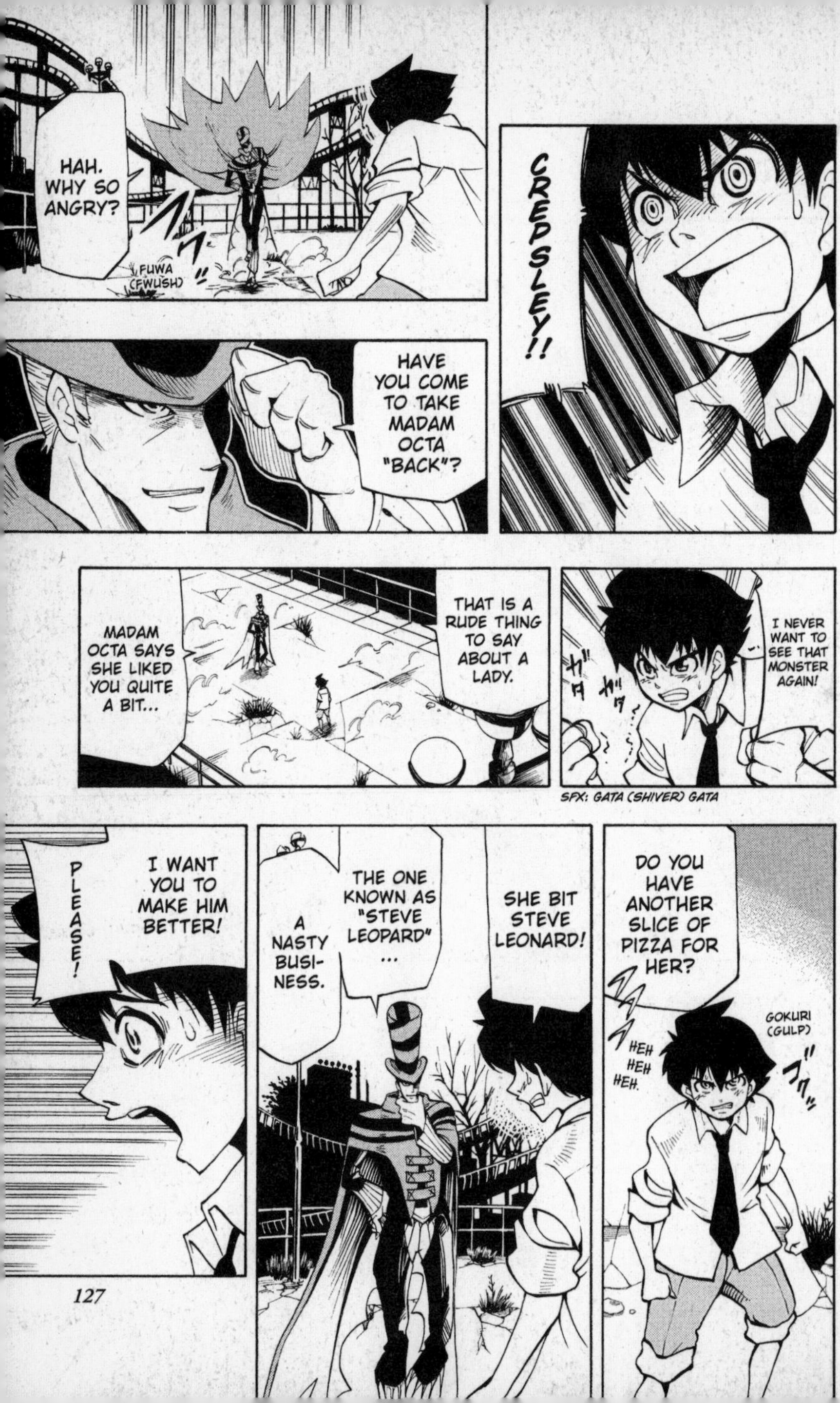
CREPSLEY!!
HAH. WHY SO ANGRY?
FUWA (FWUSH)
HAVE YOU COME TO TAKE MADAM OCTA "BACK"?
I NEVER WANT TO SEE THAT MONSTER AGAIN!
SFX: GATA (SHIVER) GATA
THAT IS A RUDE THING TO SAY ABOUT A LADY.
MADAM OCTA SAYS SHE LIKED YOU QUITE A BIT...
DO YOU HAVE ANOTHER SLICE OF PIZZA FOR HER?
HEH HEH HEH.
GOKURI (GULP)
SHE BIT STEVE LEONARD!
THE ONE KNOWN AS "STEVE LEOPARD"...
A NASTY BUSINESS.
I WANT YOU TO MAKE HIM BETTER!
PLEASE!

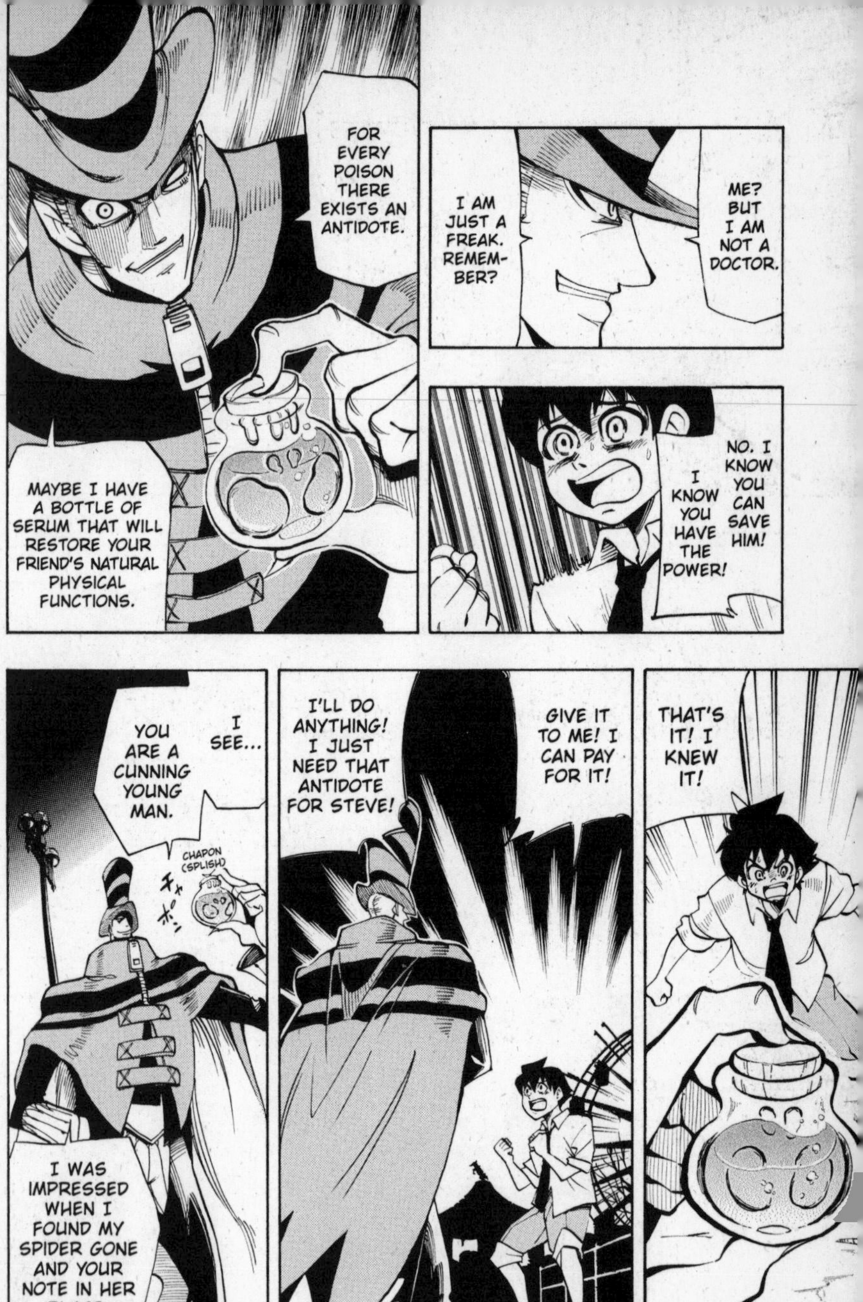
ME? BUT I AM NOT A DOCTOR.
I AM JUST A FREAK. REMEMBER?
NO. I KNOW YOU CAN SAVE HIM!
I KNOW YOU HAVE THE POWER!
FOR EVERY POISON THERE EXISTS AN ANTIDOTE.
MAYBE I HAVE A BOTTLE OF SERUM THAT WILL RESTORE YOUR FRIEND'S NATURAL PHYSICAL FUNCTIONS.
THAT'S IT! I KNEW IT!
GIVE IT TO ME! I CAN PAY FOR IT!
I'LL DO ANYTHING! I JUST NEED THAT ANTIDOTE FOR STEVE!
I SEE...
YOU ARE A CUNNING YOUNG MAN.
チャポン
CHAPON (SPLISH)
I WAS IMPRESSED WHEN I FOUND MY SPIDER GONE AND YOUR NOTE IN HER PLACE.

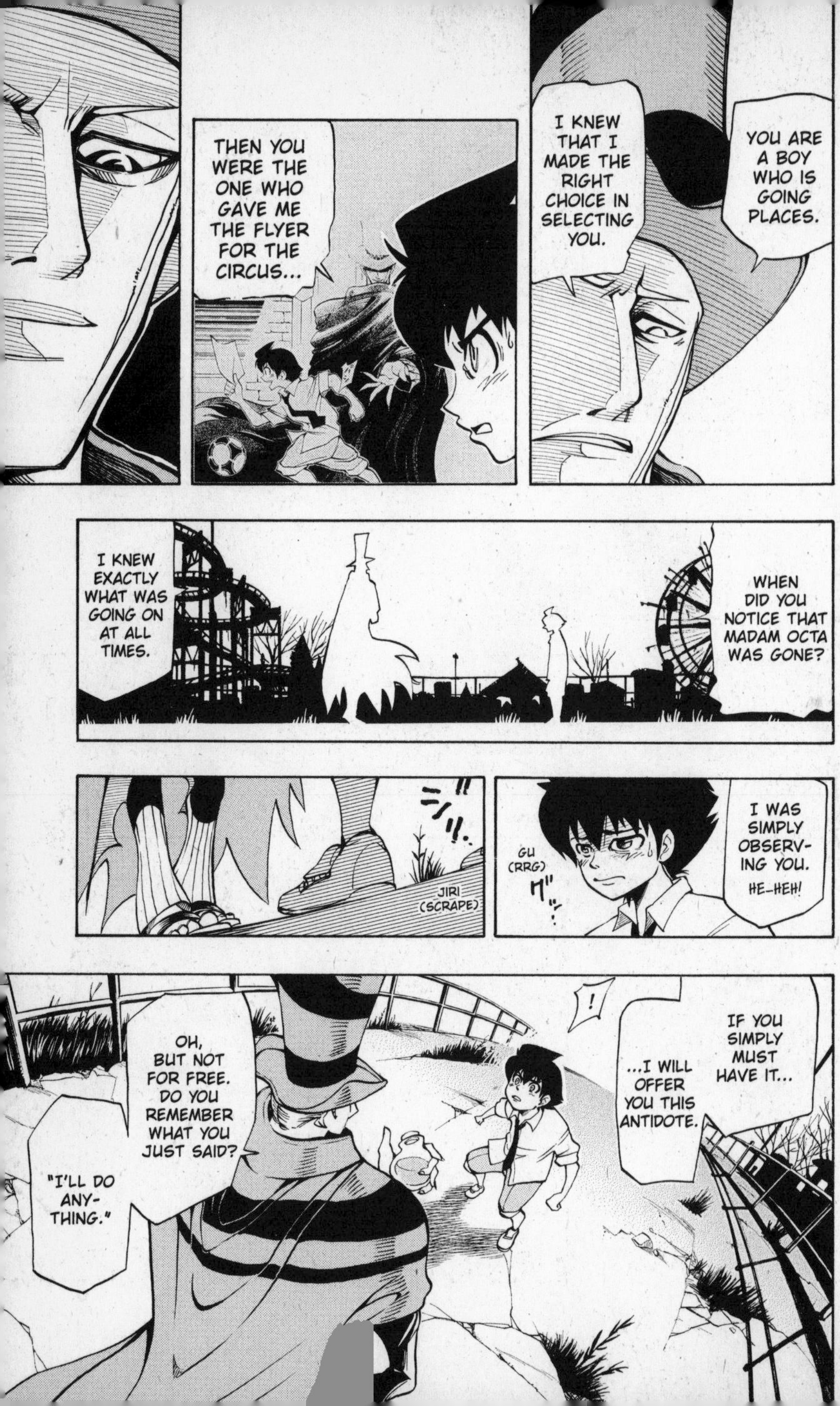
YOU ARE A BOY WHO IS GOING PLACES.
I KNEW THAT I MADE THE RIGHT CHOICE IN SELECTING YOU.
THEN YOU WERE THE ONE WHO GAVE ME THE FLYER FOR THE CIRCUS...
WHEN DID YOU NOTICE THAT MADAM OCTA WAS GONE?
I KNEW EXACTLY WHAT WAS GOING ON AT ALL TIMES.
I WAS SIMPLY OBSERVING YOU.
HE-HEH!
GU (RRG)
JIRI (SCRAPE)
IF YOU SIMPLY MUST HAVE IT...
...I WILL OFFER YOU THIS ANTIDOTE.
!
OH, BUT NOT FOR FREE. DO YOU REMEMBER WHAT YOU JUST SAID?
"I'LL DO ANYTHING."

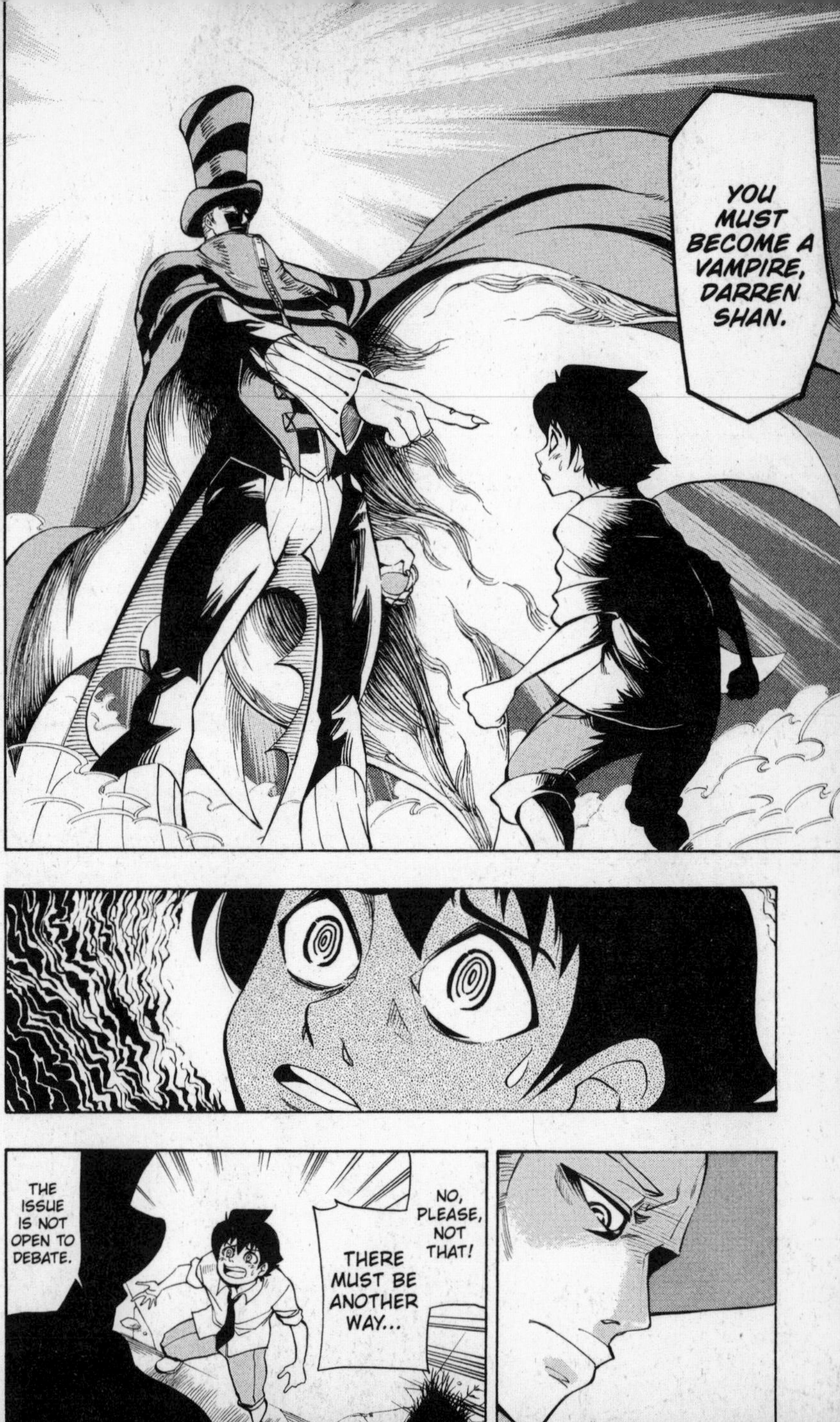
YOU MUST BECOME A VAMPIRE, DARREN SHAN.
NO, PLEASE, NOT THAT!
THERE MUST BE ANOTHER WAY...
THE ISSUE IS NOT OPEN TO DEBATE.

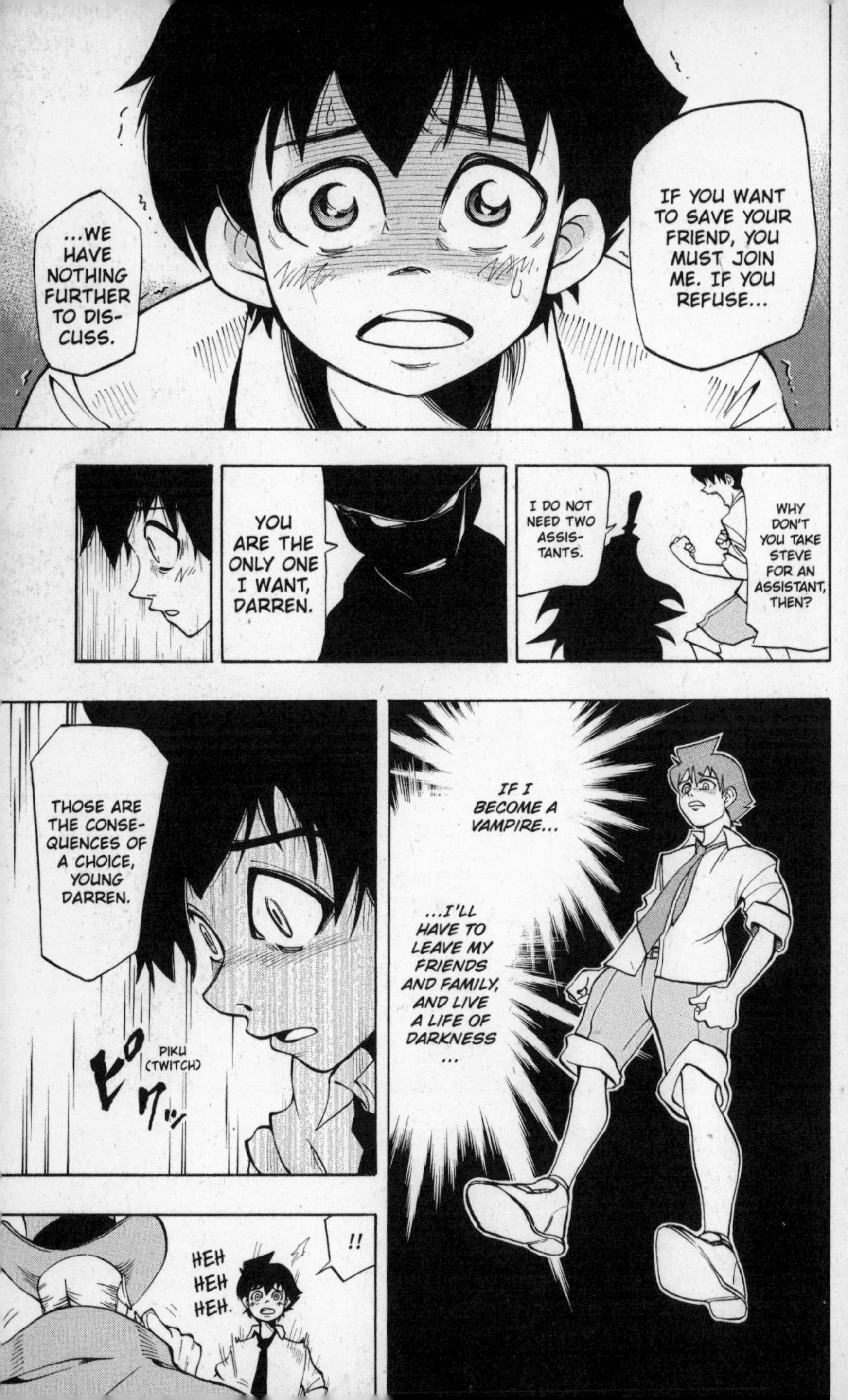
IF YOU WANT TO SAVE YOUR FRIEND, YOU MUST JOIN ME. IF YOU REFUSE...
...WE HAVE NOTHING FURTHER TO DISCUSS.
WHY DON'T YOU TAKE STEVE FOR AN ASSISTANT, THEN?
I DO NOT NEED TWO ASSISTANTS.
YOU ARE THE ONLY ONE I WANT, DARREN.
IF I BECOME A VAMPIRE...
...I'LL HAVE TO LEAVE MY FRIENDS AND FAMILY, AND LIVE A LIFE OF DARKNESS ...
THOSE ARE THE CONSEQUENCES OF A CHOICE, YOUNG DARREN.
PIKU (TWITCH)
!!
HEH HEH HEH.

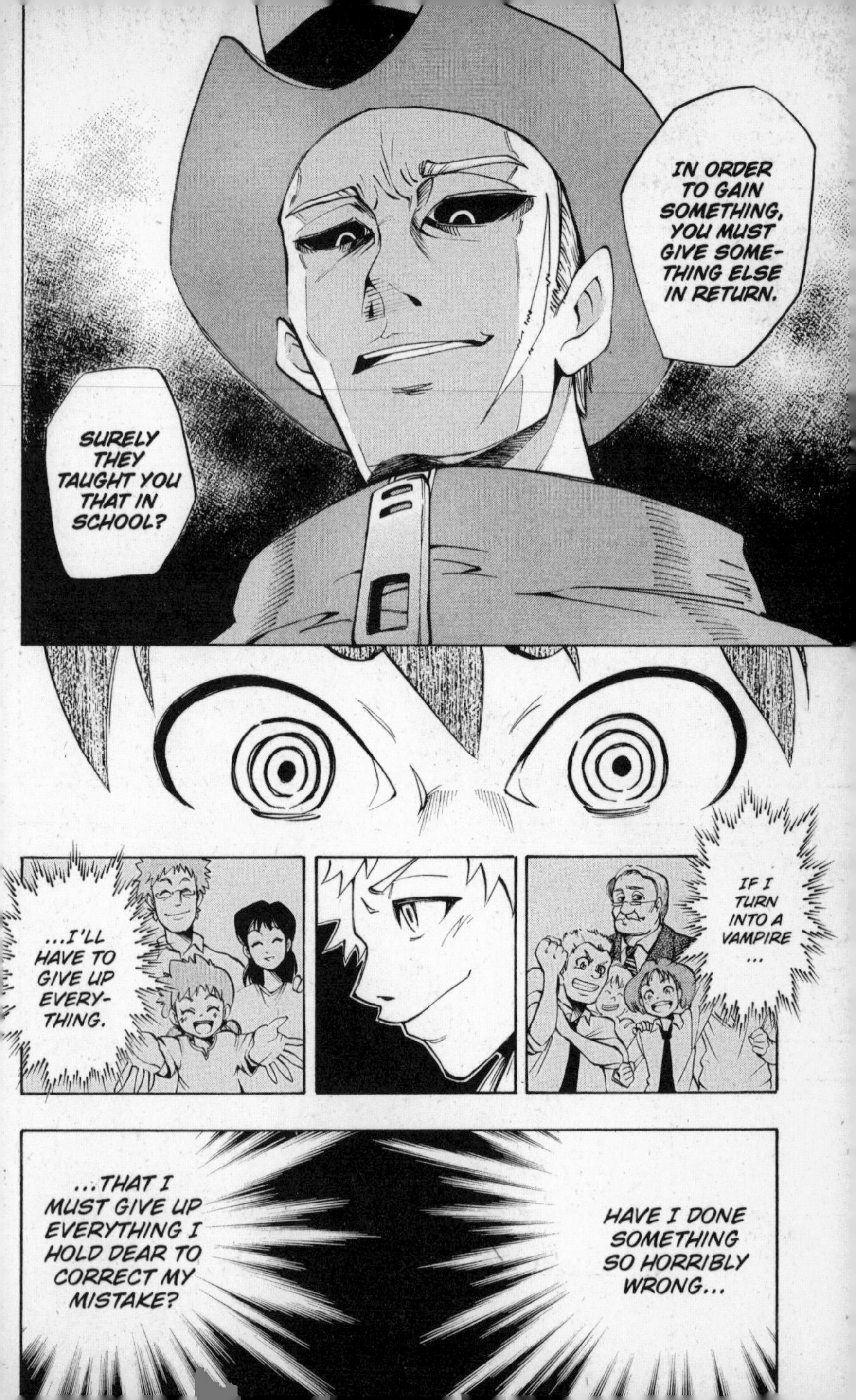
IN ORDER TO GAIN SOMETHING, YOU MUST GIVE SOME-THING ELSE IN RETURN.
SURELY THEY TAUGHT YOU THAT IN SCHOOL?
IF I TURN INTO A VAMPIRE ...
...I'LL HAVE TO GIVE UP EVERY-THING.
HAVE I DONE SOMETHING SO HORRIBLY WRONG...
...THAT I MUST GIVE UP EVERYTHING I HOLD DEAR TO CORRECT MY MISTAKE?

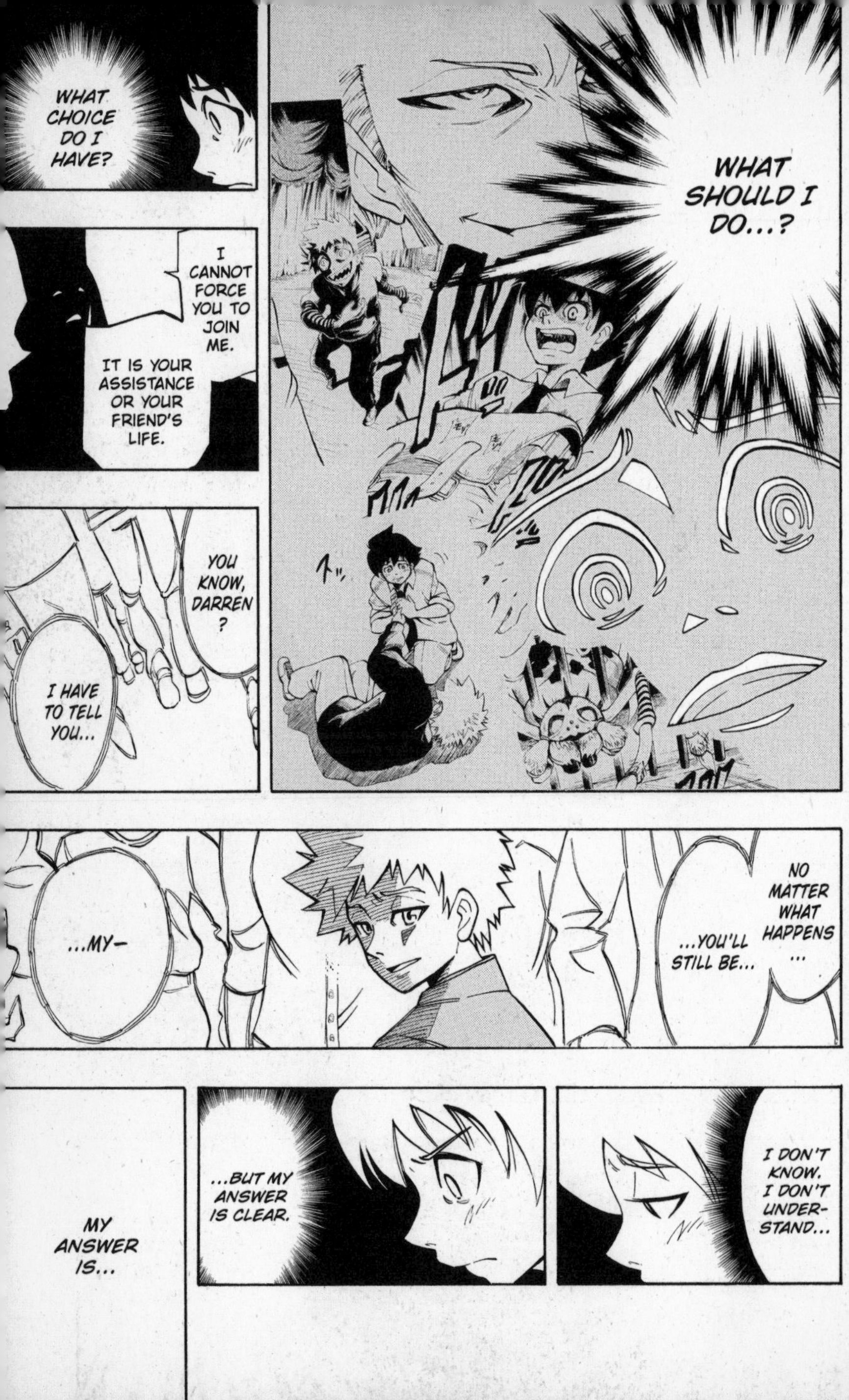
WHAT SHOULD I DO...?
WHAT CHOICE DO I HAVE?
I CANNOT FORCE YOU TO JOIN ME.
IT IS YOUR ASSISTANCE OR YOUR FRIEND'S LIFE.
YOU KNOW, DARREN?
I HAVE TO TELL YOU...
NO MATTER WHAT HAPPENS...
...YOU'LL STILL BE...
...MY—
I DON'T KNOW. I DON'T UNDER-STAND...
...BUT MY ANSWER IS CLEAR.
MY ANSWER IS...

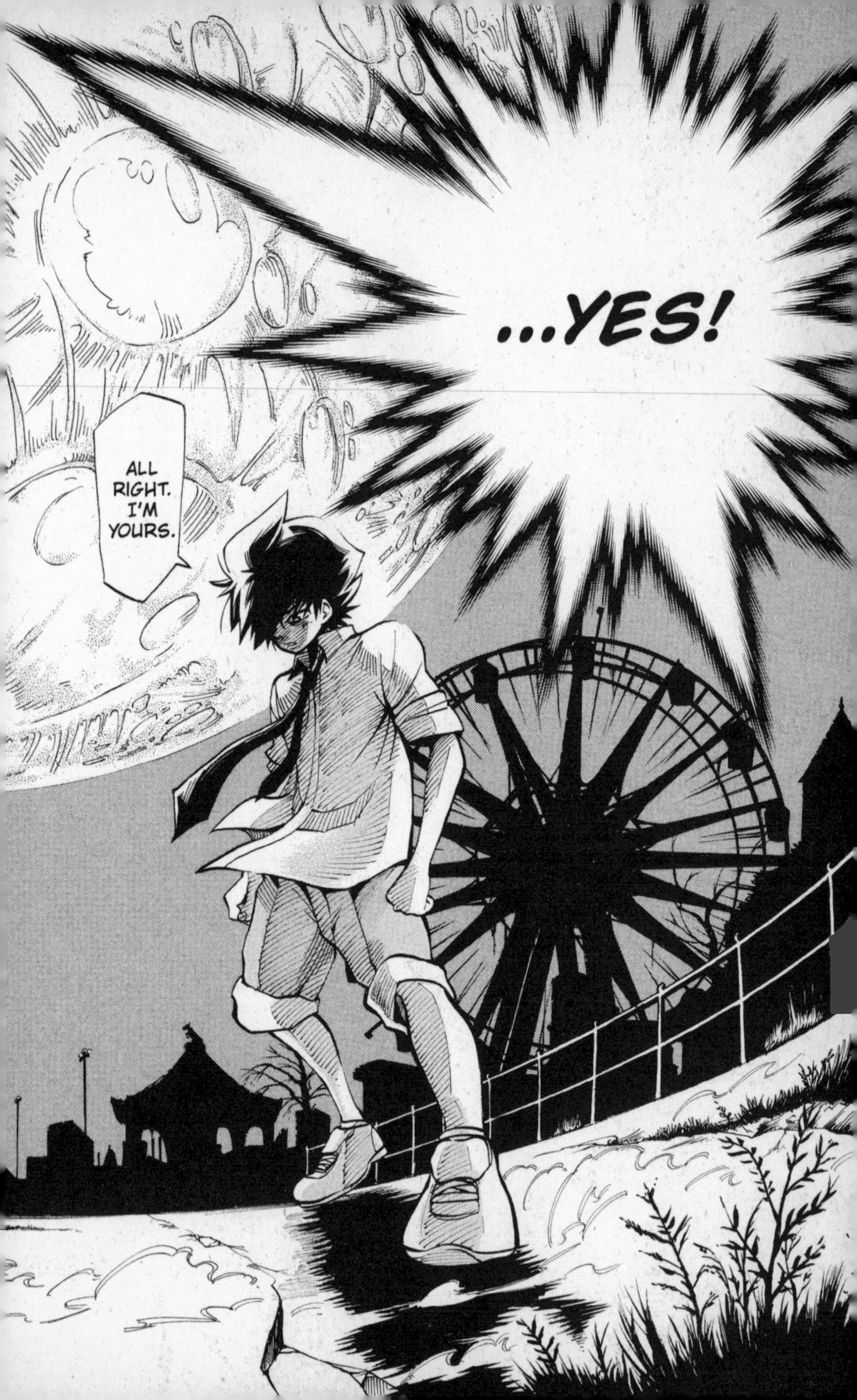
...YES!
ALL RIGHT. I'M YOURS.

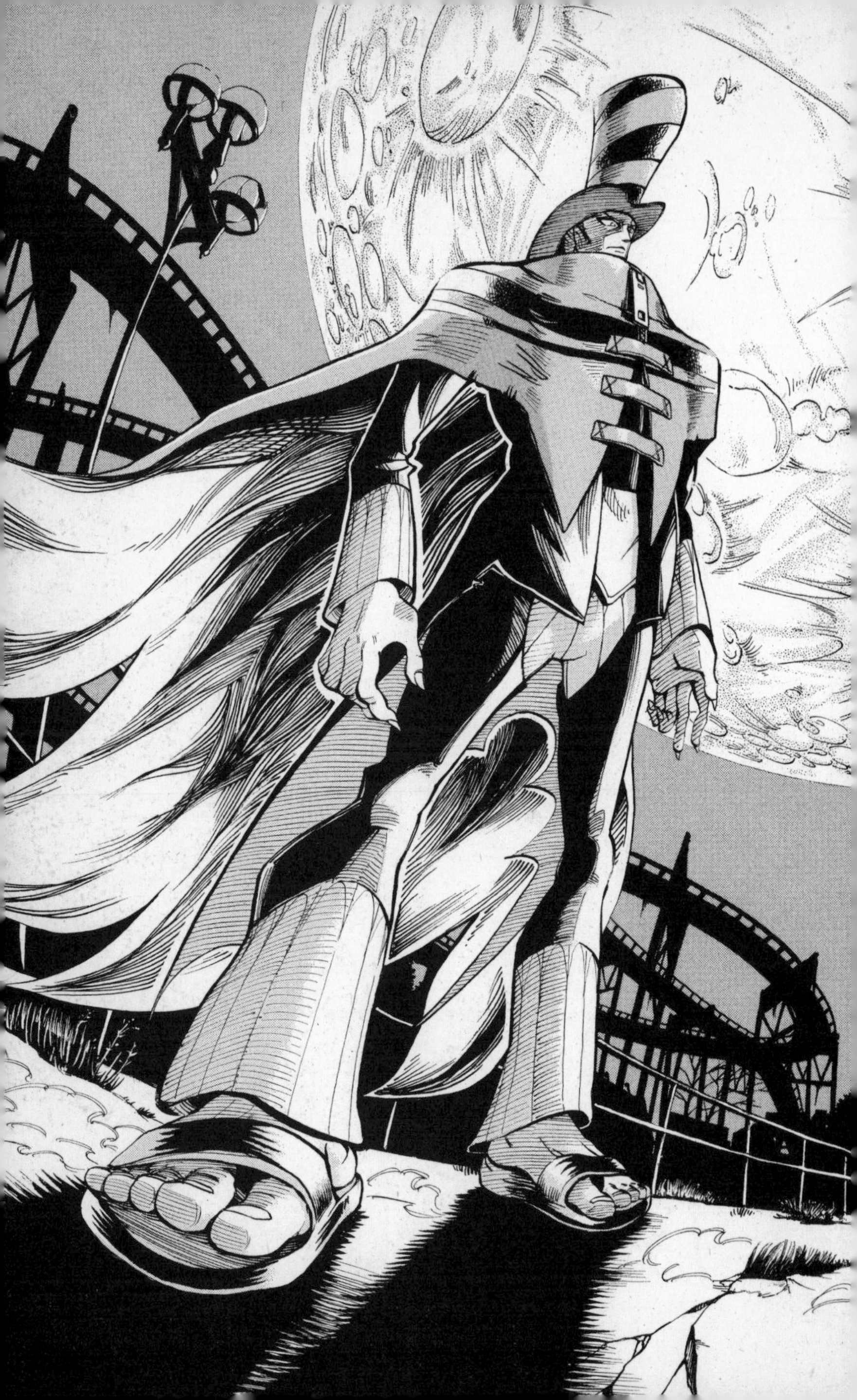

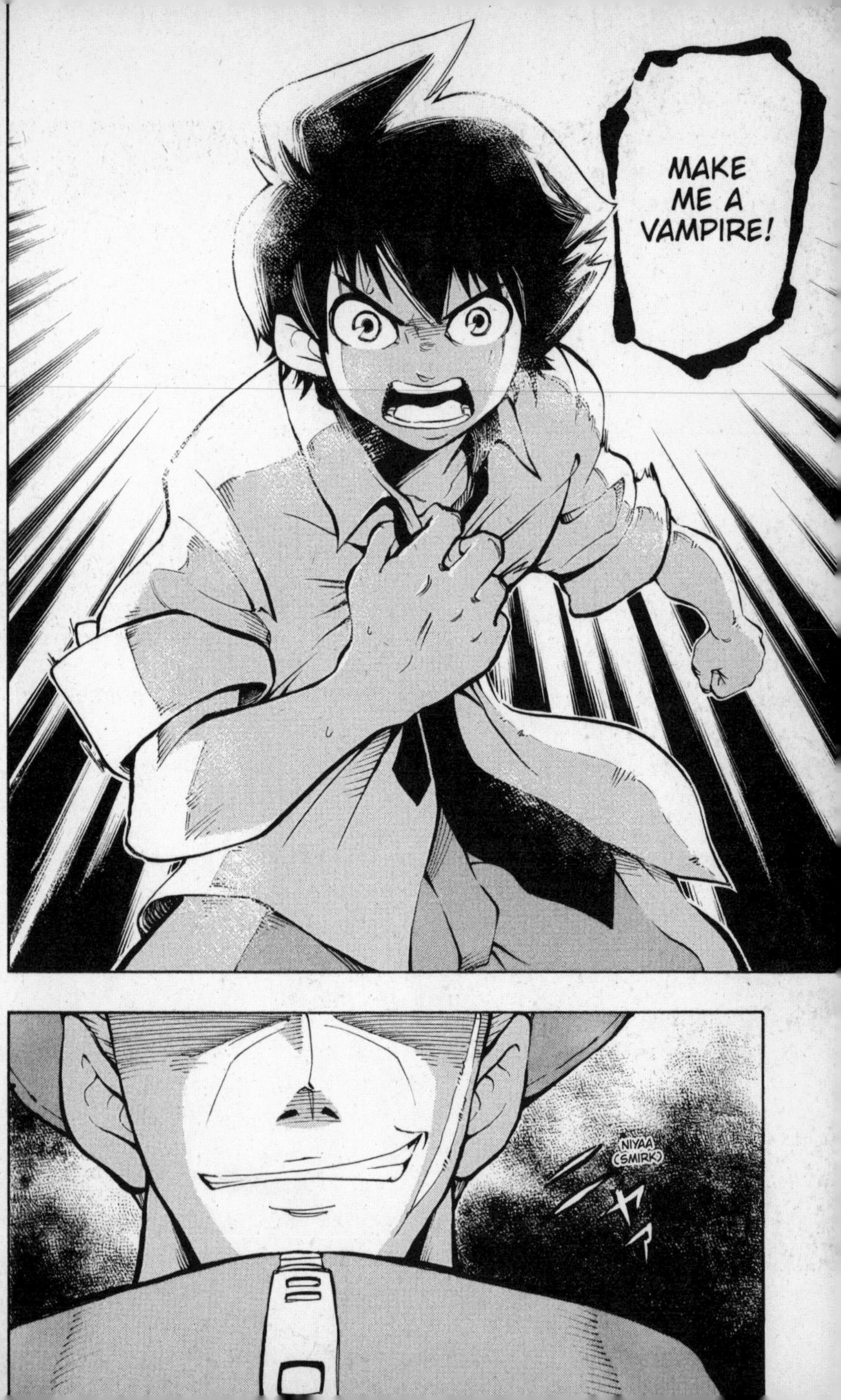
MAKE ME A VAMPIRE!
NIYAA (SMIRK)

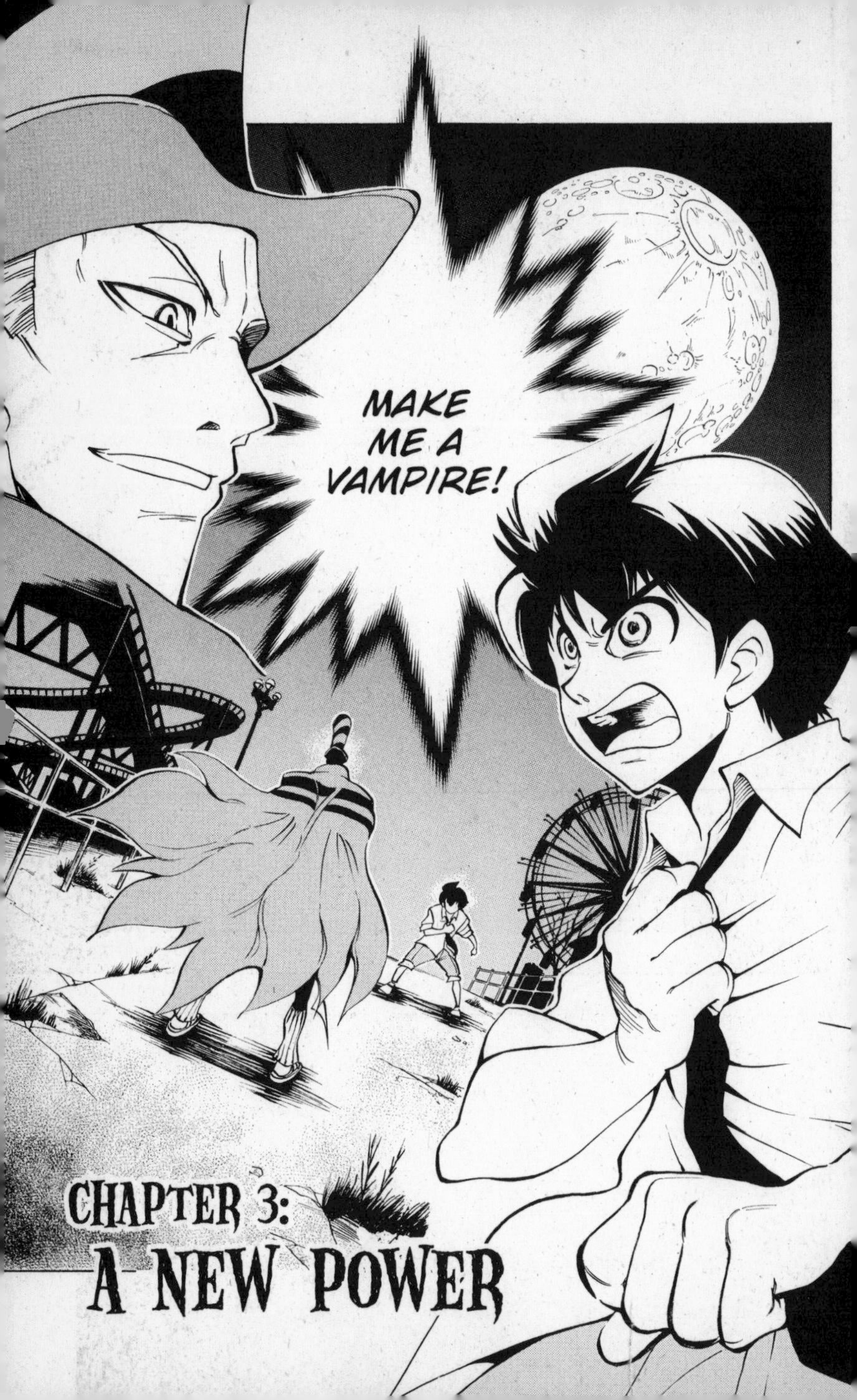
MAKE ME A VAMPIRE!
CHAPTER 3:
A NEW POWER

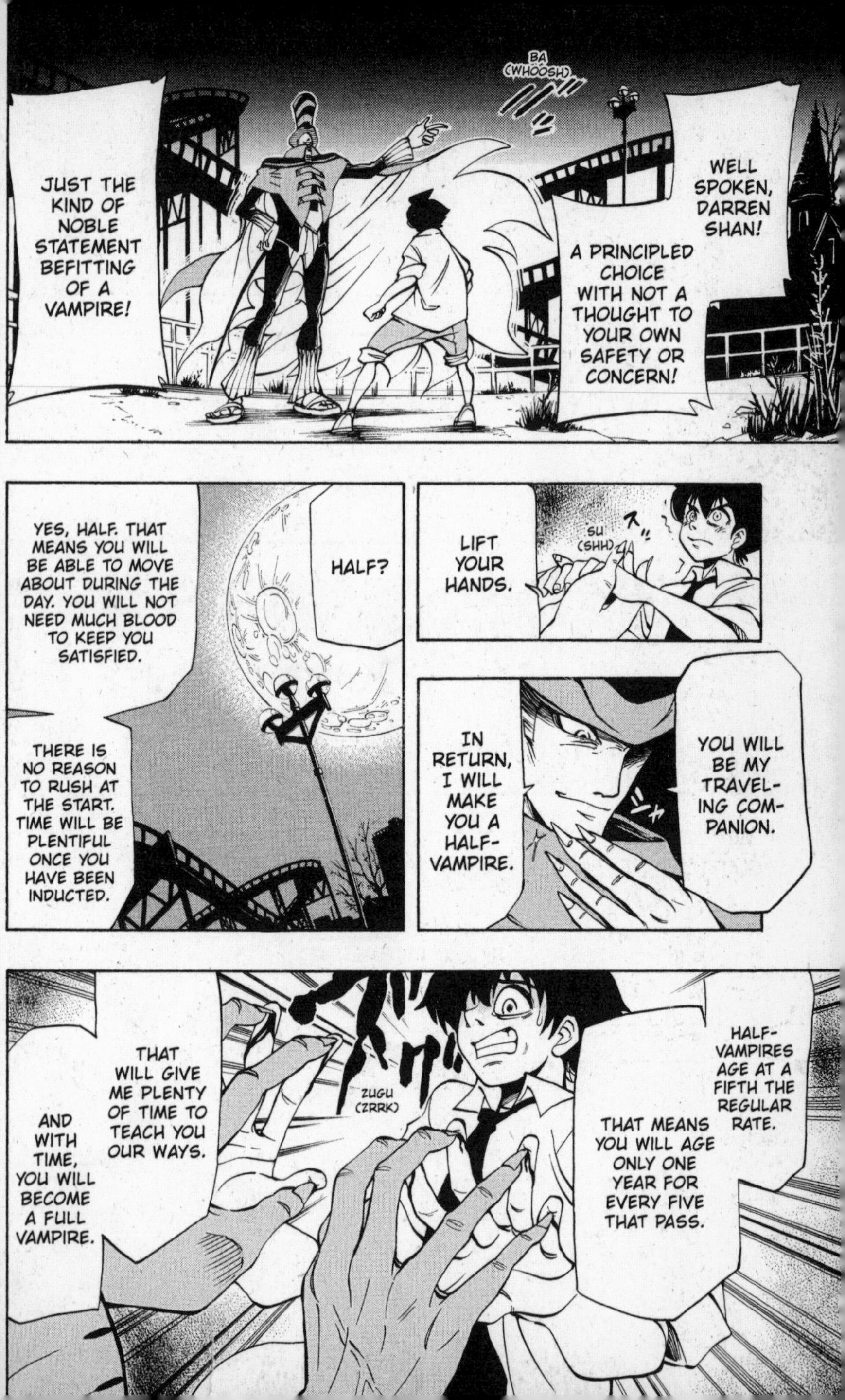
BA (WHOOSH)
WELL SPOKEN, DARREN SHAN!
A PRINCIPLED CHOICE WITH NOT A THOUGHT TO YOUR OWN SAFETY OR CONCERN!
JUST THE KIND OF NOBLE STATEMENT BEFITTING OF A VAMPIRE!
LIFT YOUR HANDS.
SU (SHH)
YOU WILL BE MY TRAVEL-ING COM-PANION.
IN RETURN, I WILL MAKE YOU A HALF-VAMPIRE.
HALF?
YES, HALF. THAT MEANS YOU WILL BE ABLE TO MOVE ABOUT DURING THE DAY. YOU WILL NOT NEED MUCH BLOOD TO KEEP YOU SATISFIED.
THERE IS NO REASON TO RUSH AT THE START. TIME WILL BE PLENTIFUL ONCE YOU HAVE BEEN INDUCTED.
HALF-VAMPIRES AGE AT A FIFTH THE REGULAR RATE.
THAT MEANS YOU WILL AGE ONLY ONE YEAR FOR EVERY FIVE THAT PASS.
ZUGU (ZRRK)
THAT WILL GIVE ME PLENTY OF TIME TO TEACH YOU OUR WAYS.
AND WITH TIME, YOU WILL BECOME A FULL VAMPIRE.

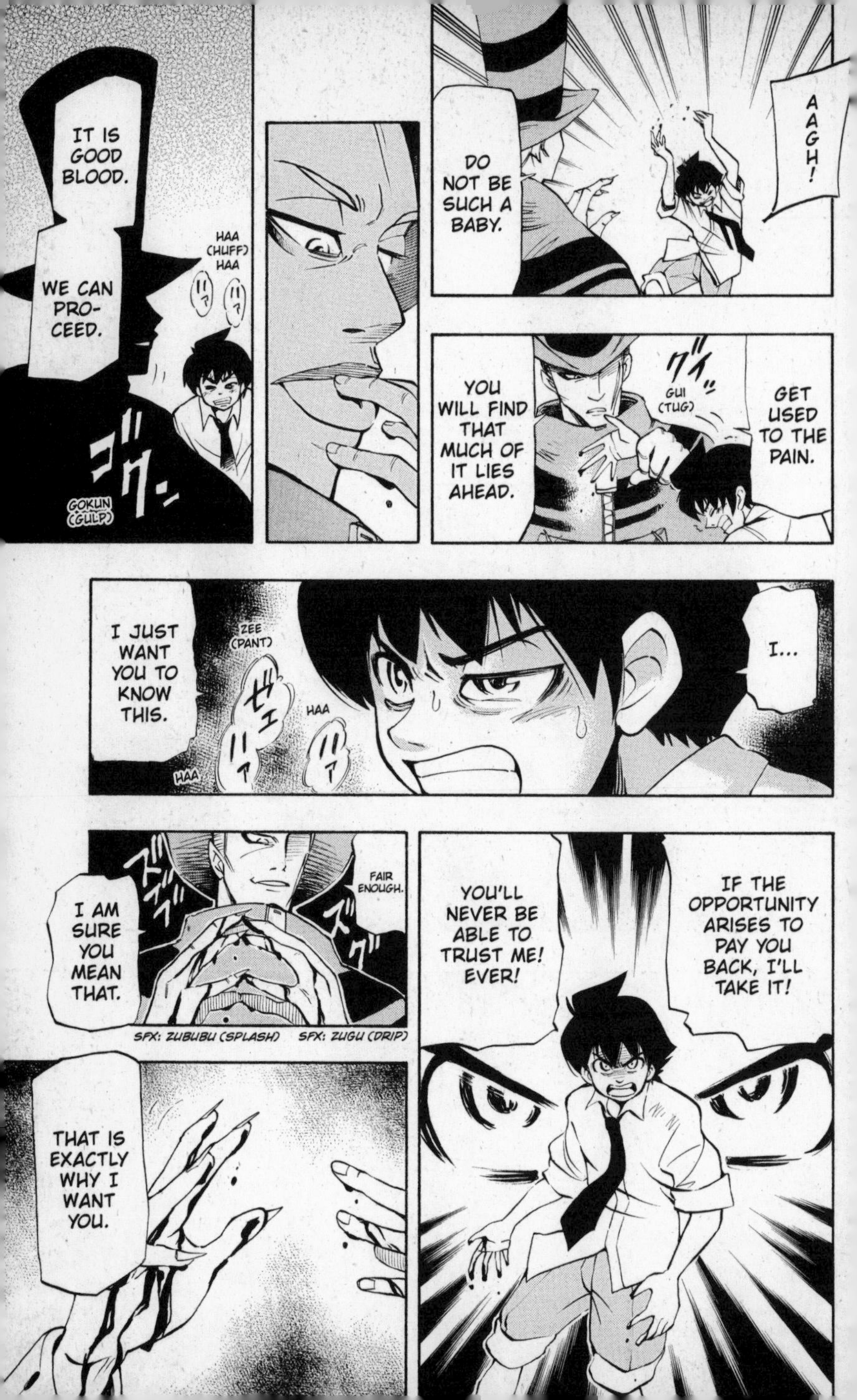
AAGH!
DO NOT BE SUCH A BABY.
GET USED TO THE PAIN.
GUI (TUG)
YOU WILL FIND THAT MUCH OF IT LIES AHEAD.
IT IS GOOD BLOOD.
HAA (HUFF) HAA
WE CAN PROCEED.
GOKUN (GULP)
I...
I JUST WANT YOU TO KNOW THIS.
ZEE (PANT)
HAA
HAA
IF THE OPPORTUNITY ARISES TO PAY YOU BACK, I'LL TAKE IT!
YOU'LL NEVER BE ABLE TO TRUST ME! EVER!
FAIR ENOUGH.
I AM SURE YOU MEAN THAT.
SFX: ZUBUBU (SPLASH)
SFX: ZUGU (DRIP)
THAT IS EXACTLY WHY I WANT YOU.

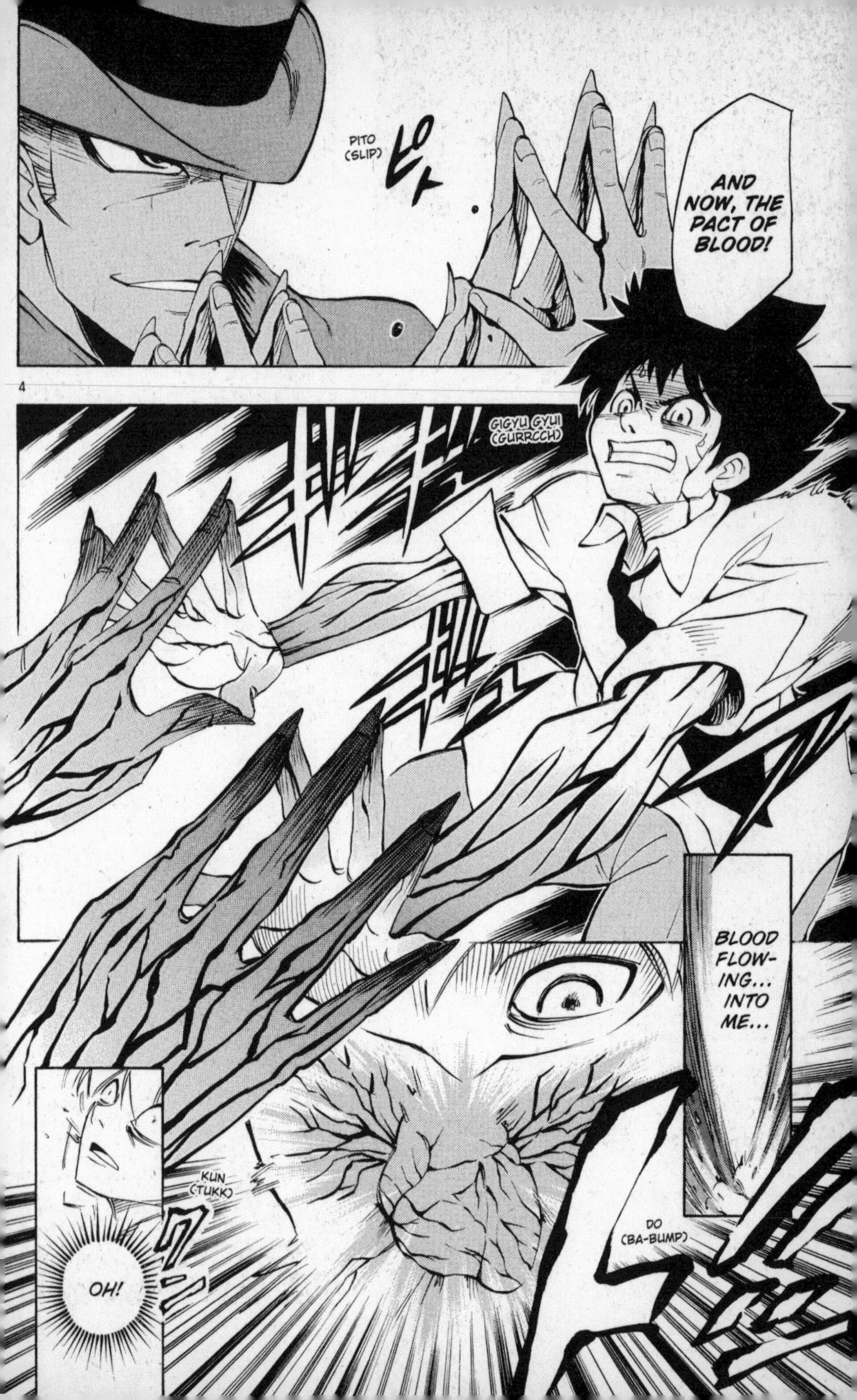
AND NOW, THE PACT OF BLOOD!
PITO (SLIP)
GIGYU GYUI (GURRCCH)
BLOOD FLOWING... INTO ME...
DO (BA-BUMP)
KUN (TUKK)
OH!

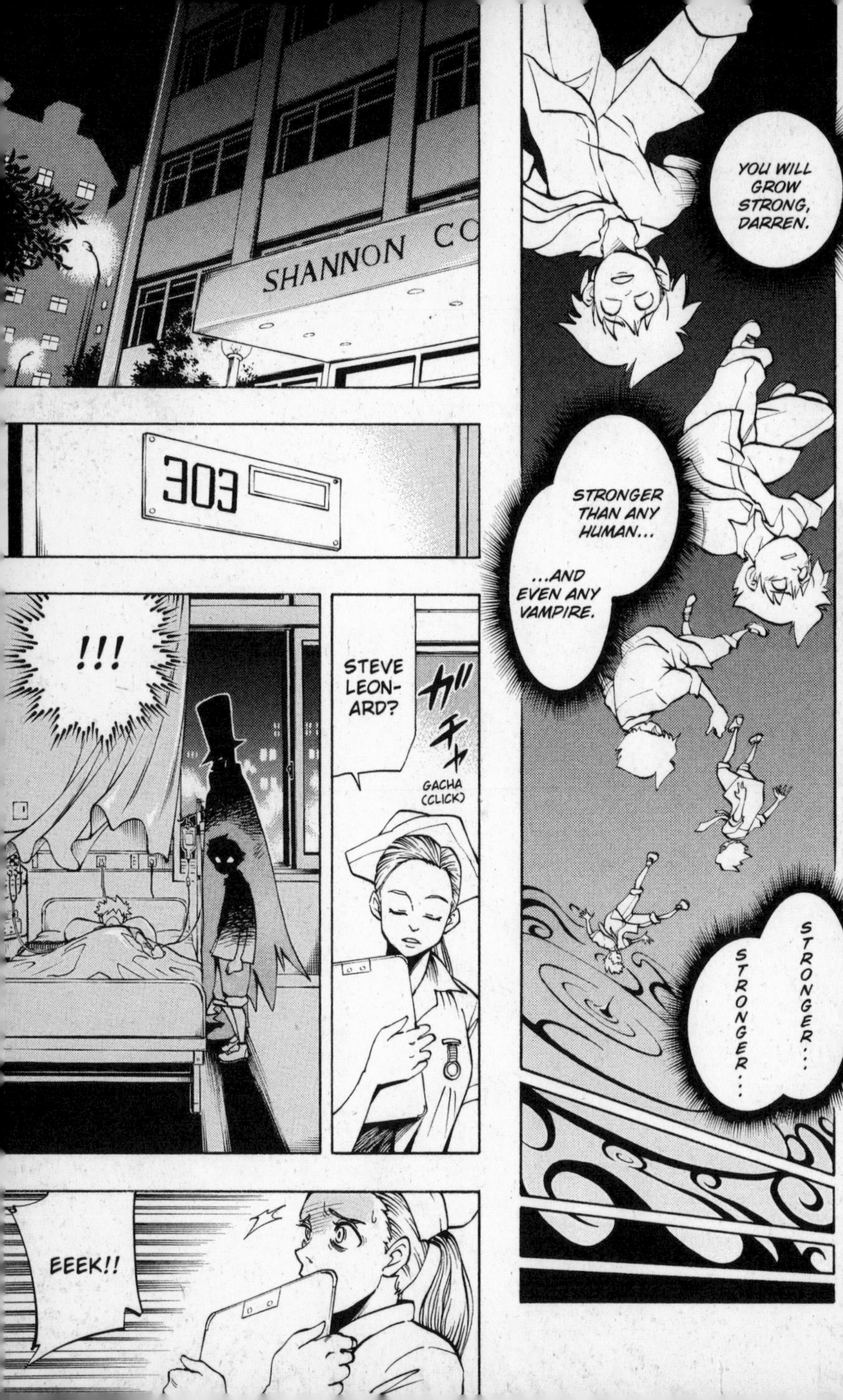
YOU WILL GROW STRONG, DARREN.
STRONGER THAN ANY HUMAN...
...AND EVEN ANY VAMPIRE.
STRONGER...
STRONGER...
SHANNON CO
303
STEVE LEON-ARD?
ガチャ
GACHA (CLICK)
!!!
EEEK!!

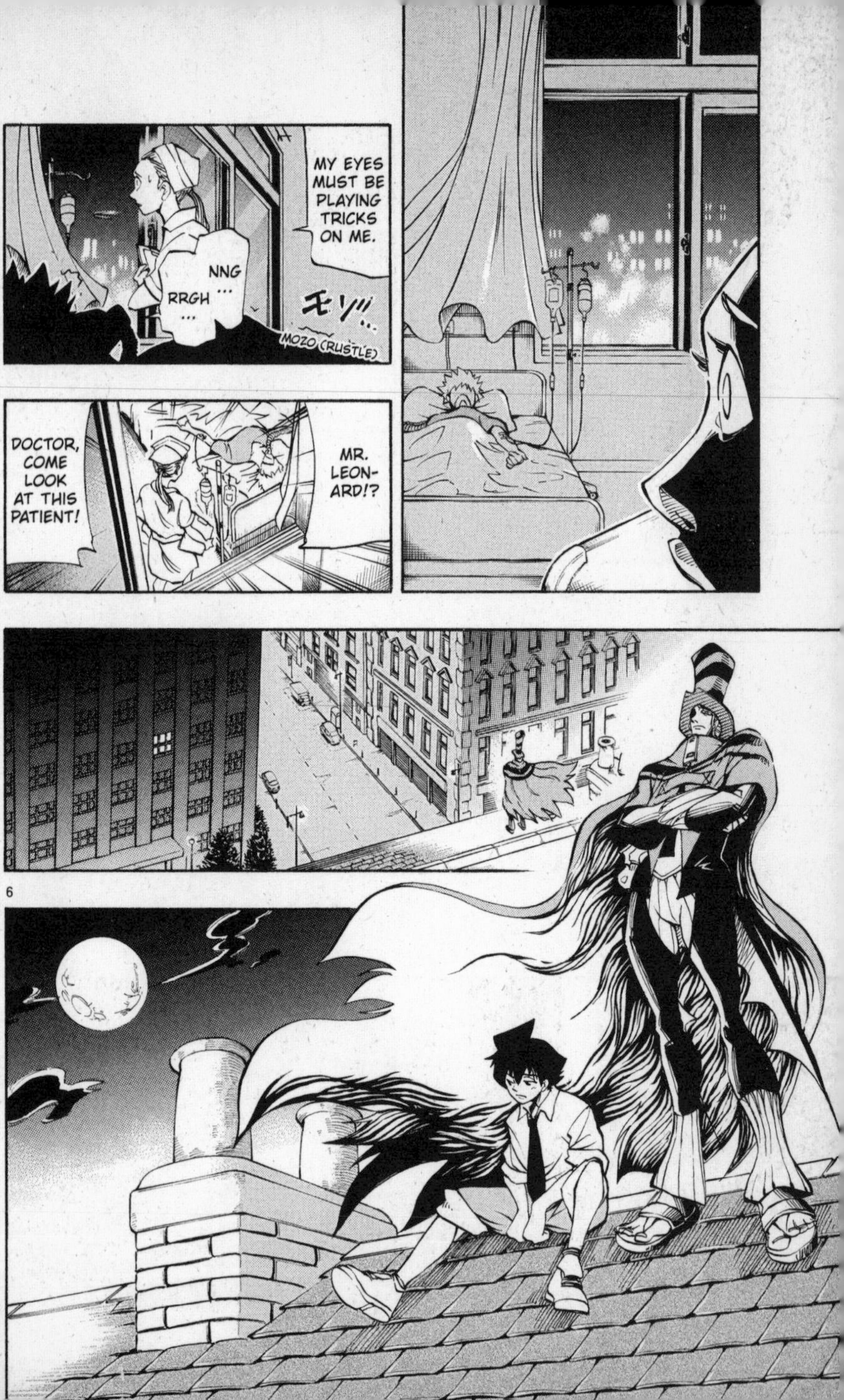
MY EYES MUST BE PLAYING TRICKS ON ME.
NNG...
RRGH...
モゾ...
MOZO (RUSTLE)
MR. LEONARD!?
DOCTOR, COME LOOK AT THIS PATIENT!
6

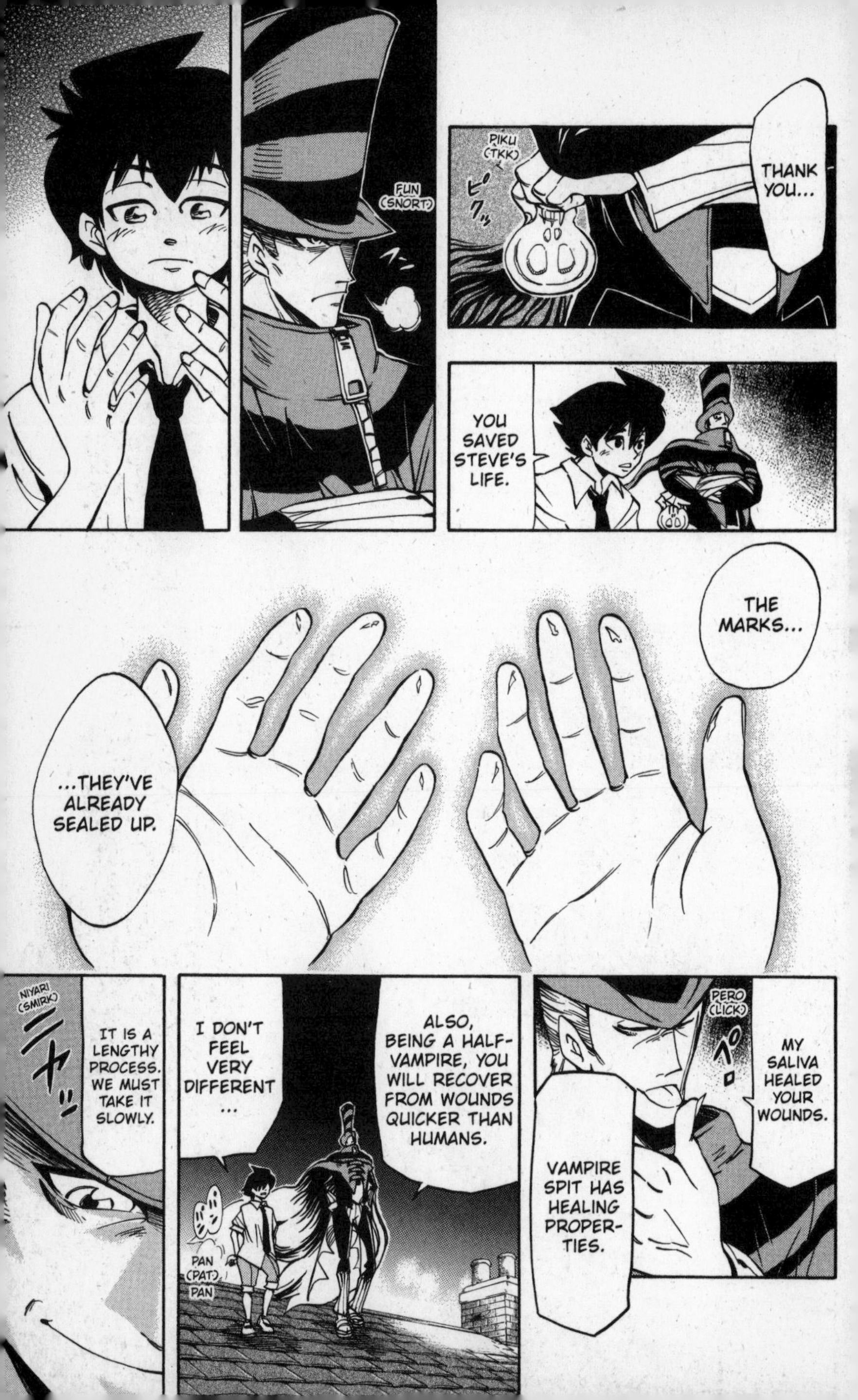

THANK YOU...
PIKU (TKK)
ピクッ
YOU SAVED STEVE'S LIFE.
FUN (SNORT)
THE MARKS...
...THEY'VE ALREADY SEALED UP.
PERO (LICK)
MY SALIVA HEALED YOUR WOUNDS.
VAMPIRE SPIT HAS HEALING PROPER-TIES.
ALSO, BEING A HALF-VAMPIRE, YOU WILL RECOVER FROM WOUNDS QUICKER THAN HUMANS.
I DON'T FEEL VERY DIFFERENT ...
PAN (PAT) PAN
NIYARI (SMIRK)
IT IS A LENGTHY PROCESS. WE MUST TAKE IT SLOWLY.

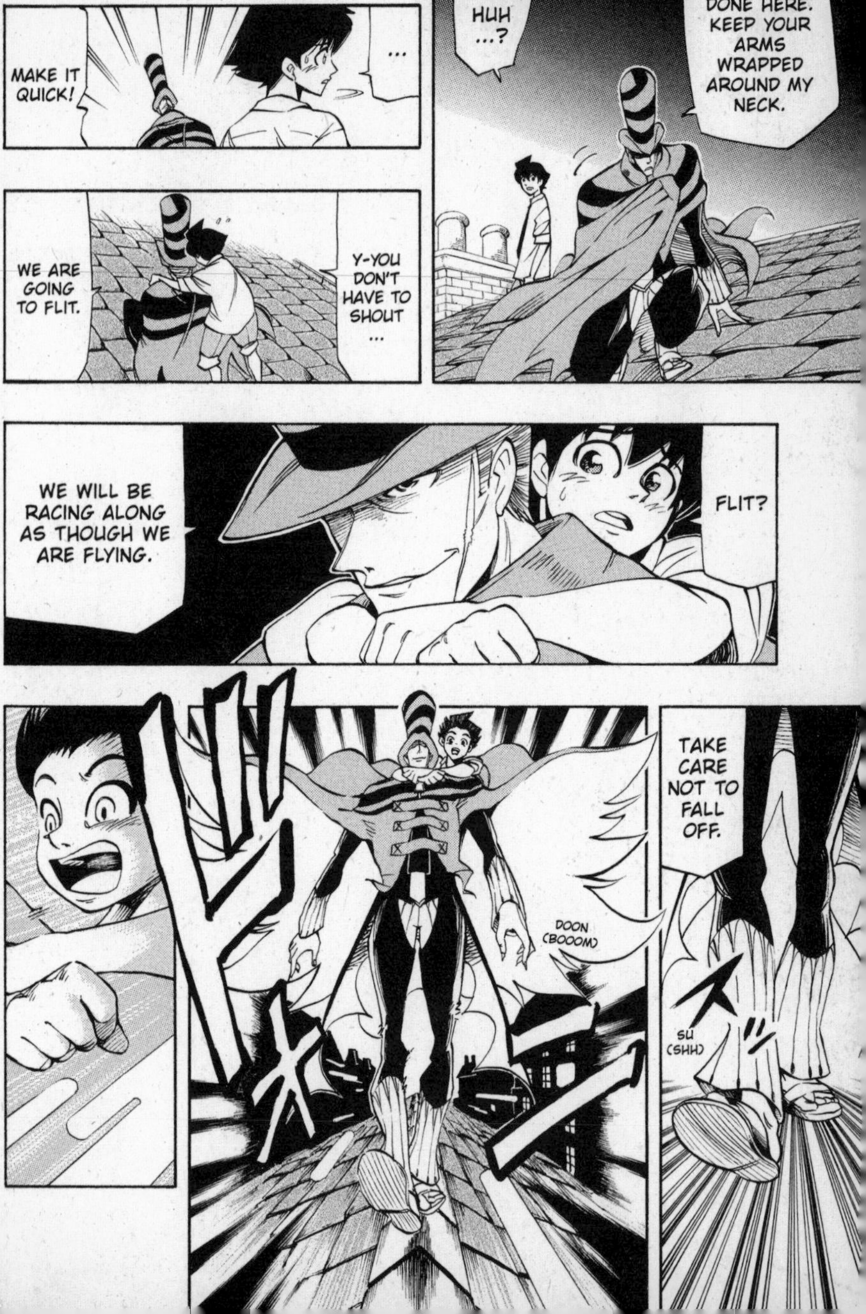
WE ARE DONE HERE. KEEP YOUR ARMS WRAPPED AROUND MY NECK.
HUH ...?
...
MAKE IT QUICK!
Y-YOU DON'T HAVE TO SHOUT ...
WE ARE GOING TO FLIT.
FLIT?
WE WILL BE RACING ALONG AS THOUGH WE ARE FLYING.
TAKE CARE NOT TO FALL OFF.
SU (SHH)
DOON (BOOOM)

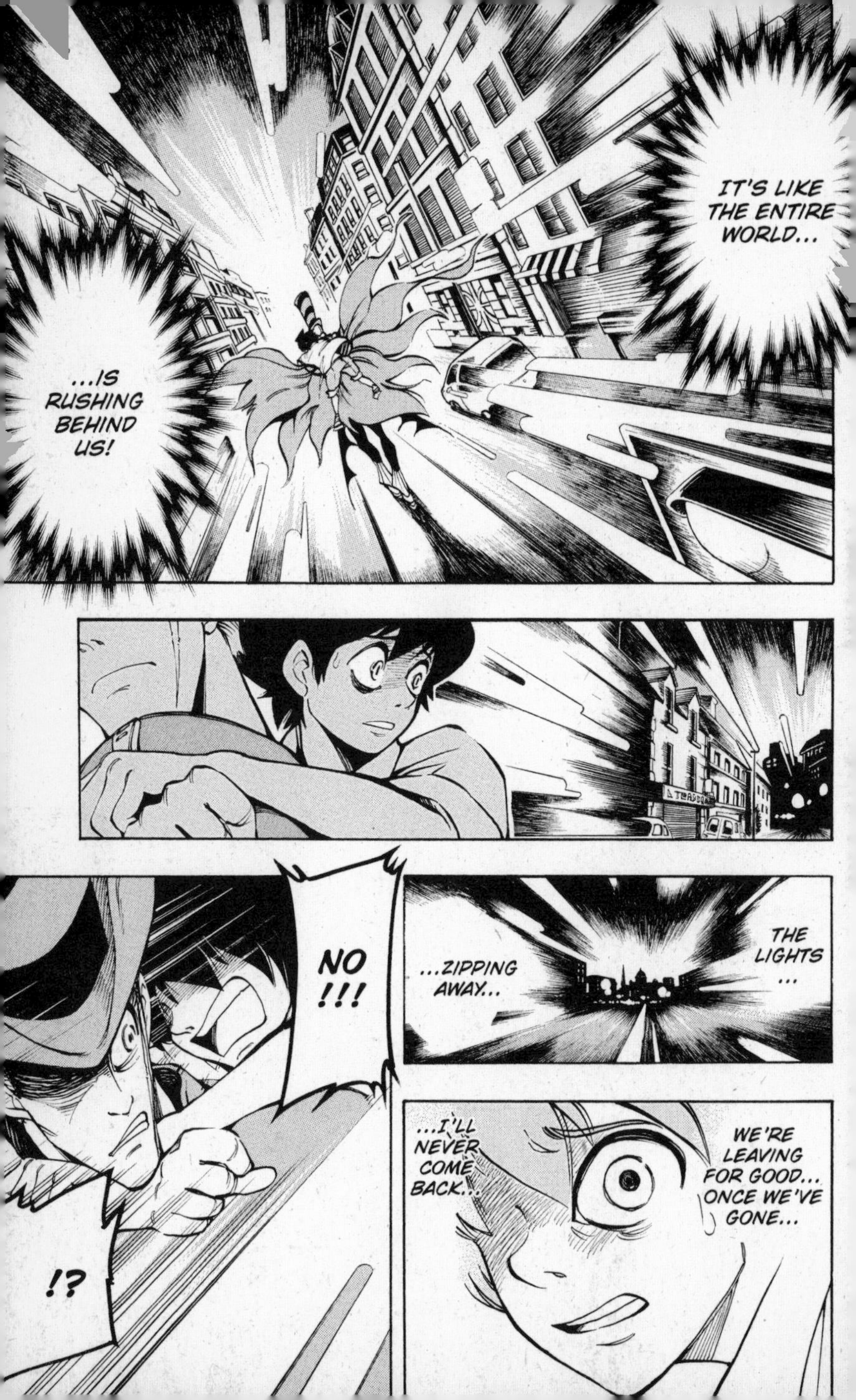
IT'S LIKE THE ENTIRE WORLD...
...IS RUSHING BEHIND US!
THE LIGHTS ...
...ZIPPING AWAY...
WE'RE LEAVING FOR GOOD... ONCE WE'VE GONE...
...I'LL NEVER COME BACK...
NO !!!
!?

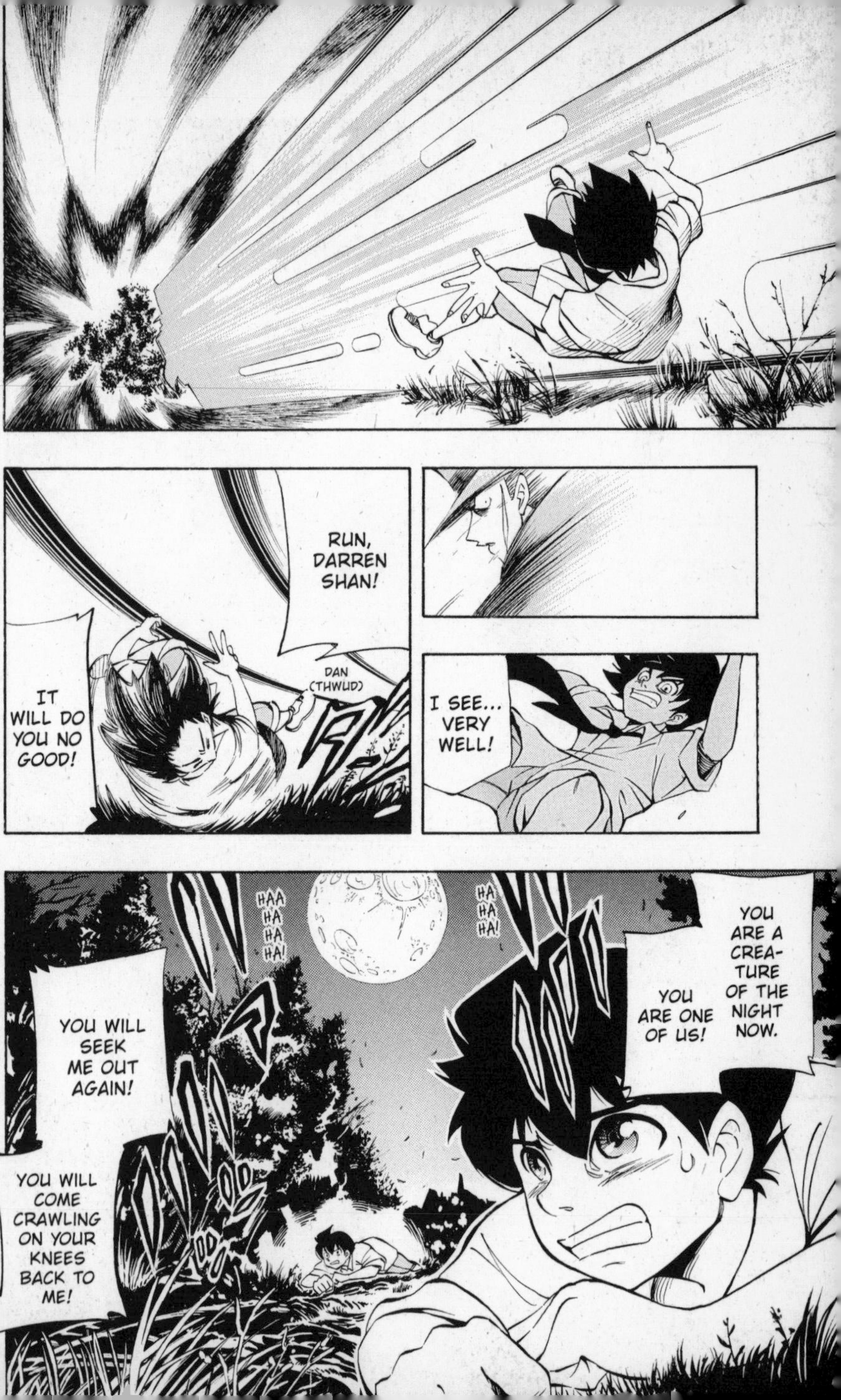
I SEE... VERY WELL!
RUN, DARREN SHAN!
DAN (THWUD)
IT WILL DO YOU NO GOOD!
YOU ARE A CREA-TURE OF THE NIGHT NOW.
YOU ARE ONE OF US!
HA HA HA!
HAA HA HA HA!
YOU WILL SEEK ME OUT AGAIN!
YOU WILL COME CRAWLING ON YOUR KNEES BACK TO ME!

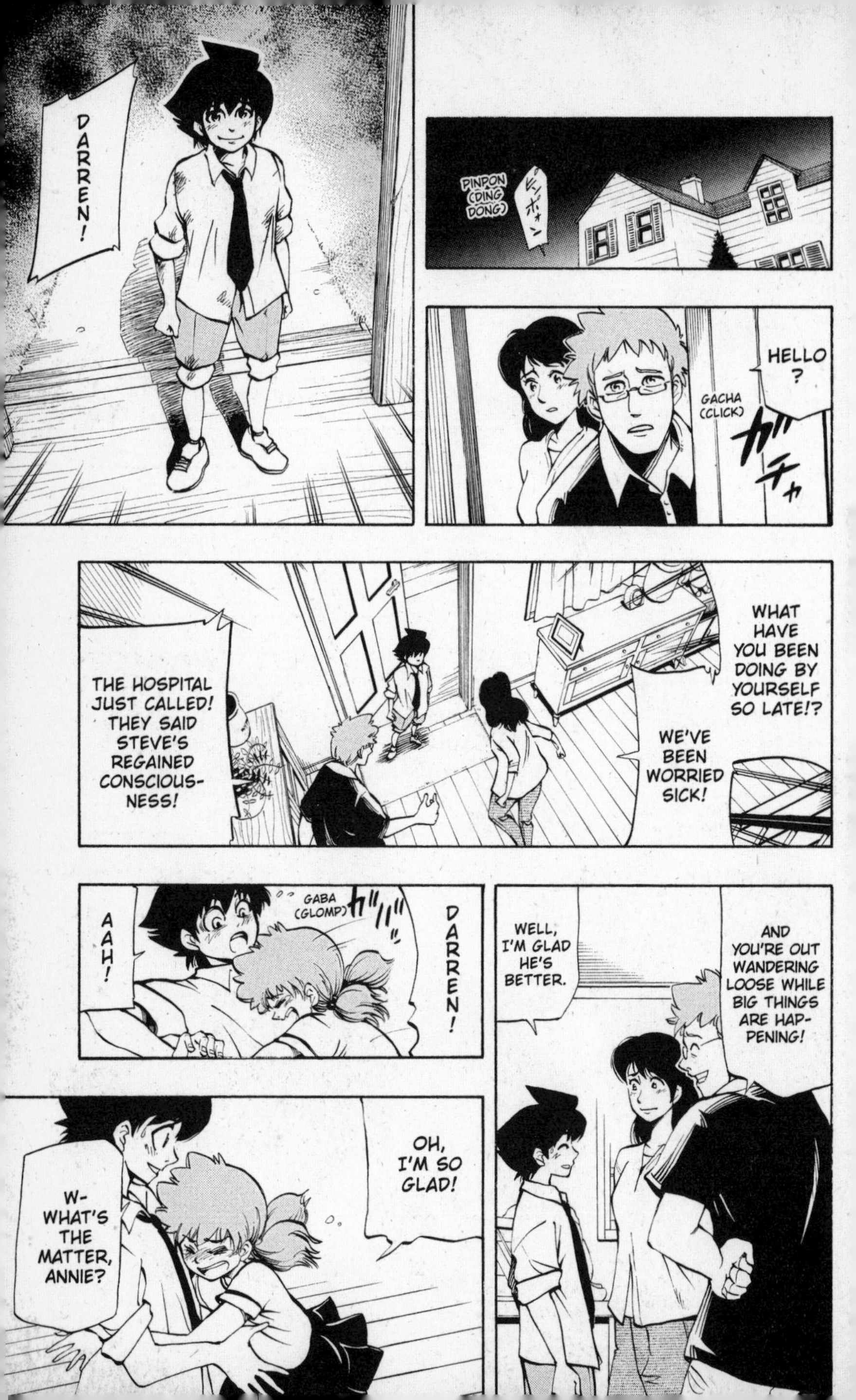
PINPON (DING DONG)
ピンポォン
HELLO?
GACHA (CLICK)
ガチャ
DARREN!
WHAT HAVE YOU BEEN DOING BY YOURSELF SO LATE!?
WE'VE BEEN WORRIED SICK!
THE HOSPITAL JUST CALLED! THEY SAID STEVE'S REGAINED CONSCIOUS-NESS!
AND YOU'RE OUT WANDERING LOOSE WHILE BIG THINGS ARE HAP-PENING!
WELL, I'M GLAD HE'S BETTER.
DARREN!
GABA (GLOMP)
AAH!
OH, I'M SO GLAD!
W-WHAT'S THE MATTER, ANNIE?

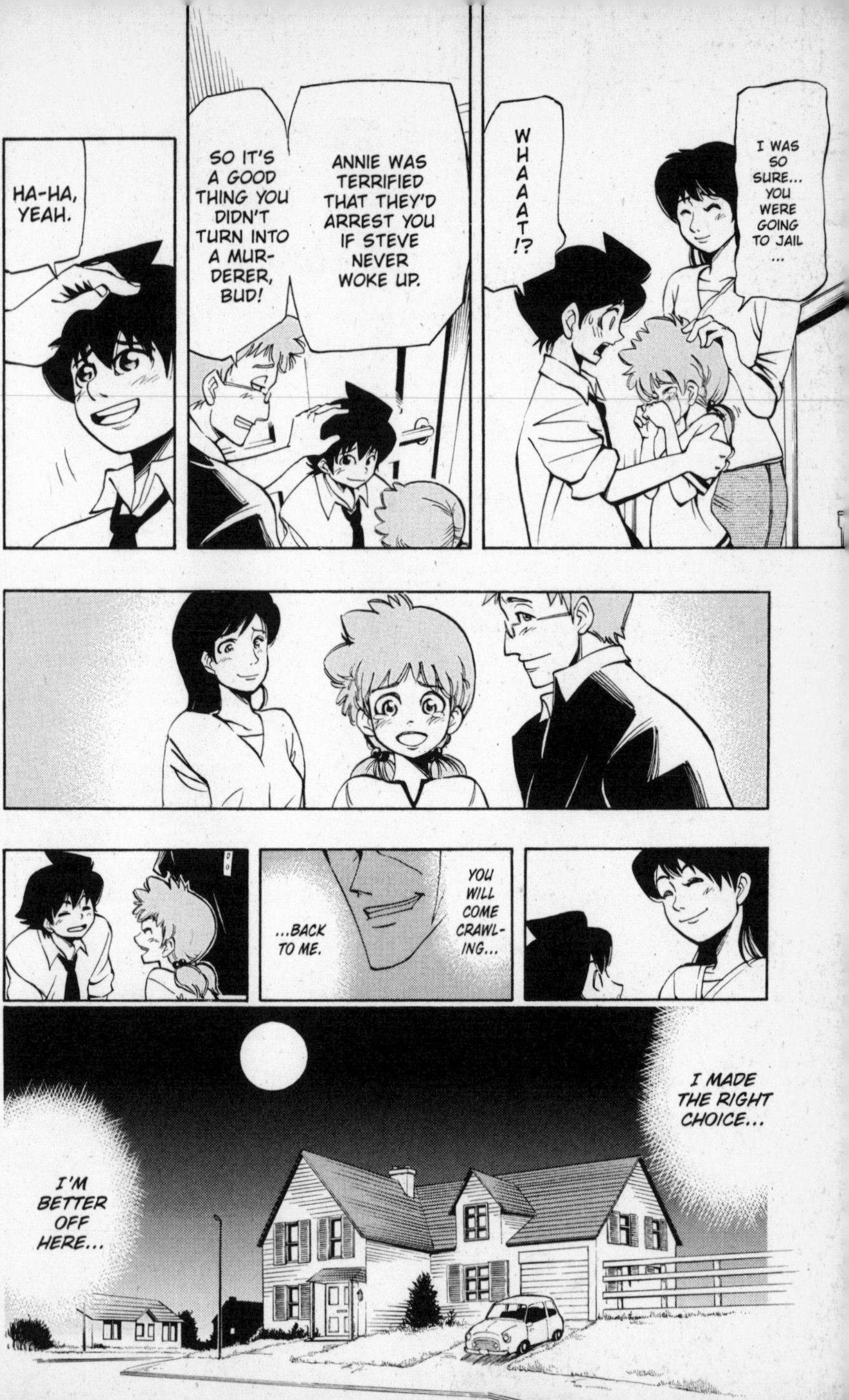
HA-HA, YEAH.
SO IT'S A GOOD THING YOU DIDN'T TURN INTO A MUR-DERER, BUD!
ANNIE WAS TERRIFIED THAT THEY'D ARREST YOU IF STEVE NEVER WOKE UP.
WHAAAAT!?
I WAS SO SURE... YOU WERE GOING TO JAIL ...
...BACK TO ME.
YOU WILL COME CRAWL-ING...
I MADE THE RIGHT CHOICE...
I'M BETTER OFF HERE...

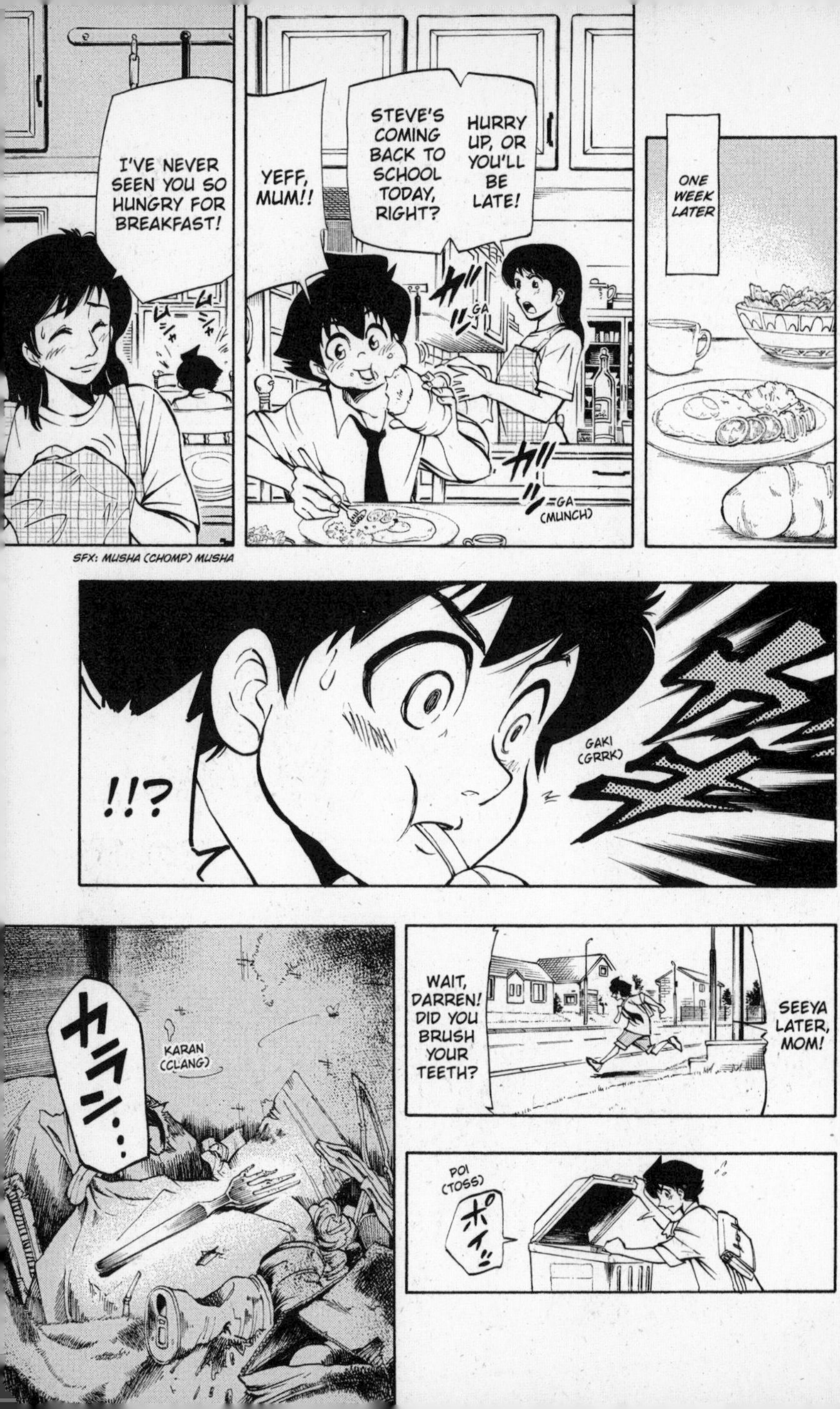
ONE WEEK LATER
HURRY UP, OR YOU'LL BE LATE!
STEVE'S COMING BACK TO SCHOOL TODAY, RIGHT?
GA
YEFF, MUM!!
GA (MUNCH)
I'VE NEVER SEEN YOU SO HUNGRY FOR BREAKFAST!
SFX: MUSHA (CHOMP) MUSHA
GAKI (GRRK)
!!?
SEEYA LATER, MOM!
WAIT, DARREN! DID YOU BRUSH YOUR TEETH?
POI (TOSS)
KARAN (CLANG)

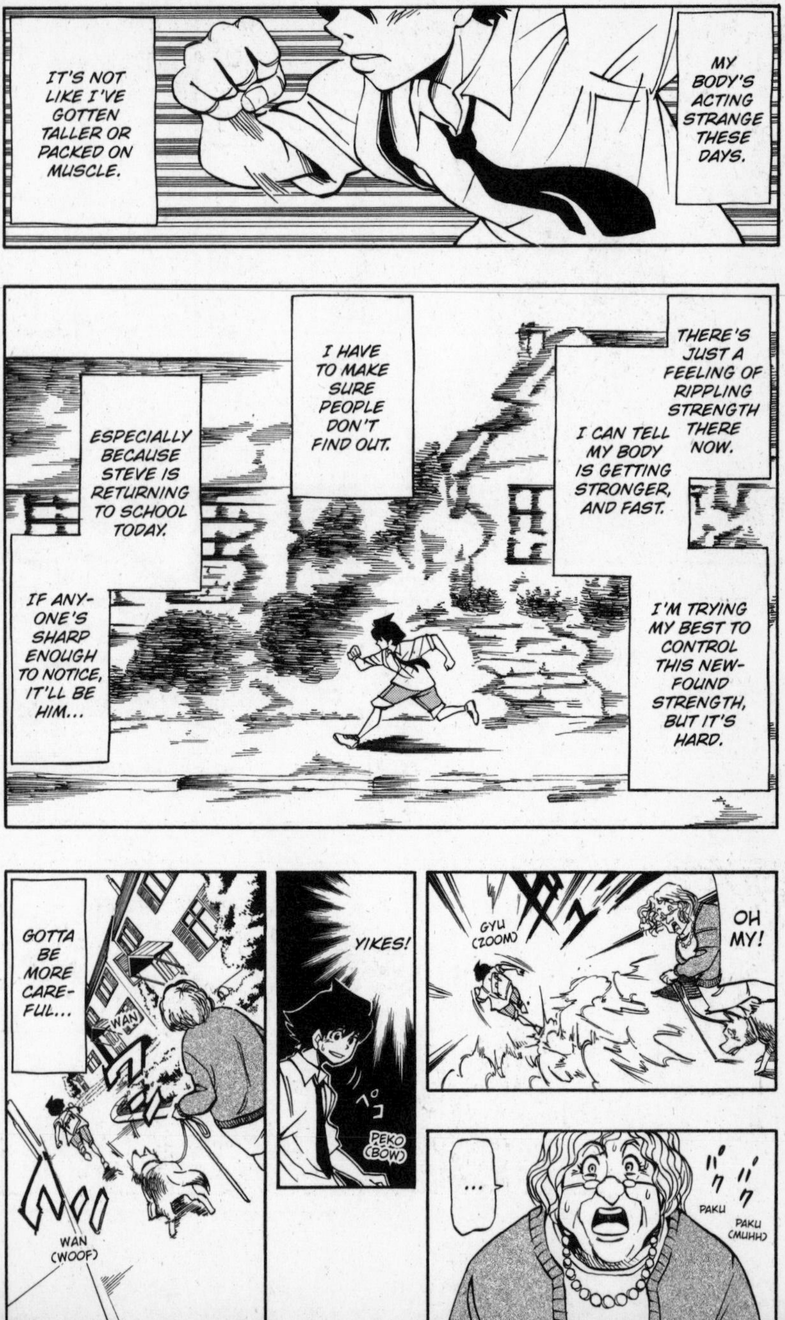
MY BODY'S ACTING STRANGE THESE DAYS.
IT'S NOT LIKE I'VE GOTTEN TALLER OR PACKED ON MUSCLE.
THERE'S JUST A FEELING OF RIPPLING STRENGTH THERE NOW.
I CAN TELL MY BODY IS GETTING STRONGER, AND FAST.
I HAVE TO MAKE SURE PEOPLE DON'T FIND OUT.
ESPECIALLY BECAUSE STEVE IS RETURNING TO SCHOOL TODAY.
I'M TRYING MY BEST TO CONTROL THIS NEW-FOUND STRENGTH, BUT IT'S HARD.
IF ANYONE'S SHARP ENOUGH TO NOTICE, IT'LL BE HIM...
OH MY!
GYU (ZOOM)
YIKES!
PEKO (BOW)
GOTTA BE MORE CAREFUL...
WAN
WAN (WOOF)
...
PAKU
PAKU (MUHH)

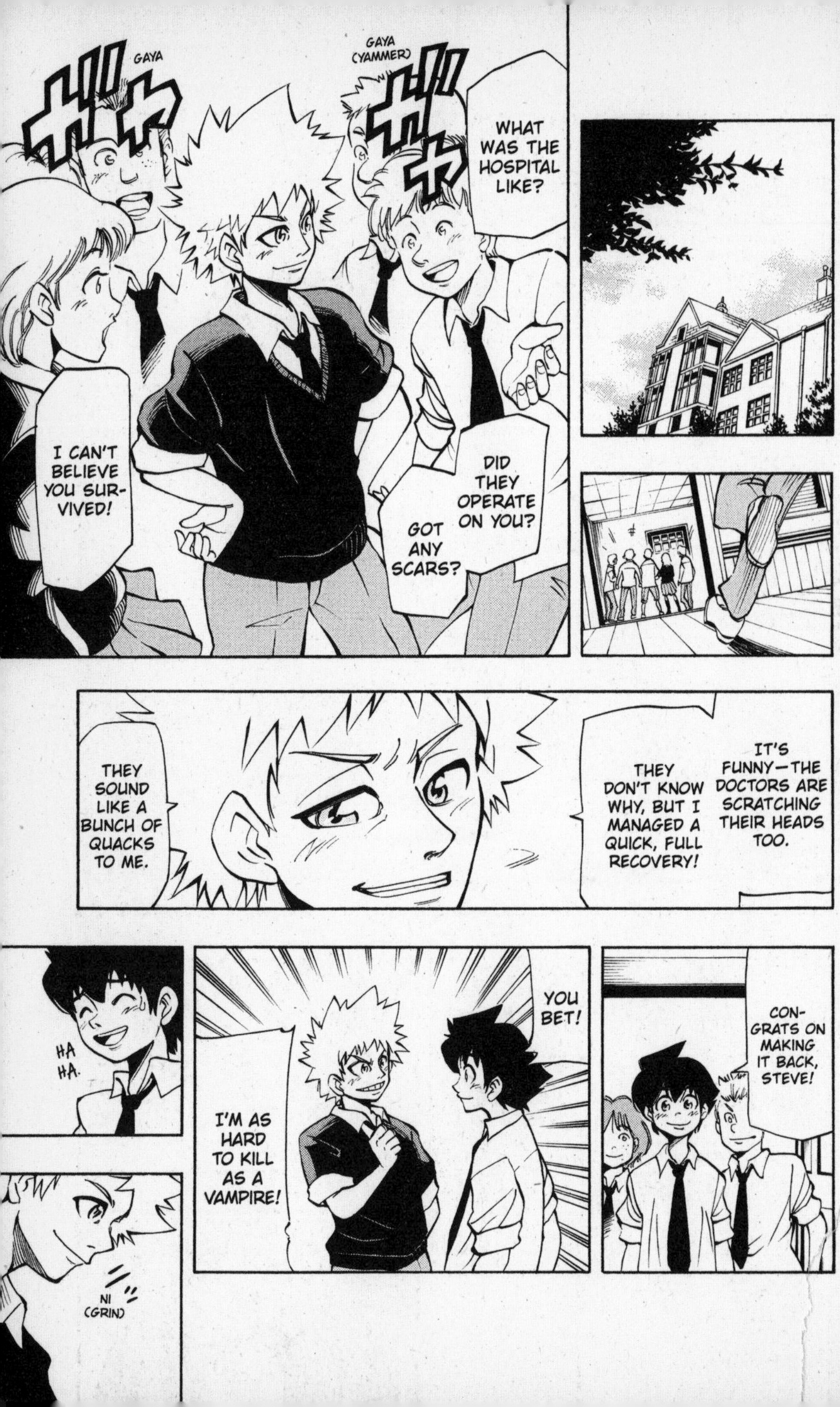
GAYA (YAMMER)
WHAT WAS THE HOSPITAL LIKE?
DID THEY OPERATE ON YOU?
GOT ANY SCARS?
GAYA
I CAN'T BELIEVE YOU SURVIVED!
IT'S FUNNY—THE DOCTORS ARE SCRATCHING THEIR HEADS TOO.
THEY DON'T KNOW WHY, BUT I MANAGED A QUICK, FULL RECOVERY!
THEY SOUND LIKE A BUNCH OF QUACKS TO ME.
CONGRATS ON MAKING IT BACK, STEVE!
NI
YOU BET!
I'M AS HARD TO KILL AS A VAMPIRE!
HA HA.
NI (GRIN)

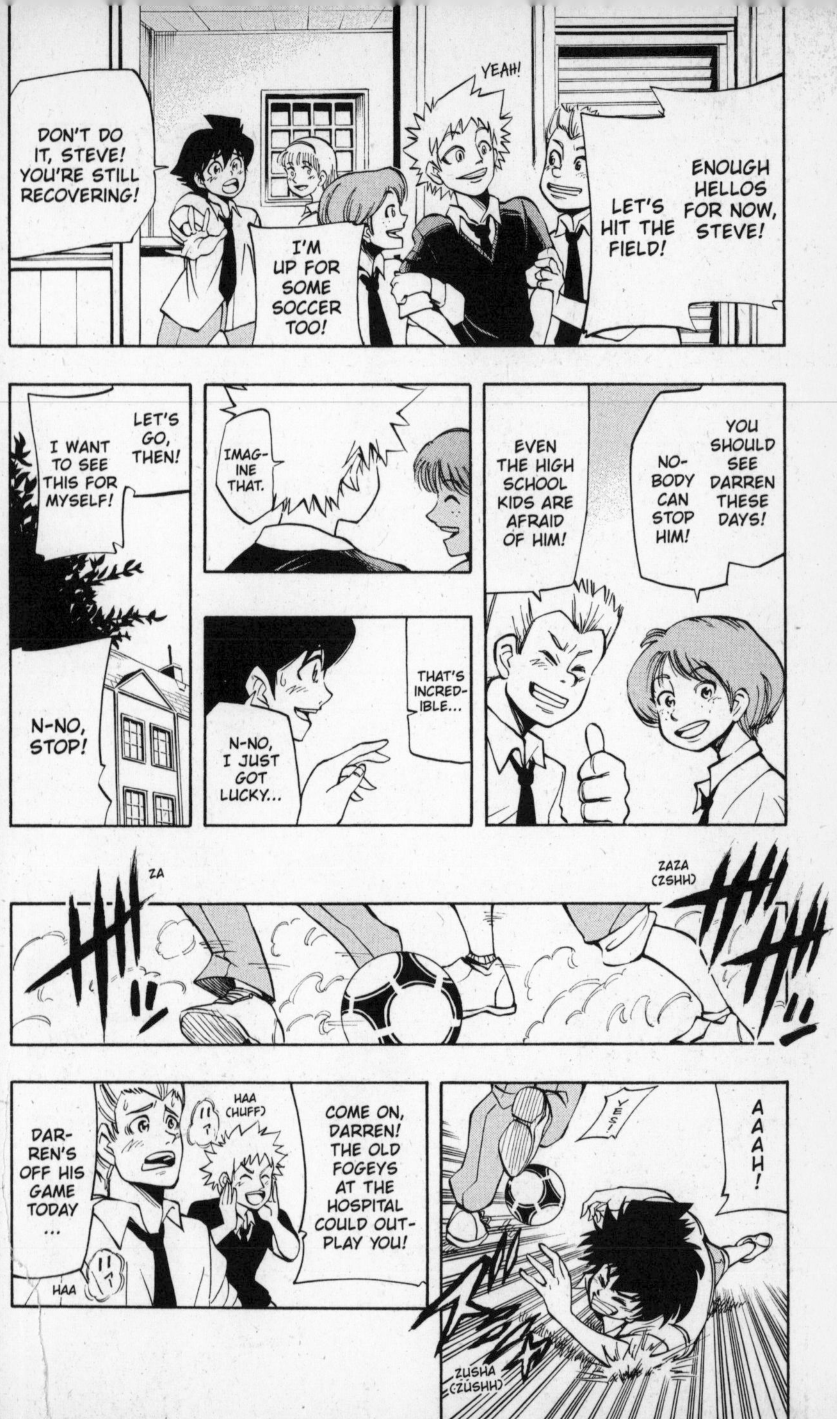
ENOUGH HELLOS FOR NOW, STEVE!
LET'S HIT THE FIELD!
YEAH!
I'M UP FOR SOME SOCCER TOO!
DON'T DO IT, STEVE! YOU'RE STILL RECOVERING!
YOU SHOULD SEE DARREN THESE DAYS!
NOBODY CAN STOP HIM!
EVEN THE HIGH SCHOOL KIDS ARE AFRAID OF HIM!
IMAGINE THAT.
THAT'S INCREDIBLE...
N-NO, I JUST GOT LUCKY...
LET'S GO, THEN!
I WANT TO SEE THIS FOR MYSELF!
N-NO, STOP!
ZAZA (ZSHH)
ZA
AAAH!
YES!
ZUSHA (ZUSHH)
COME ON, DARREN! THE OLD FOGEYS AT THE HOSPITAL COULD OUTPLAY YOU!
HAA (HUFF)
DARREN'S OFF HIS GAME TODAY...
HAA

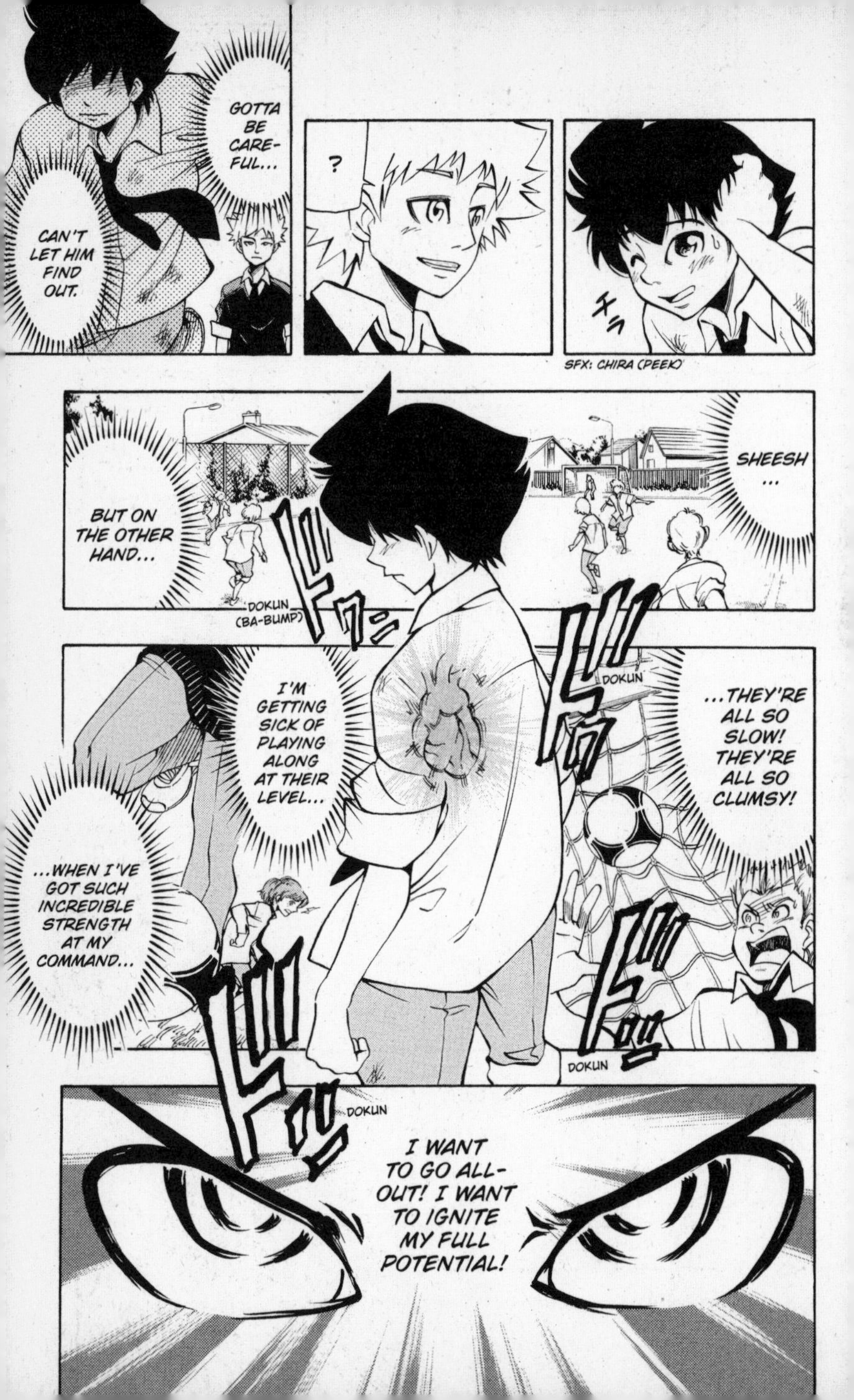
?
SFX: CHIRA (PEEK)
GOTTA BE CARE-FUL...
CAN'T LET HIM FIND OUT.
SHEESH...
BUT ON THE OTHER HAND...
DOKUN (BA-BUMP)
...THEY'RE ALL SO SLOW! THEY'RE ALL SO CLUMSY!
DOKUN
I'M GETTING SICK OF PLAYING ALONG AT THEIR LEVEL...
...WHEN I'VE GOT SUCH INCREDIBLE STRENGTH AT MY COMMAND...
DOKUN
DOKUN
I WANT TO GO ALL-OUT! I WANT TO IGNITE MY FULL POTENTIAL!

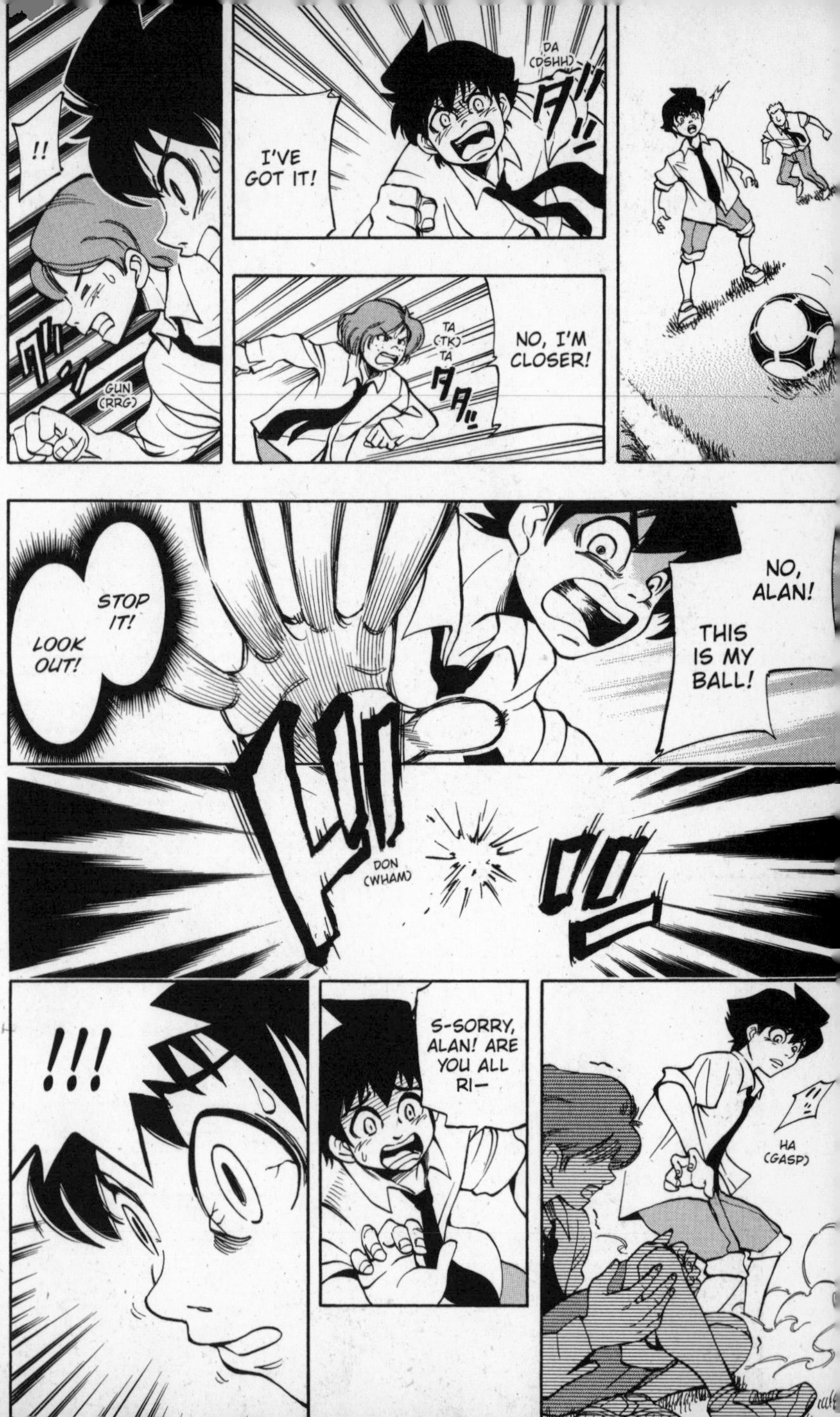
DA (DSHH)
I'VE GOT IT!
TA (TK) TA
NO, I'M CLOSER!
!!
GUN (RRG)
NO, ALAN! THIS IS MY BALL!
STOP IT! LOOK OUT!
DON (WHAM)
!!
HA (GASP)
S-SORRY, ALAN! ARE YOU ALL RI—
!!!

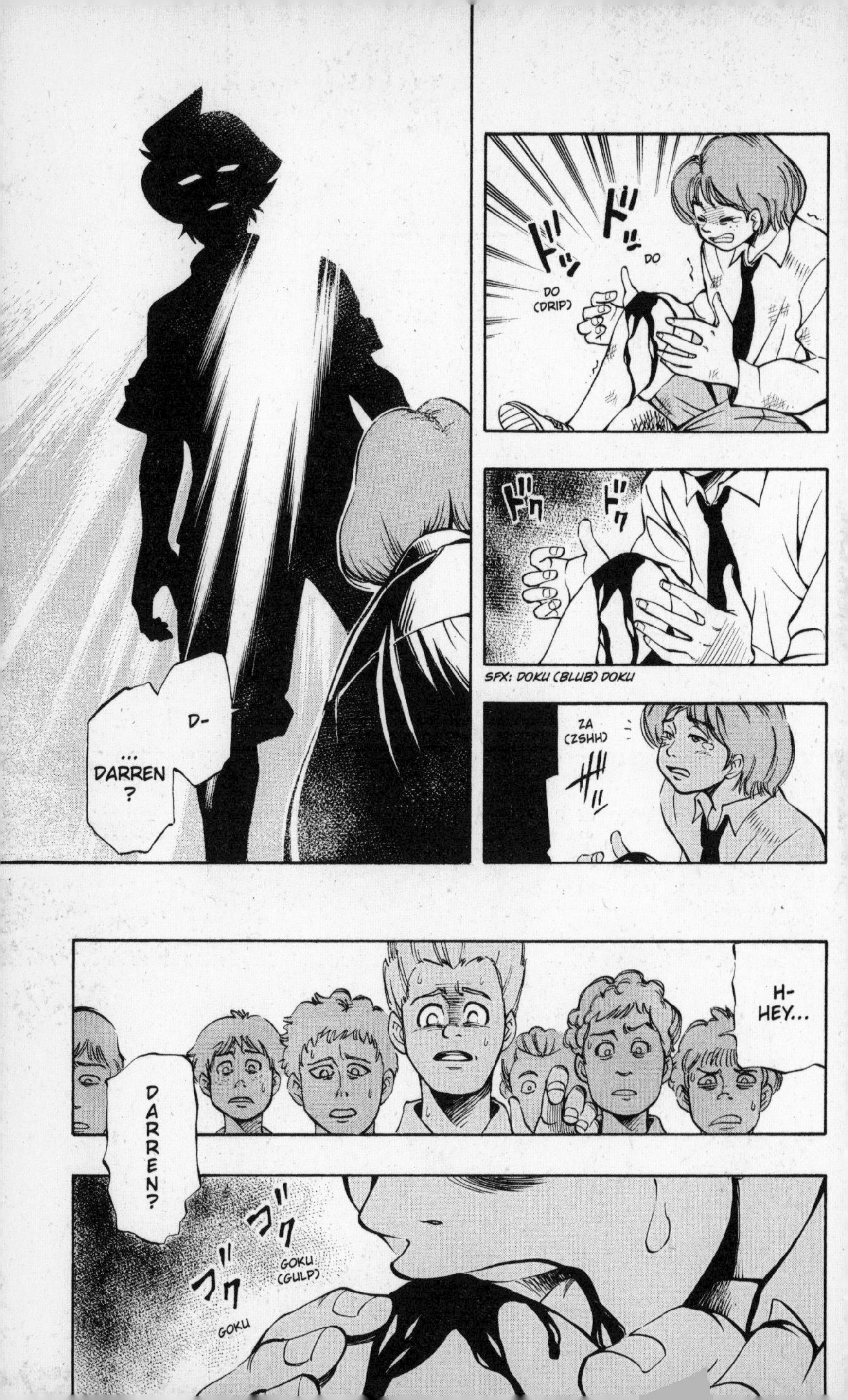
DO
DO (DRIP)
SFX: DOKU (BLUB) DOKU
ZA (ZSHH)
D- ... DARREN?
H- HEY...
DARREN?
GOKU (GULP)
GOKU

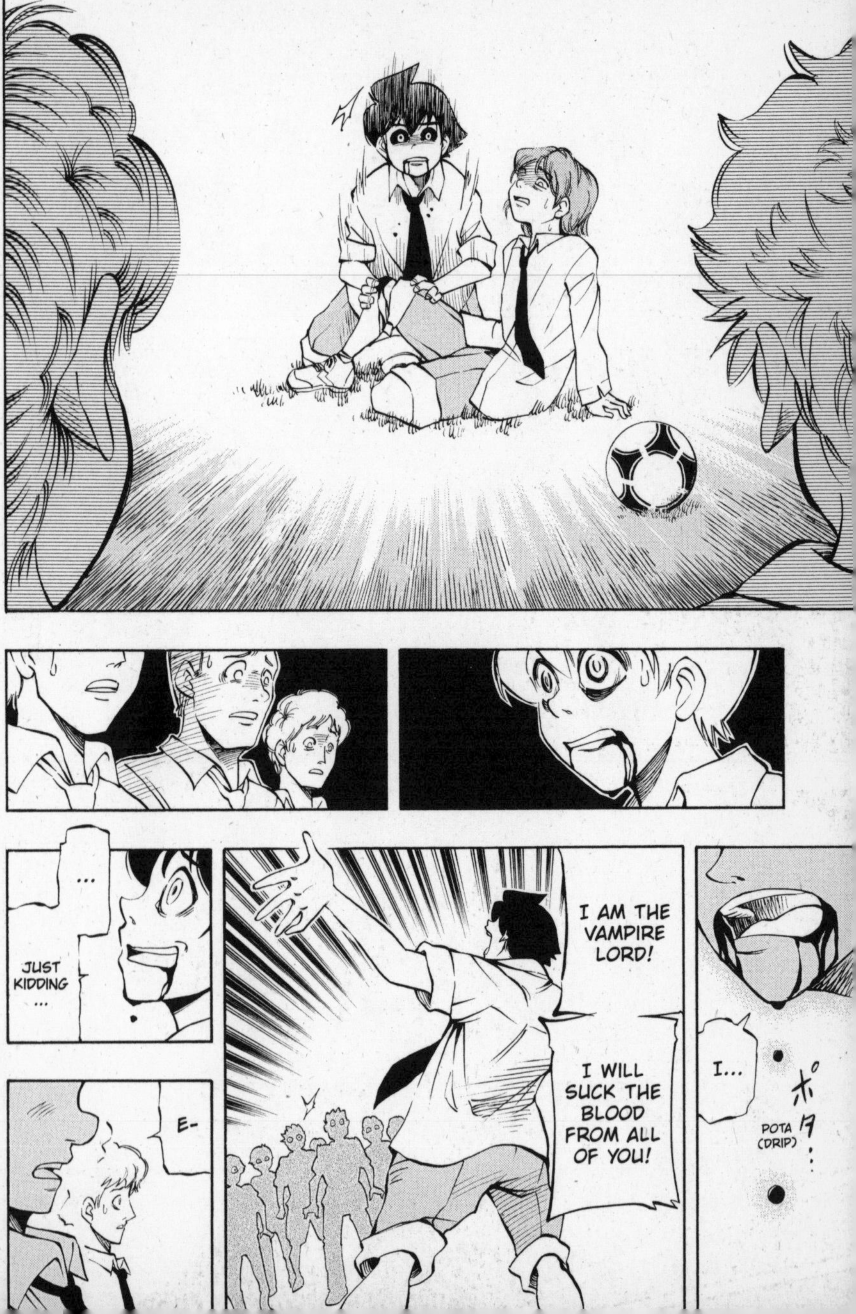
I...
POTA (DRIP)
I AM THE VAMPIRE LORD!
I WILL SUCK THE BLOOD FROM ALL OF YOU!
...
JUST KIDDING ...
E-

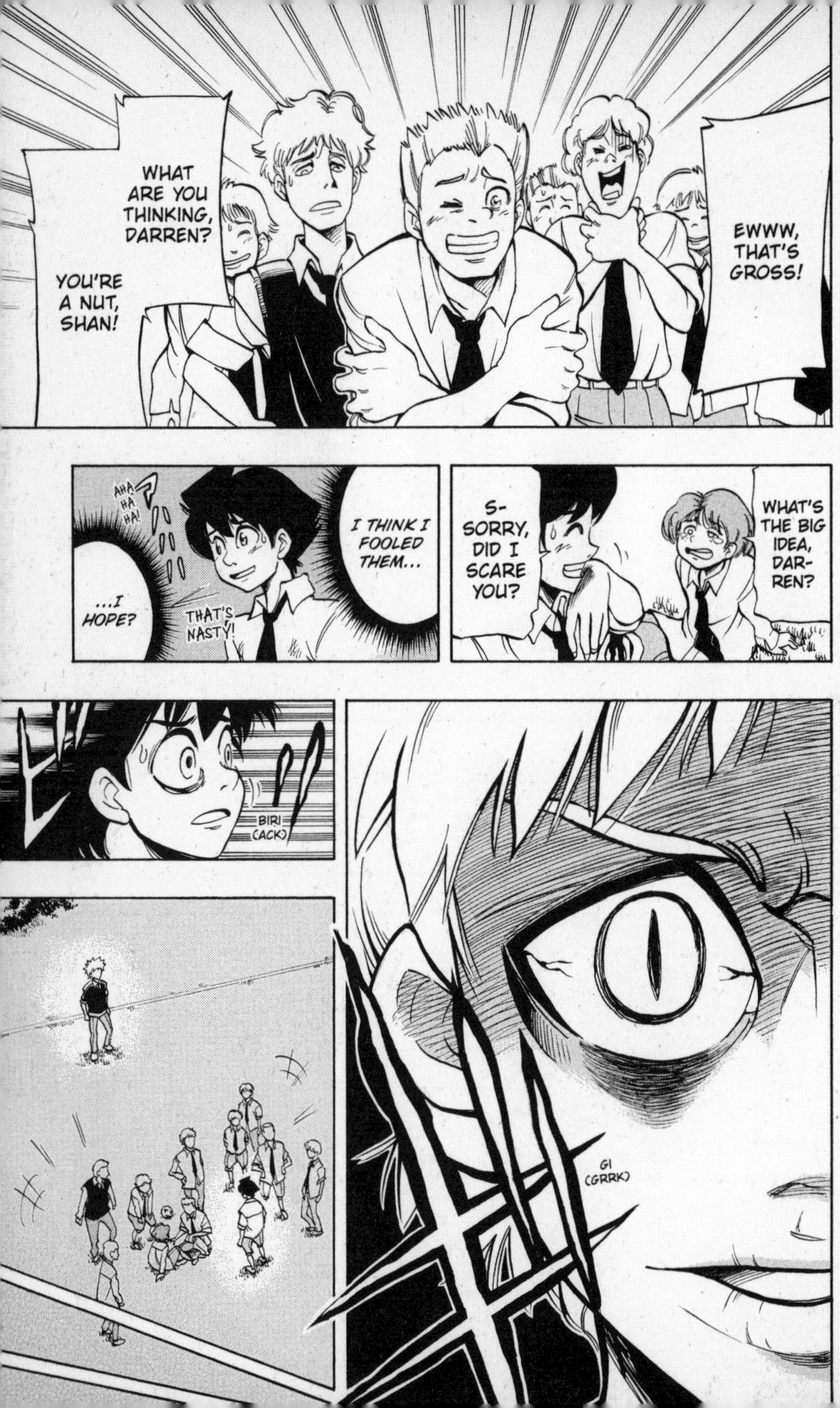
EWWW, THAT'S GROSS!
WHAT ARE YOU THINKING, DARREN?
YOU'RE A NUT, SHAN!
WHAT'S THE BIG IDEA, DAR-REN?
S-SORRY, DID I SCARE YOU?
I THINK I FOOLED THEM...
AHA HA HA!
THAT'S NASTY!
...I HOPE?
GI (GRRK)
BIRI (ACK)

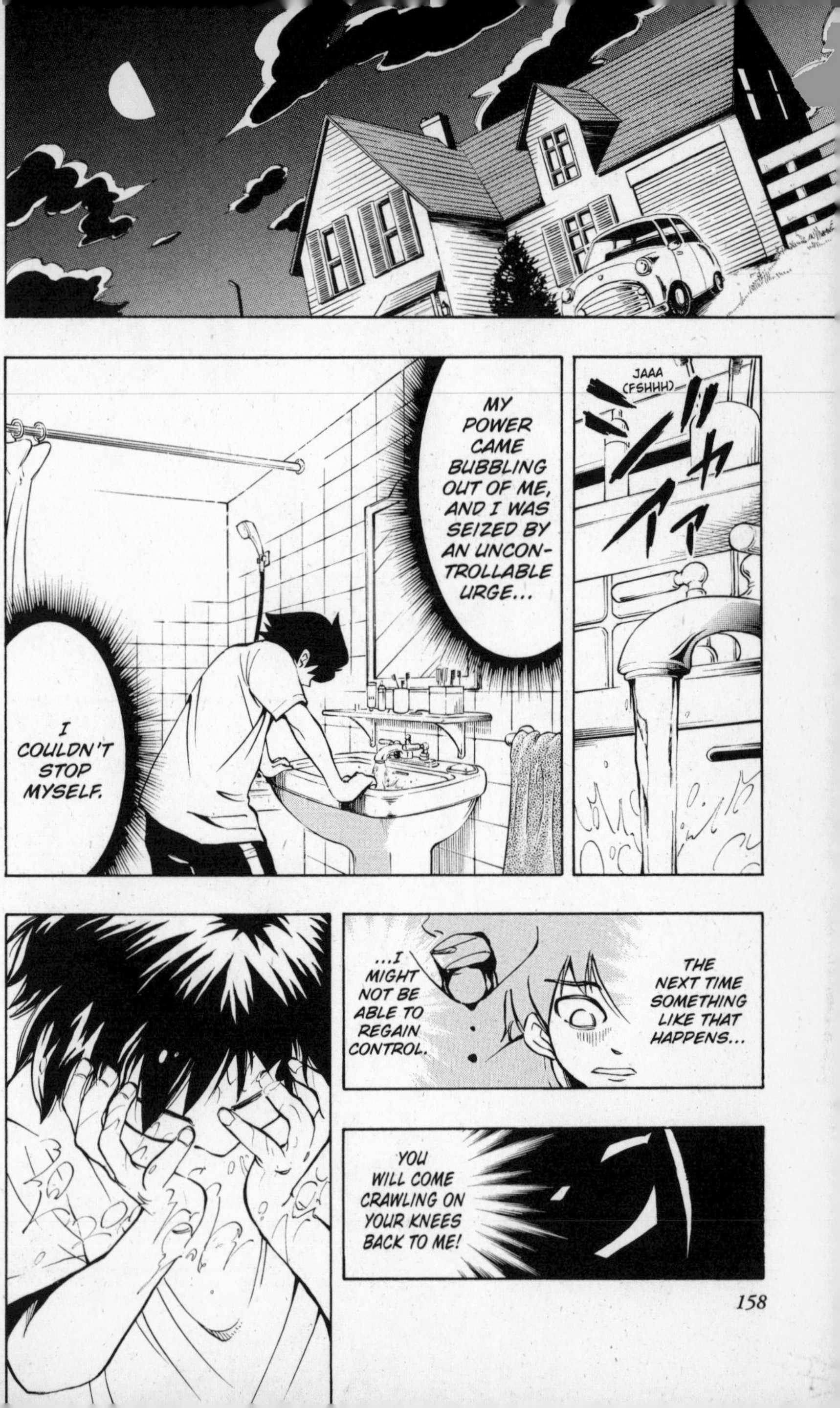
JAAA (FSHHH)
MY POWER CAME BUBBLING OUT OF ME, AND I WAS SEIZED BY AN UNCONTROLLABLE URGE...
I COULDN'T STOP MYSELF.
THE NEXT TIME SOMETHING LIKE THAT HAPPENS...
...I MIGHT NOT BE ABLE TO REGAIN CONTROL.
YOU WILL COME CRAWLING ON YOUR KNEES BACK TO ME!

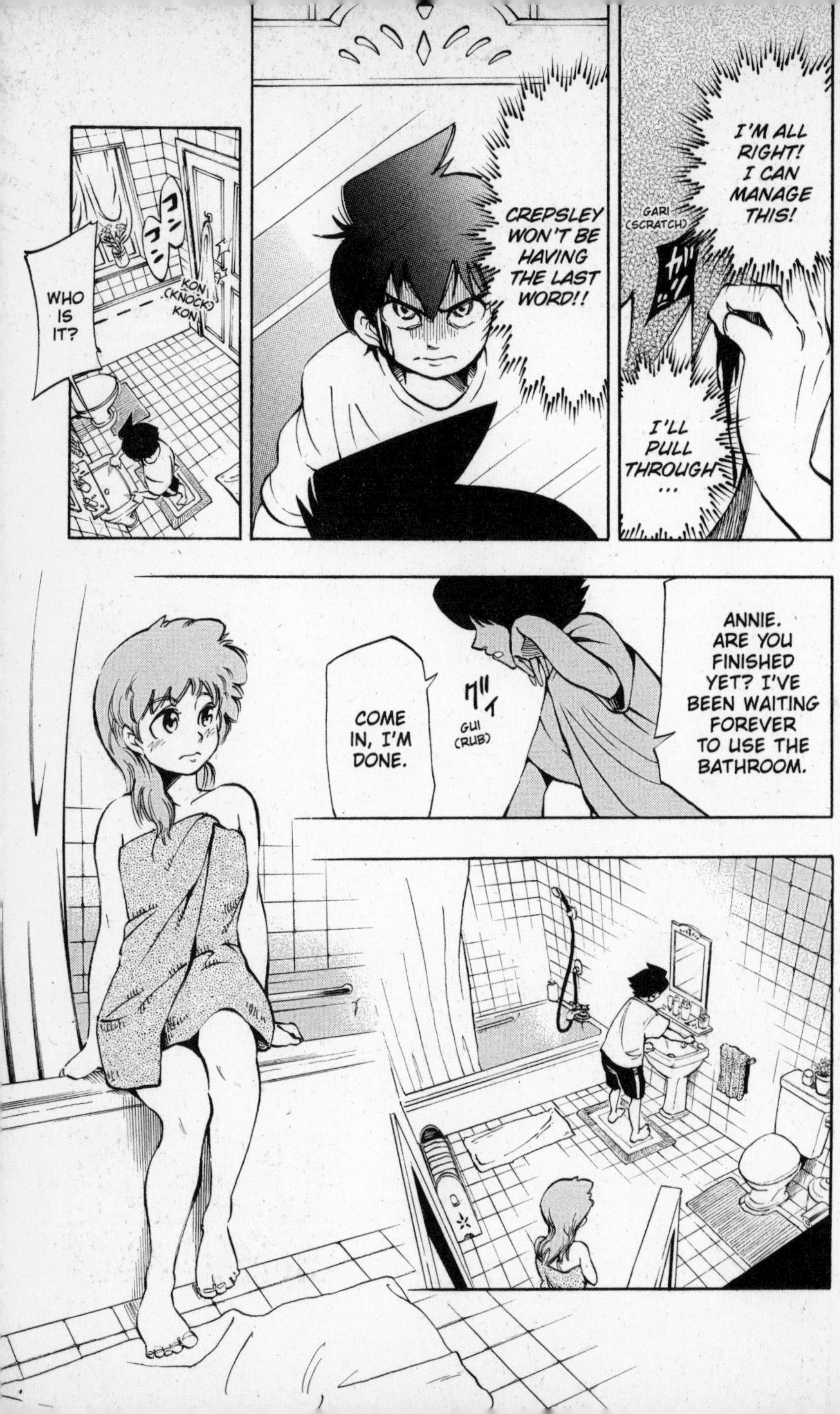
I'M ALL RIGHT! I CAN MANAGE THIS!
GARI (SCRATCH)
I'LL PULL THROUGH ...
CREPSLEY WON'T BE HAVING THE LAST WORD!!
KON (KNOCK) KON
WHO IS IT?
ANNIE. ARE YOU FINISHED YET? I'VE BEEN WAITING FOREVER TO USE THE BATHROOM.
GUI (RUB)
COME IN, I'M DONE.

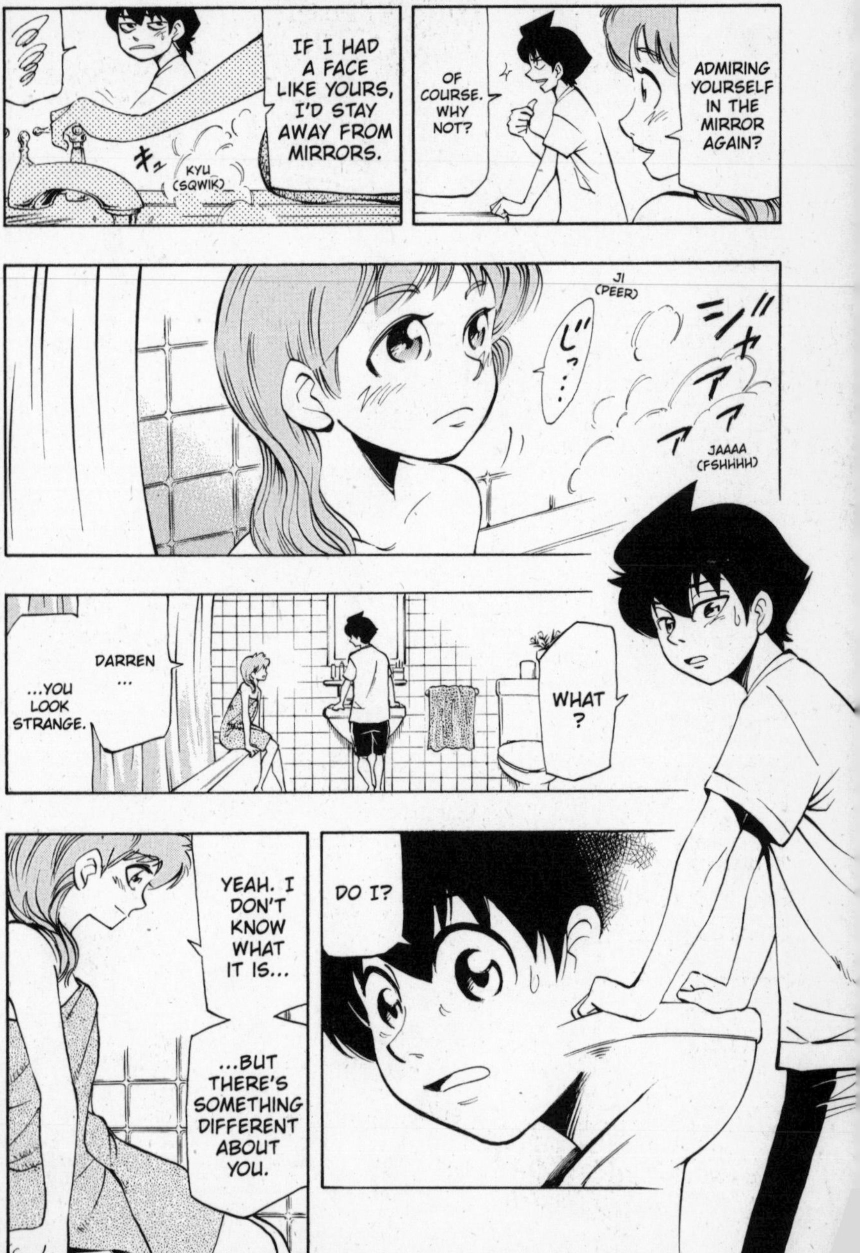
ADMIRING YOURSELF IN THE MIRROR AGAIN?
OF COURSE. WHY NOT?
IF I HAD A FACE LIKE YOURS, I'D STAY AWAY FROM MIRRORS.
キュ
KYU_ (SQWIK)_
シャアアア
JAAAA (FSHHHH)
じっ…
JI (PEER)
DARREN ...
WHAT?
...YOU LOOK STRANGE.
DO I?
YEAH. I DON'T KNOW WHAT IT IS...
...BUT THERE'S SOMETHING DIFFERENT ABOUT YOU.

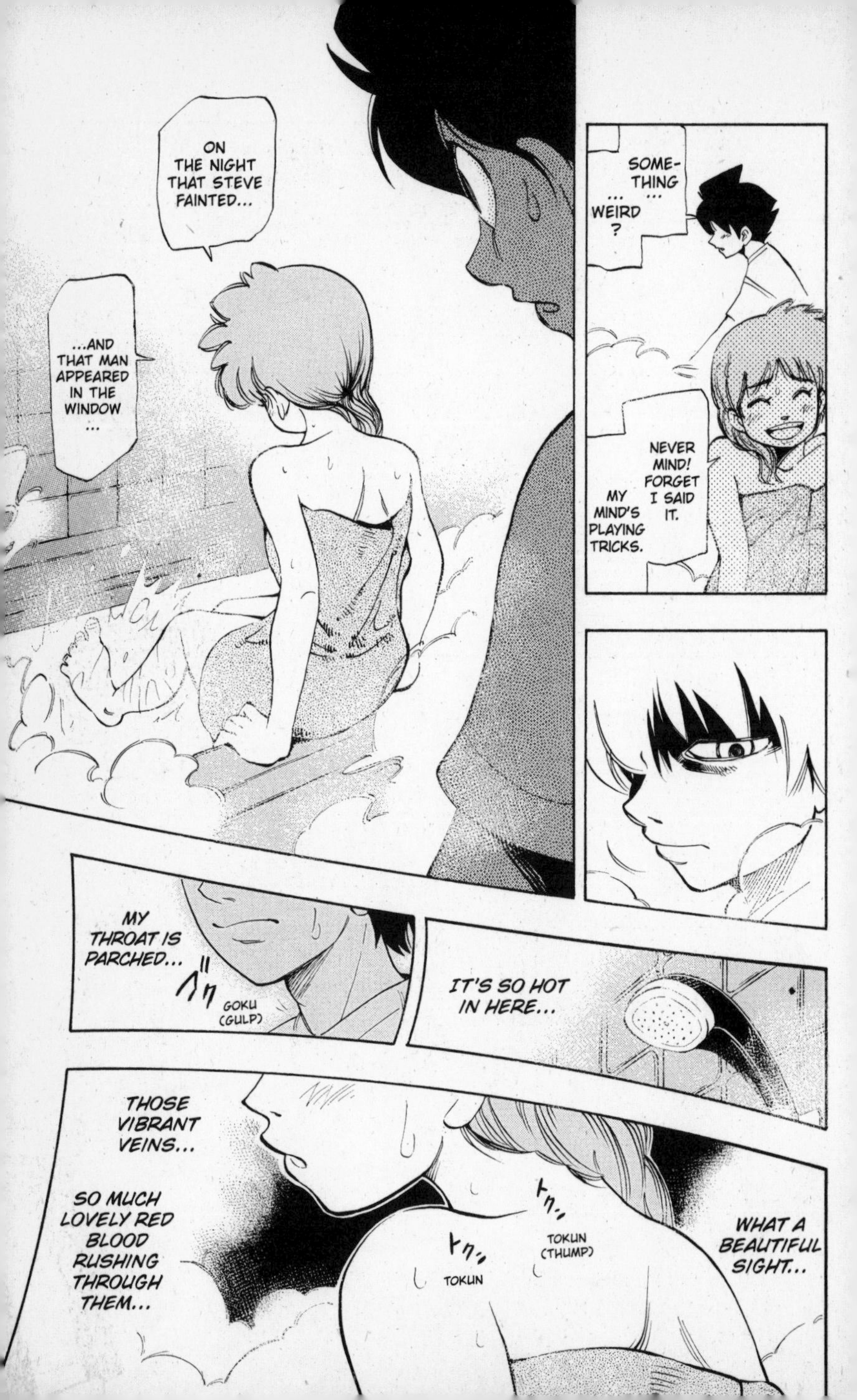
SOME-THING ... WEIRD ?
NEVER MIND! FORGET I SAID IT.
MY MIND'S PLAYING TRICKS.
ON THE NIGHT THAT STEVE FAINTED...
...AND THAT MAN APPEARED IN THE WINDOW ...
IT'S SO HOT IN HERE...
MY THROAT IS PARCHED...
GOKU (GULP)
WHAT A BEAUTIFUL SIGHT...
TOKUN (THUMP)
TOKUN
THOSE VIBRANT VEINS...
SO MUCH LOVELY RED BLOOD RUSHING THROUGH THEM...

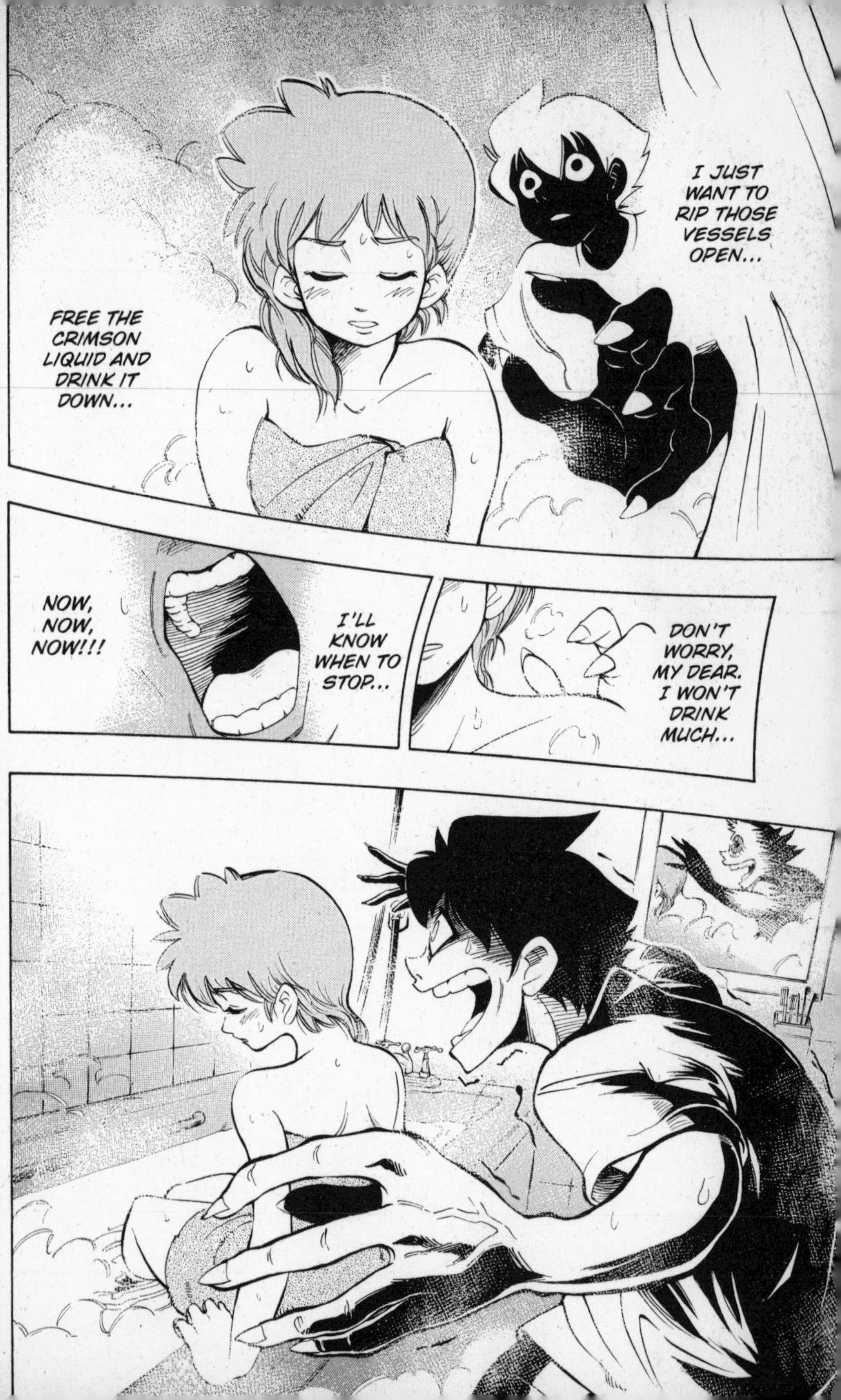
I JUST WANT TO RIP THOSE VESSELS OPEN...
FREE THE CRIMSON LIQUID AND DRINK IT DOWN...
DON'T WORRY, MY DEAR. I WON'T DRINK MUCH...
I'LL KNOW WHEN TO STOP...
NOW, NOW, NOW!!!

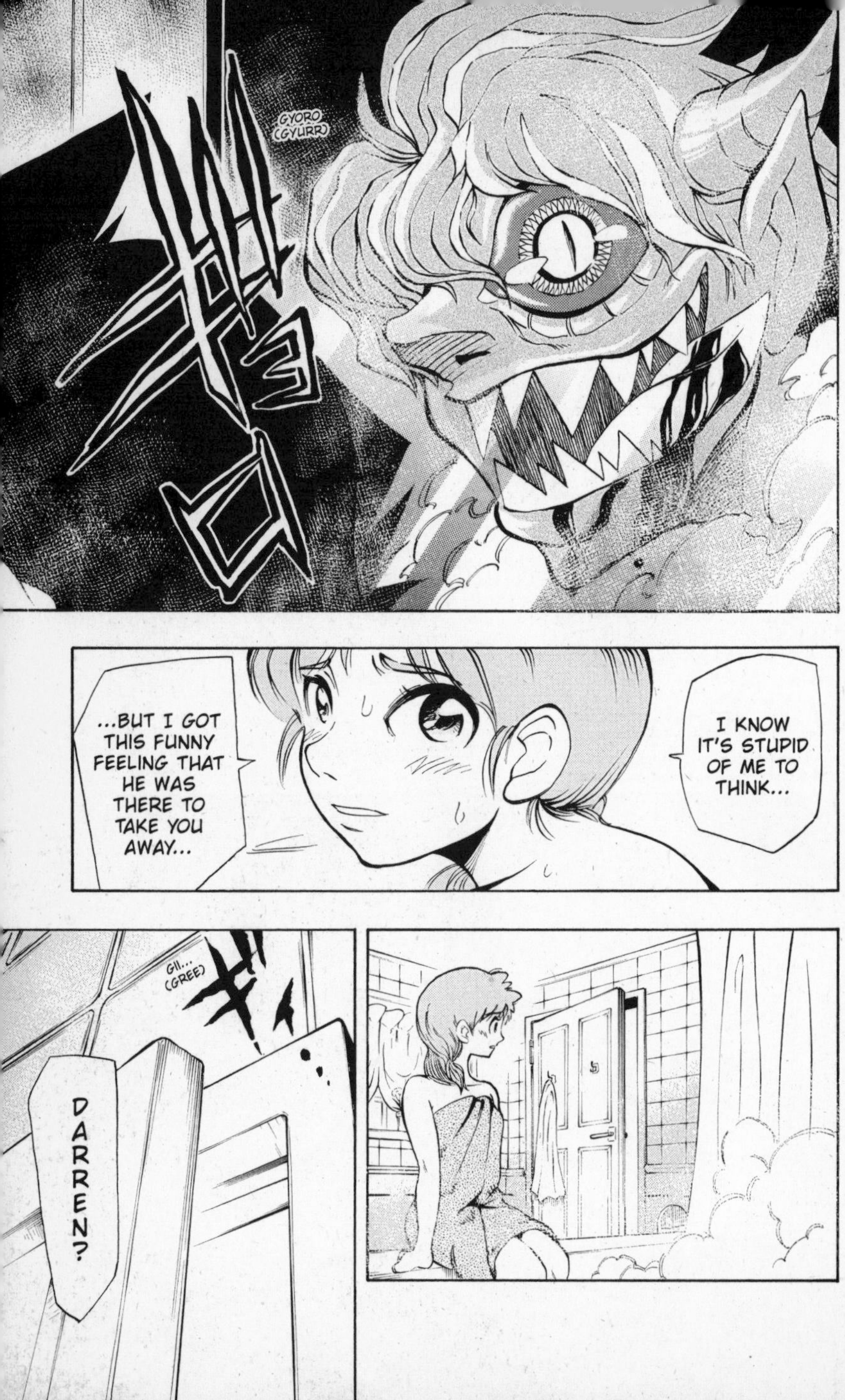
GYORO (GYURR)
I KNOW IT'S STUPID OF ME TO THINK...
...BUT I GOT THIS FUNNY FEELING THAT HE WAS THERE TO TAKE YOU AWAY...
GII... (GREE)
DARREN?

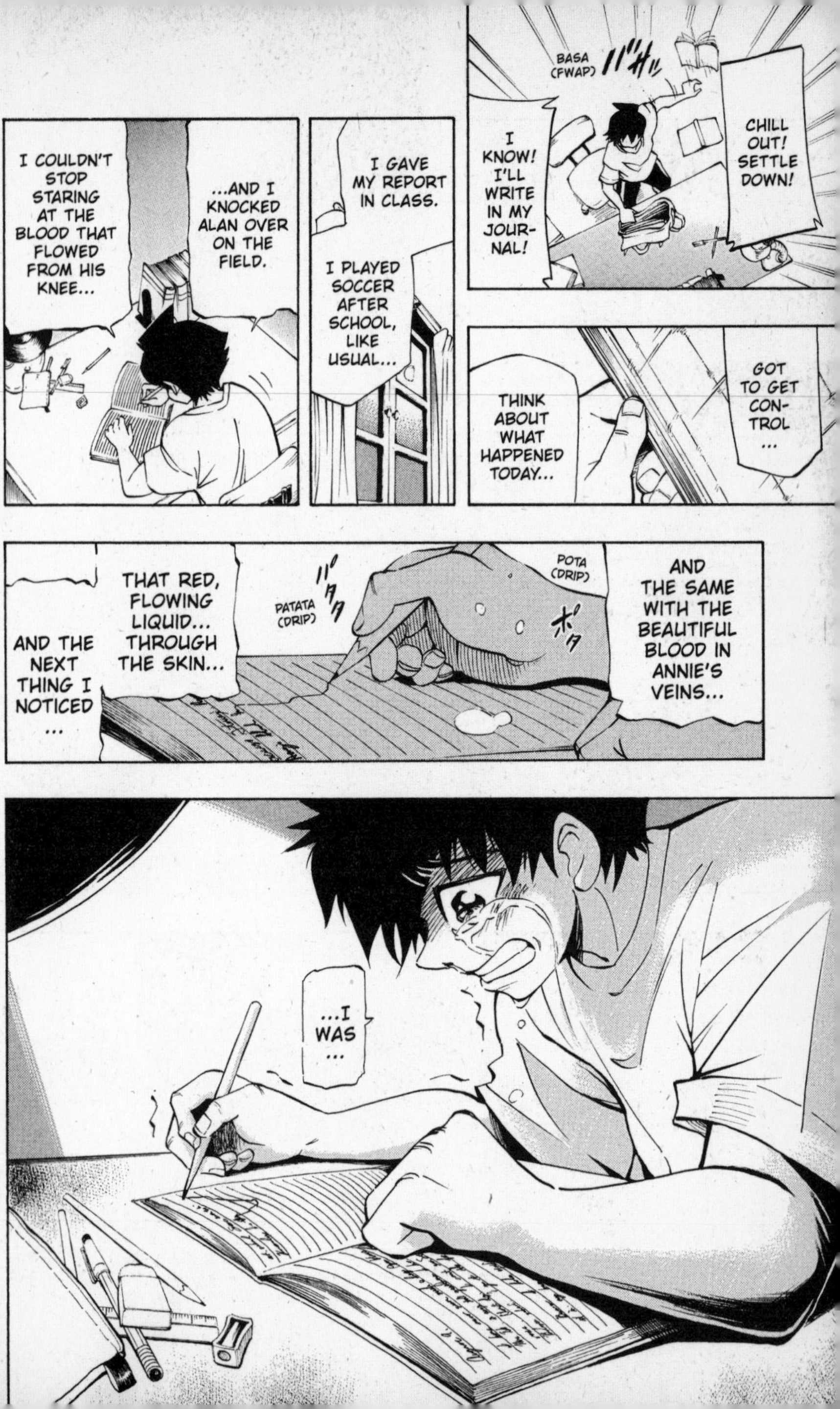
CHILL OUT! SETTLE DOWN!
BASA (FWAP)
I KNOW! I'LL WRITE IN MY JOURNAL!
GOT TO GET CONTROL...
THINK ABOUT WHAT HAPPENED TODAY...
I GAVE MY REPORT IN CLASS.
I PLAYED SOCCER AFTER SCHOOL, LIKE USUAL...
...AND I KNOCKED ALAN OVER ON THE FIELD.
I COULDN'T STOP STARING AT THE BLOOD THAT FLOWED FROM HIS KNEE...
AND THE SAME WITH THE BEAUTIFUL BLOOD IN ANNIE'S VEINS...
POTA (DRIP)
PATATA (DRIP)
THAT RED, FLOWING LIQUID... THROUGH THE SKIN...
AND THE NEXT THING I NOTICED...
...I WAS...

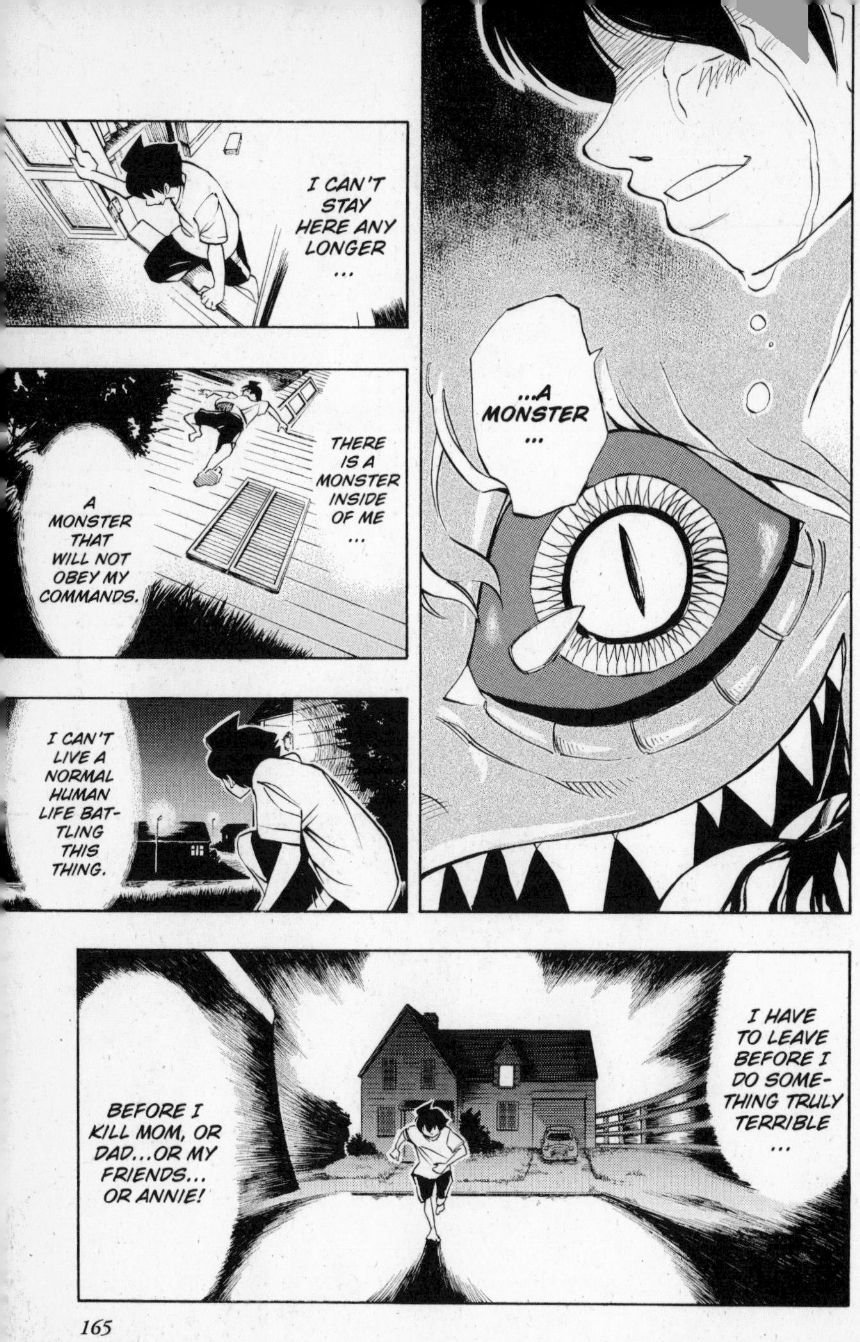
I CAN'T STAY HERE ANY LONGER ...
THERE IS A MONSTER INSIDE OF ME ...
A MONSTER THAT WILL NOT OBEY MY COMMANDS.
...A MONSTER ...
I CAN'T LIVE A NORMAL HUMAN LIFE BAT- TLING THIS THING.
I HAVE TO LEAVE BEFORE I DO SOME- THING TRULY TERRIBLE ...
BEFORE I KILL MOM, OR DAD...OR MY FRIENDS... OR ANNIE!

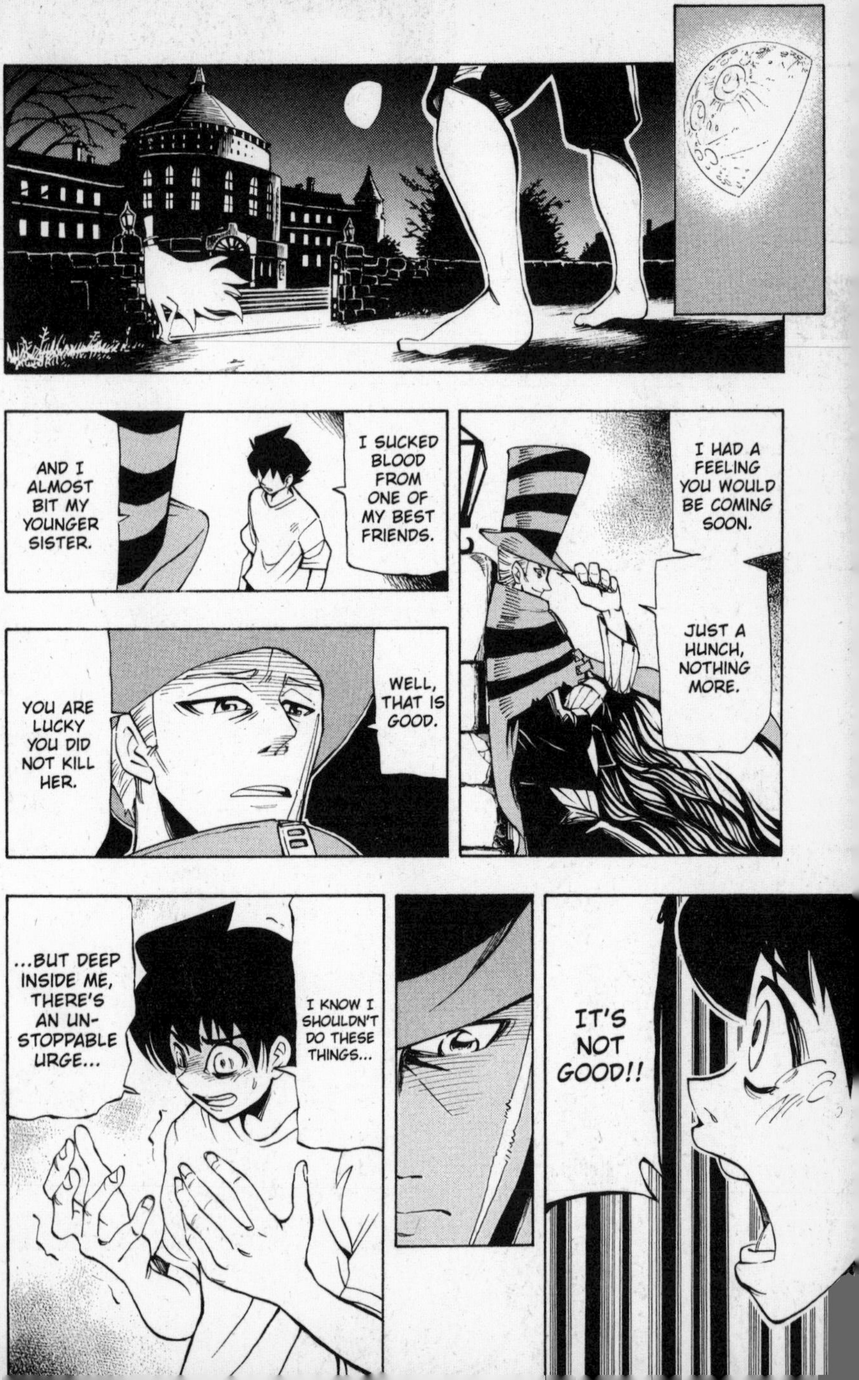
I HAD A FEELING YOU WOULD BE COMING SOON.
JUST A HUNCH, NOTHING MORE.
I SUCKED BLOOD FROM ONE OF MY BEST FRIENDS.
AND I ALMOST BIT MY YOUNGER SISTER.
WELL, THAT IS GOOD.
YOU ARE LUCKY YOU DID NOT KILL HER.
IT'S NOT GOOD!!
I KNOW I SHOULDN'T DO THESE THINGS...
...BUT DEEP INSIDE ME, THERE'S AN UN- STOPPABLE URGE...

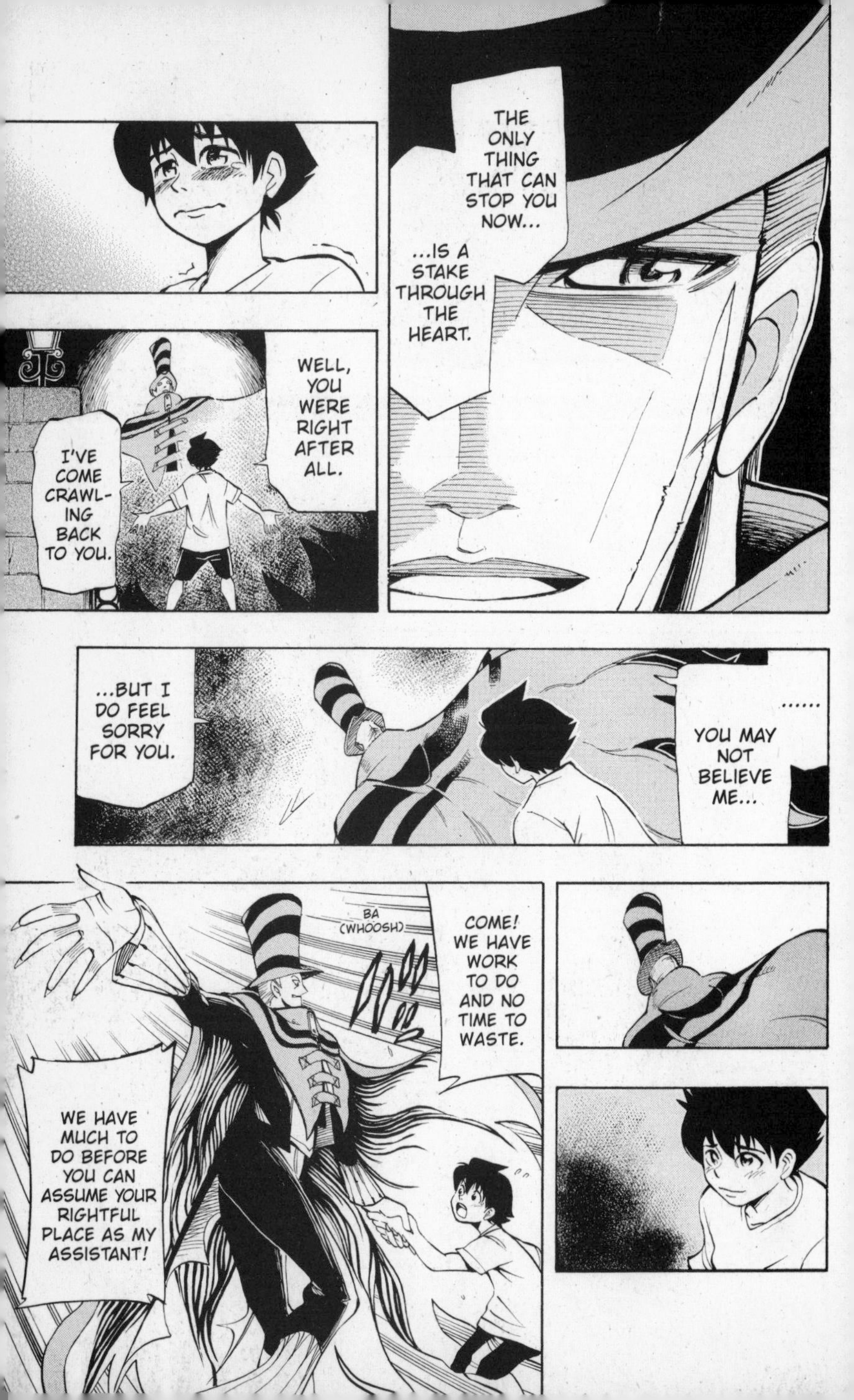
THE ONLY THING THAT CAN STOP YOU NOW...
...IS A STAKE THROUGH THE HEART.
WELL, YOU WERE RIGHT AFTER ALL.
I'VE COME CRAWLING BACK TO YOU.
......
YOU MAY NOT BELIEVE ME...
...BUT I DO FEEL SORRY FOR YOU.
COME! WE HAVE WORK TO DO AND NO TIME TO WASTE.
BA (WHOOSH)
WE HAVE MUCH TO DO BEFORE YOU CAN ASSUME YOUR RIGHTFUL PLACE AS MY ASSISTANT!

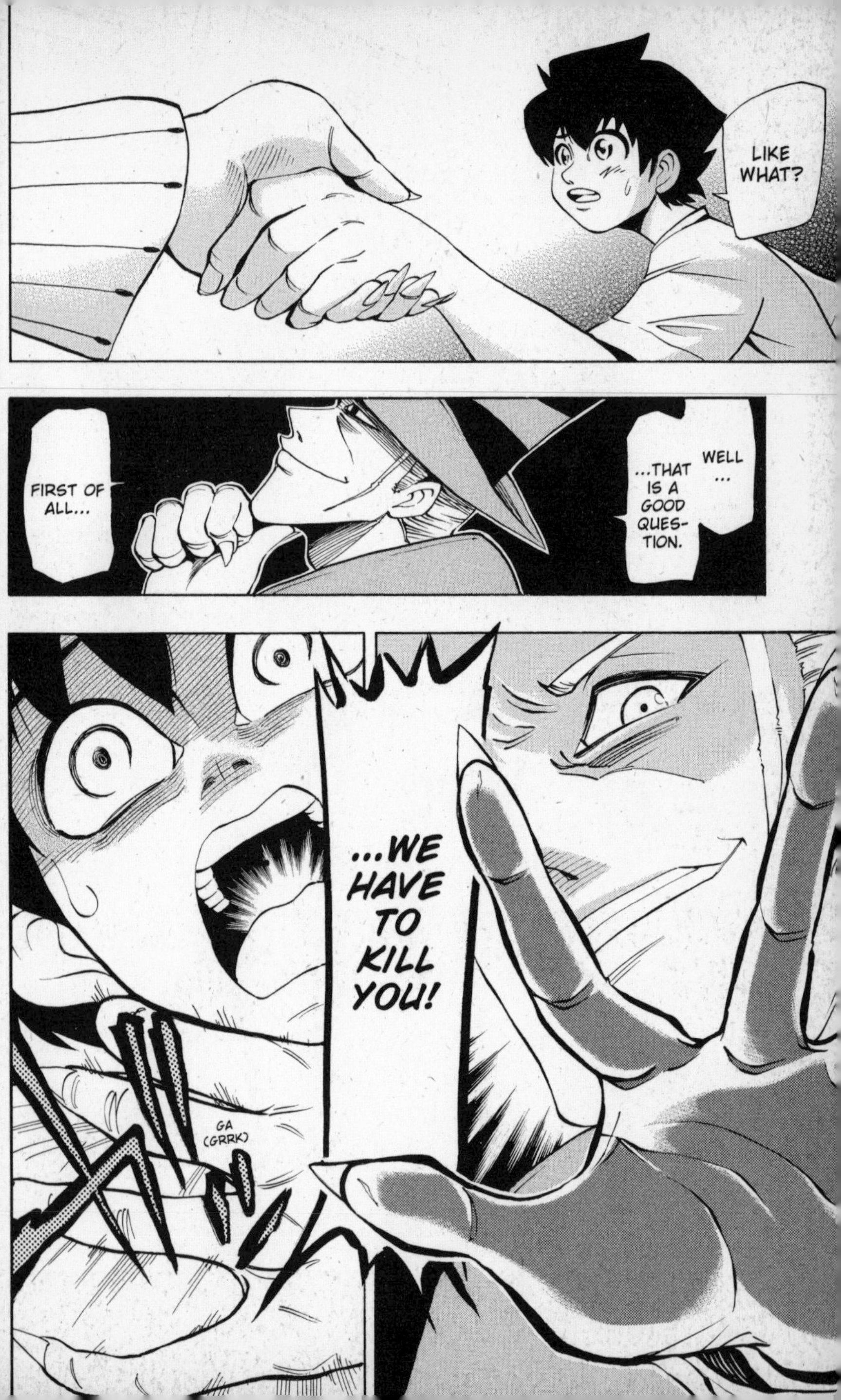
LIKE WHAT?
WELL ...
...THAT IS A GOOD QUES-TION.
FIRST OF ALL...
...WE HAVE TO KILL YOU!
GA (GRRK)

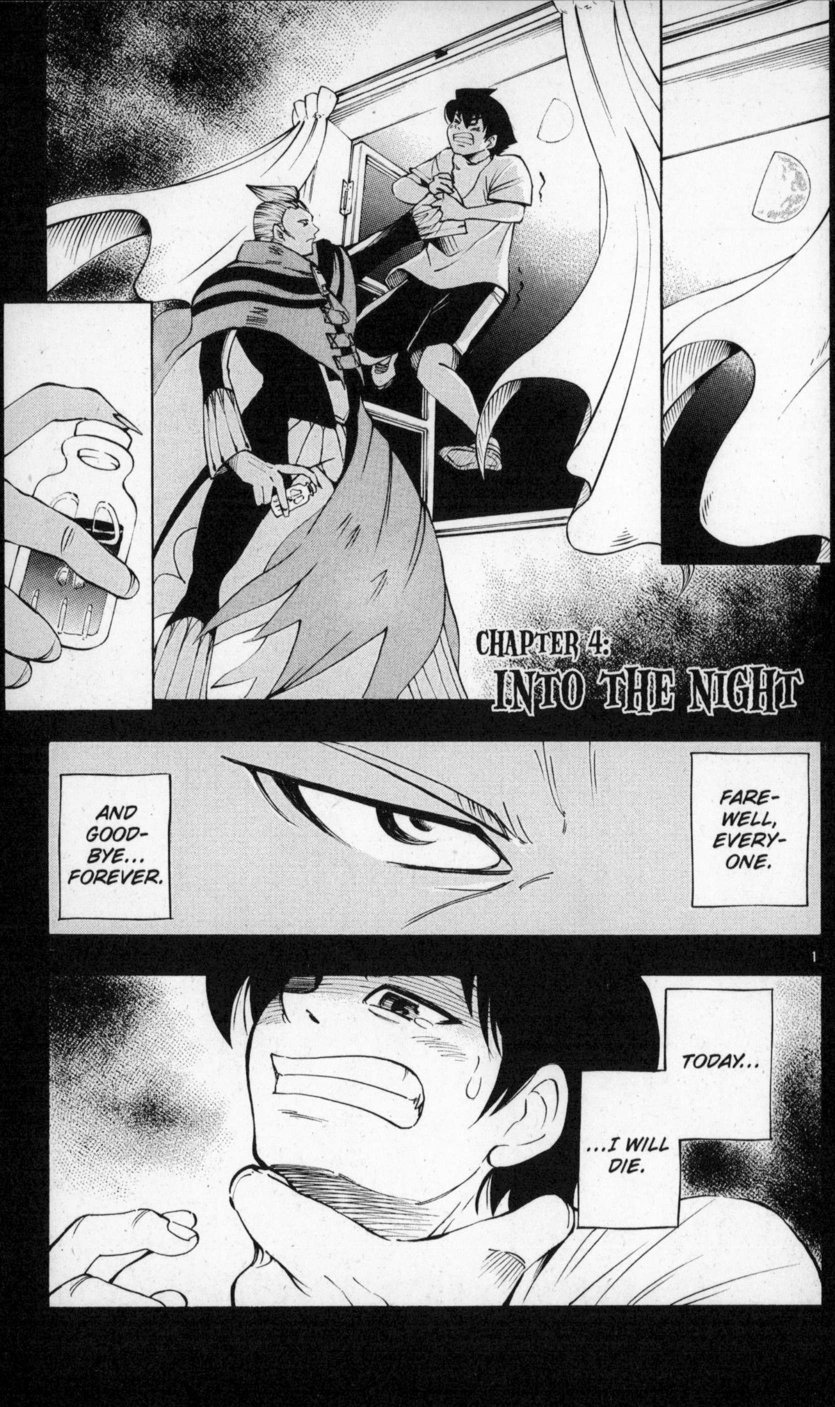
CHAPTER 4:
INTO THE NIGHT
FARE-WELL, EVERY-ONE.
AND GOOD-BYE... FOREVER.
TODAY...
...I WILL DIE.

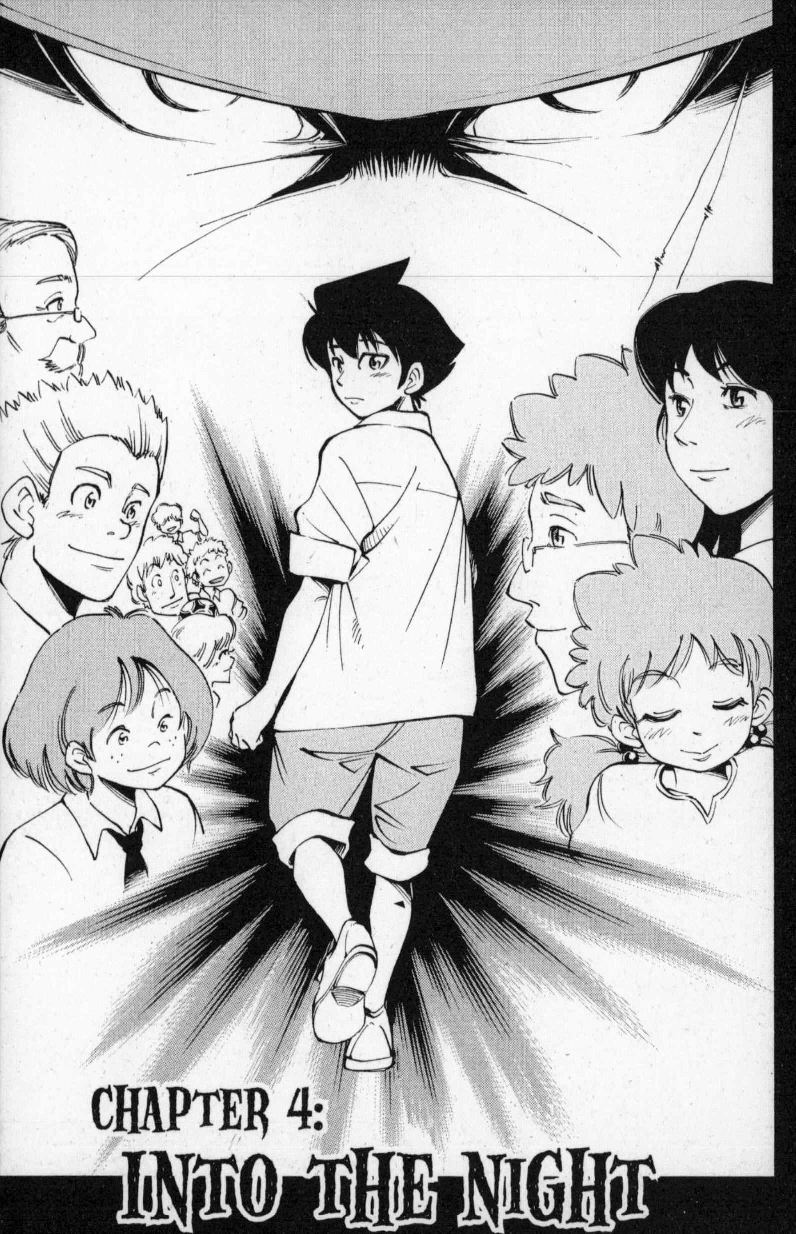
CHAPTER 4:
INTO THE NIGHT

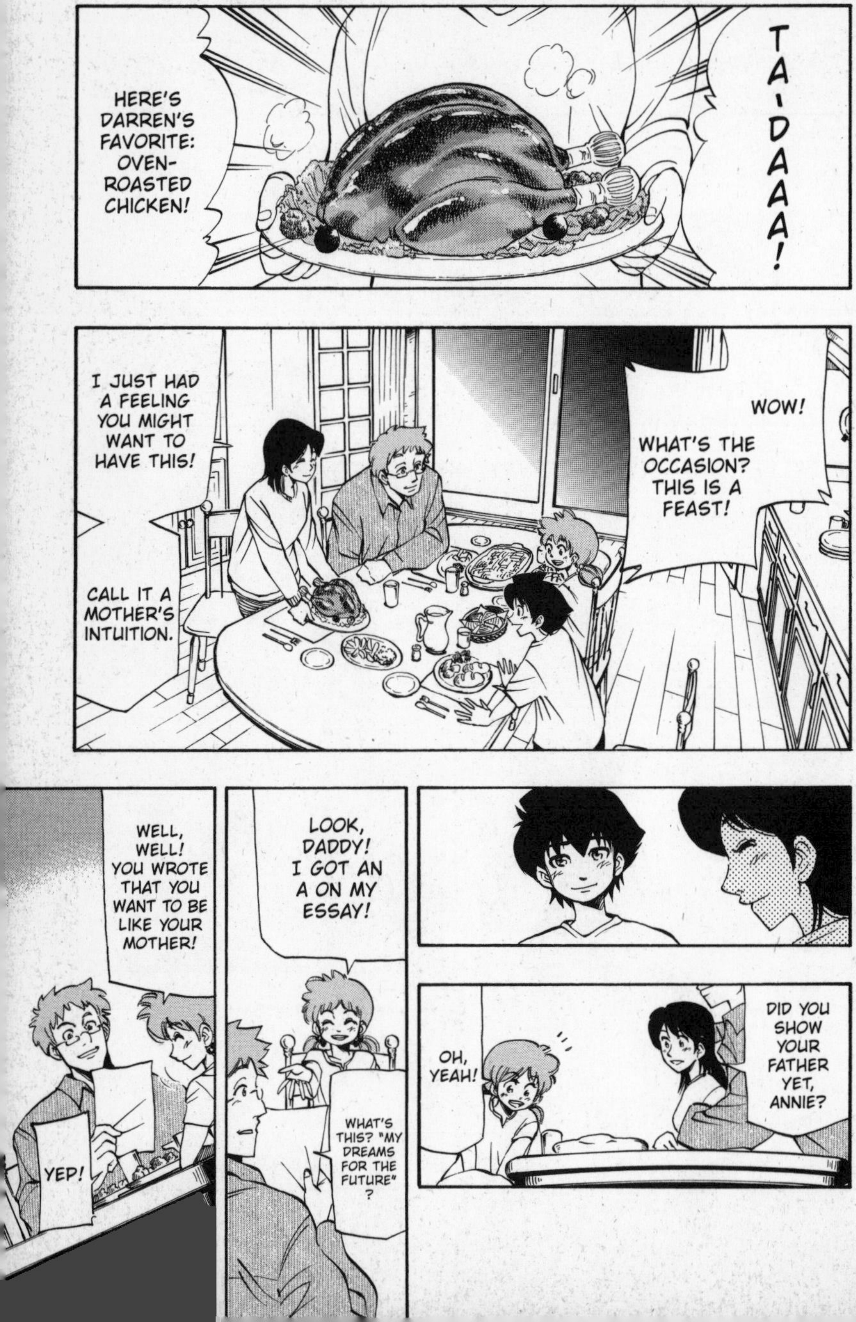
TA-DAAAA!
HERE'S DARREN'S FAVORITE: OVEN-ROASTED CHICKEN!
WOW!
WHAT'S THE OCCASION? THIS IS A FEAST!
I JUST HAD A FEELING YOU MIGHT WANT TO HAVE THIS!
CALL IT A MOTHER'S INTUITION.
DID YOU SHOW YOUR FATHER YET, ANNIE?
OH, YEAH!
LOOK, DADDY! I GOT AN A ON MY ESSAY!
WHAT'S THIS? "MY DREAMS FOR THE FUTURE"?
WELL, WELL! YOU WROTE THAT YOU WANT TO BE LIKE YOUR MOTHER!
YEP!

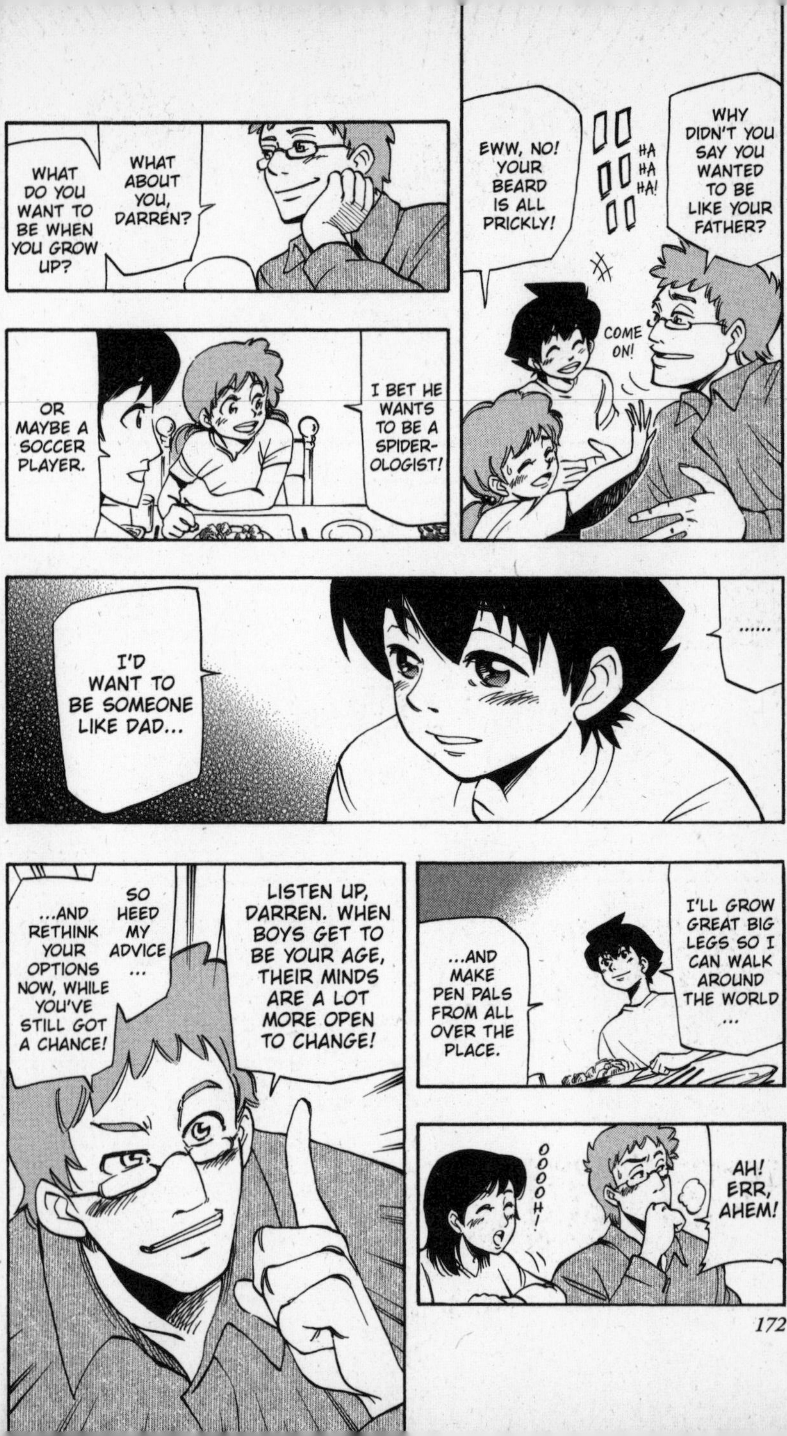
WHY DIDN'T YOU SAY YOU WANTED TO BE LIKE YOUR FATHER?
HA HA HA!
EWW, NO! YOUR BEARD IS ALL PRICKLY!
COME ON!
WHAT ABOUT YOU, DARREN?
WHAT DO YOU WANT TO BE WHEN YOU GROW UP?
I BET HE WANTS TO BE A SPIDER-OLOGIST!
OR MAYBE A SOCCER PLAYER.
......
I'D WANT TO BE SOMEONE LIKE DAD...
I'LL GROW GREAT BIG LEGS SO I CAN WALK AROUND THE WORLD...
...AND MAKE PEN PALS FROM ALL OVER THE PLACE.
AH! ERR, AHEM!
OOOOH!
LISTEN UP, DARREN. WHEN BOYS GET TO BE YOUR AGE, THEIR MINDS ARE A LOT MORE OPEN TO CHANGE!
SO HEED MY ADVICE...
...AND RETHINK YOUR OPTIONS NOW, WHILE YOU'VE STILL GOT A CHANCE!

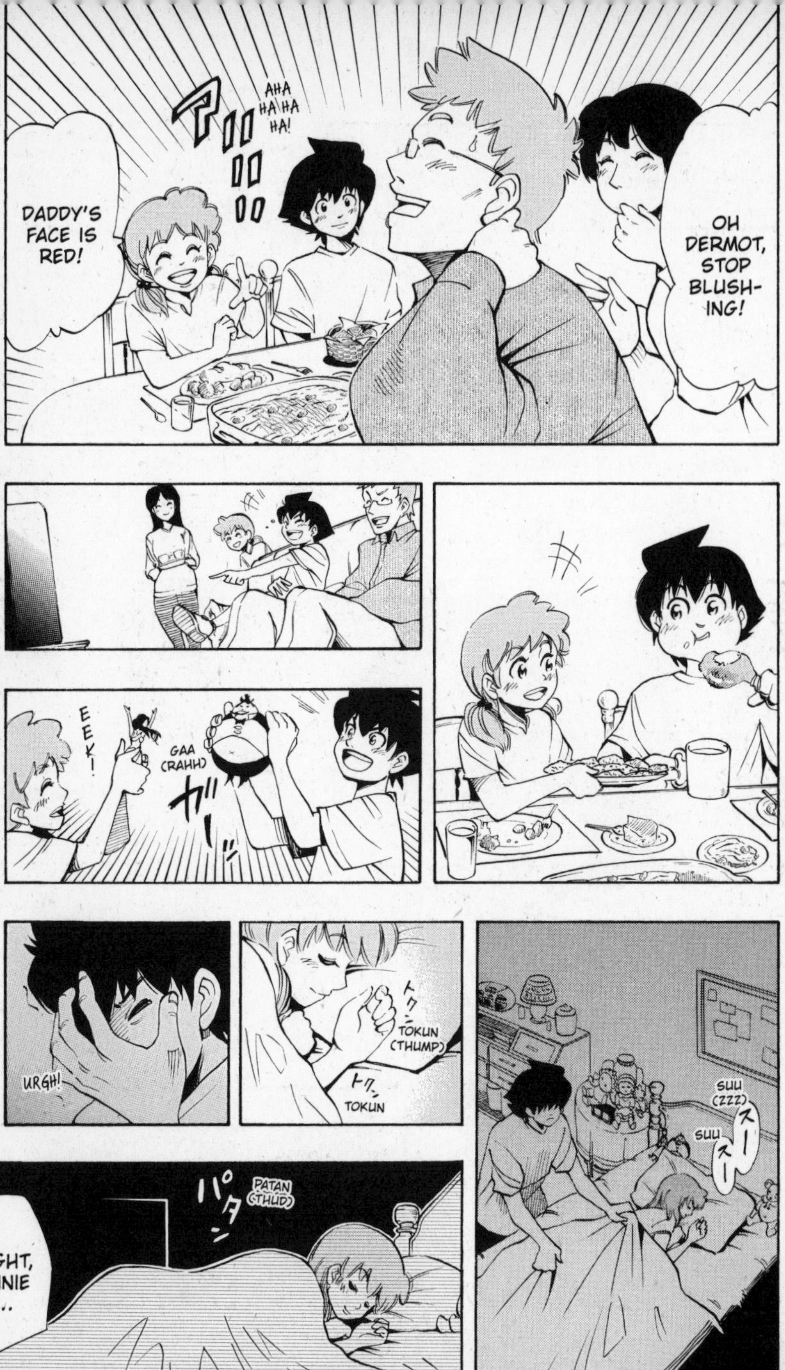
OH DERMOT, STOP BLUSHING!
AHA HA HA HA!
DADDY'S FACE IS RED!
GAA (RAHH)
EEK!
SUU (ZZZ)
SUU
TOKUN (THUMP)
TOKUN
URGH!
PATAN (THUD)
NIGHT, ANNIE ...

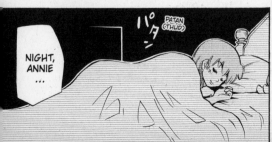

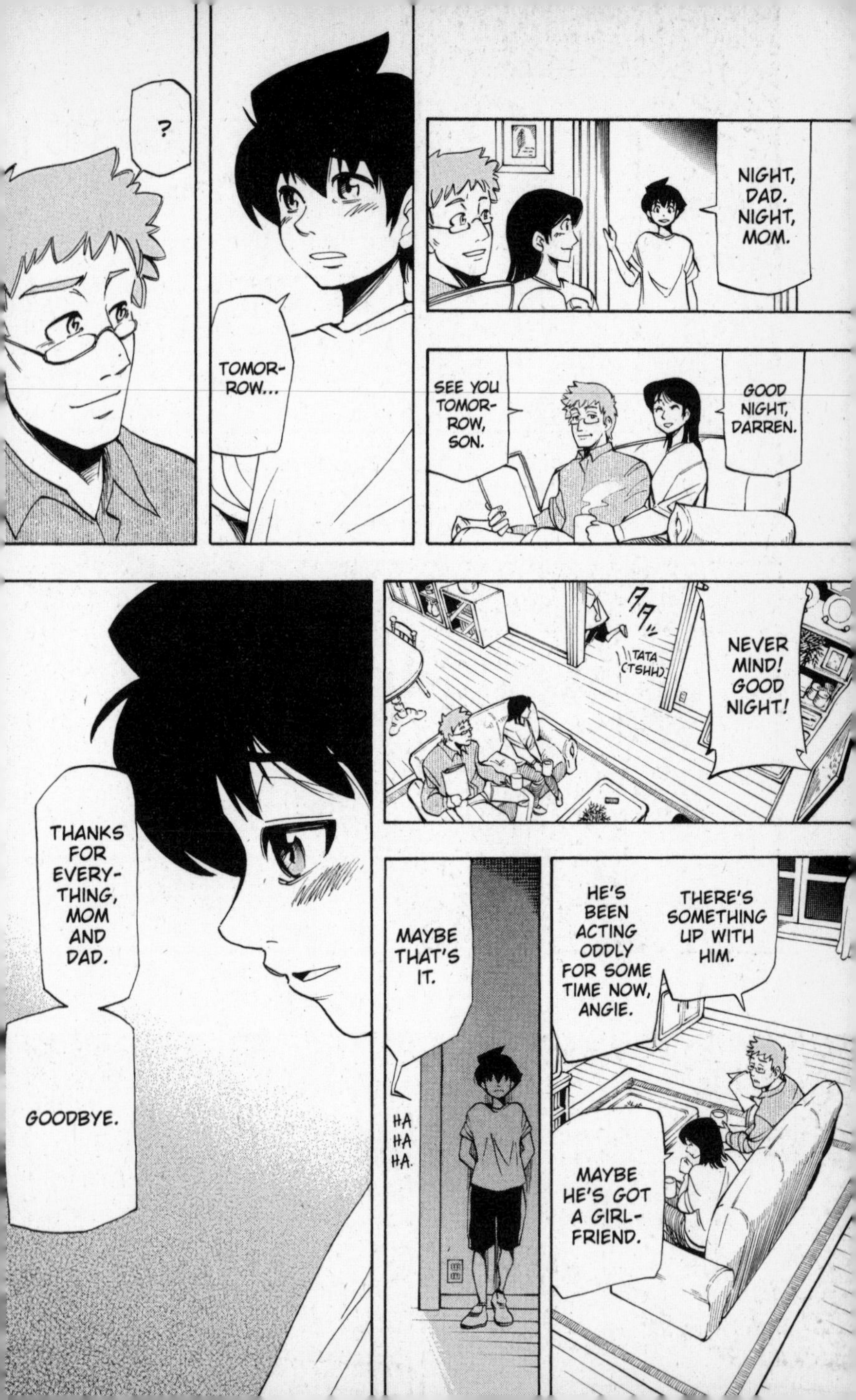

NIGHT, DAD. NIGHT, MOM.
GOOD NIGHT, DARREN.
SEE YOU TOMORROW, SON.
TOMORROW...
?
タタ
TATA (TSHH)
NEVER MIND! GOOD NIGHT!
THERE'S SOMETHING UP WITH HIM.
HE'S BEEN ACTING ODDLY FOR SOME TIME NOW, ANGIE.
MAYBE HE'S GOT A GIRLFRIEND.
MAYBE THAT'S IT.
HA HA HA.
THANKS FOR EVERYTHING, MOM AND DAD.
GOODBYE.

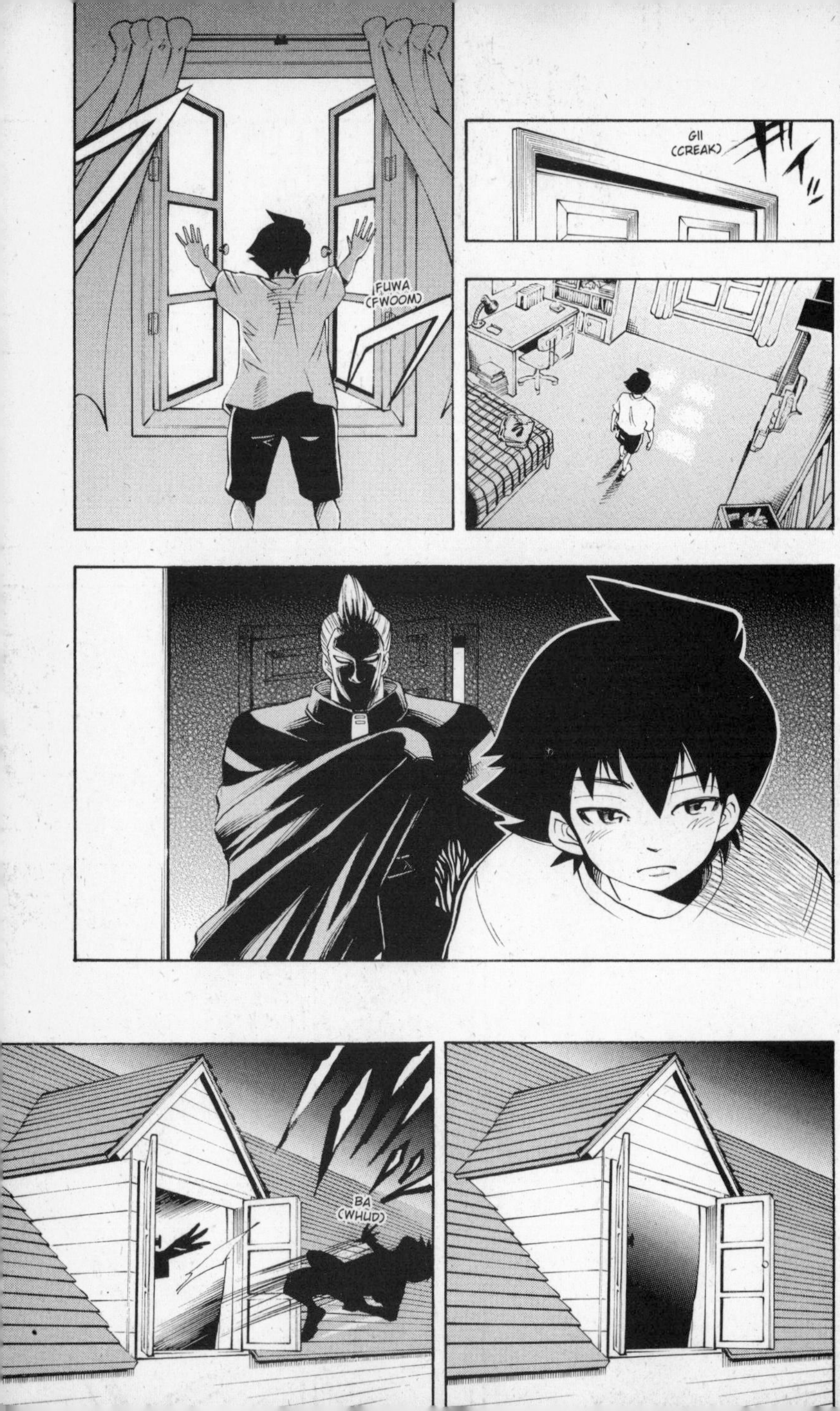
GII (CREAK)
FUWA (FWOOM)
BA (WHUD)

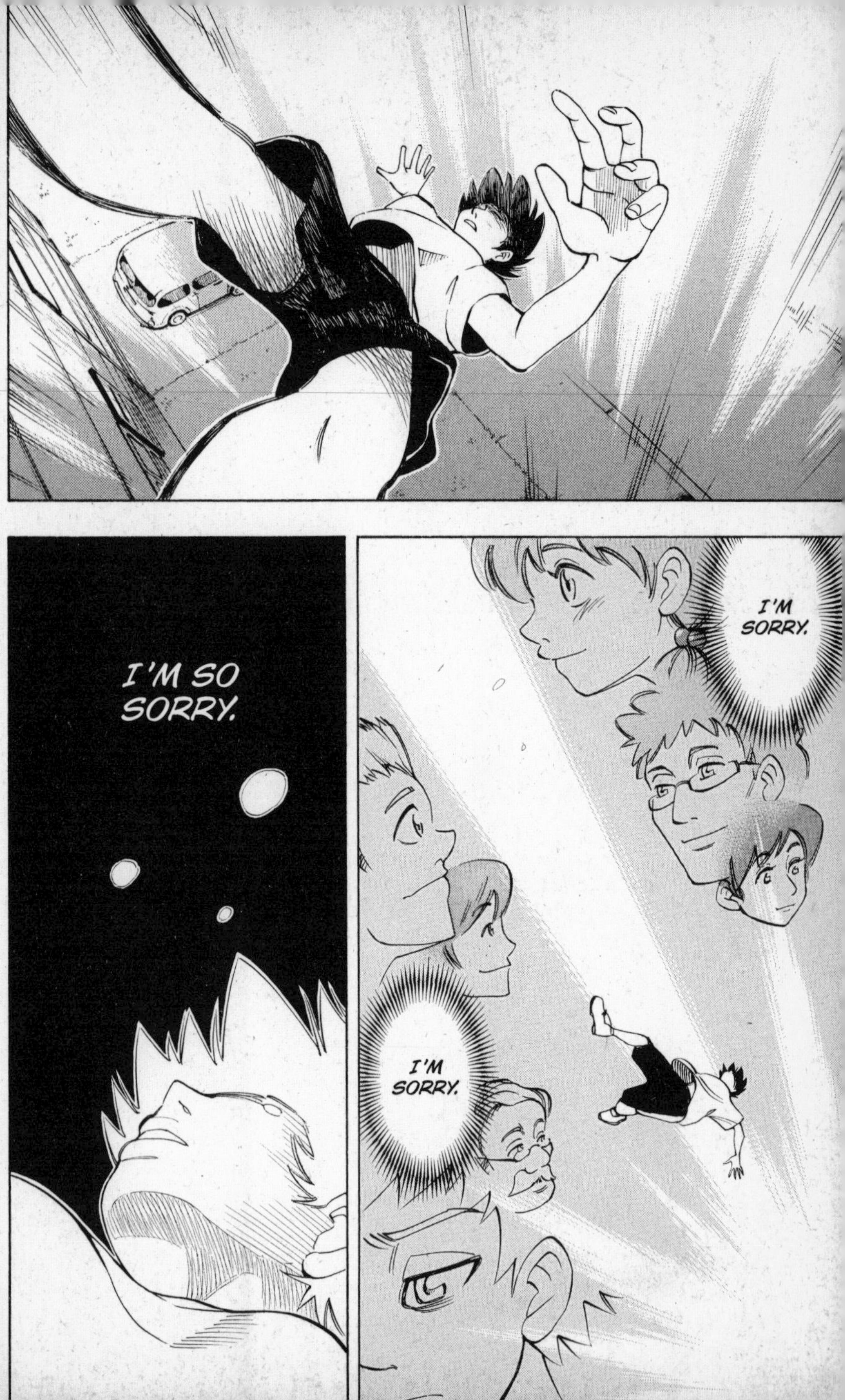
I'M SORRY.
I'M SORRY.
I'M SO SORRY.

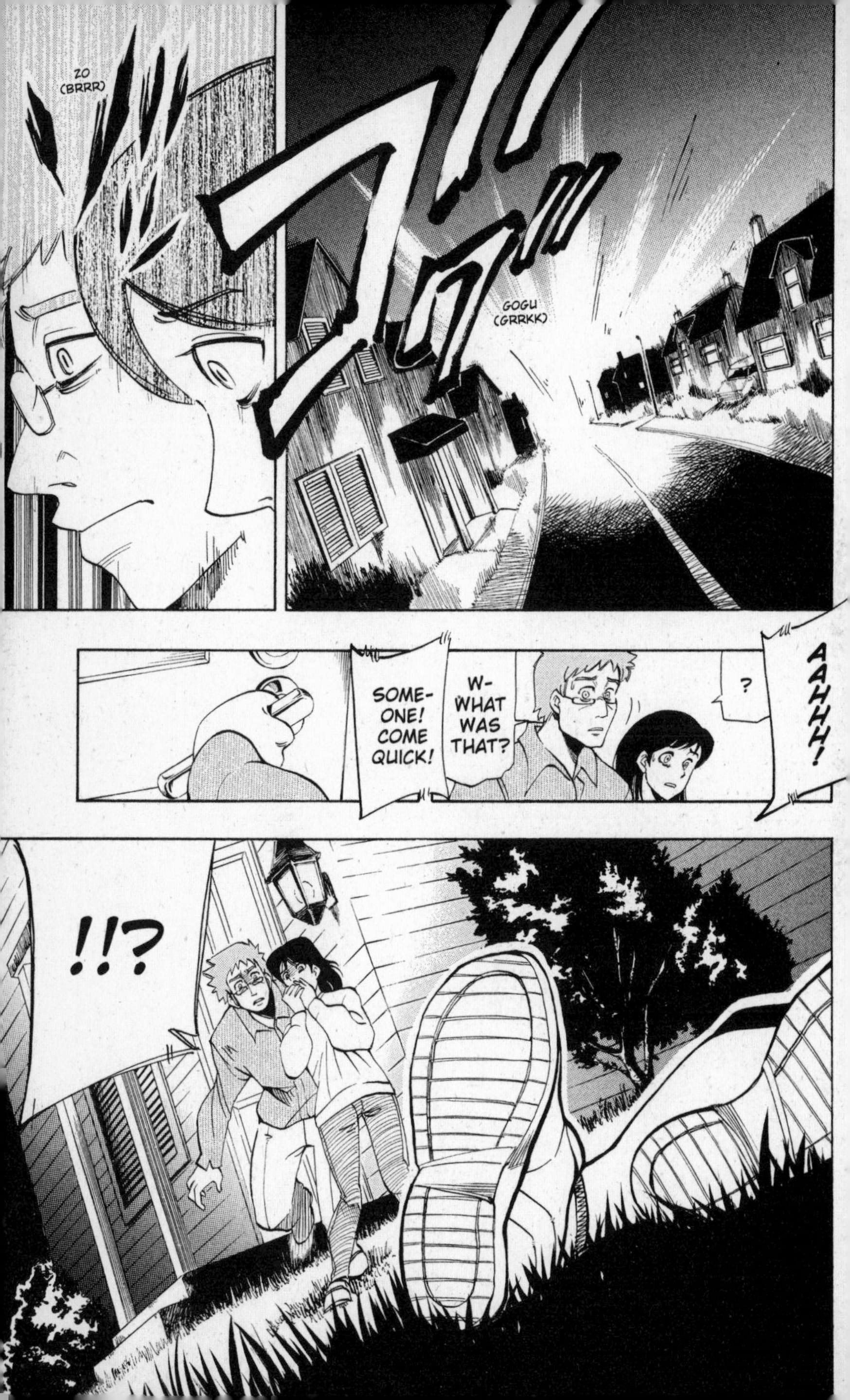
GOGU (GRRKK)
ZO (BRRR)
AAHHH!
?
W-WHAT WAS THAT?
SOME-ONE! COME QUICK!
!!?

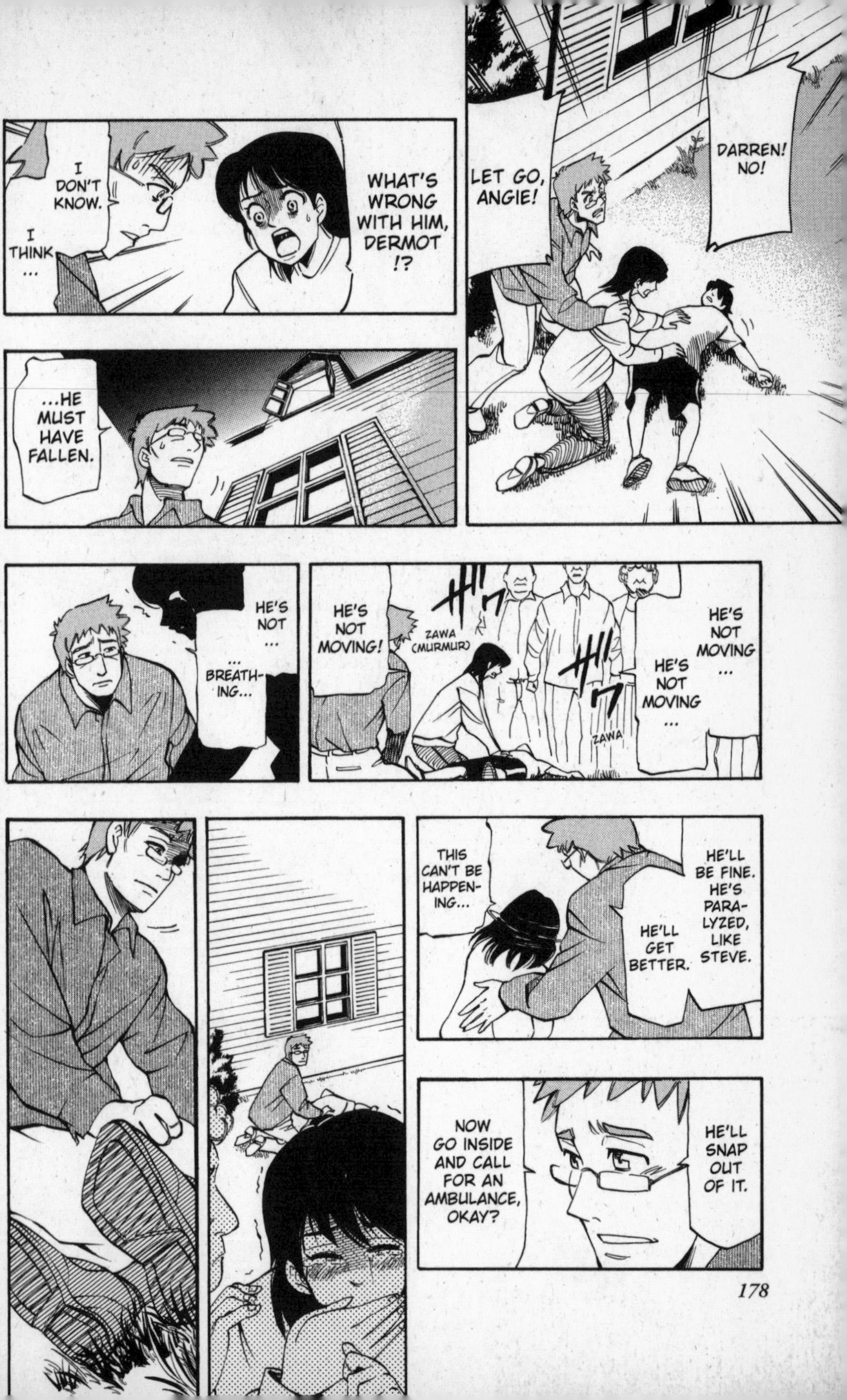
DARREN! NO!
LET GO, ANGIE!
WHAT'S WRONG WITH HIM, DERMOT!?
I DON'T KNOW.
I THINK...
...HE MUST HAVE FALLEN.
HE'S NOT MOVING...
HE'S NOT MOVING...
ZAWA
ZAWA (MURMUR)
HE'S NOT MOVING!
HE'S NOT...
...BREATHING...
HE'LL BE FINE. HE'S PARALYZED, LIKE STEVE.
HE'LL GET BETTER.
THIS CAN'T BE HAPPENING...
HE'LL SNAP OUT OF IT.
NOW GO INSIDE AND CALL FOR AN AMBULANCE, OKAY?

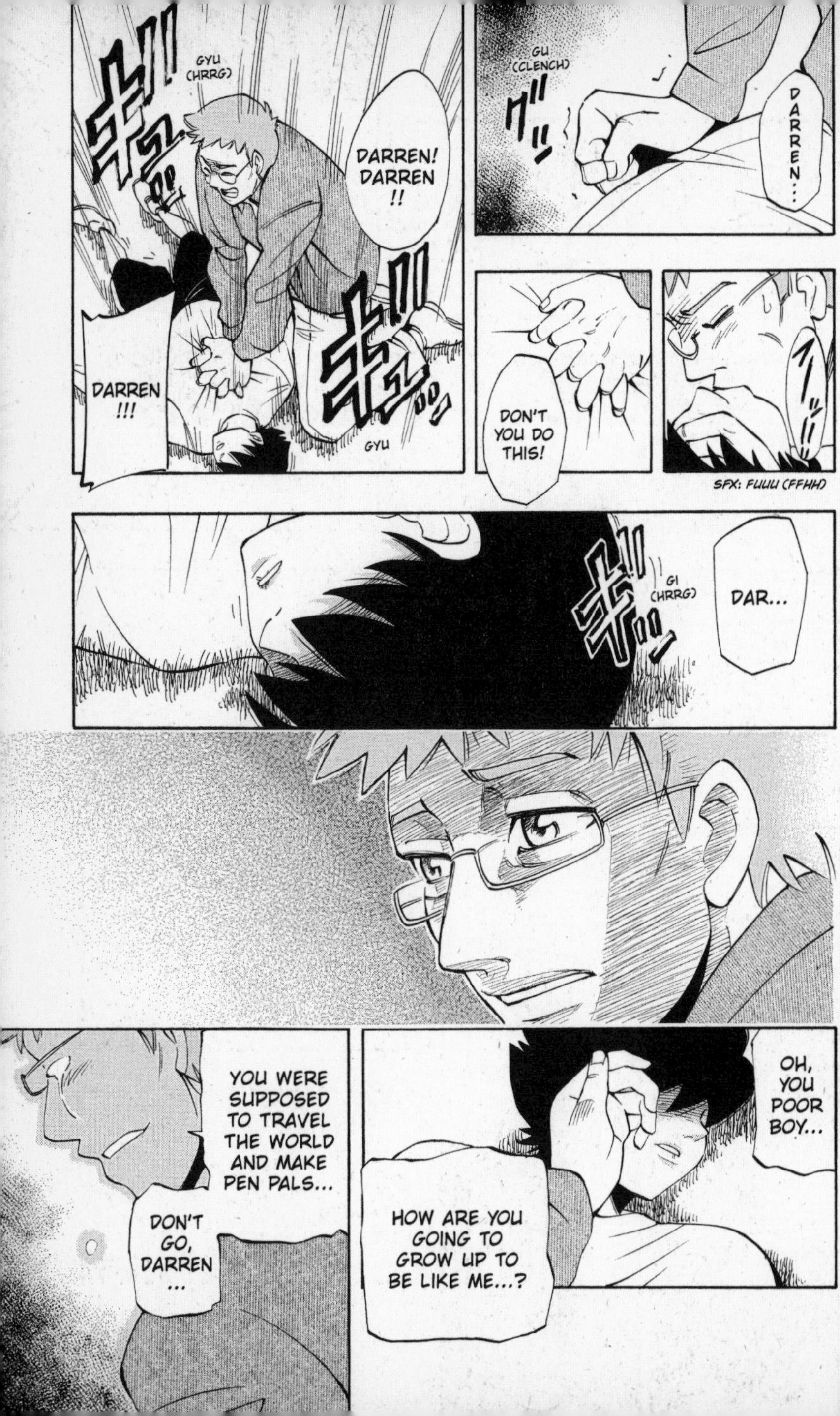
GU (CLENCH)
DARREN...
SFX: FUUU (FFHH)
DON'T YOU DO THIS!
GYU (HRRG)
DARREN! DARREN!!
DARREN!!!
GYU
DAR...
GI (HRRG)
OH, YOU POOR BOY...
HOW ARE YOU GOING TO GROW UP TO BE LIKE ME...?
YOU WERE SUPPOSED TO TRAVEL THE WORLD AND MAKE PEN PALS...
DON'T GO, DARREN...

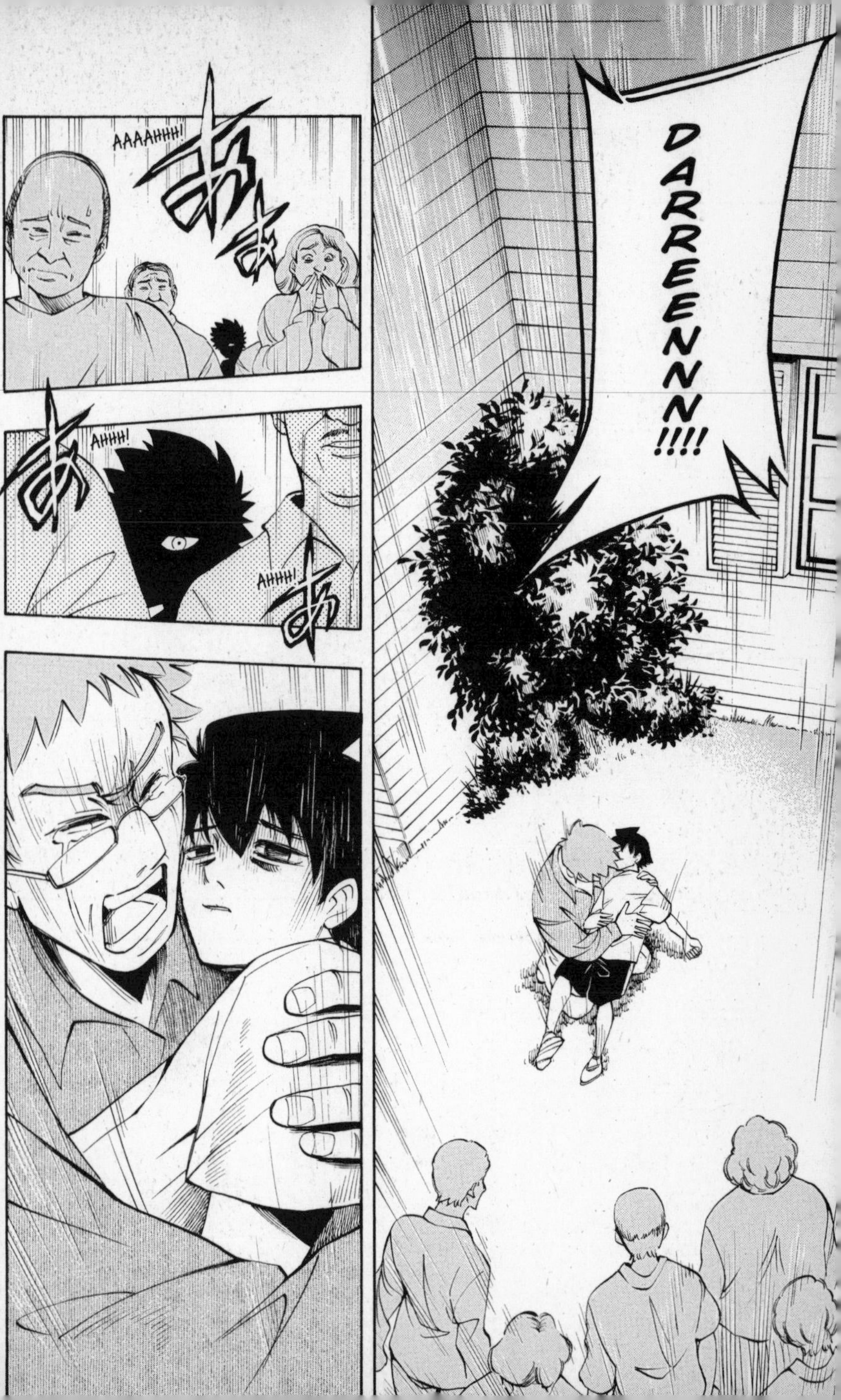
DARREENNN!!!!
あぁ
AAAAHHH!
AHHH!
あ
AHHH!
あ

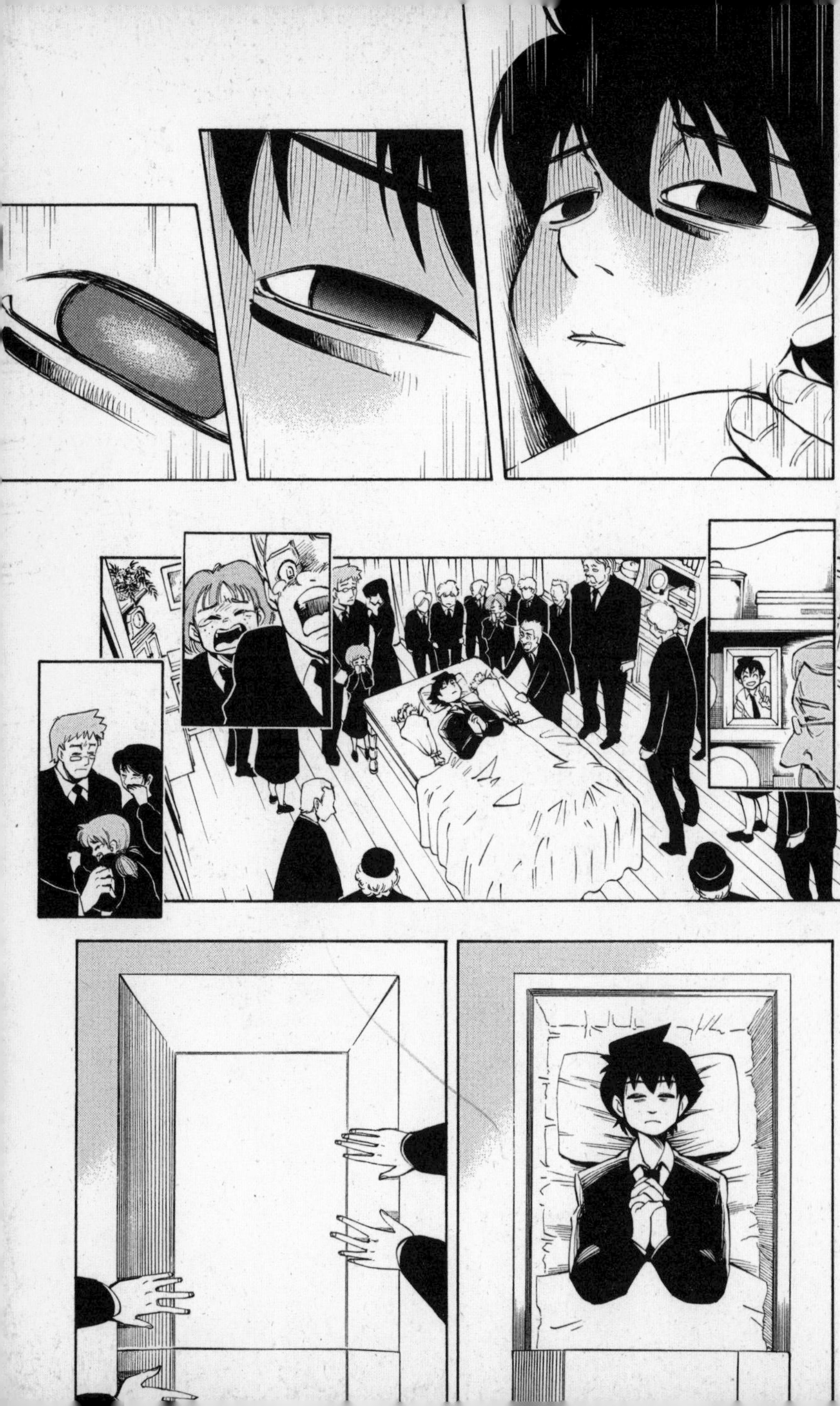

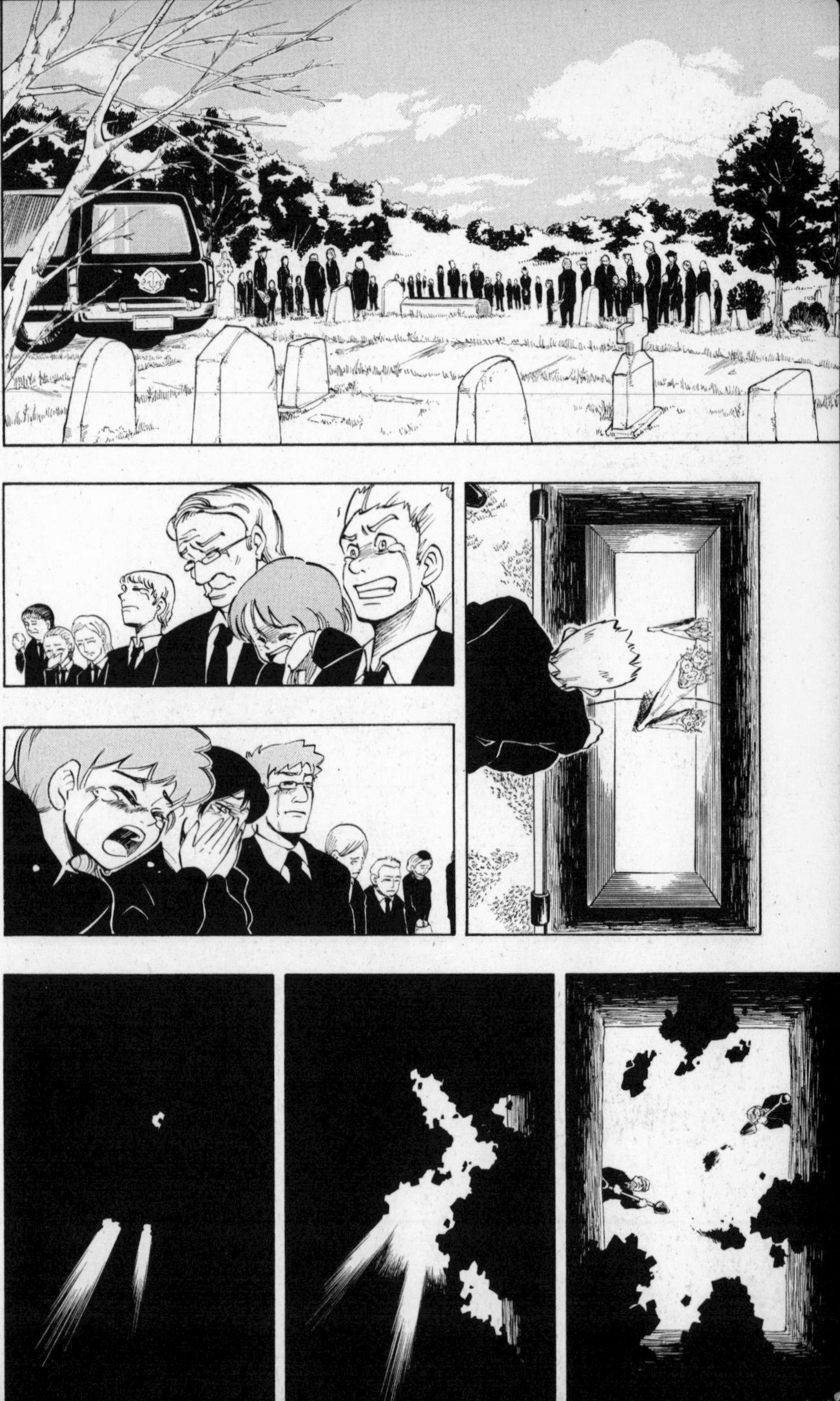

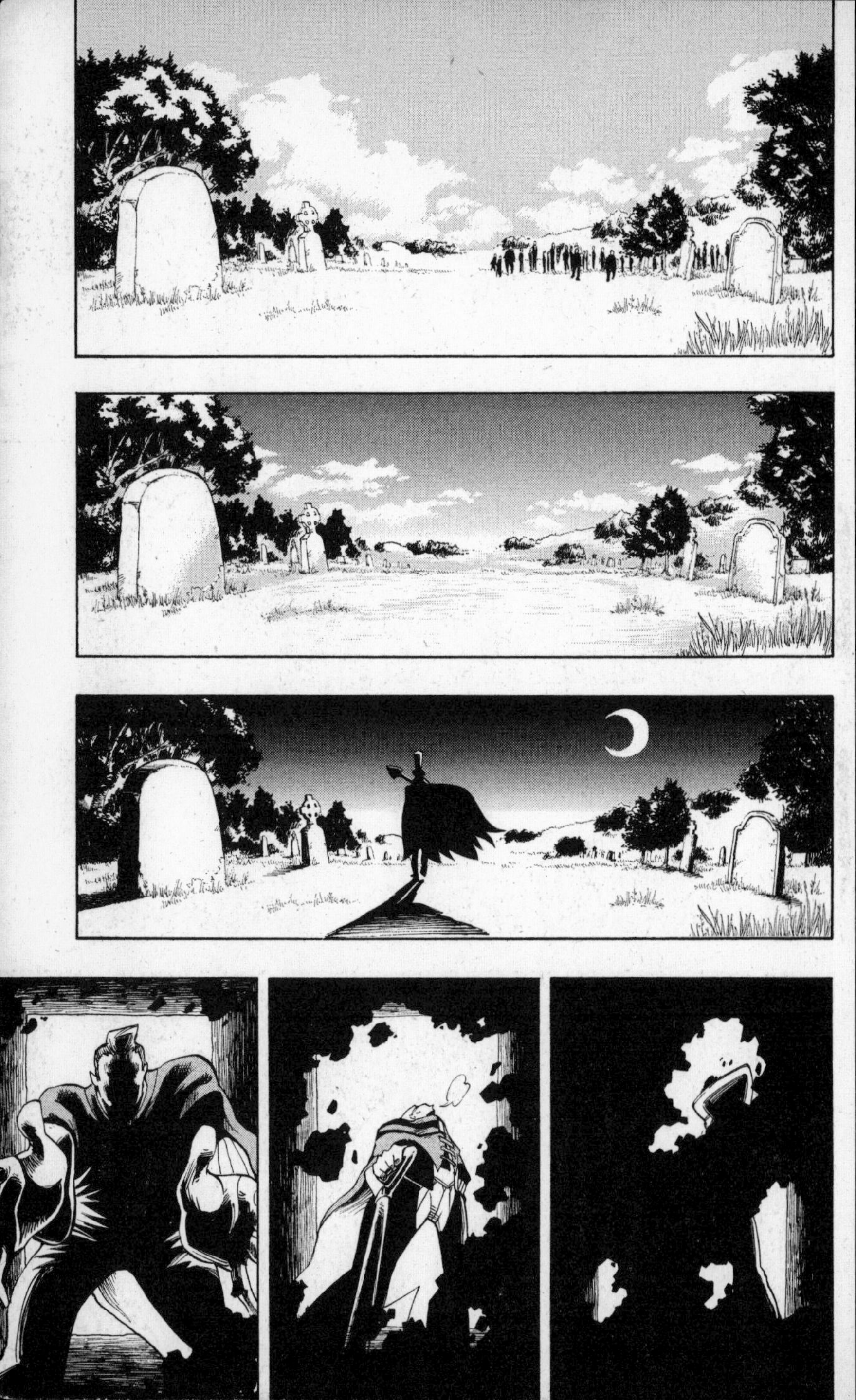

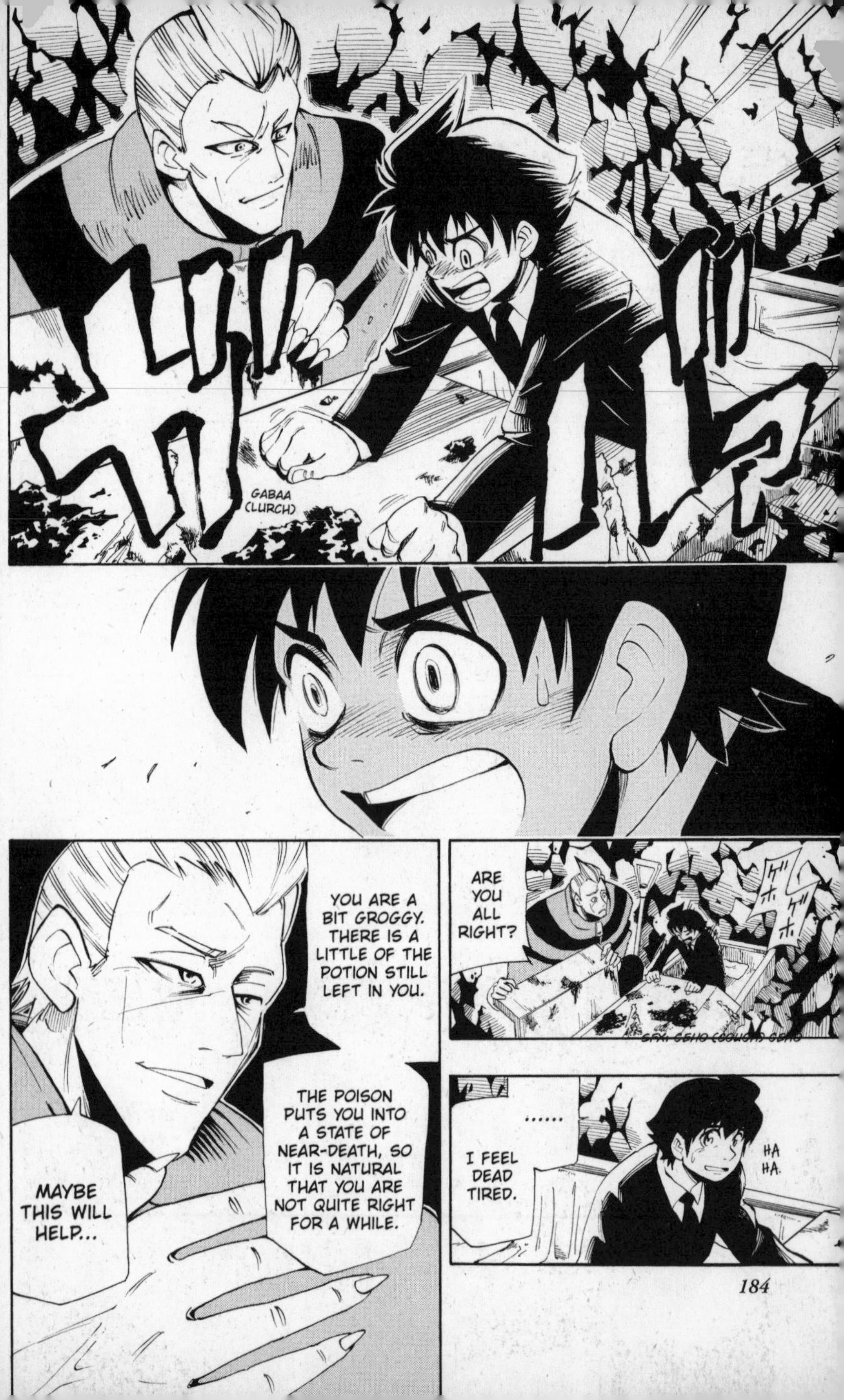
GABAA (LURCH)
ARE YOU ALL RIGHT?
SFX: GEHO (COUGH) GEHO
......
HA HA.
I FEEL DEAD TIRED.
YOU ARE A BIT GROGGY. THERE IS A LITTLE OF THE POTION STILL LEFT IN YOU.
THE POISON PUTS YOU INTO A STATE OF NEAR-DEATH, SO IT IS NATURAL THAT YOU ARE NOT QUITE RIGHT FOR A WHILE.
MAYBE THIS WILL HELP...

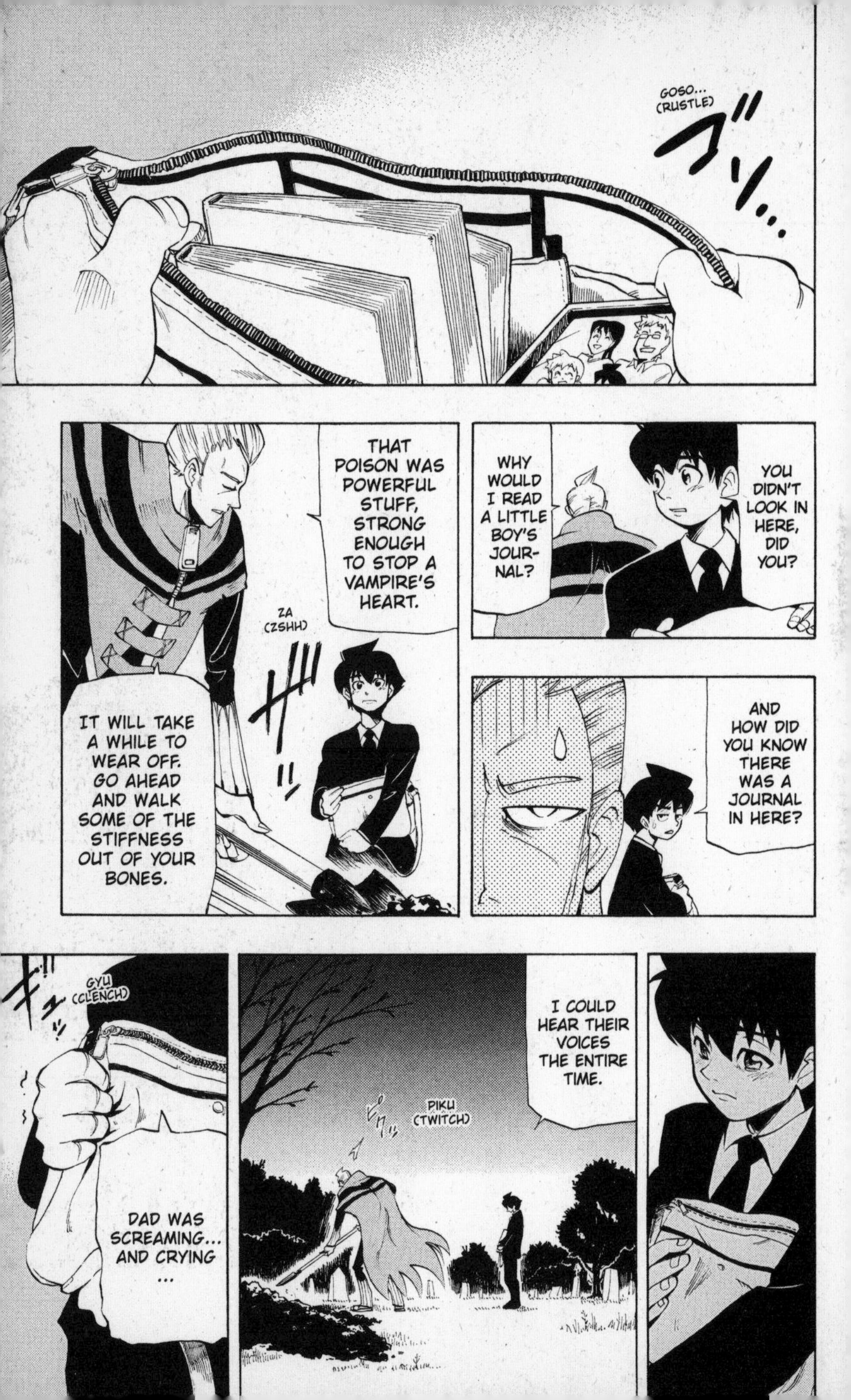
GOSO... (RUSTLE)
YOU DIDN'T LOOK IN HERE, DID YOU?
WHY WOULD I READ A LITTLE BOY'S JOURNAL?
AND HOW DID YOU KNOW THERE WAS A JOURNAL IN HERE?
THAT POISON WAS POWERFUL STUFF, STRONG ENOUGH TO STOP A VAMPIRE'S HEART.
ZA (ZSHH)
IT WILL TAKE A WHILE TO WEAR OFF. GO AHEAD AND WALK SOME OF THE STIFFNESS OUT OF YOUR BONES.
I COULD HEAR THEIR VOICES THE ENTIRE TIME.
PIKU (TWITCH)
GYU (CLENCH)
DAD WAS SCREAMING... AND CRYING ...

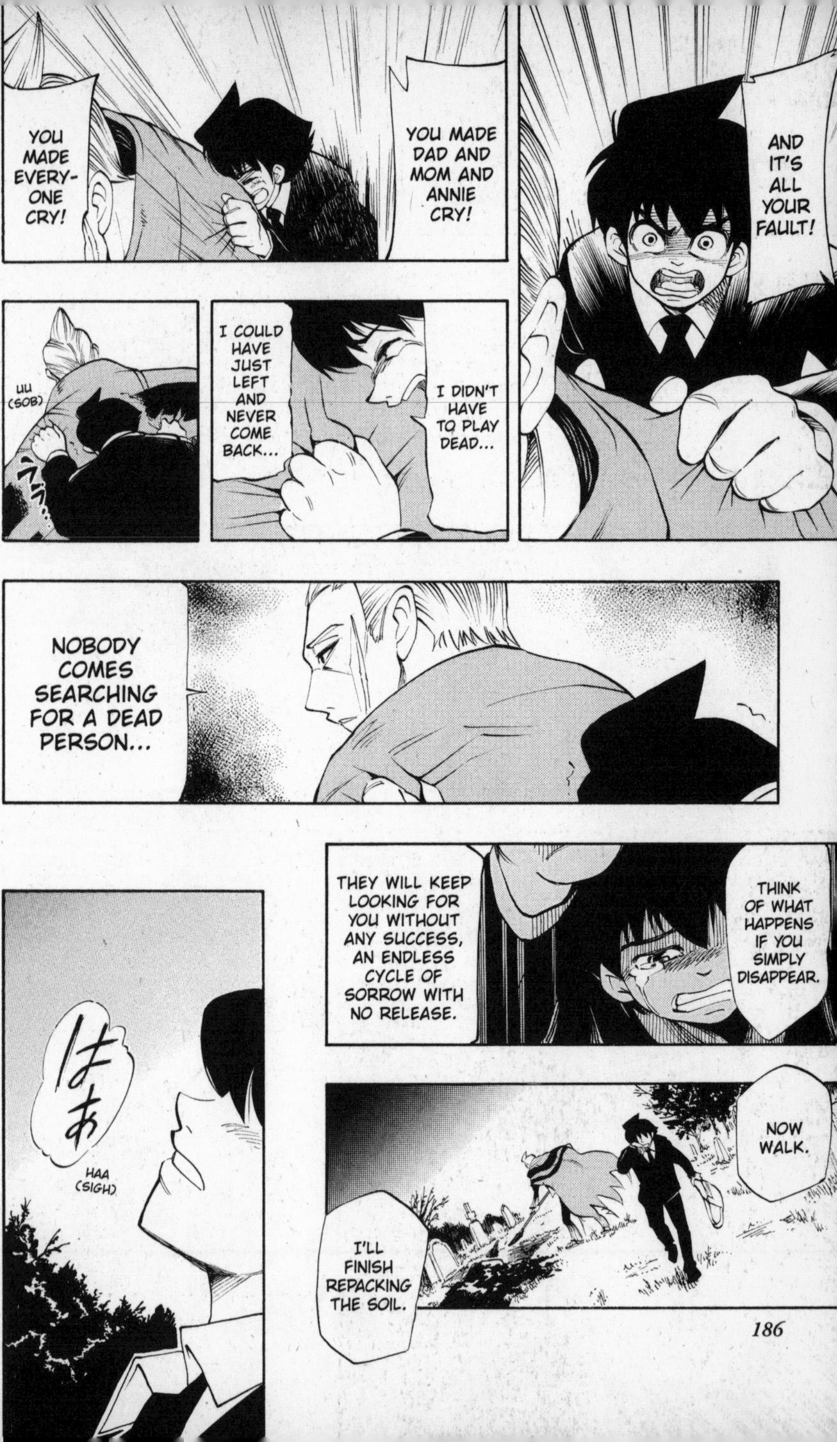
AND IT'S ALL YOUR FAULT!
YOU MADE DAD AND MOM AND ANNIE CRY!
YOU MADE EVERY-ONE CRY!
I DIDN'T HAVE TO PLAY DEAD...
I COULD HAVE JUST LEFT AND NEVER COME BACK...
UU (SOB)
NOBODY COMES SEARCHING FOR A DEAD PERSON...
THINK OF WHAT HAPPENS IF YOU SIMPLY DISAPPEAR.
THEY WILL KEEP LOOKING FOR YOU WITHOUT ANY SUCCESS, AN ENDLESS CYCLE OF SORROW WITH NO RELEASE.
NOW WALK.
I'LL FINISH REPACKING THE SOIL.
はぁ
HAA (SIGH)

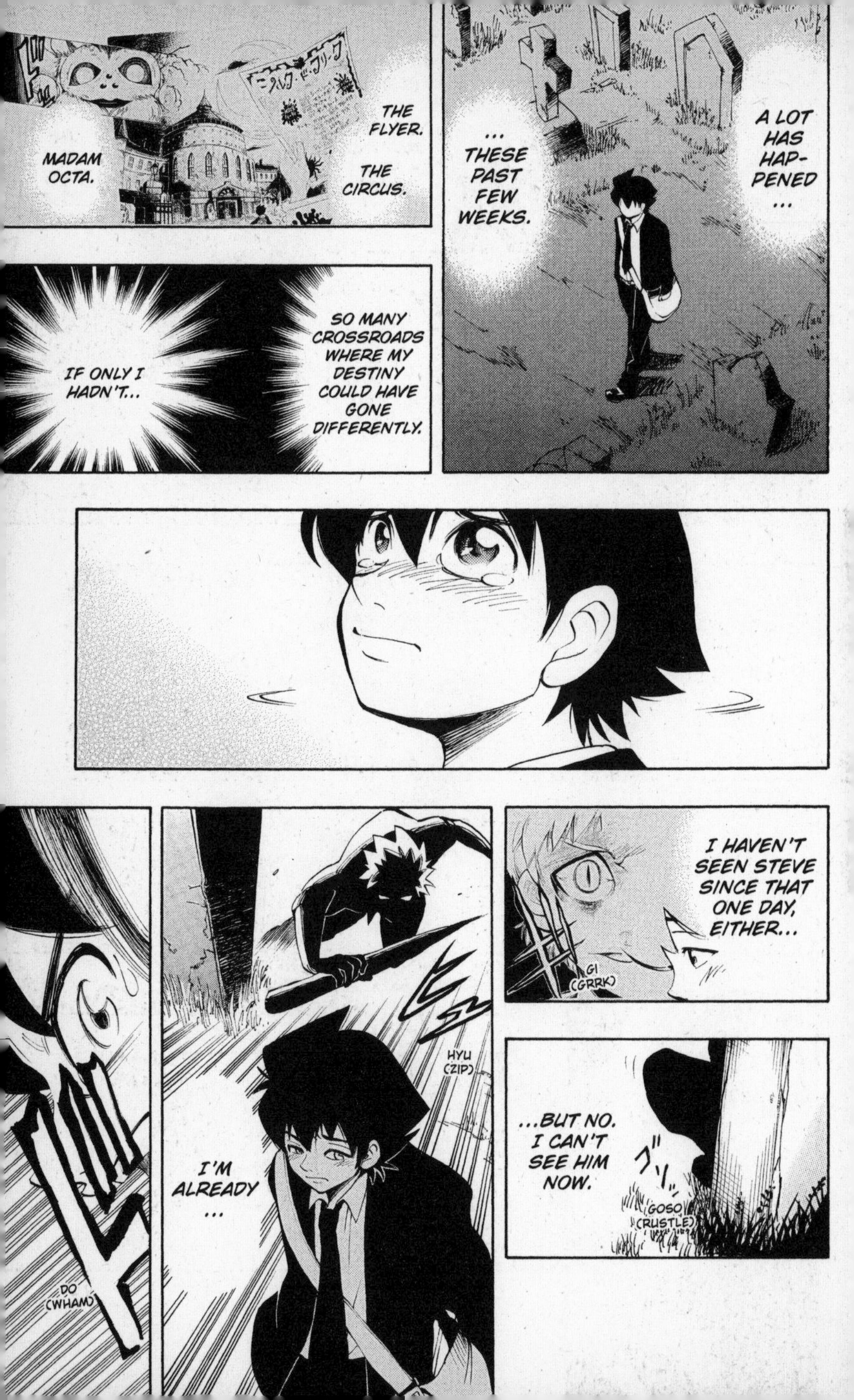
A LOT HAS HAP-PENED ...
... THESE PAST FEW WEEKS.
THE FLYER.
THE CIRCUS.
MADAM OCTA.
SO MANY CROSSROADS WHERE MY DESTINY COULD HAVE GONE DIFFERENTLY.
IF ONLY I HADN'T...
I HAVEN'T SEEN STEVE SINCE THAT ONE DAY, EITHER...
GI (GRRK)
...BUT NO. I CAN'T SEE HIM NOW.
GOSO (RUSTLE)
HYU (ZIP)
I'M ALREADY ...
DO (WHAM)

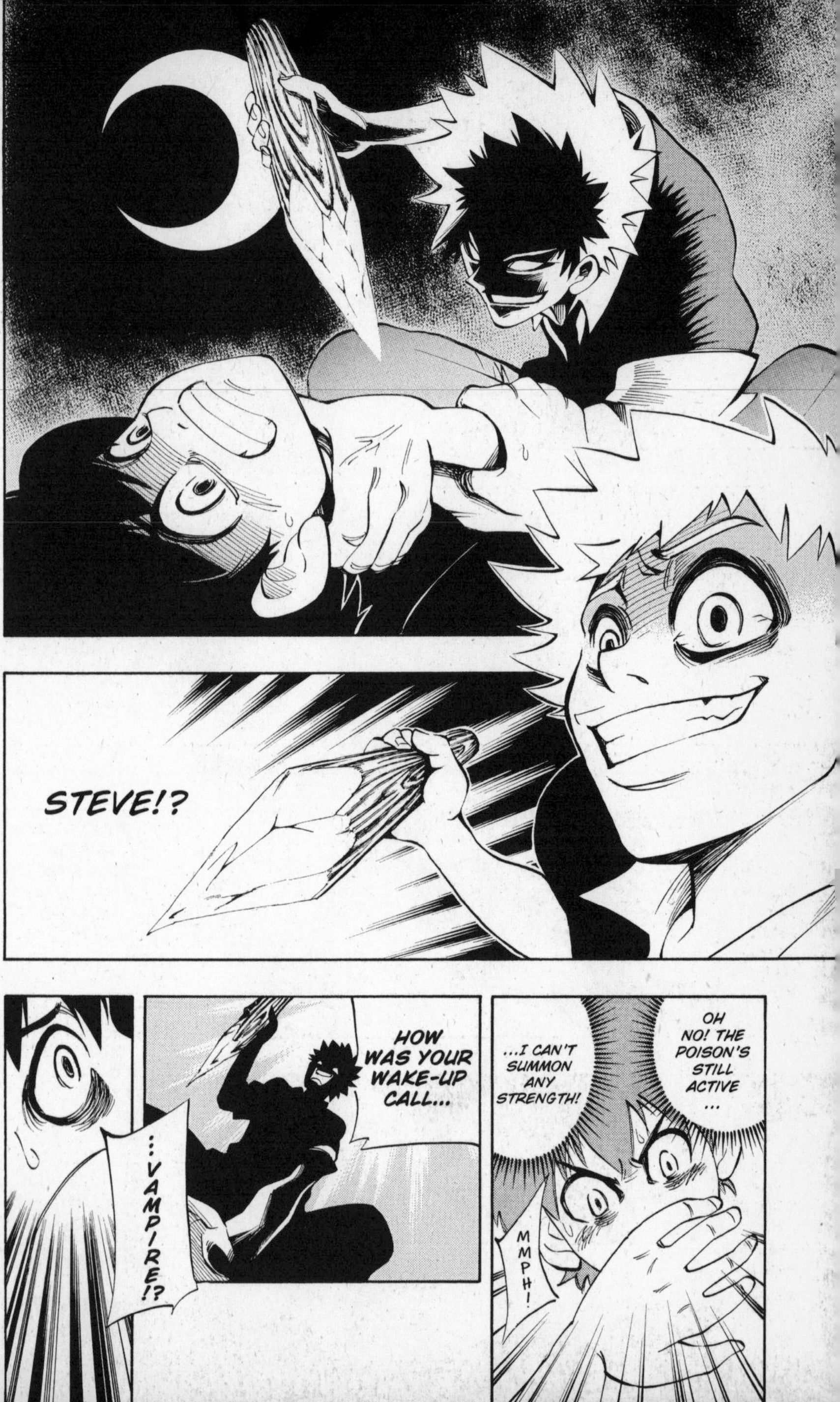
STEVE!?
OH NO! THE POISON'S STILL ACTIVE ...
...I CAN'T SUMMON ANY STRENGTH!
MMPH!
HOW WAS YOUR WAKE-UP CALL...
...VAMPIRE!?

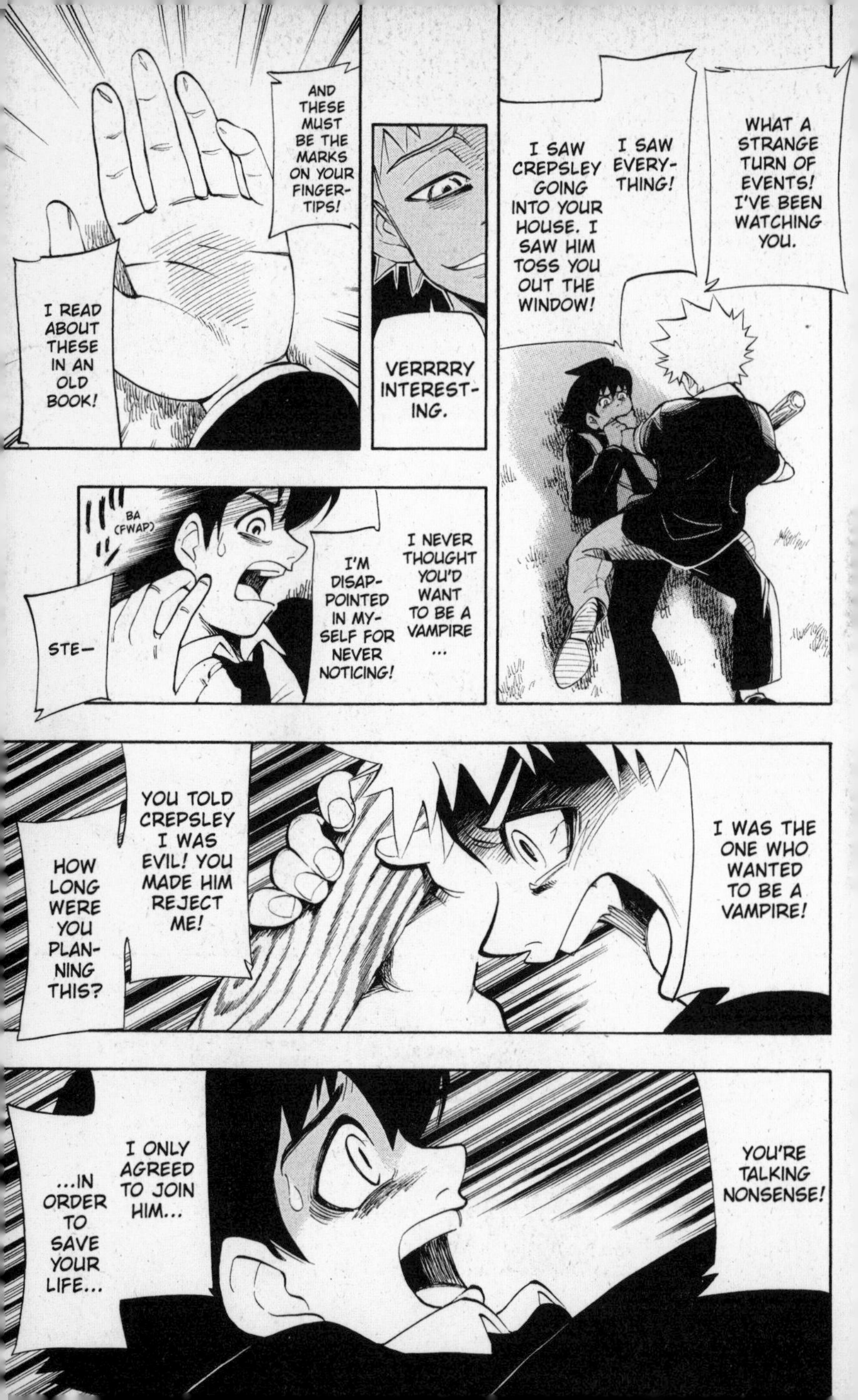
WHAT A STRANGE TURN OF EVENTS! I'VE BEEN WATCHING YOU.
I SAW EVERY-THING!
I SAW CREPSLEY GOING INTO YOUR HOUSE. I SAW HIM TOSS YOU OUT THE WINDOW!
VERRRRY INTEREST-ING.
AND THESE MUST BE THE MARKS ON YOUR FINGER-TIPS!
I READ ABOUT THESE IN AN OLD BOOK!
I NEVER THOUGHT YOU'D WANT TO BE A VAMPIRE ...
I'M DISAP-POINTED IN MY-SELF FOR NEVER NOTICING!
BA (FWAP)
STE—
I WAS THE ONE WHO WANTED TO BE A VAMPIRE!
YOU TOLD CREPSLEY I WAS EVIL! YOU MADE HIM REJECT ME!
HOW LONG WERE YOU PLAN-NING THIS?
YOU'RE TALKING NONSENSE!
I ONLY AGREED TO JOIN HIM...
...IN ORDER TO SAVE YOUR LIFE...

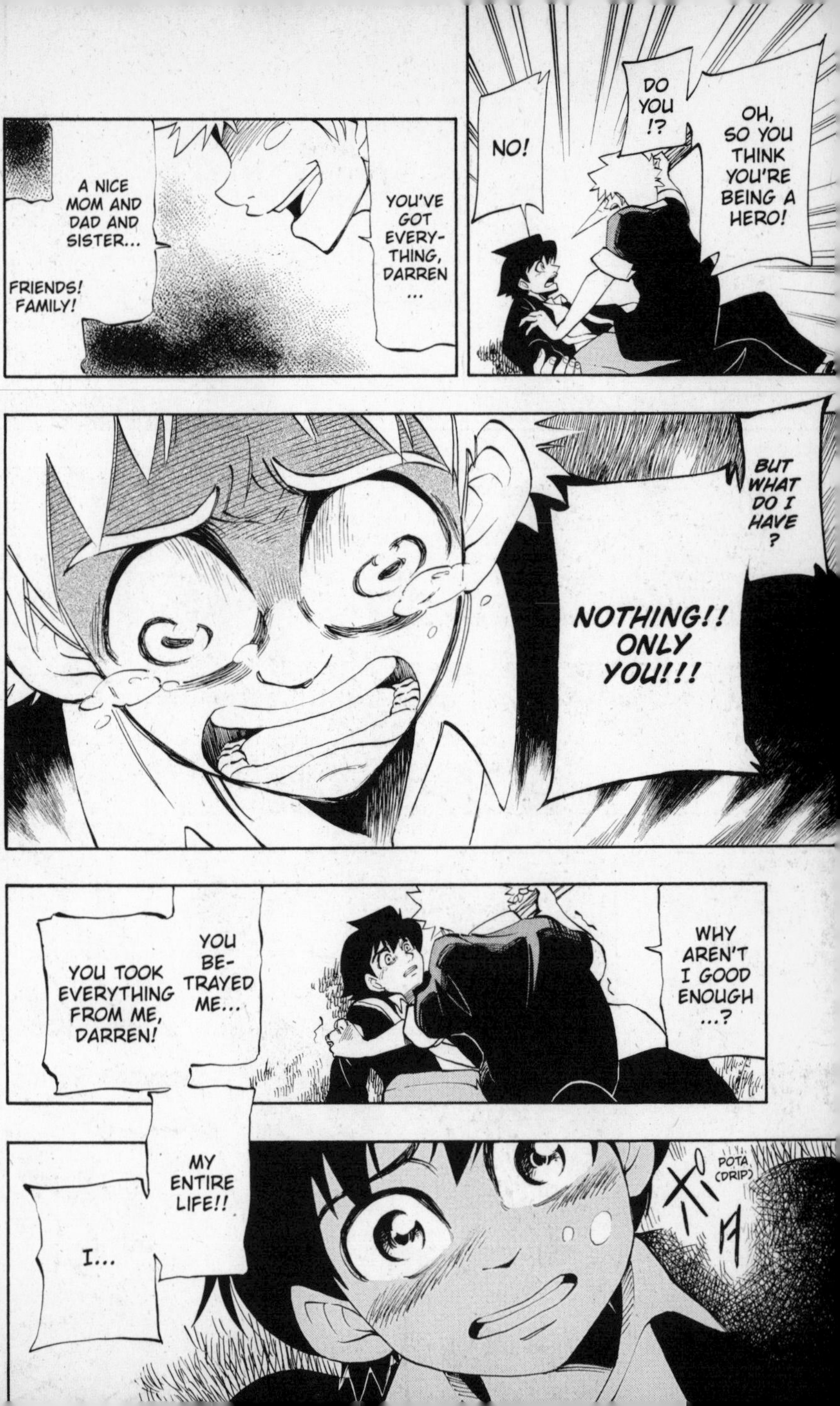
OH, SO YOU THINK YOU'RE BEING A HERO!
DO YOU !?
NO!
YOU'VE GOT EVERY-THING, DARREN ...
A NICE MOM AND DAD AND SISTER...
FRIENDS! FAMILY!
BUT WHAT DO I HAVE ?
NOTHING!! ONLY YOU!!!
WHY AREN'T I GOOD ENOUGH ...?
YOU BE-TRAYED ME...
YOU TOOK EVERYTHING FROM ME, DARREN!
POTA (DRIP)
MY ENTIRE LIFE!!
I...

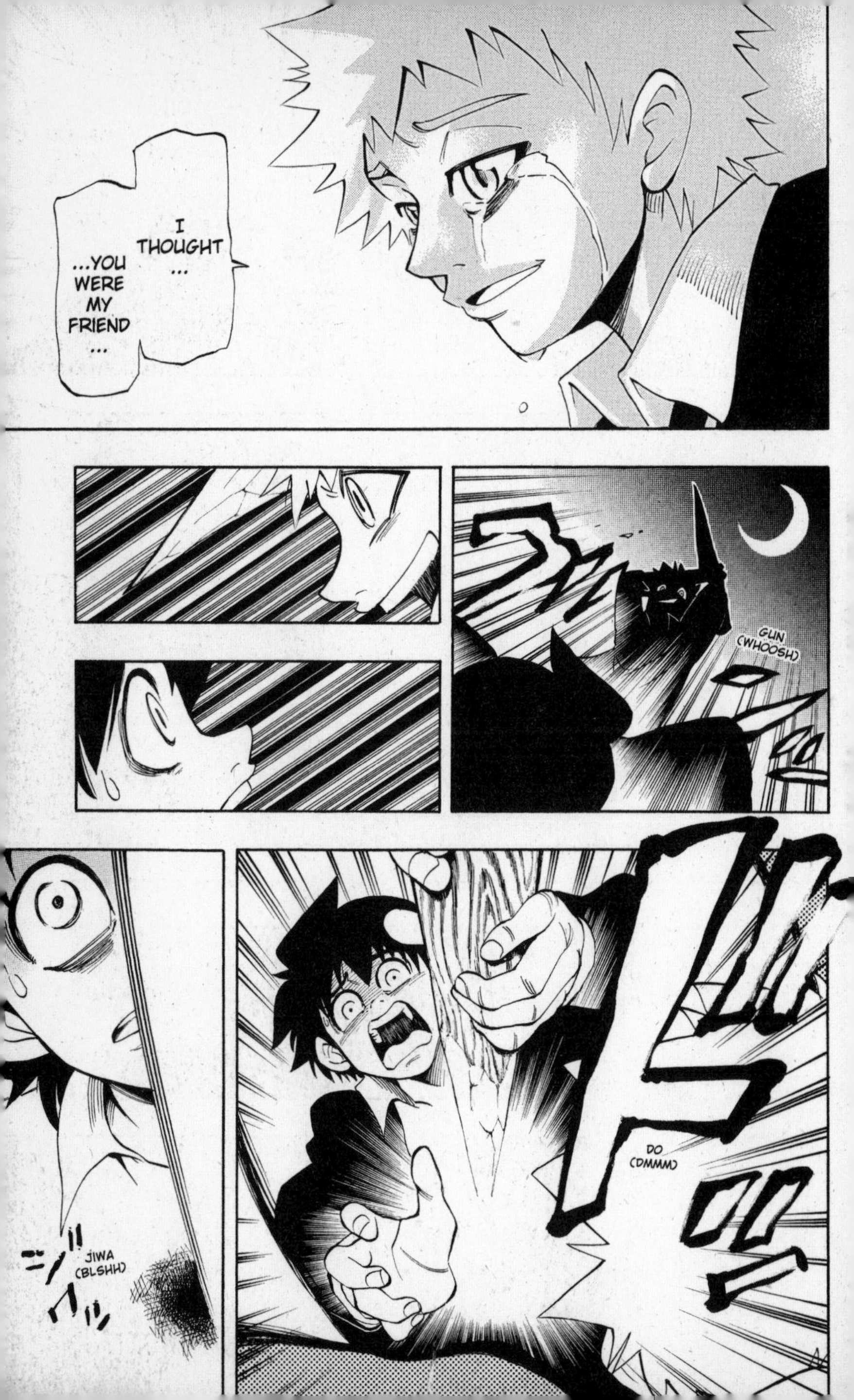
I THOUGHT ...
...YOU WERE MY FRIEND ...
GUN (WHOOSH)
DO (DMMM)
JIWA (BLSHH)

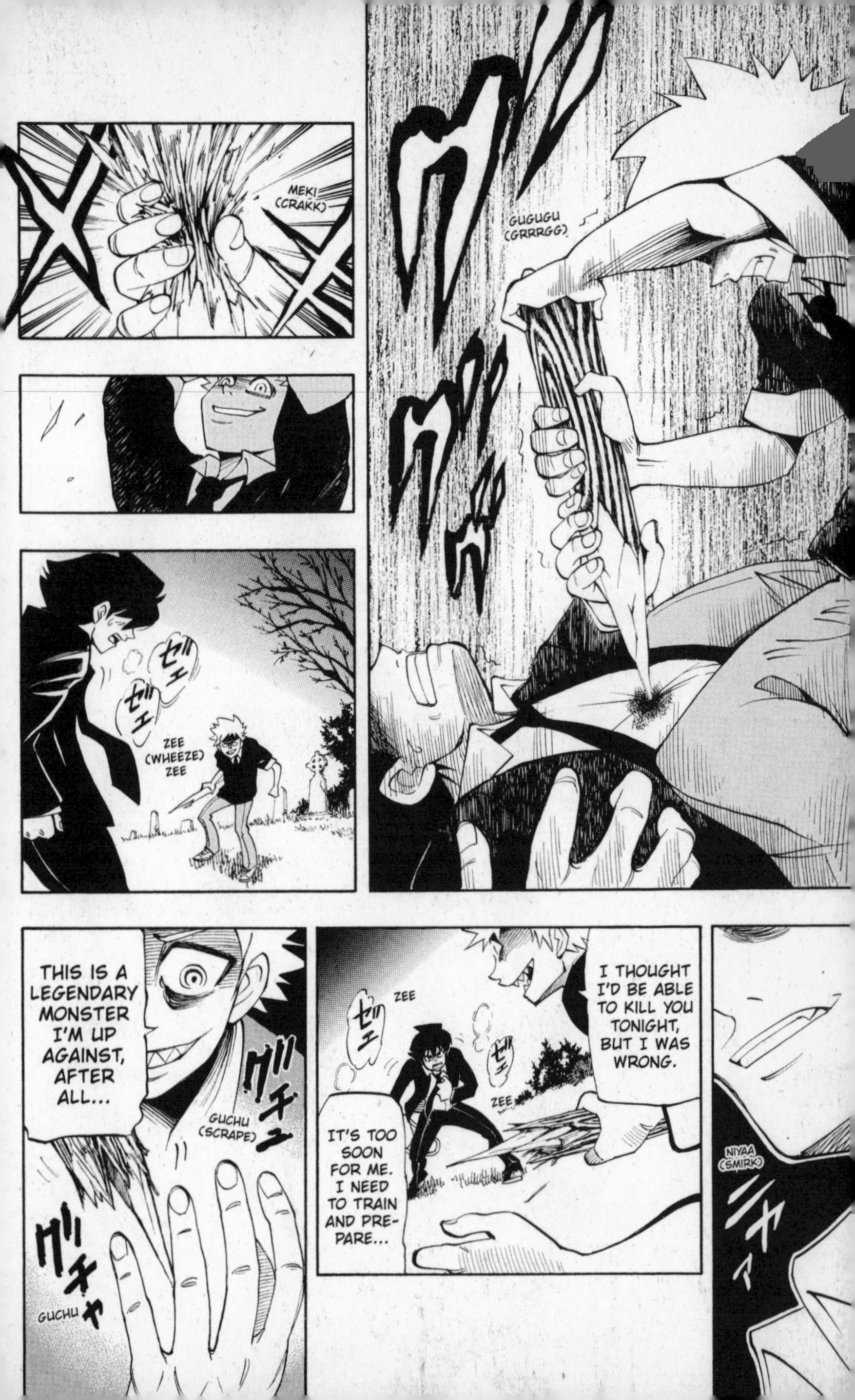
GUGUGU (GRRRGG)
MEKI (CRAKK)
ZEE (WHEEZE) ZEE
NIYAA (SMIRK)
I THOUGHT I'D BE ABLE TO KILL YOU TONIGHT, BUT I WAS WRONG.
ZEE
ZEE
IT'S TOO SOON FOR ME. I NEED TO TRAIN AND PRE-PARE...
THIS IS A LEGENDARY MONSTER I'M UP AGAINST, AFTER ALL...
GUCHU (SCRAPE)
GUCHU

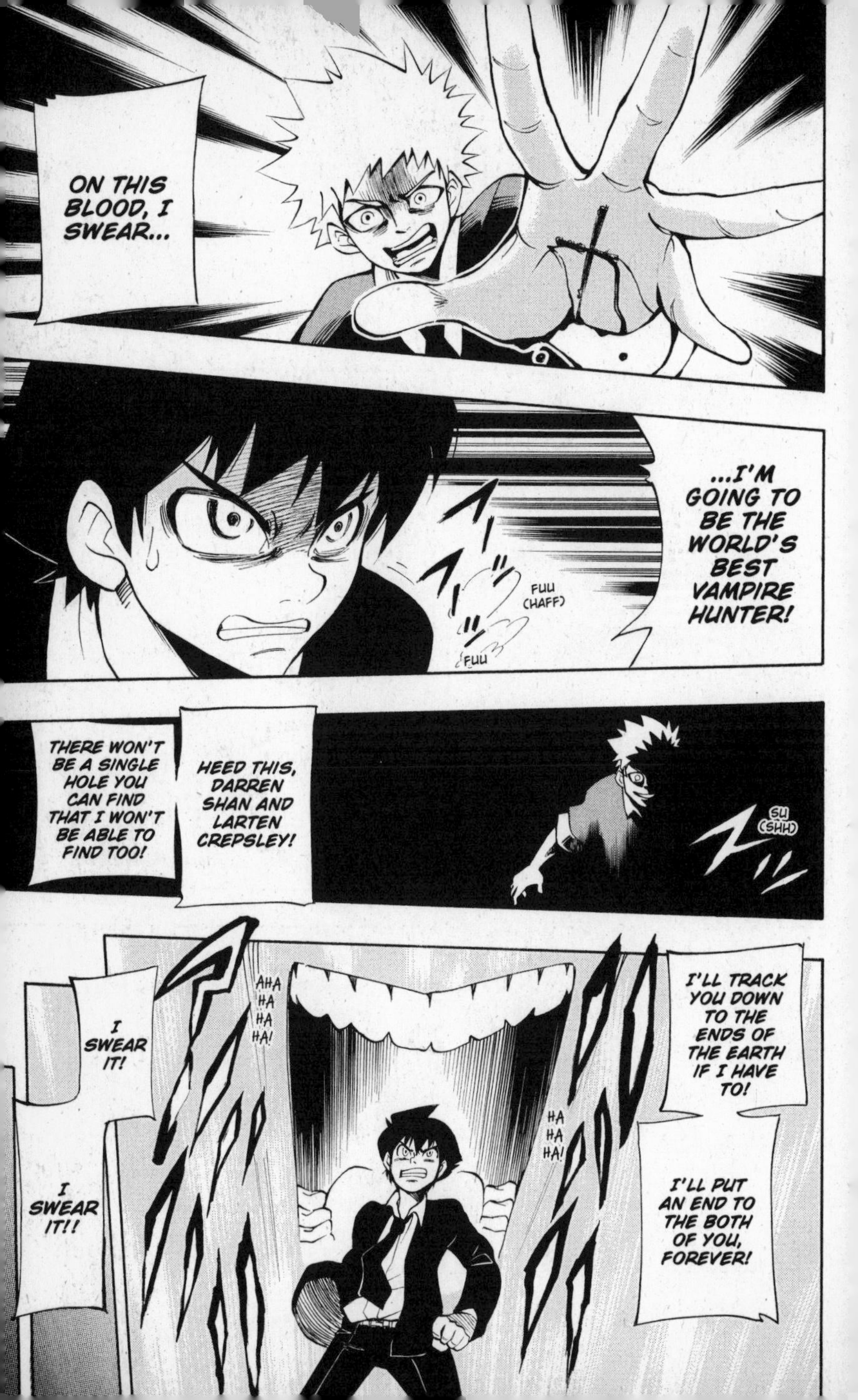
ON THIS BLOOD, I SWEAR...
...I'M GOING TO BE THE WORLD'S BEST VAMPIRE HUNTER!
FUU (HAFF)
FUU
SU (SHH)
HEED THIS, DARREN SHAN AND LARTEN CREPSLEY!
THERE WON'T BE A SINGLE HOLE YOU CAN FIND THAT I WON'T BE ABLE TO FIND TOO!
I'LL TRACK YOU DOWN TO THE ENDS OF THE EARTH IF I HAVE TO!
I'LL PUT AN END TO THE BOTH OF YOU, FOREVER!
HA HA HA!
AHA HA HA HA!
I SWEAR IT!
I SWEAR IT!!

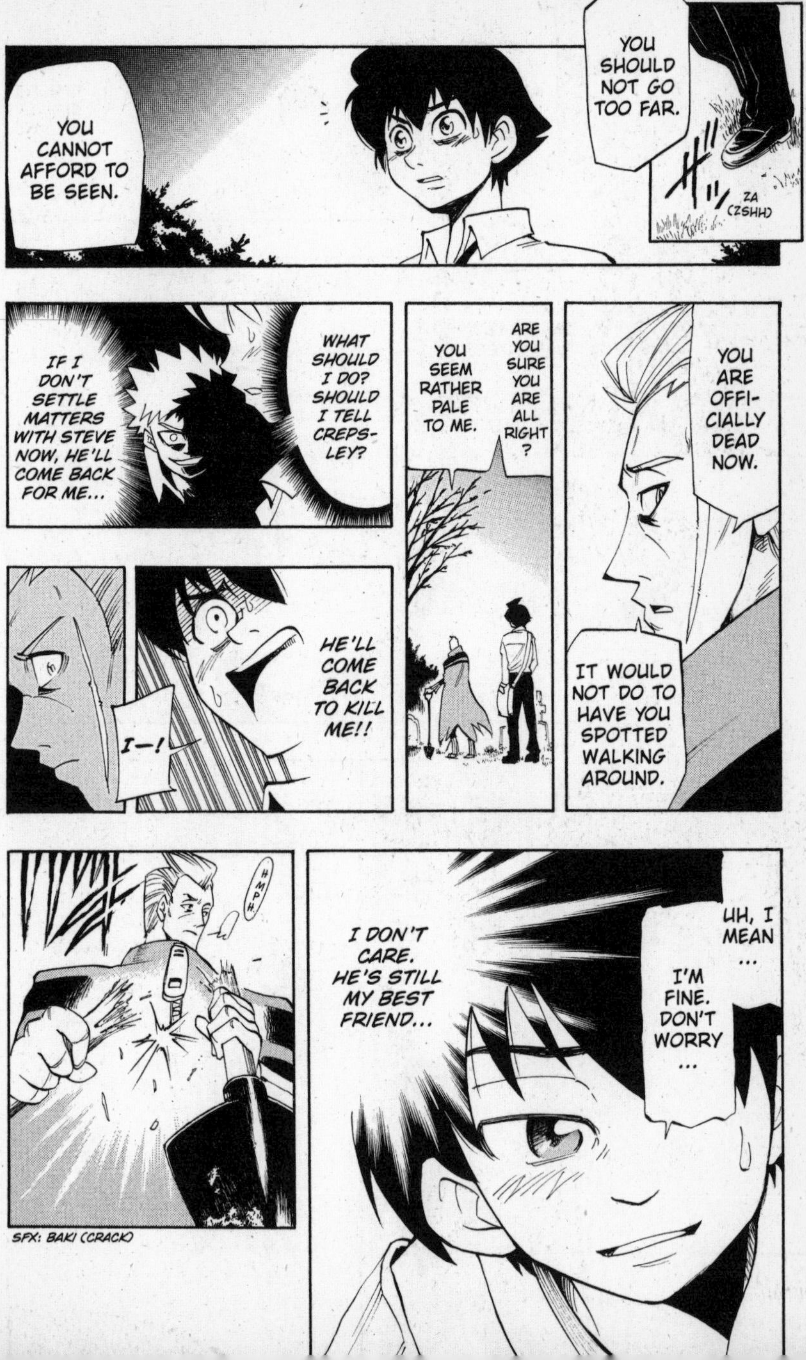
YOU SHOULD NOT GO TOO FAR.
ZA (ZSHH)
YOU CANNOT AFFORD TO BE SEEN.
YOU ARE OFFICIALLY DEAD NOW.
IT WOULD NOT DO TO HAVE YOU SPOTTED WALKING AROUND.
ARE YOU SURE YOU ARE ALL RIGHT?
YOU SEEM RATHER PALE TO ME.
WHAT SHOULD I DO? SHOULD I TELL CREPSLEY?
IF I DON'T SETTLE MATTERS WITH STEVE NOW, HE'LL COME BACK FOR ME...
HE'LL COME BACK TO KILL ME!!
I—!
UH, I MEAN...
I'M FINE. DON'T WORRY...
I DON'T CARE. HE'S STILL MY BEST FRIEND...
HMPH.
SFX: BAKI (CRACK)

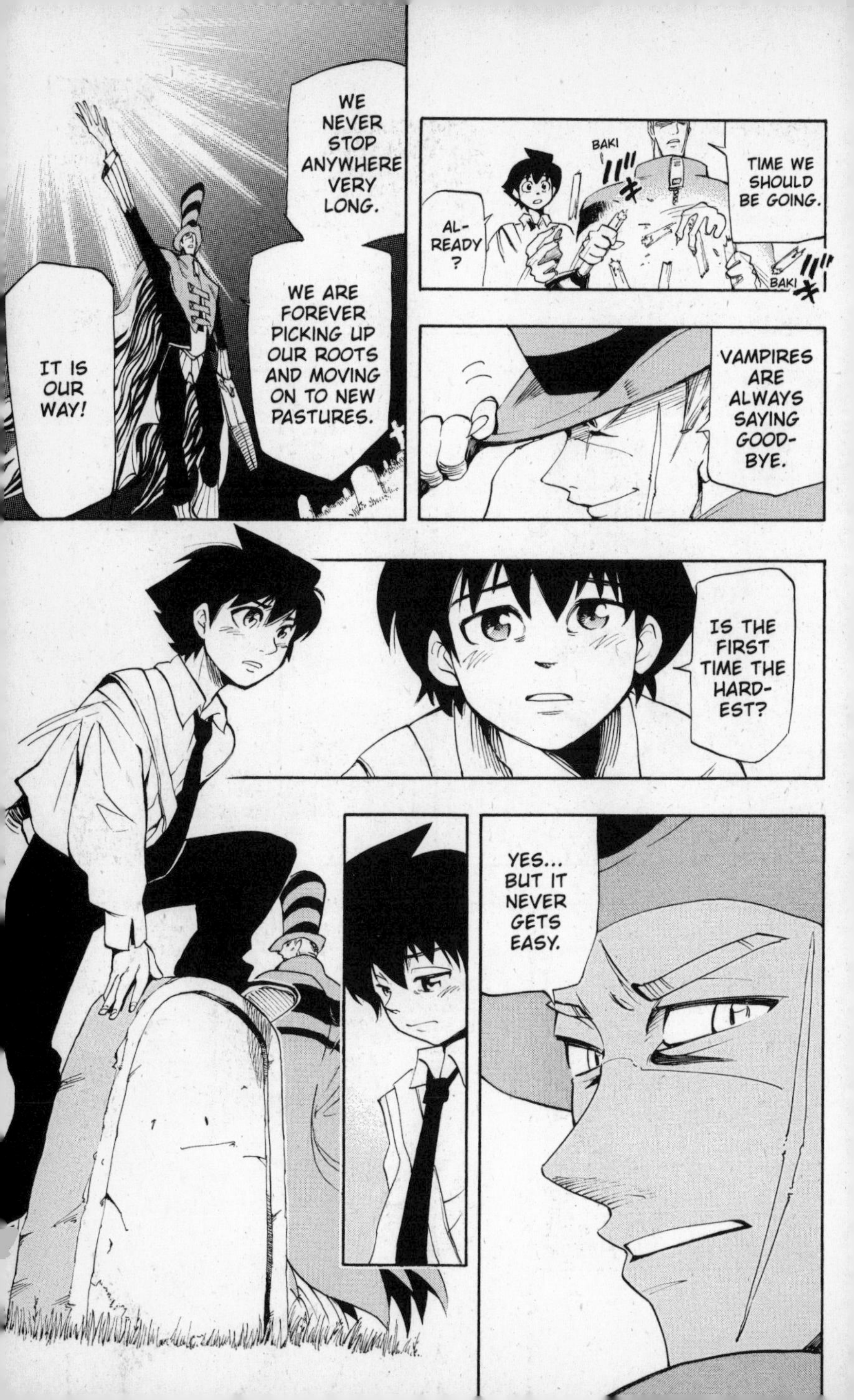
TIME WE SHOULD BE GOING.
BAKI
AL-READY?
BAKI
VAMPIRES ARE ALWAYS SAYING GOOD-BYE.
WE NEVER STOP ANYWHERE VERY LONG.
WE ARE FOREVER PICKING UP OUR ROOTS AND MOVING ON TO NEW PASTURES.
IT IS OUR WAY!
IS THE FIRST TIME THE HARD-EST?
YES... BUT IT NEVER GETS EASY.

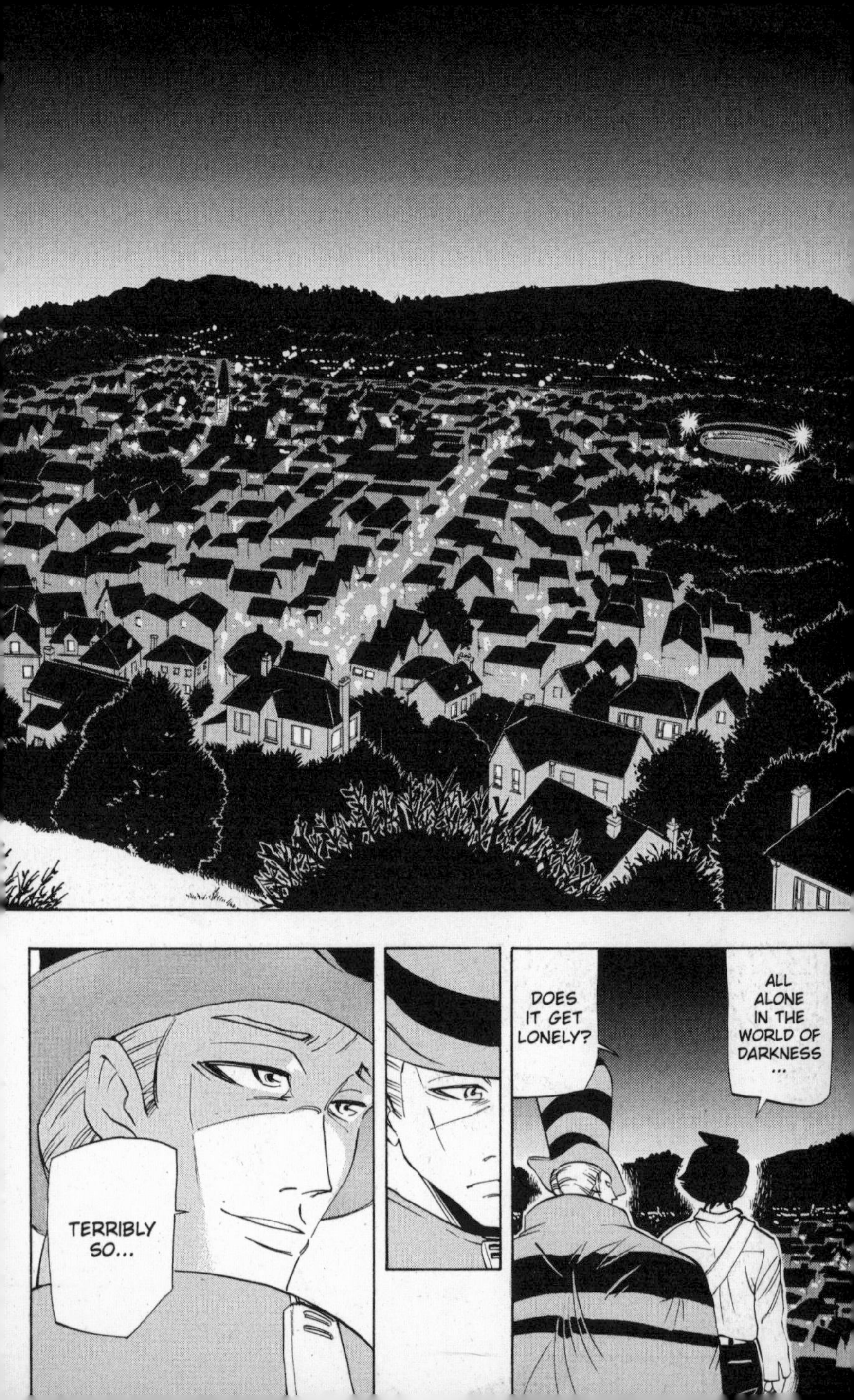
ALL ALONE IN THE WORLD OF DARKNESS ...
DOES IT GET LONELY?
TERRIBLY SO...

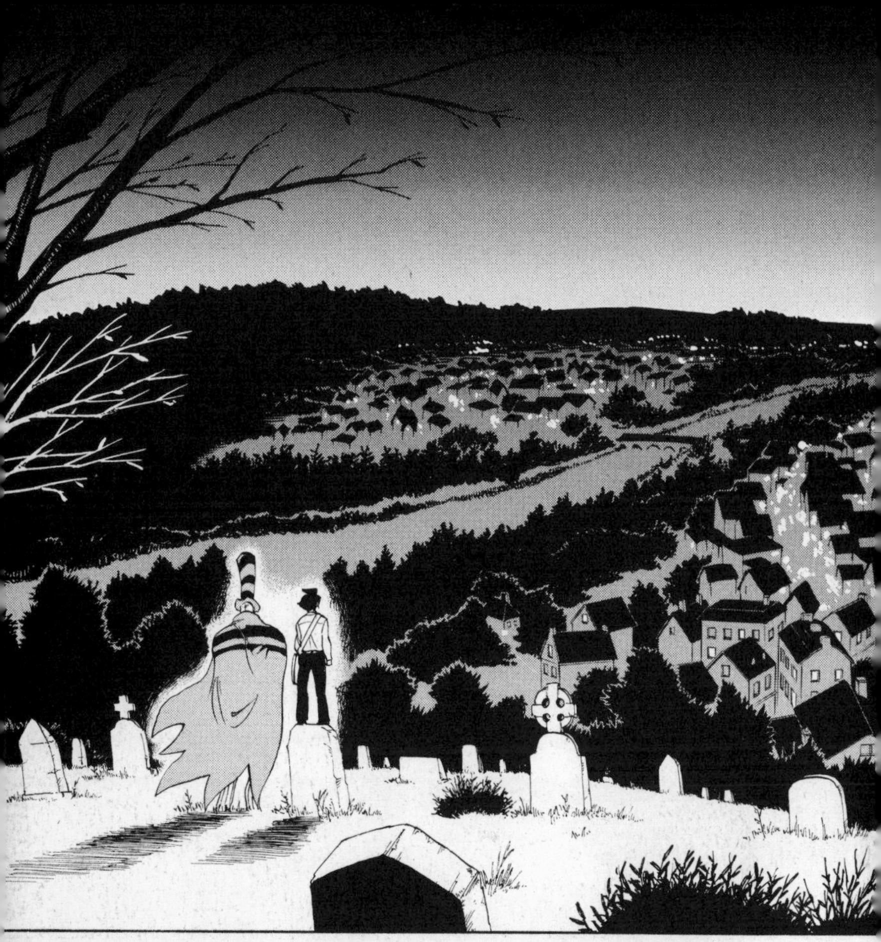
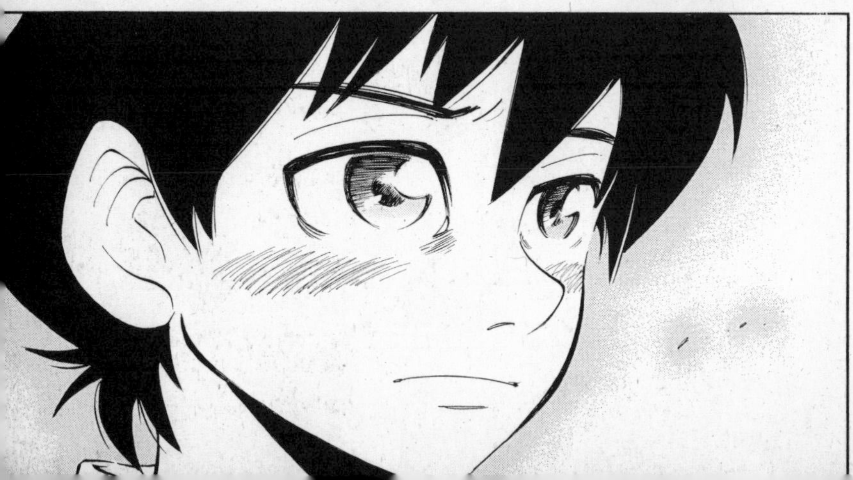

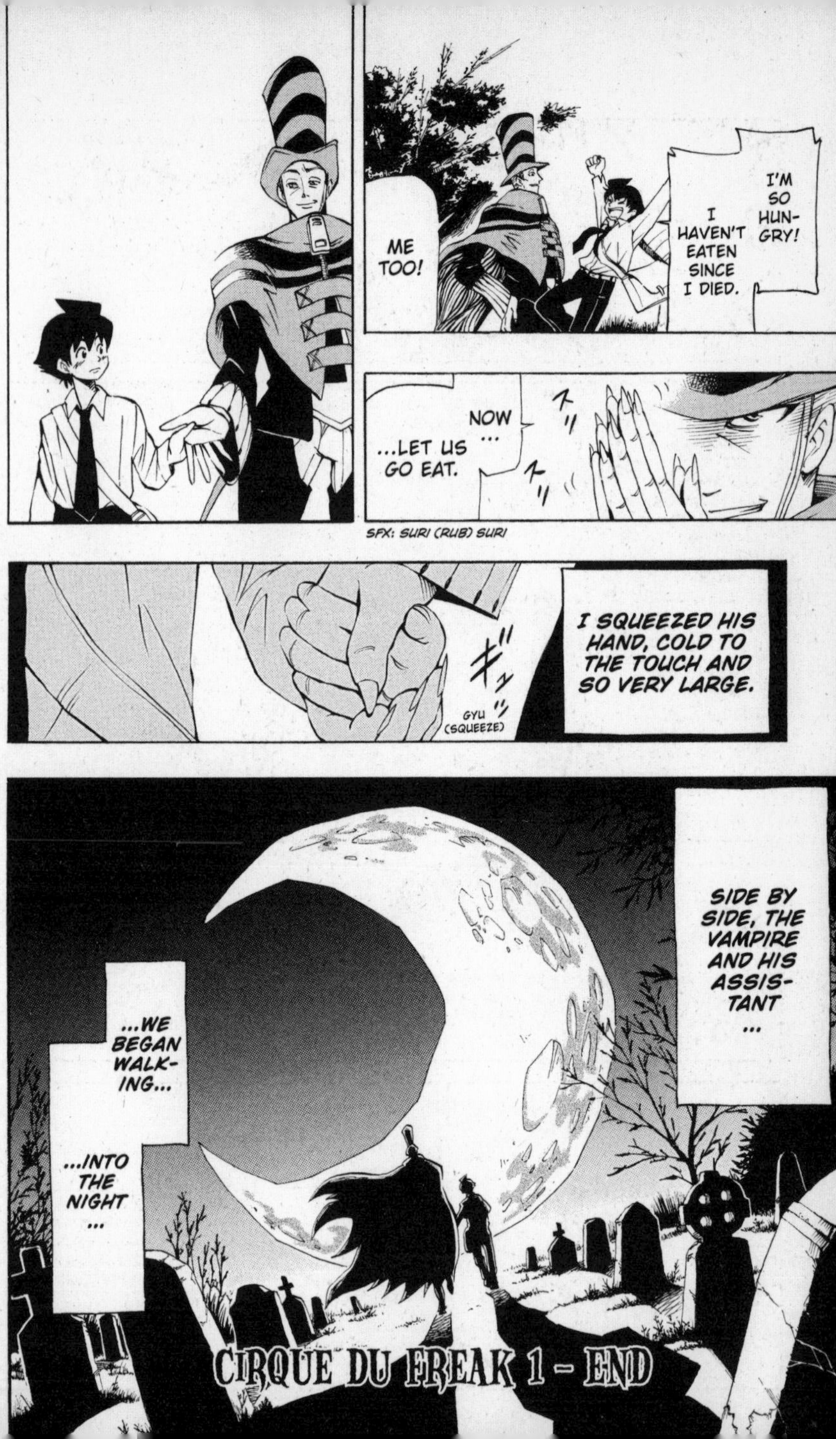
I'M SO HUN-GRY!
I HAVEN'T EATEN SINCE I DIED.
ME TOO!
NOW ...
...LET US GO EAT.
SFX: SURI (RUB) SURI
I SQUEEZED HIS HAND, COLD TO THE TOUCH AND SO VERY LARGE.
GYU (SQUEEZE)
SIDE BY SIDE, THE VAMPIRE AND HIS ASSIS-TANT ...
...WE BEGAN WALK-ING...
...INTO THE NIGHT ...
CIRQUE DU FREAK 1 - END

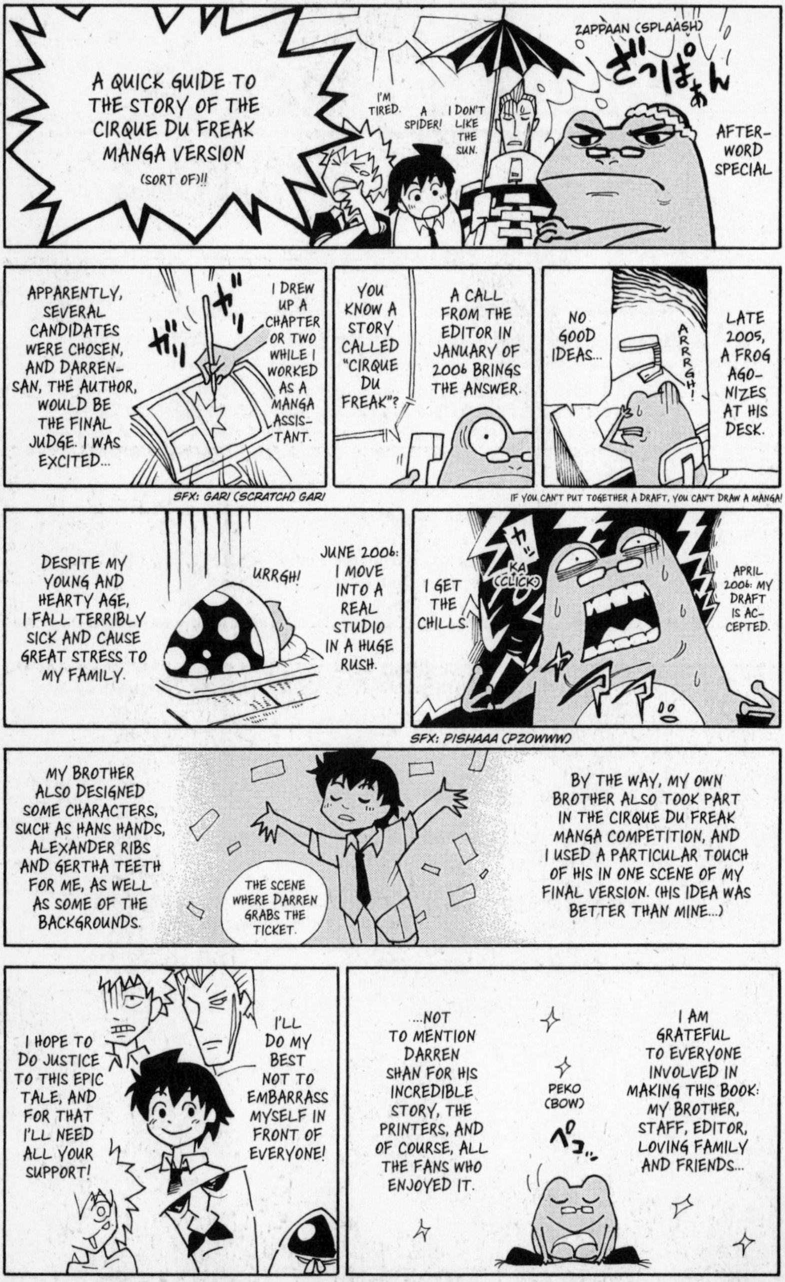
AFTER-WORD SPECIAL
ZAPPAAN (SPLAASH)
ざっぱぁん
I DON'T LIKE THE SUN.
A SPIDER!
I'M TIRED.
A QUICK GUIDE TO THE STORY OF THE CIRQUE DU FREAK MANGA VERSION (SORT OF)!!
LATE 2005, A FROG AGONIZES AT HIS DESK.
ARRRGH!
NO GOOD IDEAS...
IF YOU CAN'T PUT TOGETHER A DRAFT, YOU CAN'T DRAW A MANGA!
A CALL FROM THE EDITOR IN JANUARY OF 2006 BRINGS THE ANSWER.
YOU KNOW A STORY CALLED "CIRQUE DU FREAK"?
I DREW UP A CHAPTER OR TWO WHILE I WORKED AS A MANGA ASSISTANT.
ガリ
ガリ
APPARENTLY, SEVERAL CANDIDATES WERE CHOSEN, AND DARREN-SAN, THE AUTHOR, WOULD BE THE FINAL JUDGE. I WAS EXCITED...
SFX: GARI (SCRATCH) GARI
APRIL 2006: MY DRAFT IS ACCEPTED.
カッ
KA (CLICK)
I GET THE CHILLS.
SFX: PISHAAA (PZOWWW)
JUNE 2006: I MOVE INTO A REAL STUDIO IN A HUGE RUSH.
URRGH!
DESPITE MY YOUNG AND HEARTY AGE, I FALL TERRIBLY SICK AND CAUSE GREAT STRESS TO MY FAMILY.
BY THE WAY, MY OWN BROTHER ALSO TOOK PART IN THE CIRQUE DU FREAK MANGA COMPETITION, AND I USED A PARTICULAR TOUCH OF HIS IN ONE SCENE OF MY FINAL VERSION. (HIS IDEA WAS BETTER THAN MINE...)
THE SCENE WHERE DARREN GRABS THE TICKET.
MY BROTHER ALSO DESIGNED SOME CHARACTERS, SUCH AS HANS HANDS, ALEXANDER RIBS AND GERTHA TEETH FOR ME, AS WELL AS SOME OF THE BACKGROUNDS.
I AM GRATEFUL TO EVERYONE INVOLVED IN MAKING THIS BOOK: MY BROTHER, STAFF, EDITOR, LOVING FAMILY AND FRIENDS...
PEKO (BOW)
ペコッ
...NOT TO MENTION DARREN SHAN FOR HIS INCREDIBLE STORY, THE PRINTERS, AND OF COURSE, ALL THE FANS WHO ENJOYED IT.
I'LL DO MY BEST NOT TO EMBARRASS MYSELF IN FRONT OF EVERYONE!
I HOPE TO DO JUSTICE TO THIS EPIC TALE, AND FOR THAT I'LL NEED ALL YOUR SUPPORT!

CIRQUE DU FREAK①

DARREN SHAN
TAKAHIRO ARAI

Translation: Stephen Paul • Lettering: AndWorld Design
Original Cover Design: Hitoshi SHIRAYAMA + Bay Bridge Studio

The characters and events in this book are fictitious. Any similarity to real persons, living or dead, is coincidental and not intended by the author.

Yen Press
Hachette Book Group
237 Park Avenue, New York, NY 10017

Visit our Web sites at www.HachetteBookGroup.com and www.YenPress.com.

Yen Press is an imprint of Hachette Book Group, Inc. The Yen Press name and logo are trademarks of Hachette Book Group, Inc.

First Yen Press Edition: June 2009

ISBN: 978-0-7595-3041-6

10 9 8 7 6 5 4 3

BVG

Printed in the United States of America

CHECK OUT
AN EXCERPT OF
THE BOOK
CIRQUE DU FREAK

Please flip your book over to enjoy a couple chapters of the
prose version of *Cirque Du Freak*, currently in stores!

but the bell rang just as I was hitting my stride, so we lost nine–seven.

As we were leaving the field, Alan Morris ran toward us, panting and red-faced. They're my three best friends: Steve Leopard, Tommy Jones, and Alan Morris. We must be the weirdest four people in the whole world, because only one of us — Steve — has a nickname.

"Look what I found!" Alan yelled, waving a soggy piece of paper around under our noses.

"What is it?" Tommy asked, trying to grab it.

"It's —," Alan began, but stopped when Mr. Dalton shouted at us.

"You four! Inside!" he roared.

"We're coming, Mr. Dalton!" Steve roared back. Steve is Mr. Dalton's favorite and gets away with stuff that the rest of us couldn't do. Like when he uses swearwords sometimes in his stories. If I put in some of the words Steve has, I'd have been kicked out long ago.

But Mr. Dalton has a soft spot for Steve, because he's special. Sometimes he's brilliant in class and gets everything right, while other times he can't even spell his own name. Mr. Dalton says he's somewhat of an *idiot savant*, which mean he's a stupid genius!

Anyway, even though he's Mr. Dalton's pet, not even Steve can get away with showing up late for class. So whatever Alan had, it would have to wait. We trudged back to class, sweaty and tired after the game, and began our next lesson.

Little did I know that Alan's mysterious piece of paper was to change my life forever. For the worse!

"I thought I'd stay in here and admire the view," I said, leaning back on the toilet seat.

"Quit joking," he said. "We were down five–one when I came in. We're probably six or seven down now. We need you." He was talking about soccer. We play a game every lunchtime. My team normally wins but we'd lost a lot of our best players. Dave Morgan broke his leg. Sam White transferred to another school when his family moved. And Danny Curtain had stopped playing soccer in order to spend lunch hanging out with Sheila Leigh, the girl he likes. Idiot!

I'm our best forward. There are better defenders and midfielders, and Tommy Jones is the best goalkeeper in the whole school. But I'm the only one who can stand up front and score four or five times a day without fail.

"Okay," I said, standing. "I'll save you. I've scored a hat trick every day this week. It would be a pity to stop now."

We passed the older guys — smoking around the sinks as usual — and hurried to my locker so I could change into my cleats. I used to have a great pair, which I won in a writing competition. But the laces snapped a few months ago and the rubber along the sides started to fall off. And then my feet grew! The pair I have now are okay, but they're not the same.

We were down eight–three when I got on the field. It wasn't a real field, just a long stretch of grass with painted goalposts at either end. Whoever painted them was a total idiot. He put the crossbar too high at one end and too low at the other!

"Never fear, Hotshot Shan is here!" I shouted as I ran onto the field. A lot of players laughed or groaned, but I could see my teammates picking up and our opponents growing worried.

I made a great start and scored two goals inside a minute. It looked like we might come back to draw or win. But time ran out. If I'd arrived earlier we'd have been okay, when we first met. My mom says I was drawn to his wildness, but I just thought he was a great guy to be with. He had a fierce temper and threw scary tantrums when he lost it, but I simply ran away when that happened and came back again once he'd calmed down.

Steve's reputation had softened over the years — his mom took him to see a lot of good counselors who taught him how to control himself — but he was still a minor legend in the schoolyard and not someone you messed with, even if you were bigger and older than him.

"Hey, Steve," I called back. "I'm in here." I hit the door so he'd know which one I was behind.

He hurried over and I opened the door. He smiled when he saw me sitting down with my pants on. "Did you puke?" he asked.

"No," I said.

"Do you think you're gonna?"

"Maybe," I said. Then I leaned forward all of a sudden and made a sick noise. Bluurgh! But Steve Leopard knew me too well to be fooled.

"Give my boots a polish while you're down there," he said, and laughed when I pretended to spit on his shoes and rub them with a sheet of toilet paper.

"Did I miss anything in class?" I asked, sitting up.

"Nah," he said. "The usual crap."

"Did you do your history homework?" I asked.

"It doesn't have to be done until tomorrow, does it?" he asked, getting worried. Steve's always forgetting about homework.

"The day after tomorrow," I told him.

"Oh," he said, relaxing. "Even better. I thought . . ." He stopped and frowned. "Hold on," he said. "Today's Thursday. The day after tomorrow would be . . ."

"Got you!" I yelled, punching him on the shoulder.

"Ow!" he shouted. "That hurt." He rubbed his arm but I could tell he wasn't really hurt. "Are you coming out?" he asked then.

CHAPTER ONE

I WAS IN THE BATHROOM at school, sitting down on the toilet, humming a song. I had my pants on. I'd come in near the end of English class, feeling sick. My teacher, Mr. Dalton, is great about things like that. He's smart and knows when you're faking and when you're being serious. He took one look at me when I raised my hand and said I was ill, then nodded his head and told me to go to the bathroom.

"Throw up whatever's making you sick, Darren," he said, "then get your behind back in here."

I wish every teacher was as understanding as Mr. Dalton.

In the end, I didn't get sick, but still felt queasy, so I stayed on the toilet. I heard the bell ring for the end of class and everybody came rushing out on their lunch break. I wanted to join them but knew Mr. Dalton would be angry if he saw me in the yard so soon. He doesn't get mad if you trick him but he goes quiet and won't speak to you for a while, and that's almost worse than being shouted at.

So, there I was, humming, watching my watch, waiting. Then I heard someone calling my name.

"Darren! Hey, Darren! Have you fallen in or what?"

I grinned. It was Steve Leopard, my best friend. Steve's real last name was Leonard, but everyone called him Steve Leopard. And not just because the names sound alike. Steve used to be what my mom calls "a wild child." He raised hell wherever he went, got into fights, stole from stores. One day — he was still in a stroller — he found a sharp stick and prodded passing women with it (no prizes for guessing where he stuck it!).

He was feared and despised everywhere he went. But not by me. I've been his best friend since kindergarten,

friends, or teachers. Nobody's. I'm not even going to tell
you the name of my town or country. I don't dare.

Anyway, that's enough of an introduction. If you're
ready, let's begin. If this were a made-up story, it would begin at night, with a storm blowing and owls hooting and
rattling noises under the bed. But this is a real story, so I
have to begin where it really started.

It started in a toilet.

My parents practically hollered the roof down when they found out what I'd done — the tarantula had cost quite a lot of money. They said I was irresponsible, and from that day on they never again let me have a pet, not even an ordinary garden spider.

I started with that tale from the past for two reasons. One will become obvious as this book unfolds. The other reason is:

This is a true story.

I don't expect you to believe me — I wouldn't believe it myself if I hadn't lived it — but it is. Everything I describe in this book happened, just as I tell it.

The thing about real life is, when you do something stupid, it normally costs you. In books, the heroes can make as many mistakes as they like. It doesn't matter what they do, because everything works out in the end. They'll beat the bad guys and put things right and everything ends up cool.

In real life, vacuum cleaners kill spiders. If you cross a busy road without looking, you get whacked by a car. If you fall out of a tree, you break some bones.

Real life's nasty. It's cruel. It doesn't care about heroes and happy endings and the way things should be. In real life, bad things happen. People die. Fights are lost. Evil often wins.

I just wanted to make that clear before I began.

One more thing: my name isn't really Darren Shan. Everything's true in this book, *except* for names. I've had to change them because . . . well, by the time you get to the end, you'll understand.

I haven't used *any* real names, not mine, my sister's, my

INTRODUCTION

I'VE ALWAYS BEEN FASCINATED BY spiders. I used to collect them when I was younger. I'd spend hours rooting through the dusty old shed at the bottom of our garden, hunting the cobwebs for lurking eight-legged predators. When I found one, I'd bring it in and let it loose in my bedroom.

It used to drive my mom crazy!

Usually, the spider would slip away after no more than a day or two, never to be seen again, but sometimes they hung around longer. I had one who made a cobweb above my bed and stood guard for almost a month. Going to sleep, I used to imagine the spider creeping down, crawling into my mouth, sliding down my throat, and laying loads of eggs in my belly. The baby spiders would hatch after a while and eat me alive, from the inside out.

I loved being scared when I was little.

When I was nine, my mom and dad gave me a small tarantula. It wasn't poisonous or very big, but it was the greatest gift I'd ever received. I played with that spider almost every waking hour of the day. Gave it all sorts of treats: flies and cockroaches and tiny worms. Spoiled it rotten.

Then, one day, I did something stupid. I'd been watching a cartoon in which one of the characters was sucked up by a vacuum cleaner. No harm came to him. He squeezed out of the bag, dusty and dirty and mad as hell. It was very funny.

So funny, I tried it myself. With the tarantula.

Needless to say, things didn't happen quite like they did in the cartoon. The spider was ripped to pieces. I cried a lot, but it was too late for tears. My pet was dead, it was my fault, and there was nothing I could do about it.